Poor Little Rich Girl

C. DAVID HEYMANN

Poor Little Rich Girl

The Life and Legend
Of Barbara Hutton

LYLE STUART INC.   SECAUCUS, N.J.

Published by Lyle Stuart Inc.
Published simultaneously in Canada by
Musson Book Company,
A division of General Publishing Co. Limited
Don Mills, Ontario

Queries regarding rights and permissions should be
addressed to: Lyle Stuart, 120 Enterprise Avenue,
Secaucus, N.J. 07094

Manufactured in the United States of America

Library of Congress Cataloging in Publication Data

Heymann, C. David (Clemens David), 1945-
    Poor little rich girl.

    Bibliography: p. 365
    Includes index.
    1. Hutton, Barbara, 1912-   . 2. Millionaires—
United States—Biography. I. Title.
CT275.H796H49   1984   973.9′092′4   84-16459
ISBN 0-8184-0366-7

For Renee, Jeanne and Chloe Heymann

Poor little rich girl,
You're a bewitched girl,
Better beware!

Laughing at danger,
Virtue a stranger,
Better take care!
NOËL COWARD,
"Poor Little Rich Girl"

Foreword

In May 1977, two years before her death, I wrote to Barbara Hutton in care of her New York law firm, Cahill, Gordon and Reindel, expressing an interest in meeting with her to discuss the possibility of writing her biography. To be perfectly frank, I held out few expectations for the eventual success of this project and fewer still for the prospect of a personal encounter, much less the series of encounters that I knew were essential to any kind of meaningful life history.

Everything spoke against the venture. I was known, insofar as I was known at all, as a writer of book reviews and literary biographies, a far cry from the jet-set high society world that Barbara Hutton had once inhabited. I had also been advised by a reliable source that she was no longer in the public eye, that she was an invalid and a semirecluse who never left her tenth-floor hotel suite at the Beverly Wilshire in Beverly Hills. Furthermore, it had been years since her last meeting with a member of the working press and her last extended interview. What then were the chances of her agreeing to meet and converse with a would-be biographer?

The only aspects of my approach that seemed to offer even the dimmest ray of hope were the forthright tone of my initial inquiry, as well as a slim volume of poetry that I had written several years earlier that I sent along under separate cover. Barbara was something of a poet herself, having previously published two of her own volumes of verse. It was evidently my poetry, rather than my brazen suggestion of a biography, that elicited a response. One thing led to another. By the end of 1978 I had not only been granted a series of interviews, I had also gone through the better part of a trunkload of Barbara Hutton memorabilia—a gathering of old newspaper and magazine clippings, poems (published and unpublished), notebooks, scraps of paper, sketches, snapshots and correspondence. Barbara's writings, while neither chronological nor particularly literary, nevertheless constituted a strong personal document, a wild jumble of words on love, marriage, sex, childhood, wealth, charity, anguish and friendship. A picture of a private life emerged that seemed far more revealing of the subject than the glossy image that the public had pieced together on the basis of fifty years of sensational newspaper innuendo.

The chief merit of Barbara's writing is its attention to detail, its reconstruction of episodes, scenes and conversations that might otherwise have been permanently lost. These reflections, together with my interviews of Barbara and others who knew her, constitute the basic framework of this book. Insofar as it is possible to write the definitive biography of Barbara Hutton, it can almost be said that she actually wrote her own.*

C. David Heymann
New York City
January 1984

---

*Because of the fragmentary nature of Barbara Hutton's notebooks, the author has taken the liberty of editing them when and where necessary. The words and thoughts, however, are hers.

Contents

Part One

Society's Child

One

Did it ever occur to you that the Five and Dime stores are an indirect charity and of benefit to the people at large? While we are in business, we are also the means of making thousands of people happy. The more stores we create the more good we do humanity.

F. W. WOOLWORTH, 1905

O NE OF BARBARA HUTTON's earliest memories was of a sixty-room white marble mansion in Glen Cove on the North Shore of Long Island. The Italian Renaissance structure, named Winfield Hall after its owner, Frank Winfield Woolworth, the founder of the Woolworth Corporation, stood on eighteen acres and included stables, a carriage house, an open-air loggia of arched pillars, an eighteen-car garage, four housekeeping cottages, Borghese gardens, three greenhouses, a swimming pool and tennis courts. With ten large bedroom suites, a grand ballroom and sweeping marble staircase, Winfield Hall represented a veritable museum of variable decorating styles, raised gold letters on each bedroom door spelling out the particular period: Sheraton, Louis XIV, Louis XV, Marie Antoinette. Napoleon Bonaparte was the inspiration for F. W. Woolworth's bedroom on the second floor. In the center stood the emperor's majestic bed with gilt-edged circular canopy and hanging draperies of gold-embroidered red velvet.

It was 1917 when five-year-old Barbara Hutton, a chubby, golden-haired child with sparkling blue eyes and porcelain-white skin, was brought to Winfield Hall and placed in her grandfather's care. At sixty-four, Woolly (as everyone called him) was no longer the vigorous tycoon whose vision of a chain of five-and-dime stores had changed the entire face of merchandising in America. Age and illness had weakened his once broad frame, whitened his bushy red mustache, withered his rotund, ruddy face. In time he began to show signs of increasing

15

paranoia and melancholy, followed by prolonged alternate periods of withdrawal and extravagance.

Not only did Barbara bear witness to her grandfather's deterioration, but there was also her grandmother who seemed to dwell in her own little world, her days and nights spent in her bedroom rocking back and forth in an old-fashioned white wicker rocking chair. Jennie Creighton Woolworth, whose background as a small-town seamstress with few ambitions had poorly prepared her for the life of great luxury into which she would subsequently be thrust, was the product of a large and impoverished Canadian family. The more wealth her husband heaped upon her, the more she seemed to retreat, until by middle age she showed signs of mental debilitation, an illness that in time diminished her to a speechless remnant of her former self.

Using the medical terminology of the day, Jennie's personal physician described her illness as "premature senile dementia." Her senility, he testified in court papers, "is similar to that of a person more than ninety years of age. She is cheerful but incapable of mental processes, cannot comprehend what is going on around her, requires round-the-clock nursing care, and is unable to recognize her husband or other members of the family."

Barbara herself would later recount the poignant spectacle of meals at Winfield Hall: "They were served elegantly and punctually on fine silver and fresh napery, with flowers cut routinely from the garden, and everything polished and waxed to perfection. The dinner tableau in the imposing Georgian dining room was composed of six persons at table: grandfather and his nurse; grandmother and her attendant; myself and a governess. During meals not a word was spoken. Woolly was reduced to eating mush—strained vegetables or overripe bananas—and Jennie had a perpetual faraway smile on her face. There was never even the slightest glimmer of recognition in her eyes. It was heartbreaking and dreadful. For years Woolly dragged her to the best doctors, psychiatrists, psychologists, any expert he heard about. Finally, the day came when he had to accept the grim conclusion that there was no cure for her condition, that it could only get worse...."

Barbara could also recall the bizarre sight of Woolly in his music room, where he sat for hours at the console of his "favorite toy," a $100,000 Aeolian Skinner manual-player pipe organ. At the flick of a switch the room would be plunged into darkness. After a series of synthetic-lightning flashes, the music would burst forth and a pinkish-amber glow would illuminate the high ceiling, gradually turning to green, to deep mauve, the colors varying and changing with the sweeping tones of the composition. With every new piece of music a phantasmagorical portrait of the composer would slowly rise up from the darkness and be reflected against a specially designed screen. As the inexhaustible supply of music rolls played on, Woolworth would slide his fingers across the silent keyboard.

"I would cower in my bedroom," Barbara wrote, "while the music reverberated through the house, shaking the rafters. The coldness of my cavernous room only added to the terror I felt as the noise shattered the vaultlike silence. My room contained gloomy, thick carpeting and hunks of immense Gothic furniture. The walls were covered with limestone carvings of cherubs with demented expressions on their twisted faces. At night the dark draperies blowing in the wind looked like mourning gowns."

More comforting was her playroom with its oak-and-glass cabinet filled with a treasure trove of surprises: silver and gold rings, iridescent glass flasks, tiny carved animals of ivory and jade, charms and lockets, miniature china figurines, trinkets and coins. She had a velvet-backed rocking horse, with flared nostrils and a real mane, that moved forward when rocked and backward when reined. And there was a dollhouse, four feet high, with minuscule bearskin rugs and crystal chandeliers, a polished-brass nameplate on the front door with Barbara's name engraved, Chippendale and Adam furniture scaled to size.

She could remember a day spent in New York with her grandfather when he took her to see the Woolworth Building, then the world's tallest skyscraper, his private domain and proudest achievement. It was the day he bought her a mink-trimmed hat and coat and a matching muff to wear on a cord around her neck.

"Woolly was always a little loony, but he was sweet to me," Barbara wrote. "He was especially strange when it came to money, incredibly lax about large sums, but very chary about nickels and dimes. He would allow checks for hundreds of thousands of dollars to accumulate undeposited in his wallet, but he would keep the servants grubbing about on hands and knees long after midnight in search of a quarter that might have dropped from his purse....

"At night when he couldn't sleep he would sometimes slip into my bedroom to talk, although I can't imagine now what we must have talked about. I think he talked about his favorite composers, or maybe he described the events of the Great War to me, because he was on a Presidential committee responsible for selling Liberty Bonds. I imagine he talked about his childhood, about what it meant to grow up poor on a small farm in the near wilderness. People said that Woolly didn't own his first pair of shoes until the age of twelve. His great wealth only came to him later on. One thing I remember him saying was that having money sometimes makes people lonely. He was very lonely, steeped in personal guilt, a genius but also an outcast, a man on the edge of many worlds but belonging to none."

Frank Woolworth liked to think of himself as a simple, wholesome man, the offspring of a farm family that had originated in Woolley, England, and settled in colonial upstate New York. His grandfather, Jasper Woolworth, owned a farm in Rodman, and it was there that he was born in 1852, the eldest child of John and Fanny McBrier Woolworth. A brother, Charles Sumner (named for the Abolitionist from Massachusetts), was born two years later.

While the boys were still young their father acquired his own small plot of land and decided to go into dairy farming. At eighteen, finding the work tedious, Frank Woolworth left the farm and found employment as a general clerk in the dry-goods store of Augsbury & Moore in nearby Watertown. Hired on a three-month trial basis without pay, he worked a six-day eighty-four-hour week. After four years in the store he was earning $10 a week and taking night courses at a local business college. At this point he was lured away to work for a competitor in the same town. He had barely begun his new job when he was suddenly struck down by a mysterious illness that manifested itself in bouts of high blood pressure and nausea. To nurse him back to health his parents hired Watertown's new seamstress, a sweet and fragile-looking girl from Nova Scotia named Jennie Creighton. Frank Woolworth fell in love with Jennie and they were married on his father's farm in 1876. Woolworth returned to work at Augsbury & Moore. The store had expanded its operation to include household goods, and Woolworth was put in charge of arranging window and counter displays. On one occasion, using scraps of red cloth taken from the store's waste bin, he created a window display of pots and pans that seemed to breathe new life into these mundane utensils. The display, as he put it, "unloosed a bolt in the minds and pocketbooks of the store's customers. Within an hour there wasn't a pot or pan left on the counter."

The owners were still counting their profits from the kitchen sale when they heard of another merchant's success in selling handkerchiefs at the cut-rate price of 2-for-5¢. Determined to try their own "five-cent counter," they purchased $100 worth of miscellaneous nickel items. Woolworth carefully arranged the merchandise on two counters draped with red burlap and topped by a stenciled sign advertising the price. "The goods disappeared like snow in April," he later noted. Subsequent nickel sales proved equally profitable.

Now it was Woolworth whose bolt was unloosened. On February 22, 1879, Washington's Birthday, with $300 worth of five-cent items borrowed from his employers, he opened the "Great 5¢ Store" in Utica, New York. Owing to its poor location, the first Woolworth outlet soon closed.

Undaunted, chalking the venture up to experience, Woolworth scouted around for a better location and found it in Lancaster, Pennsylvania. The new store opened on June 21, 1879, and was an immediate success. The name was changed to "Woolworth's 5 and 10¢ store" to reflect Woolworth's new fixed-price limit. Within the first five years Woolworth created a chain of some twenty-five stores in five states with annual sales in excess of $1 million. By 1905 the F. W. Woolworth Company was grossing $10 million a year. A dozen years later the organization topped the $100 million mark and opened its thousandth store, the great New York flagship of the fleet, at Fifth Avenue and Fortieth Street. For the year 1939, sales from the 2,021 American stores rose to $319 million. Hundreds of additional stores in Mexico, Great Britain, France and Germany brought in an additional $100 million that year. The figures far exceeded Woolworth's dreams.

In making his Horatio Alger fantasy come to life, F. W. Woolworth combined a sustained capacity for hard work, a crisp manner of speech, an ability to ferret out vagaries in balance sheets, and a social philosophy intensely Darwinian. Motivated by a Protestant work ethic that equated toil and virtue, Woolworth employed thousands of young working girls, many of them immigrants or the daughters of immigrants, and paid them low wages for long hours. He defended his policy on the grounds that he was providing a paid apprenticeship to unskilled workers. Whenever challenged on this point, he responded that cheap labor was necessary if the firm could hope to keep the price of goods within reason. In one of his periodic reports to management he wrote: "You can get good honest girls at from $2-3 per week, and I would not give $3.50 for any salesladies except in special cases. It may look hard to some of you for us to pay such small wages, but there are lots of girls...too proud to work in a factory or to do housework. They are glad of a chance to get in a store for experience, if nothing more, and when they get experience they are capable of going to a store where they can afford to pay good wages."

The extent to which Frank Woolworth's commercial theories succeeded can best be measured by his steadily rising fortunes and lifestyle. There were now three children in the family, all girls: Helena, born in 1878; Edna (the future mother of Barbara Hutton), born in 1883; Jessie, born in 1886. In 1895, when the corporation's base of operations moved to New York, Woolworth bought a brownstone on Quincy Street in Brooklyn's Park Slope section. Five years later he moved his family into adjoining suites in the glittering new Hotel Savoy, on Fifth Avenue and Fifty-Ninth Street, opposite New York's grandest private residence, the 137-room mansion belonging to Alice and Cornelius Vanderbilt II. Alice kept thirty-three servants and sixteen footmen dressed in wigs and breeches, and regularly gave formal balls for 400, the figure decreed by social arbiter Ward McAllister as optimum for such occasions.

Sensitive to the fact that nobody ranked lower on New York's social scale than the merchant, Frank Woolworth took steps to correct the situation. He planned the construction of his own mansion, a four-story thirty-six-room affair at 990 Fifth Avenue on the northeast corner of Eightieth Street; it was the neighborhood of Otto Kahn, Payne Whitney, Andrew Carnegie, known as "Millionaires' Row." Designed by architect Charles P. H. Gilbert, the new house had hand-tooled gesso ceilings and golden wall panels, carved and gilded Louis XVI sofas, ornamental, overstuffed chairs with tapestry backs, Oriental rugs, stained-glass windows, bedroom suites inlaid with polished toyon wood, Old Masters, a horse-drawn carriage, a lavender Renault automobile and chauffeur in matching livery.

In addition to the mansion on Fifth Avenue, the merchant purchased four houses that stood in a row around the corner on East Eightieth Street, between Fifth and Madison avenues, a quartet of antiquated dwellings that he razed and completely rebuilt. One of them was subsequently used as a residence for Woolworth's servants. The other three he gave to his daughters as each in turn married, forming a kind of family compound. The same year he moved into the Fifth Avenue mansion, he acquired Winfield Hall in Glen Cove and simultaneously commissioned the construction of a five-story white-front mansion at 33 West Fifty-sixth Street, which he reserved primarily for visiting five-and-dime executives and store managers. But the most lavish of his construction projects was the $13.5 million Woolworth Building, at the convergence of Park Place and Broadway in lower Manhattan. Completed in 1913, the sixty-story, 792-foot structure remained the world's tallest skyscraper until the erection in 1930 of New York's Chrysler Building.

The edifice was designed by Cass Gilbert (not to be confused with Charles P. H. Gilbert), but it was Woolworth who presided over the building's construction, hoisting his lordly bulk, elegantly clad in tailored British tweeds, up into the scaffoldings to examine first-hand the work as it proceeded. King Louis XIV daily inspecting the progress of the palace at Versailles could have derived no greater pleasure than Woolworth did as he clambered about from floor to floor. The completion of the Woolworth Building was celebrated by President Woodrow Wilson in Washington, D.C., when he pushed a button that first activated in New York the skyscraper's more than 90,000 light bulbs.

૨♥

Although Frank Woolworth held out little hope for his own social vindication, he did have aspirations for his offspring, whose entry into the upper strata of aristocratic America could only be accelerated by the great fortune he had worked so hard to amass. But of his three daughters only the first-born, Helena, attained the social station that one would expect of a later-generation Woolworth. Helena's rise began shortly after her marriage, in 1904, to Charles E. F. McCann, an Assistant Attorney General for New York State, whose family was powerful and well-to-do. Initially Woolworth entertained two objections to his son-in-law: first, his uncle was Richard Croker, known as one of Tammany Hall's most corrupt bosses; second, the McCanns were Roman Catholics, whereas the Woolworths were non-practicing Episcopalians. On the other hand, McCann was a responsible, industrious young man with a solid footing in his profession. Woolworth must also have seen the advantages of having a well-trained legal mind available within the family ranks, because he later placed McCann at the helm of the Broadway–Park Place Corporation, the realty arm of his bulging empire.

The McCann-Woolworth marriage was for the most part a happy one. The couple lived at Sunken Orchard, a country estate in Oyster Bay, Long Island. They owned two yachts, a private railway car, a string of limousines, and membership in the area's most exclusive country clubs. Their rise to social respectability, including a listing in the *Social Register*, was aided by the circumspect avoidance of the kind of adverse publicity that dogged Barbara Hutton throughout her life. The McCann children were brought up impeccably and also made good marriages. Constance McCann married socialite-millionaire Wyllys Rossiter Betts, Jr., for thirty years the director of the Museum of Natural History in New York. Helena married attorney-industrialist 10-goal polo player Winston F. C. Guest, a cousin and godson to Winston Churchill. Frazier Winfield McCann, after attending Princeton, became a gentleman farmer and horse breeder in western Connecticut and then settled in New York as a successful businessman and philanthropist.

Possessing only a fraction of Helena's social ambition, her sister Jessie followed an alternate route. Blond and bouncy, she was a cheerful openhanded woman with ludicrously extravagant tastes and a zany sense of humor. She wore $75,000 Russian sable wraps and Romanov crown jewels. She had a passion for jewelry, especially emeralds and pearls, yet she was not above adorning herself with baubles picked up in her father's stores.

Her husband, James Paul Donahue, whom she first met in a New York roller-skating rink, was a high-spirited young Irish-American whose father supported a large family by rendering fats and hides on Manhattan's Upper West Side. Like Charles McCann, James Donahue was Catholic; unlike McCann, he had difficulty holding down a job. After his marriage to Jessie in 1912—a ceremony F. W. Woolworth tried desperately but unsuccessfully to prevent—Donahue went to work for his father-in-law, quickly proving himself grossly incompetent and unreliable. He became a broker for the E. F. Hutton Company, with similarly dismal results. He opened his own brokerage firm at 250 Park Avenue. His wife was his only customer, and even she felt he was wasting his time. Donahue was a spendthrift, an alcoholic and a high-rolling gambler whose losses were so excessive that one day Jessie was heard to warn him, "From now on, darling, you may lose no more than fifty thousand a night."

The Donahues lived for the joy of the moment and achieved it in the company of the night-blooming, on-the-run adherents of what then passed for café society. They made one attempt to follow in the more conventional footsteps of the McCanns by building Wooldon Manor, a million-dollar estate in Southampton, next door to the Southampton Beach Club. But "old guard" Long Island society snubbed them and they invested instead in a private railway car, "Japauldon," a condensation of the names James Paul Donahue, and constructed an elaborate mansion in Palm Beach, Cielito Lindo, which means "a little bit of heaven." They moved into the Woolworth house on West Fifty-sixth Street and redecorated it, installing a large round oak bar in the downstairs sitting room and making the top floor over into a gambling casino replete with cashier's booth, roulette wheel and gaming tables for craps, blackjack and chemin de fer. Within six months Donahue managed to accrue IOUs totaling $3 million and had to pawn much of his wife's jewelry to make good on his debts.

The Donahues rarely stayed put for more than a few weeks at a time, and when they traveled it was always with an abundance of luggage, including their own pillows, bedsheets, hot-water bottles, bottled water and portable bar. Jessie didn't have to worry about cramming her clothes into ordinary suitcases. Dresses and coats were hung in two portable leather-covered wardrobes mounted on wheels. Each ball gown had a special trunk. In addition, there were hat boxes, shoe boxes, a crocodile case holding silver-backed brushes, combs and hand mirrors, and even a travel case, long and slender, to transport umbrellas and parasols. There was also a triple-locked suitcase, as large as the average trunk, containing nothing but jewelry, or what remained of it after her husband finished paying off his IOUs.

The entourage that usually accompanied the couple included a waiter, because Jessie wanted her own to serve her even when dining out. He knew her food preferences and ensured that she got the portions she wanted. Also in the group were a lady-in-waiting, a dresser to look after Jessie's clothes, a valet to look after Donahue, two footmen, a lady's maid for the lady-in-waiting, a hairdresser, a private secretary, a security guard, and a governess and a nurse for the Donahue children.

They had two sons, Woolworth (often called Wooly, with one "l" to differentiate him from his grandfather), and James Paul, Jr. (Jimmy). They were chips off the old block, spoiled and quite different from their responsible cousins, the McCanns. One distant relative suggested that Wooly and Jimmy had been raised to succeed at being playboys and that even at this they appeared to be failures.

Jessie Donahue's life was fraught with the kind of vapid luxury that eventually wears thin and invariably takes its toll. It took its heaviest toll on her husband, who was convinced that he had ruined any social designs his wife might once have had. Guilt, business failure, and an inability to curb his vices (which by now included a series of ill-fated homosexual love affairs) were more than he could bear. One evening during a friendly poker game James Donahue excused himself, retired to his bedroom and proceeded to swallow the contents of a bottle of bichloride of mercury. He died four days later in Lenox Hill Hospital at the age of forty-four.

Jessie never remarried. She closed the East Eightieth Street house and sold the one on West Fifty-sixth Street to a bootleg syndicate that turned it into the Club Napoleon. She acquired a magnificent duplex at 834 Fifth Avenue and lived there with a lady companion named Yvonne, carrying on in her usual fashion, making frequent trips abroad and spending her money as though her husband had never left her side.

Finally there was Edna, Frank Woolworth's second-born and easily the prettiest of the three, with soft blond hair, blue eyes, pale skin and an appealing figure. She was wan, delicate, ethereal, with a sensitive and expressive face, matched by a melodic voice. Had her voice been properly trained, Edna might well have enjoyed a successful singing career. But it wasn't and she didn't. Instead she had a chance meeting one day in the lobby of the Savoy Hotel with a twenty-four-year-old stockbroker named Franklyn Laws Hutton. It was 1901, the year the Woolworths occupied a suite at the Savoy before moving into their Fifth Avenue town house. Edna was eighteen and in her father's eyes too young to marry. She settled for a long courtship instead.

The object of her pursuit, Franklyn Hutton, was of medium height and broad build, a graduate of Yale and an employee of Harris, Hutton Company, a brokerage firm with offices at 35 Wall Street. The co-founder of the company was Franklyn's elder brother, Edward Francis Hutton, a self-made financial wizard who had quit school and gone to work on Wall Street at age fourteen. A year after Franklyn Hutton met Edna, his brother's firm became the E. F. Hutton Company, with Franklyn as vice president and full partner.

Frank Woolworth's objections to the romance softened when he learned that the Huttons were also of the Episcopalian faith and that their father, James Laws Hutton, had quit his own father's Ohio dairy farm and moved to Cincinnati, where he entered the fast-growing field of pharmaceuticals. A relation, William E. Hutton, owned an investments brokerage firm by the same name in Cincinnati, and it was his influence that apparently sold Edward and Franklyn on the profession. After six years of wooing, interrupted for a year while Edna sailed off on a trip around the world, Frank Woolworth gave the couple his belated blessings. They were married on April 24, 1907, in a traditional Episcopalian ceremony at the Church of the Heavenly Rest on Fifth Avenue and Forty-fifth Street. They honeymooned in Paris and returned to New York to reside in the Woolworth town house at 2 East Eightieth Street.

If Franklyn Hutton wasn't everything that Edna's father had hoped for in a son-in-law, Woolworth nevertheless had reason to feel relieved: at least he wasn't a European fortune hunter. In 1909, while traveling in Switzerland, the five-and-dime baron wrote to his brother that "these cheap titled foreigners over here are all after the American girl and her money. You must respect their good judgment in hoping to acquire both money and a fine-looking wife. But the American father and mother have their troubles if they are not sympathetic with this sort of courtship."

On the same trip Woolworth again wrote his brother, this time while visiting Blenheim Palace, seat of the Marlborough dukedom at Woodstock in Oxfordshire, England. The ninth and latest duke, Charles, nicknamed "Sunny," had bartered title for tender by taking the hand of Willie K. and Alva Vanderbilt's only daughter, Consuelo, thereby reaping a $2.5 million dowry and a guaranteed $100,000 a year in interest. The marriage, which had been foisted upon Consuelo by her title-conscious mother, had only recently been dissolved:

> This famous estate of 70,000 acres is sadly run down because the Duke is no longer in receipt of enormous sums from his American father-in-law, W. K. Vanderbilt. The Duke spends all he can get hold of in fast living in Paris and London. He has not the power to sell his land or great works of art, sculpture or furniture. How much better it would have been for him if he had been obligated to learn the five-and-ten cent business at $6 a week and become a commercial man instead of as we see him now— no use to anyone and no satisfaction to himself.

The irony of Woolworth's forthright American attitude toward work-shy aristocrats would endlessly reassert itself in the life and legend of his granddaughter, Barbara Woolworth Hutton. Barbara, the only child of Franklyn and Edna Hutton, was delivered at home by Dr. J. Clifton Edgar on November 14, 1912. She had a full crop of lemon-blond curls and her mother's lustrous blue eyes. No mention of her birth was made in the press— "the only time in my life," she later told a friend, "they chose to ignore me."

Barbara's fragmented writings record several passing memories of being forced at an early age to take two teaspoons of castor oil three times a week, and of not being allowed to eat cooked meat until the age of four: "I can still see the governess scraping my first steak to make it as lean and tender as possible." Another account recalls a Christmas season's stroll with her father down Fifth Avenue. Santa's helpers stood on streetcorners ringing their copper bells over cauldrons of loose change. There were children carrying red balloons, garlands on doors, Christmas lights, evergreens, a tap dancer in front of a department store, brass bands, the hurdy-gurdy man, a group of young people singing carols, chestnut vendors, store windows that came alive with dolls that wagged their heads and nodded their fingers.

A third reminiscence depicts a different New York street scene: "I recall the myriad stores along Madison Avenue, the ladies parading beneath fluffy spring parasols, the antique shops, the shop windows filled with bric-a-brac and women's finery, the four- and five-story brownstones, townhouses and apartment buildings going up near Millionaires' Row. As I walked along I would look for an oriel or bay window, a bit of tiled roof, a curved glass window filled with plants or potted flowers, a pane of stained glass, stone lintels, cornices, flights of marble stairs, ceilings thirty feet high and walls two-feet thick."

In 1915 the Franklyn Huttons were living in a fifth-floor suite at the Plaza Hotel. The move from East Eightieth Street was a matter of convenience: an office of the E. F. Hutton Company had recently opened off the hotel's main lobby. The lobby itself contained a stock ticker around which investors and guests clustered to read the day's prices. The change in domicile afforded Franklyn a freedom of move-ment he hadn't enjoyed since relinquishing his bachelorhood, and his new-found mobility added an unbearable burden to a marriage that was already buckling under its own weight. The Huttons were a classic mismatch. Franklyn was an energetic, restless, striving man who drank heavily and lusted compulsively after women. Edna, like her own mother, was a homebody, too shy and insecure to indulge in the kind of social antics that attracted her husband, too unsure of herself to oppose his blatant womanizing.

Revenge and loneliness finally drove Edna Hutton into the arms of another man. Bud Bouvier was the youngest brother of John Vernon ("Black Jack") Bouvier, the father of Jacqueline Kennedy Onassis. Although there was never any question of marriage between them, their friendship gradually evolved into a full-blown romance. But over the long run her affair proved as distressing as her marriage. It ended when Bouvier married a younger woman, Emma Louise Stone, and went off to Europe to fight in the war.

In the summer of 1916 Edna took her daughter to live in a large rented house in Bar Harbor, Maine. Franklyn Hutton spent a week with them and passed the rest of the summer at a country estate he kept at Glen Cove, Long Island. The estate became a retreat for Hutton's male friends, who would pack their tackle boxes and tell their spouses they were going off for a little fishing, when in reality they were going off to free-spirited weekend parties at Hutton's house, which usually in-cluded a crowd of young single women.

One of the regulars at these weekend galas was an exceptionally attractive twenty-five-year-old Swedish actress, Monica von Fursten, whose father was an envoy to the United States. Hutton and the Swedish actress were soon seen all over town together, attending balls, dinner parties, public functions. Even the *Wall Street Journal* made note of Hutton's resplendent new companion and of Hutton's ability "to clog the night away," a dance in which the performer wears clogs and beats out a clattering rhythm on the floor.

Nobody was more baffled or enraged by the situation than Frank Woolworth, whose repeated efforts to convince his daughter to initiate divorce proceedings against her unfaithful husband went unheeded. Finally the five-and-dime magnate himself confronted Hutton, eliciting a promise from him to end the affair. But in late March 1917 when Franklyn went to California for four weeks on business, his companion was Monica von Fursten. A few days after arriving in San Francisco they were photographed dancing together at a country-club dinner party. Edna found it impossible to ignore the photo, which ran on the society page of the New York *Sun.*

Franklyn Hutton was back in New York and staying in Bay Shore when his wife took her final act of revenge. She had made plans, procuring a small bottle of strychnine crystals and laying out her most flattering evening gown for the occasion, a straight chemise of white charmeuse, embroidered with gold irises from waist to hem. She was wearing the gown and a double strand of pearls when her body was found on May 2 in her bedroom at the Plaza Hotel. The New York *Times* for May 3 ran a short and misleading obituary:

> Mrs. Franklyn Laws Hutton, 33, who was Miss Edna Woolworth, daughter of F. W. Woolworth, was found dead yesterday in her apartment at the Hotel Plaza. Mrs. Hutton was the wife of Franklyn L. Hutton, a member of the firm of E. F. Hutton & Co. and a prominent member of the Stock Exchange. When found in her room by her maid, Mrs. Hutton had probably been dead several hours. According to New York City Coroner David Feinberg, who later asserted that an autopsy was unnecessary, death was due to a chronic ear disease, which resulted in the hardening of the bones of the ear, causing severe contraction of the tongue muscles and eventual suffocation.
>
> Mr. Hutton reached the hotel shortly after his wife's death from a visit to his summer home at Bay Shore, L.I. Mrs. Hutton was married to Mr. Hutton April 24, 1907, at the Church of the Heavenly Rest. Mrs. Hutton leaves behind one child, Barbara, aged four.

Although it was true that Edna suffered from mastoiditis, a disease characterized by a hardening of the bones in the middle ear, the illness had been diagnosed and arrested sometime before. If Edna suffocated, it was most likely the result not of a middle-ear ailment, but of a lethal dose of strychnine poisoning, a chemical whose effects are felt in the respiratory and central nervous systems. According to the police report, an empty vial of the poison was found in the deceased's bathroom, as well as a glass containing the residue of strychnine crystals mixed with

water. Another disclosure made by the police was that the body was
discovered not by the maid, but by Edna's daughter.

What is most peculiar about the death of Edna Hutton is that the
medical examiner's office ordered no autopsy or inquest into the cause
of death. The death certificate, signed by New York City Coroner David
Feinberg, indicates that she died of a cerebral thrombosis, with asphyx-
iation (from mastoiditis) listed as a contributing factor. The same
document, however, contained a built-in disclaimer: *"The Department
of Health does not certify to the truth of the statements made thereon,
as no inquiry as to the facts has been provided by Law."* The common
assumption among the press was that Frank Woolworth had paid off
certain key city officials to avoid an investigation into the causes
surrounding his daughter's death, an investigation that in all proba-
bility would have landed the family in the midst of a public scandal.
This theory gained support with the disclosure a year later that the
New York City coroner's office had mysteriously misplaced their files
on the case. The files were never recovered.

After Edna's death, Frank Woolworth's few remaining moments of
happiness were provided by the diminutive presence at Winfield Hall of
his granddaughter, whose care he willingly undertook while her father
went off in search of beautiful women and high adventure. Yet
somehow it was all slipping away for Woolworth, the zest and wonder
of that fantastical night just a few years earlier when President Wilson
turned on the lights, when Charles M. Schwab of Bethlehem Steel and
Elbert Gary of U.S. Steel and Otto Kahn, the titan of finance, all paid
homage at a dinner party to the man who had built the world's tallest
building and made millions by selling merchandise for nickels and
dimes.

One of the merchant's final gestures, undertaken not long after
Edna's death, was the construction of a $100,000 mausoleum in New
York's Woodlawn Memorial Cemetery. The ornate neo-Egyptian
bronze-and-marble tomb, fronted by grandiose pillars and sphinxes,
seemed grotesquely inappropriate to one whose typically American
success was predicated on an understanding, if not an appreciation of
homely things and homely people. "The Pyramid," as Barbara Hutton
later called it, was very simply the last word in mortuary chintz.

When Frank Woolworth died on April 8, 1919, just five days short of his
sixty-seventh birthday, he was at work on a last will and testament that
proposed to leave a large share of his fortune to various charities, with a
series of smaller, interlocking trusts to be distributed among his

children, grandchildren and ailing wife. But because this document was incomplete and unsigned at the time of his death, the attorneys for his estate were forced to turn back to a two-page handwritten will dashed off in 1889 in which he left everything to Jennie Woolworth.

Whatever the reasons for his failure to execute the later will, the testament of record, filed for probate in Mineola, Nassau County, theoretically enabled a mentally infirm woman, unaware of her surroundings, to become a millionairess many times over and the Woolworth Corporation's major stockholder. The deceased's brother, Charles Sumner Woolworth, was named director of the corporation, while Hubert Parson, a trusted executive, took over as president of domestic operations, a position that then entailed supervision of 1,050 branch stores and a total payroll of more than 50,000 employees. Parson was also named, together with Woolworth's two surviving daughters, Helena McCann and Jessie Donahue, administrator of the Woolworth estate. This was done in accordance with the legal dictates of a petition of dower filed during Woolworth's lifetime.

A catatonic Jennie Woolworth outlived her husband by exactly five years and forty-three days, passing away intestate at Winfield Hall on May 21, 1924. Had she died forty-four days sooner, millions of dollars would have been saved in estate and inheritance taxes. Because she survived her husband by this brief period beyond five years, the Woolworth estate was subject to additional federal taxes, quite apart from the $8 million in taxes levied in 1919, immediately following Woolworth's death.

The total estate after taxes came to $78,317,938.47, or $26,105,979.49 for each of three heirs: Helena, Jessie and Barbara Hutton (as the sole surviving heir of Edna Woolworth Hutton). In addition to her grandfather's bequest, Barbara inherited $2.1 million from the estate of her mother—$411,000 of it in cash, the remainder in stocks and bonds—bringing her total trust to well over $28 million, a sum worth approximately twenty times as much in today's currency.

Two

F.W. WOOLWORTH'S death marked the beginning of a long and unsettling period in Barbara's life, during which she was moved around from one house and caretaker to another. At the age of seven she was taken to Altadena, a suburb of Los Angeles, and placed with Grace Hutton Wood, her father's older sister. Aunt Grace, who had formerly been married to West Coast businessman Benjamin Wood, was gregarious and friendly, an appealing woman in her early forties whose major interests included garden parties, dinner parties, sewing circles, book clubs and flower shows. She was a collector of fine objects of art with an emphasis on French and Oriental antiques. She painted landscapes and still lifes and gave them away to friends or sold them at auction to raise money for charity.

Her hectic social schedule prevented her from spending much time with her niece. Aside from a spinsterish private tutor named Miss Alice Day, who saw Barbara several times a week, the little girl was almost totally isolated in her new environment and was glad to hear from her aunt that they would soon be joining Franklyn Hutton in San Francisco, where he was in the process of opening a new branch office for the E. F. Hutton Company. But it came as a disappointment for her to learn that she and her aunt would be living on an estate in outlying Burlingame, while her father occupied a suite at San Francisco's Drake Hotel.

The property that Hutton leased for them was large with well-kept gardens and long sloping lawns, but isolated behind tall, ivy-covered stone walls. Barbara's sole companion for many months was a Shetland pony given to her for her ninth birthday. She named it Princess, though in fact it was a male pony. Although a fair number of well-to-do children lived in Burlingame, it took Barbara time to make her first acquaintances.*

One of her closest early companions was a redheaded girl named Consuelo "Nini" Tobin (today Mrs. Francis A. Martin), whose grandfather, M. H. de Young, was a pioneering California newspaper publisher. Barbara befriended a second girl, Harrie Hill (the future Mrs. Stanley Page), daughter of railroad baron Harry Hill. The three girls played together on the grounds of their homes and imagined they saw medieval archers and knights weaving through the surrounding woods; they created dramatic epics enlivened by real makeup and grown-up clothes. In these childhood dramas Barbara always assumed the role of a queen or princess, while Nini and Harrie played the parts of her ladies-in-waiting.

"Barbara never outgrew the princess role," Harrie Hill Page remarks. "She was an odd mixture of tomboy and dream princess. She climbed trees but had a fairy-princess complex. Her grandfather had always called her 'Princess.' She wanted the servants to call her 'Princess' too, and when they refused or forgot she would cry. Her aunt's chauffeur made a point of addressing her as 'Your Royal Highness,' and for a long time he was her favorite.

"She was a wistful, imaginative, lonely child with no family and few friends. Her father, while showering her with material possessions, fundamentally neglected her. He was almost never home, and most people in the neighborhood were just as glad. The man had a terrible temper, and the most trivial thing could set him off—a misplaced key, a stalled car, a few specks of dust on the floor. Whenever he was around, everyone else stayed away. He was a cruel and spiteful man. Brilliant in the brokerage business, I suppose, but he had no compassion for anyone, least of all his daughter. Nothing she did pleased him. He was cold, forever complaining, always yelling at people. Barbara was scared

*For his managerial duties as Barbara's trustee, Franklyn Hutton received 2 percent of his daughter's annual allowance, which was regulated by the Surrogate Court of Suffolk County, Long Island. When she was six, her allowance was $5,000 a year. At seven, it was $7,000. At nine, her father petitioned the court to raise it to $12,000. At thirteen, it went to $35,000 annually. At sixteen, she received a $60,000-a-year allowance. Thereafter it continued to rise in regular increments, reaching $300,000 before her twenty-first birthday.

to death of him. She wanted to impress him, win his approval, but she also hated his guts. He was very opinionated and dogmatic and if he couldn't convince you of something by reason, he could drum it home by raising his voice. Franklyn Hutton's worst feature, I suppose, was his drinking. He was an alcoholic.

"If Barbara had difficulty making friends at first, it was because of her wealth. A number of the children in the neighborhood came from prosperous homes, but Barbara's inheritance was of an altogether different order. Some of the kids taunted her because of it. They wanted to be her friend but were either intimidated or jealous. She was remote and rich and that frightened them, although she eventually made some friends: Christine Henry, Jane Christenson, Bobbie Carpenter. They were less close to Barbara at that time than in later years. She and Bobbie, for instance, had rather drifted apart, until Bobbie married a naval officer, Carpenter Tennant, in the mid-1930s. Then came beautiful diamond-and-ruby clips from the one who never forgot. Barbara always had a loving quality to her memory. She managed to blot out the bad and remember the good."

Nicoll Smith, son of Susan Smith, the San Francisco *Examiner* society columnist, also knew Barbara during this period: "Burlingame was an artsy-ginsy suburb with lots of parties and a very tight social clique. Everyone knew everything about everyone else. Most people felt sorry for Barbara. She had no family life. Her father was home only on holidays. And even then they didn't get along. I remember when he brought Barbara over to our house for a Christmas Eve dinner. In the middle of the meal he started spouting how he had never wanted a child in the first place. 'Let's face it,' he said, 'ninety-nine percent of the people on this planet were born out of a bottle of whiskey on a Saturday night. Why lie about it?' He said it right in front of Barbara. He was drunk. I don't remember ever seeing him when he wasn't intoxicated.

"My mother liked Barbara and began taking her with us whenever we went anywhere. They showed silent movies in those days at the Burlingame Country Club and every Saturday afternoon we went to see Theda Bara, the Gish sisters, William Hart, Pearl White, Charlie Chaplin, and the other screen immortals of the day. Barbara loved the movies. She had a great affinity for anything removed from reality.

"She had another great love—a store in San Francisco called Gump's, a magnificent jewelry parlor that handled mostly Oriental artifacts. The owner of the store, Mr. A. L. Gump, was an amazing man. He was blind but he was an expert in his field. He would give Barbara impromptu lectures on what to look for in jade, how to tell a genuine court piece from a counterfeit, how to appraise jewelry by touch rather than by sight. Her interest in Orientalia started at Gump's and stayed with her always. Over the years she became the store's best customer."

Barbara was presently enrolled at Miss Shinn's School for Girls, where many of her classmates showed signs of hostility. "Those girls used to tell me that people would always hate me because I had so much money," she claimed in later years. "Back then I didn't even know the meaning of money. Once when Aunt Jessie visited, I asked her if we could give all our money away. Jessie tried to explain why this couldn't be done. I couldn't grasp it and out of frustration began to cut up all my clothes with a pair of scissors."

Barbara's truest allies in Burlingame were drawn from among the household help employed by her father. There was always someone on the payroll to follow around. For several months it was Mrs. Jeanne Peterson, the family laundress, to whom she sent Christmas and birthday packages long after her retirement. Then there was Sophie Malluck, a German-born maid, who was later fired by Franklyn Hutton because of a dispute over wages. Another employee, a French governess named Mlle. Germaine Tocquet, who was known to the family as Ticki, became Barbara's closest confederate. A tiny cream puff of a woman, Ticki was first hired as a temporary replacement for Barbara's vacationing full-time nurse. When Ticki left at the end of her term, Barbara threw such a violent tantrum that her father quickly rehired her. She was to remain permanently with Barbara, first as governess and chaperone, and in later years as a social secretary and companion.

Barbara was eleven when Aunt Grace married Thomas Alston Middleton, a broker with the E. F. Hutton firm, and moved with him to Pleasantville, New Jersey. Franklyn Hutton returned to New York, and Barbara was sent off to the then fashionable Santa Barbara School for Girls, a half-day's drive from the few friends she had managed to make in Burlingame. Her two semesters at Santa Barbara were ill-spent. Her housemother at the school, Mrs. George Coles, indicated in an interview with San Francisco newspaperman Dean Jennings (the author of a 1968 profile of Barbara, *Barbara Hutton: A Candid Biography*) that she showed no interest in her classmates: "She was a lovely little girl, but she just never seemed to have a chance. She had so much money but no one to guide her or listen to her. She was lonely and very shy and spent a lot of time writing poetry that she did not show to anyone. No one ever came to see her at the school, not even at Christmas."

The only incident of note at Santa Barbara reported by Jennings involved a pair of students who took malicious pleasure in teasing

Barbara because she insisted on wearing expensive, tailored clothes. On one occasion Barbara heard them chattering about her and giggling outside her dormitory room. She opened her door and confronted them. "Did you come down to see my pretty dress?" she asked. The girls ran away and didn't trouble her again.

It was 1926 and Barbara, now fourteen, had returned to New York and was living with the Donahues; she attended classes at Miss Hewitt's School in Manhattan. Although she didn't care for the stuffiness of the school, she was pleased to be back on the east coast. The city was exhilarating. It shimmered with excitement, whereas California (as she wrote) was "all grapefruits and orange groves, sloth and slick."

Two events of note took place at this time. The first involved Barbara's father. Weary of bachelorhood, Hutton had remarried. His new wife was Irene Curley, a divorcée from Detroit and the former operator of a beauty salon. Barbara found her a bit loud and crass but eventually came to appreciate her. There was little not to appreciate about her. She was a warm, compassionate, not unattractive woman who happened to enjoy the good life, and was consequently better suited to it than Hutton's first wife. She also happened to be very fond of Barbara, and during family arguments always took Barbara's side. Another of her motherly deeds was to start a Barbara Hutton scrapbook, clipping articles and photographs of Barbara that appeared in the press and pasting them into a leatherbound album. "Those albums," Barbara noted, "were the only books my father allowed in the house. He didn't trust people who wrote books, and he trusted people who read them even less."

The second event was a financial one. At the beginning of 1926 the banking firm of Lehman Brothers, on the basis of Franklyn Hutton's timely recommendation, had placed 50,000 shares of Barbara's common-stock holdings in the Woolworth Company on the market. The offering constituted one of the largest transactions of its kind. At slightly more than $200 a share, the sale netted Barbara $10 million, which her father reinvested in a diversified portfolio of public stocks, bonds and securities, placing a portion of the assets in interest-bearing blue-chip stocks, speculating with the remaining funds in electronics, utilities and marginal commodities.

The disbursement of such a large block of common stock had a disastrous effect on the market in general and on the Woolworth Company in particular. Two months after the sale, the net value of the stock plunged dramatically, and those who had bought into the firm took a thorough drubbing. But for Barbara the sale and subsequent reinvestment of funds proved highly lucrative. A portion of her windfall was used to purchase a pair of adjoining duplex apartments at 1020 Fifth Avenue. It was decided that Barbara would occupy her own twenty-six-room duplex, and the Huttons theirs.

To cover the cost of Barbara's new apartment, her father filed a petition with Surrogate Court. The underlying tone of the document can be best described as haughty:

> Barbara's two aunts on her mother's side, Mrs. McCann and Mrs. Donahue, are ladies of wealth at least equal to hers, and my brother (E. F. Hutton) and his wife (Marjorie Merriweather Post) also possess extremely large means. Each of them maintains a large and expensive establishment in the neighborhoods of the apartments which I have purchased.
>
> My daughter, for her own safety and welfare in later years, must be brought up surrounded by the luxury and comfort to which her income entitles her, so that upon attaining the age of 21, at which time her fortune is to be turned over to her unrestricted control, she will have no desire or reason to embark upon a scale of expenditures in living to which she has not been accustomed during her formative years.

It is instructive to note that the E. F. Huttons counted as their New York residence the top three floors of a fourteen-story apartment building at 1107 Fifth Avenue, on the corner of Ninety-second Street. The triplex, consisting of seventy rooms, was the largest residential apartment in New York City and included an indoor swimming pool, ballroom, gymnasium, bakery, solarium and two private elevators. The apartment Barbara wanted seemed almost modest in comparison. The Surrogate Court agreed to her father's request. Barbara was granted $90,000 to purchase the duplex, $250,000 for renovations and improvements, and an extra $25,000 a year for maintenance.

Outwardly Barbara's life seemed well in hand. She was attractive (if somewhat pudgy), exorbitantly wealthy, bright, polite and sophisticated. She now had her own apartment, replete with Louis XIV furniture and a string of retainers. She had begun spending her summers abroad. She had a surrogate mother in the person of Ticki Tocquet, as well as a new stepmother. Yet for all her obvious advantages and all her money, Barbara was a disillusioned teenager. Her scrapbooks for this period contain entries that reflect a longing for something she can not quite grasp:

...I long for a friend, somebody to understand me, an intimate with whom to share my innermost thoughts and terrors.

...I am too reserved, too afraid of people. I am too sensitive and have too much pride. I must learn to be more open, less guarded...I should like best of all to be loved.

...Deep down I feel inadequate. I am ugly, fat, awkward. I am also dull. To be dull, says Aunt Jessie, is a cardinal sin. "Be mean, be stupid, but don't be dull!"

...I shall be an old maid. Nobody can ever love me. For my money but not for me. I am doomed. I will always be alone.

Barbara's childhood poetry reveals an alternate side of her personality, her deep conflicts and ambivalence over her wealth and privileged position. "Why?"—written when she was thirteen—succinctly poses the unanswerable question:

> *Why should some have all*
> *And others be without,*
> *Why should men pretend*
> *And women have to doubt?*

In another poem of this period, "Big Business," she explores the same theme while expressing a certain distaste for the more commercial aspects of capitalism:

> *I have no doubt you think you're smart*
> *Big Business*
> *With all your money*
> *But to others and me*
> *You're damn funny.*
>
> *Poor man, you'd scream with laughter*
> *If you could see your face,*
> *It bulges over your collar*
> *Like a boot that burnt its lace.*
>
> *But the silliest thing of all*
> *To me and all the fellers,*
> *Is the way you sing in church*
> *"God help us miserable sinners."*

At age fifteen Barbara was introduced by her Aunt Jessie to Cobina Wright, the imposing, elegant wife of socialite stockbroker William May Wright. In her autobiography, *I Never Grew Up*, Cobina described a lifestyle that was "all tinsel, all unreal...materialism to the nth degree. We both wanted everything bigger and better. That was the tempo, the watchword of our times."

Nothing demonstrates Cobina's claim better than the way her daughter, Cobina Junior, was brought up in the family mansion, Casa Cobina, on Long Island's North Shore. The estate came complete with a four-room playhouse for the child, a golf course for the father, a bathroom lined with mink for the mother. It was said of the Wrights' chauffeur that he owned his own chauffeur-driven Rolls-Royce. The family used one of their own Rolls-Royces just to take their poodle to the hairdresser every day. Cobina Junior had a specially built miniature Rolls in which she was driven to the polo matches at Sands Point by a midget chauffeur. She took her friends sailing on her father's yacht, was attended by fourteen servants, and owned a stable full of horses.

In their Sutton Place town house the Wrights threw parties that attracted not just New York society but some of the leading entertainers, actors and musicians of the day. A typical guest list was usually an odd coupling of money and talent, featuring names such as the Walter Chryslers, Tallulah Bankhead, Jules Bache,[*] Fred Astaire, Gertrude Vanderbilt Whitney, Arturo Toscanini, Bernard Baruch, Lawrence Tibbett, Mrs. Vincent Astor, Jimmy Durante.

Barbara Hutton attended several of these gatherings and on other occasions visited alone with the Wrights. "Barbara would sing," recalls Cobina Junior, "and Mother would accompany her on the piano. She was no Caruso, but she enjoyed singing. She was plump but very pretty with perfect facial features and alabaster skin. My mother's friends found her shy but pleasant. She sometimes brought along her cousin Jimmy Donahue, the only person who could consistently make her laugh. They were always together. Barbara was the same age as Woolworth Donahue, Jimmy's older brother, but she was closer to Jimmy."

Another frequent guest at the Wrights' was Doris Duke, a tall, thin, well-groomed girl with a protruding chin, which was later modified through plastic surgery. Dee-Dee, as she was known to friends, was the daughter of James Buchanan Duke, founder of the American Tobacco Company and of Duke University. When she was thirteen, Doris' father died and left her more than $70 million, a slew of town and country

---

[*]Following the death of F. W. Woolworth, it was Jules S. Bache, founder of the Wall Street brokerage firm and a friend of the Huttons, who purchased the Woolworth mansion at 990 Fifth Avenue in New York.

mansions, a private railroad car named "Doris," and thousands of shares of stock in the family business.

Although they were to become friends, Barbara and Doris had completely different orientations toward their respective inheritances. The essential difference was one of attitude. While Barbara had not the slightest interest in overseeing her finances, Doris had been brought up to believe that money was a responsibility. As a trustee of the influential Duke Foundation (which today still controls Duke University) she attended its monthly meetings, investigating its work, going so far as to make incognito inspections of the campus (in Durham, North Carolina) in tattered clothing and driving an old jalopy. She had the managers of the foundation administer her commercial interests but maintained a controlling hand in her personal affairs, disbursing her charities through a special nonprofit foundation established specifically for that purpose. Although her critics accused Doris of parsimony, she gave freely to assorted university and educational programs and helped support a number of art and musical societies. She was once quoted as saying, "When you are rich and careful you sometimes get a reputation for stinginess. I'm not stingy. I'm just afraid of being an easy mark. People wouldn't have money long if they didn't ask how much things cost and then refuse to buy half of them."

Barbara, with her later reputation for nonstop spending, was far less practical-minded than Doris, delegating all responsibility for her financial dealings to lawyers and business advisers. She never, to anyone's knowledge, attended an executive-board meeting of the Woolworth Corporation. Despite their sharply defined differences, the press insisted on lumping the two heiresses together. The papers christened them "the Gold Dust Twins" and "the poor little rich girls," the girls who had everything but love.

Three

A RECENT BROCHURE describes Miss Porter's School for Girls, located in Farmington, Connecticut, as a place where students "work in close contact with caring adults," who encourage them "to take pride in themselves as women and to develop leadership qualities that will help them take active and responsible roles in a new world." Although it has grown in size, Farmington (as the school is usually called) hasn't changed much from what Miss Sarah Porter, a girls' school headmistress in the classic New England mold, intended when she founded it in 1843. Despite Miss Porter's parochial background, the school has always catered to the rich and worldly, the girl whose parents wanted her to graduate polished but also educated.

The atmosphere at Farmington when Barbara matriculated in 1928 was distinctly high-minded, correct, superior, competitive, snobbish, cold and arbitrary. First-semester students were required to attend Sunday-night devotional meetings in the school chapel and were permitted to board their own horses in the school stables. There was no school uniform, but students were expected to dress conservatively. There was no smoking, drinking, cardplaying or gum chewing. The girls were prohibited from leaving the school grounds in term time unless special permission had been cleared through proper channels. There was even a regulation concerning the type of fiction the girls were allowed to read in their spare time. They were not permitted to read the popular novels of the day, a rule that Barbara broke repeatedly, and that led to several confrontations with Farmington's headmistress, Mrs. Rose Day Keep.

Those who attended Miss Porter's with Barbara remember a temperamental, standoffish teenager who liked to take long strolls by herself around the periphery of the campus, an area lined with old houses and giant elm trees. Although she rarely socialized with her classmates, she had a well-deserved reputation as a fashion plate, wearing the latest styles and outfits—tweed skirts by Chanel with inverted pleats, frilly jabot blouses; angoras with lynx collars and cuffs; the briefly popular "Franklyn" knits. The school did not approve; nor did her classmates. "It was as though she wanted to show us up," said one of them.

The dormitories for the then hundred-or-so students consisted of plain old-fashioned New England residences, each named after the family that had last owned it. During her first year Barbara lived in Lathorp House, sharing a large room with Eleanor Stewart Carson, a quiet, unassuming girl who made her debut the same year as Barbara and later married William B. Kraft, Jr., a socialite from Haverford, Pennsylvania. Eleanor died in 1972, but Kraft recalls that Barbara and his late wife were good friends. "Eleanor would listen to Barbara's nightly confessionals, her reminiscences of being sent off as a child from relative to relative, her father's indiscretions and alcoholism, her mother's mysterious death. More than once she brought up her father's dire prophecy that when she finally came of age nobody would want to marry her.

"One can hardly blame Barbara for feeling insecure about herself. Her father never lost an opportunity to chide or upbraid her. Once, in a moment of great candor, Barbara told Eleanor that she was convinced her father would actually rejoice were something drastic to happen to her. At some point during her first year at Miss Porter's, Barbara had to be taken to Hartford for an emergency appendectomy. Before going under, she scrawled out a one-page will and gave it to Eleanor for safekeeping. She wanted to be sure that if something happened, her father wouldn't get a penny of her money. It was a whimsical document, not at all legal, but it illustrates the extent of Barbara's alienation.

"She apparently wanted friends but couldn't bring herself to take the initiative in making them. So she convinced herself that she was different. She fantasized a lot. She covered her walls with laminated maps ordered from *National Geographic* and dreamed of exploring the strange and exotic places of the world—the places where girls at Farmington would never go and ostensibly where money didn't matter. Maybe that explains her ceaseless travels later in life."

Barbara's compulsion "to be different" took various forms. She refused to use the hairdressers from nearby Hartford whom the school brought in, preferring to cut and style her own hair. For a while she resorted to some strange hair dyes—bright gold on one occasion, platinum on another. During her more somber moments Barbara could be heard playing Brahms on an old upright piano located in the student lounge. For her weight problem she went on coffee-and-cracker binges. She finally telephoned Ticki in New York and made her purchase a pair of large weight-reduction rollers, then a popular method of slimming down. To the great amusement of her classmates Barbara would stretch out on the floor of her dormitory room atop the two wooden rollers and put herself through the painful exercises every evening.*

One of Barbara's classmates at Farmington was her McCann cousin, Helena, whose mother made frequent trips to the campus, often bringing along Jessie Donahue. Aunt Helena, less ostentatious than her younger sister, was visible nonetheless in her costly Paris designers' originals. But it was Aunt Jessie with her decorative jewelry who manifested the more noticeable image of new wealth. It was one thing for Barbara to wear the latest fashions around school; it was something else to have an aunt prancing about in finery and jewels better suited to opening night at the Met.†

It was another aunt, Marjorie Merriweather Post, a woman of supreme self-confidence and fierce optimism, who gave Barbara her first taste of hope for the foreseeable future. Born in Springfield, Illinois, in 1887, Marjorie was the daughter of Charles William Post, a farm-machinery repairman and itinerant inventor who started out selling suspenders door to door. In 1894, at age forty, C. W. Post went into a sanatarium in Battle Creek, Michigan, suffering from nervous exhaustion. While there, he became interested in health foods. Once recovered, he began to market a caffeine-free coffee substitute called Postum, followed by a breakfast cereal known as Grape-Nuts. These two products made C. W. Post a very rich man and formed the nucleus of the General Foods Corporation, the parent company of such products as Jell-O, Swan's Down Cake Mix, Minute Tapioca and Birds Eye Frozen Foods. From the day of her father's death in 1914, it was Marjorie Post who ran the organization, aided by her first husband, Edward B. Close, member of a socially prominent New England family. Their marriage lasted fifteen

*See Dean Jennings, *Barbara Hutton,* p. 40.
†See Philip Van Rensselaer, *Million Dollar Baby,* p. 30.

years, until 1919; a year later Marjorie married Edward F. Hutton, who had also been married once before. Taking a leave of absence from his brokerage firm, Hutton became director of General Foods and developed it into the largest food-processing corporation in the world. The E. F. Huttons had one child, Nedenia, later known as the actress Dina Merrill; Deenie, as her parents called her, was Barbara Hutton's first cousin.

Edward F. (Ned) Hutton was slightly taller and less broad-shouldered than his brother, Franklyn. His rugged profile and wavy, prematurely gray hair made him immensely appealing to members of the opposite sex. Marriage was never a deterrent to E. F. Hutton's pursuit of sexual fulfillment. Like Franklyn, he flaunted his extramarital affairs as though they were trophies amassed in his favorite outdoor sports: deep-sea fishing and big-game hunting. Both brothers were sportsmen. Both owned vast plantations and game preserves near Charleston, South Carolina. Both also bred a variety of exotic East Indian partridge twice the size of the familiar domestic breed.

Marjorie Post Hutton became famous for her exuberant display of riches, her capricious spending, her preoccupation with power, parties and possessions. Yet she did not believe in owning emptily. She was both an ardent clubwoman and an altruistic benefactor, supporting all manner of charitable and educational organizations, the best known being the Hell's Kitchen soup dispensary that fed thousands of New Yorkers during the Depression.

On the other hand, this was the same woman who thought nothing of hiring the entire Ringling Bros. Circus or the cast of a Broadway play to entertain at one of her massive bashes. She owned estates along the North Shore of Long Island; in Greenwich, Connecticut, in the heart of the Adirondacks, and in Palm Beach, as well as the acclaimed triplex in New York City. The Palm Beach palace, which she and Hutton built jointly, was named Mar-a-Lago, meaning sea-to-lake in Spanish, appropriate considering that the eighteen-acre property stretched from Lake Worth on one side to the Atlantic on the other. Built by architect Marion Simms Wyeth and set designer Joseph Urban, the 123-room structure cost its owners $10 million and another million a year in maintenance. It was the second largest private residence in the United States, the first being William Randolph Hearst's San Simeon in California.

When Barbara Hutton first saw Mar-a-Lago, apparently during spring recess of 1929,* she was most impressed by the fact that each guest

---

*Philip Van Rensselaer describes the visit in *Million Dollar Baby*, but sets the date as Christmas vacation of 1928.

bedroom contained a panel of buzzers representing a variety of services. If you pushed one buzzer a waiter appeared carrying a glass of freshly squeezed orange juice; another buzzer brought a maid with a vase of flowers; a third buzzer alerted the chauffeur that he was to drive the guest to Worth Avenue for shopping.

Barbara went down to Palm Beach that year with the Donahues, including her cousins, Jimmy and Woolworth Donahue. Her favorite activity was purportedly swimming, which she did at any of the resort's three leading country clubs: the Bath and Tennis (located a block from Mar-a-Lago); the Seminole (of which E. F. Hutton was president); the Everglades (Barbara's favorite of the three).

The highlight of Barbara's stay must have been a gala luncheon at the Bath and Tennis that Aunt Marjorie gave in honor of Grand Duke Alexander of Russia, the brother-in-law of former Czar Nicholas II. The guest list, which was published in several newspapers, included the names of the rich and famous: H.R.H. Prince Cyril of Bulgaria, Lady Wavetree, Baron and Baroness von Einem, Mr. and Mrs. Edward A. Stotesbury, Mr. and Mrs. John S. Pillsbury. Whatever else the luncheon might have demonstrated, it conveyed the message that Marjorie Merriweather Post knew the right people and felt at home in their company.

Back at Farmington, Barbara's social fortunes rapidly improved. Now that she was in her second semester, she was accorded a few extra privileges, including the right to attend college functions, not overnight but with extended curfews. She went on several prearranged dates with Yale undergraduates. Two of her escorts were Allen Hapke and Fred Gilmore, who were both members of the Yale football team.

There was another Yale man at this time named Dick Bettis, a scholarship student who professed to know little about the Woolworth millions. He invited Barbara to the Yale-Harvard-Princeton triangular track meet held at New Haven that spring; the two of them went on several picnics together. One weekend when she was visiting Aunt Marjorie in New York, Bettis came down from New Haven to escort Barbara to the theater. They went dancing afterward at the Embassy Club on East Fifty-seventh Street, where Bettis drank bootleg wine and Barbara drank lemonade. The next evening they went to the Central Park Casino and danced to the music of Eddy Duchin.

Barbara liked Bettis. He was tall and angular, with regular but sensitive features. He was from a large New England family more interested in literature than money, which may have accounted for Barbara's interest in him. Too often the men forced upon her were of her own background. Bettis was the first man she was even moderately serious about.

The only problem was the rapid approach of the summer of 1929. As in summers past, Barbara was expected to accompany her parents to Europe. She suddenly balked at the prospect, informing them that she preferred to stay in New York. Hutton tried every means at his disposal to change her mind, offering the usual parental caveat that if Dick Bettis truly cared he would wait until she returned; and if he didn't wait, neither should she. To sweeten the pot, Hutton accompanied Barbara to Cartier. Two trays, each containing fifty ruby rings, were brought out and placed before her. If she agreed to go along without further fuss, he would buy her the ring of her choice. Barbara surveyed the rings and then pointed to the one she wanted.

"Are you sure?" inquired Hutton.

"I'm sure," said Barbara.

The salesman beamed. Barbara had chosen the most expensive ruby in the collection, one of the finest rubies in the Cartier vaults. When Hutton heard the price the blood drained from his face. He had counted on spending at most $5,000, not $50,000. His only consolation was the knowledge that his daughter had developed an exquisite taste in jewels.

In Paris, Barbara soon forgot about Dick Bettis and after several weeks she and Ticki traveled to Biarritz, where they stayed with William and Buelah Fiske, friends of Franklyn Hutton. The Huttons remained behind in Paris to tie up some unfinished business. It was at the Fiskes' that Barbara first met Elsa Maxwell, whose nominal profession was journalism but whose fame emanated from her parties and her successful introductions of wealthy American heiresses to impoverished but pedigreed Europeans.

Elsa recorded her initial impressions of Barbara in her autobiography, *R.S.V.P.**: "When I arrived [at the Fiskes] the only other person on the terrace was a girl who was wearing a dress too tight for her. It was too hot to make conversation with a strange child, who I guessed was about fifteen or sixteen. I merely nodded to her and waited for my host. With perfect poise, the girl came across the terrace and introduced herself as Barbara Hutton, explaining that she was staying with the Fiskes... It was not until she made a passing reference to her aunt, Jessie Donahue, that I placed the girl, whose body was exaggerated by her tiny hands and feet. I was also struck by her large, lustrous eyes,

---

*The Elsa Maxwell scenes that follow are redacted from several sources, including *R.S.V.P.* and Elsa Maxwell's three-part *International-Cosmopolitan* article, "The Truth About Barbara Hutton," as well as *Barbara Hutton*, by Dean Jennings.

which remained curiously expressionless while she prattled in an obvious effort to talk like a sophisticated grownup."

Barbara spoke about music with Miss Maxwell. The child was an admirer of George Gershwin, Noël Coward and Cole Porter, and knew many of their songs by heart.

"What else are you interested in?" Elsa asked.

"Poetry and Chinese art," said Barbara. She recited a poem of her own and talked about China. Then the Fiskes appeared and lunch was served. When it was over, Elsa, who was staying with Jean Patou, the Parisian couturier, invited Barbara to attend a cocktail party at Patou's Biarritz house the following afternoon. Barbara accepted the invitation.

That evening Elsa and Patou looked over the guest list together. Eventually they reached a name that caught Elsa's attention: Prince Alexis Mdivani. Although she knew most of the émigré Russian princes, here was a name she failed to recognize.

"Is the title legitimate?" she asked.

Patou laughed and explained that the Mdivanis came from Tiflis in Georgia, a part of the world where anyone with three sheep was considered royalty. "In the West they have another title," he explained. "Alexis and his brothers are known as 'the marrying Mdivanis.' At the moment Serge Mdivani is married to the actress Pola Negri. David Mdivani is also married to an actress—Mae Murray. And Alexis, the baby of the family, is engaged to Louise Astor Van Alen, a young American heiress whose family tree bulges with Astors and Vanderbilts. Louise also has two brothers and one of them is James Van Alen, the former U.S. amateur tennis champion."

"Getting back to the Mdivanis," said Elsa, " —isn't their sister the Roussadana Mdivani who stole the Spanish painter José Maria Sert away from his wife?"

"Exactly!" cried Patou. "Roussie Sert is a tall, graceful, bone-thin beauty with silver-blond hair, whose taste in fashion is impeccable. She's as cunning as her brothers, more so. The strain runs pure through the entire clan. There's another sister as well, Nina, whose husband, half her age, is Charles Henry Huberich, an American lawyer with a practice in Holland. He's the mastermind behind the marriage contracts and divorce settlements. They may sound pernicious but they're really not that wicked. Besides, they're much in vogue."

In fact, the Mdivanis were no better or worse than a hundred other White Russian émigré families living in Europe. They were originally from Imeritia, one of three Georgian kingdoms later annexed by Russia. The name Mdivani (silent "M"), from the Persian word *divan*, meant "he who sits on the divan," an Oriental circumlocution for "secretary to a potentate." It suggests that an ancestor must have served one of the ancient Moslem rulers of Georgia. Zakharias Mdivani, the patriarch of "the marrying Mdivanis," had risen to the rank of colonel in the Georgian army and at one point served as an aide-de-camp to Czar Nicholas II. It seems, however, that the colonel met the Czar on but a single occasion. There existed a photograph of this momentous encounter, Colonel Mdivani standing at attention, Nicholas seated like a peacock upon his throne. This photograph, smuggled out of Russia when the Mdivanis fled, was dragged out at the least provocation as proof of the clan's aristocracy.

Despite their regal airs, the Mdivanis never possessed the rank to which they laid claim. It was a title they adopted only after leaving Russia and arriving in post-World War I Paris, a means of gaining entrée to the rarefied salons of French society. Only the colonel, insisting on the valor of his own accomplishments, refused to go along with the little hoax. One of the stories associated with the Mdivanis had it that when anybody in Paris called the house and asked for Prince Mdivani, the father responded, "You must mean one of my sons." In a similar vein he once informed the press that he was the only man in history who had inherited a title from his offspring.

Genealogy was hardly the motivating force that brought Barbara Hutton to Jean Patou's villa on that sunny summer afternoon. Elsa Maxwell tried to engage her in conversation, but Barbara quickly repaired by herself to a distant corner, her face hidden behind a frozen mask.

The guests were strewn about the large salon in small intimate eddies, many dressed in the latest mode of informal resort wear— lounging pajamas. Patou had devised his own line of daytime bedwear and people went around day and night dressed either for bed or for the beach. Barbara seemed content to sit and watch Patou's guests carousing in their gaily patterned garb.

> Then something very strange happened [writes Elsa Maxwell in *R.S.V.P.*]—something so strange that I cannot give a rational explanation for it. I was standing near Barbara and I saw her suddenly stiffen with anticipation as an enormous Rolls-Royce drove up emblazoned with a coronet that couldn't have been more conspicuous had it been outlined in neon. Prince Mdivani...bounded out the car followed at a discreet distance by Miss Van Alen. He glanced around the large room crowded with sixty people—and headed for Barbara in the corner as though he had an appointment with her. Mdivani couldn't possibly have known Barbara

was to be at the party. Neither Patou nor I had told anyone she was invited. Barbara since has told me she never had met Mdivani.

The simple truth is that Barbara was lying. Not only did she know Alexis Mdivani, she also knew Louise Van Alen, the latter from Bailey's Beach, the center of summer high life in Newport. As teenagers growing up in New York, Barbara and Louise had both attended many of the same parties and social events.

Barbara's friendship with Alexis dated to 1925 when they were introduced by a mutual friend, Silvia de Rivas (later Silvia de Castellane), a girl three years older than Barbara who lived in Paris with her titled Spanish-born father (Count de Castille Jaet) and Colombian mother. Silvia and her elder brother, Philippe, were among Barbara's first acquaintances in Europe. Silvia, a dynamic and self-assured young lady, stood at the center of a tight circle of youthful members of international café society, which every summer seemed to gravitate to Biarritz. Barbara Hutton's friendship with Silvia enabled her to gain quick entrance into this fast-moving crowd.

Alexis Mdivani also came to this crowd through Silvia. Like most girls her age, Silvia found Alexis disarmingly attractive. He had a wide Russian face, a full lower lip that protruded in a pout, a small straight nose, and curly sandy-colored hair and deep grayish-green eyes; his voice was throaty and seductive. His early skill at polo had enabled him to play from a young age on some of the leading international teams, with teammates no less prestigious than the Prince of Wales and Lord Louis Mountbatten. He was precocious in another respect. His first sexual encounter, while only fourteen, was with Mistinguett, the leggy star of the Folies-Bergére. This was followed by a tempestuous fling with the American actress Kay Francis; a passing affair with Louise Cook, a black bellydancer; and a romance with Evelyn Clark, a leading junior member of Newport society. But it was with Silvia Rivas that he fell in love.

Their romance created problems. Silvia's overprotective, aristocratic parents were opposed to Alexis, who didn't live up to their standards. When Silvia's father learned that the young couple planned to elope, he threatened to disinherit his daughter. He hired a private detective to follow her around and went personally to speak with Mdivani's father. Such behavior spurred the headstrong Georgian youth on. But in 1929, when the New York stock market crashed, the Rivas family was all but wiped out. Silvia's parents wanted her to marry Henri de Castellane, Duke of Valençay, the aging and tubercular but wealthy nephew of the noted Count Boni de Castellane who so successfully and cynically glorified the male art of fortune hunting by his turn-of-the-century marriage to Anna Gould, daughter of the American railroad baron Jay Gould.* In the French manner, Silvia's was to be an "arranged" marriage, eminently "proper" and not at all unusual according to Latin custom.

Alexis quickly turned his attention to Louise Van Alen, whose brothers, Jimmy and Sam, he had befriended in England. Louise was not only much wealthier than Silvia but more immediately available. This, too, was to be an "arrangement," an affair of convenience. But if Alexis was an opportunist, he was also a romantic. He had telephoned Barbara the morning of the Patou party and had arranged to meet her there to discuss his frustrating relationship with Silvia. Nobody knew Silvia better than Barbara. During their summers together at Biarritz, the two girls had grown as close as sisters.

Barbara and Alexis huddled in the corner of Patou's living room, completely absorbed in conversation. Alexis ignored Louise, who sat elsewhere and tried to feign indifference. Always the attentive hostess, Elsa walked over to the couple and asked Barbara if she wished to join the crowd in the swimming pool. Barbara declined and turned back to Alexis. But Alexis was already on his feet. He took Barbara's hand and kissed it. Then he turned on his heels and walked out of the house, trailed by Louise Van Alen. During the hour that he was there he had not spoken a word to his host or, for that matter, to anyone else except Barbara.

After Mdivani's departure, Barbara's eyes began to brim with tears. "What's wrong? Did he say something that offended you?" asked Elsa.

Barbara shook her head. "No, no. He was very kind," she said. "I—I just have something in my eye."

Elsa felt intuitively what Barbara could not bring herself to admit. Alexis, with his impetuous bravado and charismatic good looks, appealed to her. Her confusion was fairly evident. She had never before given Mdivani a serious thought. Why should she? He was engaged to marry Louise Van Alen and at the same time was in love with one of Barbara's closest friends. She left Biarritz without seeing him again.

❧

By the middle of July, Franklyn and Irene Hutton had returned from Paris to Biarritz to retrieve Barbara and Ticki, and together they

---

*The marriage of Anna Gould and Count Paul Ernest Boniface de Castellane, who was known simply as Boni, gained Anna a title and Boni a fortune. After their divorce Boni summed up the marriage: "It was very simple—our eyes met, our hands met, our lips met, and our attorneys met."

traveled by train to the twin-towered Carlton Hotel in Cannes. A photograph of Barbara playing croquet on the hotel's back lawn shows a plumpish girl, looking older than her sixteen years in a clinging dress and high-heeled pumps, gripping a maple mallet with both hands and addressing a croquet ball. Her hair is cropped and styled in the post-flapper fashion of the day. Her face is handsome rather than pretty, though other photographs stress the winsome quality in greater detail. Author Alice-Leone Moats in her book *The Million Dollar Studs*, describes Barbara at this time: "The combination of regular, fine features, large gray-blue eyes under eyebrows like wide black velvet strips that contrasted dramatically with her blondness could never have made her anything but pretty."

When not playing croquet Barbara read, tearing through much of modern French literature, perusing a book a day, reading all in the original, underlining unfamiliar words and phrases and going over them later with Ticki. She read wherever she happened to be—by the pool, on the strand, in her hotel room.

Franklyn Hutton, attempting to distract her, signed Barbara up for a series of private tennis lessons. One of the tennis instructors at the Carlton, Peter Storey, was tall and reedy, with dark curls, lively blue eyes, broad brow and strong jaw. A graduate of Cambridge, Storey came from an upper-class English family. Barbara was intrigued, but then, so were a number of the girls and women who took private tennis lessons from him.

One afternoon after her lesson, Barbara made a point of loitering around the clubhouse under the pretext of purchasing a new tennis racquet. For a few minutes she and Storey debated the pros and cons of the various models. Gradually the conversation turned personal.

He was born and raised in London, he said, but since graduating had lived and worked in Paris, an employee in the French branch of his family's banking firm. Only recently had he left the firm to become a writer. He was working on a novel, supporting himself by teaching tennis, writing nights and on days off.

It was a romantic notion, Barbara pointed out, especially since it was so difficult to succeed as an author. Did he regret not pursuing his original career?

"No," he said, "no regrets." He had joined the bank only to appease his father, who had entered the business only to appease *his* father. He was relieved he had left the job when he did.

And did he like Cannes? she inquired.

Cannes was a bastion of privilege, a haven for the rich. He had liked it better when it was only a small fishing village and no one had ever heard of it. "Once a place becomes special," he said, "it's no longer special."

The next evening he invited Barbara to a small, romantic, out-of-the-way restaurant. It was pleasant to sip wine on the terrace, chatting and watching the sun slowly sink, the last rays turning the Mediterranean gold. The sommelier brought more wine. Later they went for a ride in an open horse-drawn carriage. "It was a cool and star-filled evening," Barbara remarks in her notebooks. "And it was pretty heavenly to hold hands and kiss and think away all the bad thoughts in the world. He put his hands on my throat and on my breasts. He was excited, tender, and I was happy. 'I feel wonderful,' I said. 'I can't believe how wonderful I feel.' 'You sound surprised,' he said. To be honest, I think I was."

The next evening he invited her to his home in Antibes, a few miles east of Cannes. Ticki provided an alibi, informing the Huttons that she and Barbara were going to the movies, then attending the film herself, while Barbara disappeared with her date.

Antibes was a stamp-sized village, much more sedate than Cannes, with pebbled beaches and tiny houses set among dark hills. Wild-flower gardens dotted gentle slopes, and sailboats bobbed lazily in the harbor. They ate cheese and crackers and held hands, and as Barbara put it, "played footsies while staring at the sea." It was all very thrilling because Barbara felt she had "earned this man, earned the right to be alone with him."

The entry for August 2, 1929, tells the rest. "The house was comfortably cool, and Peter said we should climb into bed, under the sheet. Peter is all rib cage and no chest, with jagged edges that hurt, but his skin is baby smooth. It was my first experience with a man who devoured me. I have never felt like this before. It is like being captured and drained. It is not altogether pleasant, and it certainly isn't very graceful. Peter is 26 and must be very experienced..."

Barbara stayed until dawn: "It was just getting daylight as we drove back to the hotel on the road that ran along the sea. The sea was peaceful. And the birds started singing. The colors were muted. It was a dewy morning, a bright new day."

Four

T HE SUMMER of 1929 represented a turning point in Barbara
Hutton's life, her emergence from the confining cocoon of adolescence
into the free flight and rapid transformation of young adulthood. Men
were to take on a new significance. Already Barbara seemed to relate to
them as though her experiences represented an interlocking series of
passion plays, with herself as heroine and the man (or hero) as the
unattainable object of her desire. The play endured only as long as the
hero remained just out of reach; the moment he capitulated, the
moment he revealed his feelings, he was discarded and ultimately
replaced.

A pattern of behavior had clearly been established and it was first
enacted that fall on Barbara's return from Europe. Dick Bettis had been
relegated to the role of comrade, and Peter Storey was a mere memory.
Of her night with Storey, she confided only in Ticki Tocquet and her
cousin Jimmy Donahue. She told them also of her attraction to Alexis
Mdivani, the newest hero in her pantheon of white knights. Fearful
that her revelations might reach the ears of her vindictive classmates at
Farmington, she told no one else, not even Eleanor Carson, with whom
she once again shared a dormitory room.

As morose in school as she had been the year before, Barbara
summed up her feelings in a letter to a friend: "Finishing school picks
up where the governess left off. Girls are sent to these places to attain a
smattering of book knowledge and a large measure of social etiquette.

When she finishes, the student supposedly knows how to enter and leave a room, carry on insignificant conversation with complete strangers, and worm her way into the heart of Mr. Right."

The recipient of this acerbic brief was Foster Blakely, a student at Yale whose brother Jimmy was also a friend. The Blakely brothers, Jimmy Donahue, and another fraternal duo, George and Louis Ehret, were among her closest companions during this period. All five, for that matter, escorted her to her debutante ball in 1930. The Ehret boys, like the Blakelys, were earnest young gentlemen-about-town, Ivy Leaguers whose family fortune derived from oil and real estate.

"At that time Barbara had few girlfriends," Louis Ehret recalls. "She had mostly male friends and suitors. She was fun to be around, loved going to the theater and out to dinner. She seemed quite proper, very much the lady, but she was attracted even then to eccentric characters. Her cousin Jimmy Donahue, whom she adored, was bright as a dime and very witty but his sense of humor was of the washroom variety, full of cloacal references and four-letter words. He never stopped talking about orifices, of what went into and came out of them. This was partially the fault of his mother, Aunt Jessie, who dressed him in girls' clothing until he was eight or nine. His brother Wooly also had a strange sense of humor. He would go swimming and take a crap in your swimming pool. But at least he was straight. Jimmy was a flaming fag. Barbara was titillated by all his talk. Even at that age he was queering half the big-name homosexuals in New York, people like Maury Paul, the gossip columnist. And he wasn't too discreet about it. It was a good diversion for Barbara from that uptight school she was going to, which she hated so much.

"She had several girlfriends in New York—Doris Duke, Gretchen Upperçu, Virginia Warren—but her closest girlfriend at the time was probably Jane Alcott, a very attractive and slim brunette she used to visit at home in East Hampton. Jane complained that Barbara talked only about diets and boys. Barbara didn't get along with most girls because they were jealous of her money. Or maybe that's just a rationalization Barbara invented to protect herself.

"There were so many fictions and myths that sprouted up around Barbara that it's hard to say what's true and what's not. It wasn't true that she and her father were mortal enemies. They didn't always get along but they certainly didn't hate each other. He called her 'babykins' and 'Bobbie,' which she didn't like, but otherwise they seemed compatible."

This view of Barbara and her father is shared by J. D. Webb, a Florida sportsman who was friendly with Franklyn Hutton. "Their relationship improved as Barbara matured," says Webb. "And Barbara matured early, both physically and mentally. When she visited Palm Beach with her father and stepmother over Christmas vacation of 1929, she was already a woman. I saw her standing alone in front of a shop on Worth Avenue in a *Vogue*-model pose, looking much wiser than her years. She was ravishing looking. And she had nothing but nice things to say about her father."

Despite the well-intentioned assertions of Ehret and Webb that all was peaceful within the family unit, there was evidence of continued and even mounting pressures between Barbara and her father. In the spring of 1930 a series of strange events underlined the basic differences that existed between Barbara and her immediate family. The first of these occurred in early May, toward the end of Barbara's last semester at Farmington, while she was visiting with the McCanns at Sunken Orchard. At some point during her weekend stay she and several friends of her McCann cousins attended a party at somebody's home in East Hampton. "It was a clambake," wrote Barbara in her notebooks, "with corn on the cob, [bootleg] beer and a loud band that played one brassy song after another. There were these boring boys, Harvard freshmen and Columbia sophomores mostly, and it was just yak-yak-yak until I couldn't stand it anymore. So I left and walked up the street. It was late and very still. I kept going until I reached somebody's dock, and that's when I saw the boat.

"I'd perched on the jetty and was dangling my feet in the water, which felt unusually warm considering the time of year, and this great white sloop, moored out fifty yards or so, seemed to beckon. I didn't have to think about it very long. I lowered myself into the water and swam out, and to my surprise, the sails hadn't been unzipped. I pulled them up. Then I reeled in the mainsheet and the whole thing pivoted on its keel and went off with a woosh. I must have been a mile away before I realized what I had just done: I had stolen somebody's boat.

"I can't imagine what went through my mind at that moment. I knew my way around a boat, but I had never been on one by myself before. I was soaked to the bone, so I wrapped myself in a blanket I found on board. I located the compass, but I began to worry about things such as rocks and reefs and other vessels—but mostly, I suppose, I worried about drifting out to sea. It was only after I saw that I could pretty well control the sloop that I began to relax. I sat back and enjoyed myself. The moon and the stars were as bright as I had ever seen them. I had always wanted to be an explorer. I thought about that, and I thought about *Robinson Crusoe*, which had always been a favorite book, and I wondered what it would be like to be shipwrecked on a tropical island.

"It was perfect sailing weather, the wind up but not too strong, the sea gently hitting the sides of the 40-foot craft. It was a euphoric feeling being alone on the water like that, sailing along, waiting for the sun to rise. The night passed quickly, and the sun rose slowly, bringing with it a ragged crew of seagulls. It was a red sunrise, more perfect than the most perfect painted sunrise. I was in my boat, and it was so beautiful in the early morning sea, all brass and mahogany, everything shipshape, not a blemish, the white of the boat as white as bleach, the mast bending slightly in the sea breeze. It occurred to me that I could probably cross the Atlantic in that boat. As I held the tiller, I imagined all sorts of possibilities. I wasn't afraid. I had a boat under me, and I only had to tug on the tiller and the cords would pull taut and send the craft off in another direction.

"I was still lost in my revery of adventure when I saw the Coast Guard cutter off my port bow, cruising toward me. The sloop had been reported missing, and they had been plotting me for hours. They were very gentlemanly and didn't ask any questions as they took me aboard and prepared to turn around. I hadn't drifted more than fifteen miles from East Hampton. I took a shower, ate a large breakfast and was out like a light. The next thing I knew we were back on shore."

Although Barbara had no regrets, her father was hardly amused by the incident. He reimbursed the boat's owner for minor damages incurred during Barbara's little sea voyage and pulled strings to keep the story out of the press. In an effort to contain his rebellious daughter, Hutton waited several weeks, until she was graduated from Miss Porter's, and then hired a security guard to keep an eye on her—a direct assault, she maintained, on her privacy. She also regarded it as a deliberate attempt on her father's part to control her social activities and to keep her under wing.

Within a few days of the bodyguard's arrival Barbara proceeded to seduce the man in the privacy of her Fifth Avenue duplex. Although the individual remains nameless in her notebook, Barbara spares nothing in the way of graphic detail: "He was rampant as a bull, literally tearing himself out of his clothes, then diving on top of me. His recuperative powers were admirable. We made love repeatedly and for hours. I was black and blue and torn and tattered and covered with stickiness."

This, her second one-night stand in as many affairs, was an out-and-out act of mutiny against her father. To ensure that he learned of it,

Barbara "confessed" to Irene Hutton, who in turn told her husband. Hutton reacted in predictable fashion: "At first he said nothing at all to me; he just looked at me as if I were an insect of some kind. But after a few days he began to bombard me with questions—he wanted to know *why* I had done it and *how* could I have done it and *what if* it got out and had I told anyone else and how *inconceivable* the whole thing was to him, and he even said how *repulsive* he found it and how unlike me. Then he wanted to know if I had ever been with a man before, and of course I lied and said I hadn't. I don't think he believed me. 'Why a security guard,' he said, 'why not a chimney sweep or a garbage collector or the husband of the chambermaid? You have such elegant taste, my dear.'"

After dismissing the bodyguard, Hutton hired a chauffeur, Clinton Gardiner, with the agreement that Gardiner would keep an eye on Barbara, though not as close an eye as his predecessor. Gardiner was married and his wife, Lilian, was invited to join Barbara's budding entourage. It was not long after this that Franklyn Hutton petitioned Surrogate Court in his daughter's name, pointing out Barbara's urgent need to own her own private railway car:

> I have finished school and am now about to make my debut at a large dance which my father is giving for that purpose at the Ritz-Carlton.
>
> In addition to our apartments on Fifth Avenue, my father maintains a home in Palm Beach, a plantation and shooting preserve near Charleston, South Carolina, and we usually spend summers at Newport, Rhode Island, when not abroad. During the next few years I anticipate that my father will entertain extensively for me at Palm Beach, New York, Charleston and Newport, and our family will make frequent trips between those places, and I expect to accompany them with guests of my own. My own personal fortune is infinitely greater than that possessed by my father, and in view of the great amount of traveling the family expects to do during the next few years, I am desirous of having my father purchase for me, out of my income, a private car.
>
> I am informed by my father, and verily believe, that the cost of this car will not exceed $120,000, and that the annual maintenance or expense will not be in excess of $36,000. While this sum is a large one, the maintenance expense of the first year will be less than one-tenth of my income, and the purchase of the car will give me, as well as other members of the family, so much pleasure that I do not consider it an extravagance for one of my position and means.
>
> My two aunts have and maintain private cars, chiefly for the purpose of making trips back and forth from Palm Beach and their summer homes, and having my father and guardian purchase one for me will only give me

what other members of my family have, and at the same time will be spending only a small part of my income, and giving employment to others instead of adding to my own fortune, which is already amply large.

The prospect of providing "employment to others" as justification for the six-figure purchase price of a private railway car, especially in light of the deepening financial crisis, gave rise to a considerable amount of debate in the press. Another bone of contention concerned the inclusion of a second request in the same document, this one relating to Barbara's pending debut, in which the debatable issue of employment was again raised:

> I ask that my father be allowed to reimburse himself for the expenses of my debut to the extent of $10,000 out of my income, this amount to be given in our family's name to this most worthy charity (unemployment relief) which I am most anxious to see aided, believing as I do that, in view of the great unemployment that now exists, it is the duty of people situated as fortunately as I am, to aid in the relief of those less fortunately situated.

The $10,000 donation seemed like nothing more than a convenient way to salve the family conscience. The venture took on nepotistic overtones with the disclosure that the relief fund's co-chairwoman was Barbara's aunt, Marjorie Post Hutton. But the petition's most unfortunate aspect was that Franklyn Hutton devised it in his daughter's name; when critics attacked the family for their oppression of the poor, it was Barbara who reaped most of the blame.

The conservative court endorsed the petition in all its particulars. The private railway car was built according to Franklyn Hutton's specifications. For $125,000 the Berwick Car Company of Berwick, Pennsylvania, produced a Pullman with a bedroom suite, three baths, dining salon, galley, glass-enclosed observation platform and a sitting lounge. The car was named "Curleyhut" —Curley was Irene Hutton's maiden name; "Hut" was Franklyn's nickname. "Curleyhut" seemed appropriate, since Franklyn and Irene used the coach far more than Barbara.

The wealth of the various Huttons was so widely and wisely invested that the family emerged from the Great Depression barely bruised by it. In this respect they were more fortunate than many of their friends. There were numerous cases of people who awoke millionaires one

morning and went to bed penniless that night. It was not uncommon to
see ladies offering their fur coats for sale in hotel lobbies; yachts, polo
ponies and Rolls-Royces were being sold for quick cash. High-society
princesses suddenly found themselves behind the sales counters and
cash registers of department stores. Or they took jobs as hostesses in
restaurants, receptionists in offices, nurses in hospitals. Cobina Wright
and her daughter donned Daniel Boone raccoon caps and formed a
supper-club singing act. "WRIGHTS PERFORM IN FRONTIER GARB: SO-
CIETY IS DEAD!" roared one headline. Cobina's husband was wiped out,
the marriage dissolved, and she and her daughter relocated to California, where Cobina eventually became a successful society columnist.
She also received generous financial support from friends, including a
gift of $50,000 from Jessie Donahue.

"Soc-i-i-i-i-i-ety," as nineteenth-century social commentator Julia
Ward Howe termed it, was not yet quite dead. It was mortally wounded
and in a state of flux, but it still existed, even if it existed in a vastly
altered form. Those whose fortunes had been shrewdly invested, or who
simply had too much money to be affected by the collapse, survived
handsomely. Contrary to popular myth, there was little deprivation
among the dowagers of Newport or along Millionaires' Row in New
York. Yet even the most solidly entrenched families, those at the top of
the social totem pole, were forced to regroup their ranks and rethink
their priorities. Out of the rubble a new class arose, a revitalized faction
that included old wealth, new money, and a large contingent of movie
stars, gossip columnists, socialites and heiresses. At once less exclusive and more visible, this new cabal became known as café society.
The New York cafés where they held court were former speakeasies,
which, after Prohibition was repealed in 1933, re-emerged as chic
restaurants and liquor-licensed night spots: the Stork Club, El Morocco, 21, and the Copacabana. Suddenly all the Wrong People were
about to become the Right People: high society, in the old sense of the
term, ceased to exist anywhere except in a few sentimental Broadway
plays and on the society pages of the New York *Times*, where its
adherents languished and grew gray in slightly frayed accounts of the
Charity Ball.

One of the few enduring traditions that society managed to continue
was the Coming Out party, supposedly the presentation or introduction of one's daughter to one's friends, and hence to society. During the
fall of 1930, in preparation for her own coming-out party, Barbara
turned up at some forty receptions, brunches and dinner balls, among
them the debut of her friend Eleanor Carson. Barbara also attended the
Newport debut of Doris Duke, an affair that attracted clusters of Astors,

Bowdoins, Cushings, Rhinelanders, and Winthrops, many of them former classmates of Doris at Brearley, the élite New York finishing school. The same crowd turned out for Louise Van Alen's coming-out party, also in Newport. Louise's escort that evening was Alexis Mdivani.

"In black swallowtails and neat white piqué shirt front, Alexis was easily the most attractive man there" Barbara wrote, "the others all being pimply-faced and drunk, throwing up into their top hats. They threw up on the steps and every place else. It was appalling. All the liquor you wanted...Nobody too sure of what they were drinking, but a lot of champagne. The girls didn't drink much. Mostly the boys drank and did a thorough job of it. They were all in college and not very eligible. Alexis very humorously compared the ritual of the debut to registering one's prize canary at the annual Madison Square Garden bird show. The reception line was miles long. On cue Louise did her court bow, a very low curtsy that made her look like a pup tent folding over in a high wind."

Barbara's debut followed shortly and was conducted in three stages, starting with a tea party for five hundred guests at the Fifth Avenue triplex of Edward and Marjorie Hutton, featuring the music of the Meyer Davis orchestra. The second stage took place at the Central Park Casino and consisted of dinner and dancing for another five hundred guests. The main event was held on December 21, 1930, at the Ritz-Carlton on Forty-sixth Street and Madison Avenue, a formal ball for a thousand, including Louise Van Alen (*sans* Alexis Mdivani, who had returned to Paris), Doris Duke, Silvia de Castellane (brought over from Paris for the occasion), the Blakely brothers, the Ehret brothers, Tony Biddle, Douglas Fairbanks, Jr., Bobby La Branche, Jane Alcott, Virginia Thaw, Gladys Rockefeller, Mary Pierrepont, Sarah Woodward, Peggy Moffett, Frederica Frelinghuysen, Edith Betts, John Jacob Astor, Alice Belmont, John H. de Braganza, the Torlonia sisters, Peggy LeBoutillier, Mr. and Mrs. Francis Hitchcock, Mr. and Mrs. Kenelm Winslow, and Brooke Astor, who described the party as "to die from—the epitome of the big money deb affair."

The $60,000 extravaganza was by far the outstanding social event of the season. Four orchestras, two hundred waiters, ten thousand American Beauty roses, twenty thousand white violets, two thousand bottles of champagne (Prohibition notwithstanding), one thousand seven-course midnight suppers, one thousand breakfasts, and a jungle of silver birch trees, scarlet poinsettias, mountain heather, and tropical greens (from Florida and California) went into the making of this grand spectacle.

For two days and nights hundreds of workmen labored to transform the entire lower floor of the Ritz into an opulent bower of flowers and trees. Max Schling, the fashionable Fifth Avenue florist, supplied the greenery and flowers. The bosky, many-petaled, roses-thrown-on-stairs coming-out party took over not only the hotel's main ballroom, but the large, oval restaurant, the smaller ballroom, and the huge crystal room. The balustrades of the marble staircase were entirely concealed by trailing wreaths of smilax and birches. Star-spangled dark-blue gauze covered the ceiling of the main ballroom to represent a night sky. A full electrical moon and a web of electrical stars completed the indoor firmament. Mounds of artificial snow engulfed everything, including the reservations desk in the lobby of the hotel.

As the guests arrived they were greeted at the entrance to the ballroom by Maurice Chevalier, dressed as Santa Claus, assisted by a team of Santa's Helpers who handed out party favors of pocket-size gold jewelry cases containing unmounted diamonds, emeralds, rubies and sapphires. The music was provided in part by crooner Rudy Vallee and his band and by the Meyer Davis orchestra, as well as by Howard Lanin's orchestra and a Russian ensemble that circulated from table to table during dinner. Lester Lanin, who played the drums that evening in his late brother's band, remembered the ball as the most outstanding he had ever played— "and I've played for Presidents, Kings, Queens, and Maharajahs, but I've never seen a party like this one."

If there was a single uneasy moment, it came shortly after dinner during a performance by the Spanish dancer, Mme. Argentinita, whose exotic ballroom numbers failed to interest the guests. The disrepect the crowd showed the performer so irked Marjorie Hutton, whose idea it had been to hire her, that she interrupted the band, took the microphone and issued a warning that she would end the party unless the guests kept quiet until Argentinita's number was finished. Thereafter the affair ran like clockwork. According to one of the guests, "it was the night Bobbie became Barbara Hutton—debutante, Glamour Queen, Playgirl of the Western World."

If the ball was an artistic success, it nevertheless failed to yield a suitable mate for Barbara. One of the problems was that younger men— college students, Wall Street apprentices, law-firm trainees—were insecure around Barbara. Aware of her great fortune, they were afraid of being labeled fortune hunters or gigolos. One potential suitor summed up for all when he told Dean Jennings, "She's attractive, all right, and a nice kid, but I haven't got the money to keep that girl in postage stamps and I'll be damned if any woman is going to keep me in postage stamps." Barbara began to think of herself as something of a "plague princess" — "I only had to look once at a decent, attractive man and he would run as fast as he could in the opposite direction."

Shortly after her debut she did find herself involved with a man named Phil Morgan Plant, a sportsman and playboy who had been left a $25 million trust fund by his stepfather, Commodore Morton Plant. From Barbara's point of view, Phil Plant's major attraction was his previous marriage to Constance Bennett, an actress Barbara idolized for her svelte good looks. Otherwise Plant had few attributes. He was a prodigious gambler, a renowned womanizer, and a heavy drinker. He went night-clubbing with a different glamour girl or movie starlet every night, and rarely tried to avoid photographers or bothered to deny gossip columnist rumors that a romance was brewing. More often than not the rumors were true.

From the beginning Franklyn Hutton opposed Barbara's attachment to Phil Plant and did everything he possibly could to discourage the relationship. When he heard that Plant had actually had the temerity to propose to his daughter, he arranged to have her presented at court before the King and Queen of England, an honor bestowed only upon the highest-ranking British and American debutantes. The stratagem was calculated not only to bolster Barbara's social stock, but to get her away from her present suitor. What Hutton didn't realize was that Plant had booked passage on the same ocean liner that was to take Barbara and her stepmother to England. Hutton's plan threatened to backfire in his face. He moved quickly, catching the next boat to Europe and arriving in London only days after the others. His blustering presence must have convinced Barbara's admirer that he was wasting his time because Plant packed his bags and returned to New York.

Barbara Hutton made her obeisance to Queen Mary and King George V at Buckingham Palace on May 19, 1931. She wore a heavy shimmering ivory satin gown embroidered with seed pearls, a six-foot train slung over her arm, and a tiara of sparkling diamonds. Her writings describe this most formal of social occasions: "At a given moment the military band pays 'God Save the King' and Their Majesties enter, with their attendants backing before them. The Royal family takes its place on a dais under a canopy of crimson velvet, and standing, receives the obeisance first of Ambassadresses and then Ambassadors. Their Majesties now sit, with ladies on one side of the throne and peeresses on the other. Then the presentees are led in, while the orchestra plays softly. Occasionally a debutante trips, or steps on the train in front. The debutante is escorted forward by a series of ushers, her card of introduction handed from one to another until finally it reaches the Lord Chamberlain, who announces her name to Their Majesties. She curtsies, usually badly and with a frozen smile. The King bows; the Queen bows—the game is over. Or maybe it has just begun."

It occurred to Barbara when her turn came that the King was half asleep: "His face was twisted behind an expression of supreme indifference. He could barely keep his eyes open." Queen Mary, buxom and plain-looking, seemed weary as well but forced herself to see the charade through until the last debutante had passed before her and into oblivion. "And yet," adds Barbara, "this is certainly the most prestigious ritual of its kind in the world."

Barbara's presentation was followed the next day by a garden party attended by Edward, Prince of Wales, on the grounds of Buckingham Palace. "He was deft and light on his feet, a good dancer," Barbara noted. "He was also very cheerful, almost too cheerful, a bit tipsy maybe. It's hard to imagine him as the future King of England."

Edward's cheerfulness, it turned out, may have been due to his recent introduction to Wallis Warfield Simpson, an American divorcée of moderate means whose second marriage, to English businessman Ernest Simpson, had begun to come undone about the time she met Edward. That propitious encounter was to mark the end of the Prince's long-term affair with Thelma Lady Furness and the beginning of a liaison between Edward and Wallis that would make Barbara Hutton's notebook entry look nearly prophetic.

Fleet Street, finding Barbara a more appealing figure than the less glamorous Mrs. Simpson, did its utmost to unearth tidbits of hearsay from beneath the Buckingham Palace rosebushes, and in so doing blew up an innocent fox trot between Barbara and the Prince into something far more unsavory. A slew of rumors flew around London charging Barbara with trying "to land" a certain royal personage. The *Daily Express* dubbed Barbara "a celebutante" and compared her, though not favorably, with a former season's Buckingham graduate, Margaret Wigham, the daughter of a Scottish industrialist, whose 1930 debut was the most publicized social event that England had seen in a decade. Margaret, later Mrs. Charles Sweeny and still later the Duchess of Argyll, had known Barbara when both were growing up in New York. They became friends in England—nearly sisters-in-law, for that matter—but held consistently disparate views. Margaret described her debut at Buckingham Palace as "a whirl through wonderland," whereas Barbara characterized hers as "a quick trip to Hades."*

From the day of her introduction at court, the British press was relentless in its pursuit of Barbara. The matrimonial angle was played to the hilt. Barbara was depicted as "the prototypical American export, a heavily chaperoned eighteen-year-old heiress who has come here to steal the vaulted throne of the British Empire and return with it to the United States." At other points she was described as "an American reject, a spoiled brat whose rejection by New York's most eligible bachelors has brought her to England in search of more select pickings."

Delving into Barbara's background, the British press came up with several stories of more substantive value; none of them, however, were directly related to anything that the American heiress had done or not done. The most significant of these pertained to the recent acquisition by the E. F. Huttons of a new yacht, the *Huzzar V* (later renamed the *Sea Cloud*), a 350-foot oceangoing version of Mar-a-Lago. The million-dollar vessel, with its four full masts and four diesel engines, featured wall-to-wall carpeting, electric fireplaces, pink marble bathrooms with gold fixtures, sleeping quarters for 280, a movie-projection room, a barbershop and beauty salon, a gym, a game room, a classroom for their daughter Dina, and a full ballroom.†

The British newspapers launched a broadside attack on the Huttons for their unprecedented extravagance at the height of the Depression. E.F. Hutton made matters worse for himself by falling back on what had become the standard line—namely, that these expenditures collectively kept numberless persons directly or indirectly employed. What

---

*Following her British debut, Barbara wrote "Expectation," one of her livelier poetic sequences:

> I must sing a song of ecstasy,
> They expect it of me;
> And I must laugh
> To fill the world with glee,
> They expect it of me.
>
> A thousand joyous things
> I must do,
> They expect me to.
>
> Well, the devil take them
> And their expectations,
> All they will get from me
> Is lamentations.

†A more detailed description of the vessel is contained in William Wright's *Heiress*, a biography of Marjorie Merriweather Post.

Hutton neglected to mention was that the *Huzzar V* was built to order in 1931 at a shipyard in Kiel, Germany, and that during its early years in operation the ship was manned by an all-German crew. The *Daily Mail* ran an irony-tinged editorial, which read in part: "There is probably no rich person who upon quaffing a glass of champagne doesn't experience a happy glow of pleasure at the thought of all the vintners, bottlers, freighters, and servants to whom his simple act gives livelihood."

Such attacks did little for Barbara's fragile self-image, particularly because she had no way of responding to the charges. By the end of June she and her parents had left London and were staying at the Ritz in Paris, where they encountered the ubiqitous Elsa Maxwell. Elsa, who was about to leave for Biarritz, invited Barbara along.*

"Will Alexis Mdivani be there?" asked Barbara.

"Why, yes," chimed Elsa. "He recently married Louise Van Alen, and I believe they're honeymooning in Biarritz."

Elsa suddenly remembered the meeting between Barbara and Alexis at Jean Patou's house in Biarritz.

"You do know they're married?" she asked.

Barbara nodded: she knew. Her pocketbook was crammed with letters from Alexis. The engagement to Louise had been announced January 10, 1931. The marriage had taken place in Newport four months later, only days before Barbara's presentation at court.

Following the ceremony the honeymooners had turned up in London, where the first thing they did was to establish a joint-checking account. They next purchased Mdivani's wedding presents: a half-dozen polo ponies, a set of diamond-and-pearl shirt studs, and a new Rolls-Royce. The buying spree continued in Paris, where the groom acquired a new wardrobe—custom-tailored suits, coats and shirts, as well as a hundred sets of monogrammed silk underwear. Alexis was now ready for Biarritz and presumably Barbara Hutton. The question remained: Was she ready for him?

---

*This particular Maxwell–Hutton meeting is also described in Philip Van Rensselaer's memoir, *Million Dollar Baby*, p. 43.

Part Two

The Enchanted

Five

Barbara Hutton lived a fairytale existence, a second-rate fairytale at that. She was like the Cincinnati shopgirl who goes to the movies for the first time, sees a distorted celluloid image of the world, then swallows it hook, line and sinker.

DOUGLAS FAIRBANKS, JR.

ALEXIS MDIVANI spent his summer at Biarritz galloping up and down a polo field. Of the three Mdivani brothers he was by far the most skillful polo player and at times seemed intrigued by very little else. That summer his only other interest was Barbara Hutton. He and Barbara were often seen in each other's company, and on too many occasions Louise Van Alen Mdivani was nowhere in sight.

Alice-Leone Moats, while vacationing in Cannes, noted that gossip about Alexis and Barbara had reached her on the Riviera: "My mother and I quarreled when she said, 'You'll see, he will walk out on Louise and marry Barbara.' I accused her of being a cynic, insisting that Alexis was a nice fellow who couldn't possibly be that unkind to someone as sweet and gentle as Louise."

The rumors continued to fly, but Barbara was having too good a time to notice. There was a glamour in the air, a careless cabaret chic that appealed to her sensibility. The sidewalk cafés in Biarritz were always crowded. Vacationers sipped cocktails in the late afternoon and watched the procession of international society strolling along the breeze-cooled promenade. The Hotel du Palais was filled with celebrities. There was a polo field, a race track, a gambling casino; there were dinner parties and balls. When tourists grew bored with Biarritz they could always drive off to nearby St. Jean de Luz for a picnic, or to Lourdes to view and explore its hauntingly beautiful cathedral.

Toward the end of the summer of 1931 Barbara made her way to Italy to stay at the sprawling Villa Madama outside Rome, the residence of Count and Countess Carlo di Frasso. Alfred Hitchcock described the di Frasso house, with its Raphael frescoes and large collection of Hubert Robert paintings, as "an open house for celebrities, dignitaries, and royalty on the loose, as well as other congenial characters." Another frequent visitor maintained that "it was hard to tell whether the Countess threw one party that lasted all summer or a series of weekend parties that lasted all week. Guests just came and went as if the Villa Madama were a Grand Hotel."

Countess Dorothy Dentice di Frasso (née Taylor) was an American whose grandfather had been a New York State governor, and whose father, Bertrand L. Taylor, was a leather-goods manufacturer and early Wall Street shark who amassed a fortune of $50 million. In 1912 Dorothy had married Claude Graham White, a British aviator best remembered as having landed a plane on the White House lawn during their courtship. They were divorced in 1916, shortly after Dorothy came into an inheritance variously estimated at between $10 million and $15 million. Her brother, Bertrand L. Taylor, Jr., a member of the Board of Governors of the New York Stock Exchange, inherited the remainder of the estate.

In 1923, when she was in her mid-thirties, Dorothy married an impoverished but distinguished Roman nobleman, Count Carlo di Frasso, thirty years her senior, yet active enough to be named Master of the Roman Fox Hounds. Dorothy spent well over $1 million restoring the count's family home, the sixteenth-century Villa Madama, making it into an international gathering spot where she regularly gave sit-down dinners for two hundred or more. The di Frassos also maintained houses in London, New York and Beverly Hills.

On meeting the di Frassos, Barbara was immediately struck by the openness and nonchalance with which they managed their lives, even when it came to their frequent extramarital affairs, particularly Dorothy; her black hair, blue eyes and voluptuous figure were bait that few men could resist. Asked by a reporter to describe her vision of Paradise, Dorothy responded: "The English writer Max Beerbohm said that Paradise to him was a four-post bed in a field of poppy and mandragora. I say it depends who's between the sheets." Dorothy's taste in men can best be described as eclectic. Among her lovers were author Ben Hecht, gangster Bugsy Siegel and actor Gary Cooper, whose arrival as a houseguest at the Madama in the summer of 1931 signaled the start of her most sensational affair.

Gary Cooper was taller and even more powerful in person than he appeared on screen. He lacked great elegance but he had a cool, cynical, detached air about him that excited women. Until he met Dorothy di Frasso, the two most vivid and high-powered women in his life had been Clara Bow and Lupe Velez. Dorothy outdid them both. She nearly outdid Cooper, squiring him around Italy with an authority the likes of which he had never before encountered. When it came time for him to leave she threw a going-away party at the Villa Madama, attended by His Royal Highness Prince Umberto, Crown Prince of Italy; the Earl and Countess of Portarlington; and Prince Christopher of Greece. Also present was Barbara Hutton, accompanied by a dashing Italian nobleman, Prince Girolamo Rospigliosi, introduced to her by Countess di Frasso as a favor to Aunt Marjorie Hutton. The Italian prince had once owned seventeen palaces, but lacked the wherewithal to hold on to them. The minute he met Barbara he proposed to her— "and never stopped," she complained to Dorothy. She was more impressed by Gary Cooper— "handsome, calm, laconic…in many respects the quintessential American."

By September Barbara was back in Paris, staying at the Ritz. Alexis and Louise Mdivani were also in Paris. The Mdivani family Rolls-Royce was spotted all over town, transporting Prince Alexis and his bride to sumptuous luncheons and dinners, sporting events, and concerts, and on shopping sprees that frequently resulted in the purchase of tens of thousands of dollars' worth of jewels, furs, and finery. Mdivani's delight in these latest acquisitions was almost humorous. Alice-Leone Moats, living in Paris at this time, wrote: "He had to show each new thing off, and before a polo match at Bagatelle, he dragged his friend Chico Kilvert to the stable so that she could see his ponies. The horse blankets were adorned with closed crowns about the size of a witch's cauldron. Chico, doing her best to keep a straight face, asked, 'Aren't the crowns a bit small?' That worried him. 'Do you really think so?' he replied."

If he found it difficult to interest himself in the personality of his wife, he found it less difficult to interest himself in her inheritance. The couple rented a well-staffed house on Place des Etats-Unis, and spent thousands refurbishing it. Alarmed by the influx of bills and the outflow of money, Louise's mother, who had openly opposed the marriage, arrived in Paris to have a talk with her daughter. Mrs. Van Alen's arrival set Mdivani off on a round of screaming and yelling. He was given to making scenes and commenced to make his mother-in-law's stay as unbearable as possible. Alexis had no intention of allowing Mrs. Van Alen to tie his wife's purse strings and even less intention of letting her turn Louise against him. His brash display worked. Mrs. Van Alen stayed only a week and left without having made a noticeable impression on her love-stricken daughter and none at all on her money-stricken son-in-law.

While there was a certain charm to Alexis's money-madness, he tended at times to carry it to extremes. Alice-Leone Moats was alone with the young couple at dinner one evening when Alexis insisted that the meal be served at the dining table normally reserved for company. "The dining table," Miss Moats commented, "would have held its own in length at Buckingham Palace, but Alexis wouldn't allow any leaves to be removed even for an intimate gathering... Alexis sat at one end of the table, Louise at the other, and I was in the middle. We were so far apart that we should have been supplied with microphones in order to communicate."

The parties that Mdivani and Louise hosted at Place des Etats-Unis attracted the most fashionable men and women in Paris, all eager to catch a glimpse of the town's latest *nouveau arrivé*, whose ability to charm and captivate rich American heiresses was rapidly becoming part of the legend. Barbara Hutton was often invited to these weekly bashes and was sometimes accompanied by her friend Lord Warwick. Warwick's presence as escort was mostly a ruse to help Barbara in her ongoing struggle with her difficult father. Franklyn Hutton had no intention of allowing his daughter anywhere near Alexis Mdivani. But with Lord Warwick's help, getting to see him was no great problem.

Barbara and Alexis picked up in Paris where they had left off in Biarritz, never bothering very much to disguise their mutual attraction. At the Mdivani parties that Barbara attended they would cuddle up together, nuzzling by the fireplace, while Louise simmered in some distant part of the house and tried not to notice. Everybody else did.

One of the major factors in the Hutton-Mdivani romance was the presence of Alexis' sister, Roussie Sert, whose ability to manipulate and bewitch was practically an act of art. Having assumed complete responsibility for her brother's welfare, Roussie found out everything she could about Barbara Hutton, from the full measure of her wealth to the most intimate details of her private life. Always in attendance at her brother's parties, Roussie made it a point to take Barbara aside and draw her out. She learned of Barbara's secret attempts at writing poetry, the strain of her relationship with her father, the suicide of her mother, her hatred for Farmington, everything that had any bearing on her character and personality. Barbara was much taken with Roussie's beguiling manner, her steady patter, her hypnotic gaze, her intriguing smile, her tall and spare figure, her pageboy hairdo, her exquisite taste in fashion and jewelry. Like the rest of her family, Roussie's social graces were acquired rather than inherited. Her savoir-faire and poise, both developed through much effort on her part, enabled her to win the favors of the rich and powerful. She had a gift for establishing an immediate intimacy that bordered on the conspiratorial, whispering malevolent asides that allied her with whomever she was addressing against all the other guests in the room.

It was this same winning manner that had catapulted Roussie into the life of José Maria Sert, the famous Spanish painter, then still married to the equally celebrated Misia Sert, a leading light on the Paris arts scene. It was a testimonial to Roussie's manipulative prowess that she was able not only to oust and replace Misia, but also to befriend her. She now employed her skill in maintaining the delicate balance that existed between Barbara Hutton and Louise Van Alen. Roussie somehow convinced the outside world that all was well between the two American heiresses, when in fact they were both vying for the attentions of Alexis Mdivani.

In December 1931, much to Louise's relief, Barbara departed for London to visit Morley and Jean Kennerley. Jean, the daughter of Lord Alfred Simpson-Baikie, honorary Lieutenant Governor of Orkney and Shetland Islands, first met Barbara at Biarritz in the summer of 1926. Jean was vivacious and outgoing, every inch the outrageous patrician debutante of the thirties. Morley Kennerley, an American publishing executive who became director of Faber and Faber in London, was more cautious and conservative than his wife. Together they exercised a stabilizing effect on their highly emotional and unpredictable young friend.

"When Barbara came to visit us in 1931," recalls Morley, "she had Alexis Mdivani on the brain. He was charming and so forth but not very substantial. Barbara's interest, I suspect, was aroused by his marriage to Louise Van Alen. She thrived on pursuit. If a man was available and offered no resistance, she lost interest and found herself a new challenge. If she saw something she wanted, she went after it. We told her to take a trip and give the matter some thought. She immediately booked passage for herself, Ticki and her stepmother aboard the *Empress* on one of those around-the-world-in-eighty-days cruises. Three months and thirty thousand nautical miles later she was back in New York, as confused as ever."

Barbara Hutton was not only the most traveled young lady in New York society, but also the most talked-about. In the 1920s Noël Coward penned the popular song "Poor Little Rich Girl," which gave Barbara fair warning: "Poor little rich girl,/You're a bewitched girl,/Better beware!/...Better take care!" Now there was a new Bing Crosby recording of "I Found a Million-Dollar Baby (in a Five and Ten Cent Store)," lyrics by Billy Rose and Mort Dixon, a song hit whose title again focused attention on Barbara. Marjorie Hutton had formulated a plan to counter some of this negative publicity. As honorary chairwoman of the annual charity carnival for the New York Judson Health Center, she was in a position to offer her niece the lead role in the carnival pageant, which she had booked into Madison Square Garden.

The pageant was held on May 3, 1932, before a capacity crowd of 20,000 paying spectators. Barbara appeared as "The Spirit of Adventure," the female lead in a grandiose song-and-dance production that included such "name" performers as Johnny Weissmuller and Charles "Buddy" Rogers, the future husband of Mary Pickford. Barbara's efforts did not go unnoticed. "She can sing and dance," said the reviewer for *Time* magazine. The *Daily News* mentioned her "luminous smile, girlish charm, big blue eyes, and thick glossy hair," then went on to castigate the pageant itself as "one more empty gesture on the part of the rich to appease the poor."

❧

Shortly after the pageant Barbara and Irene Hutton sailed for Europe, spending two weeks in Madeira before joining Franklyn Hutton at the Ritz in Paris.When she arrived Barbara found a gift waiting for her, a volume of poems by the Bengalese poet Rabindranath Tagore, whose work had become popular in Europe. The collection contained a handwritten dedication by Alexis Mdivani. Some of Barbara's friends recall that within days of receiving the gift, she had committed the entire volume to memory.

A day later she received an invitation to a dinner at the home of Alexis and Louise Mdivani. Barbara's father greeted the invitation with a stream of invective. His animosity toward the Mdivanis, which in the long run seemed only to encourage his daughter, had been reinforced by recent newspaper accounts concerning the divorce proceedings of Pola Negri and Serge Mdivani. Having lost most of her assets in the stock-market crash, Pola and her fading film career were summarily discarded by the opportunistic Serge in favor of a new wage earner, the opera singer Mary McCormick, a Texas-bred prima donna approaching middle age but still known as the "baby diva," presumably because her bee-stung lips gave her the look of youthful innocence.

Despite her father's protestations Barbara attended the party and even reciprocated toward the end of June by inviting Alexis, Louise, Roussie, Serge, Mary McCormick and several others for dinner at Maxim's and then to a small night club in Montmartre, where Alexis ignored his wife to fawn over Barbara. The more Barbara saw of the Mdivanis, the more Franklyn Hutton railed against them. In the *wagon-lit* from Paris to Biarritz that Barbara shared with her parents in early July, he blasted the entire clan of "Russian interlopers," reserving his choicest words for Roussie, in his eyes a vile bloodsucker and procurer of young and wealthy flesh for the delectation and enrichment of her brothers.

Barbara acquired her own Rolls-Royce that summer, dark blue with an outfitted interior of rosewood and ivory. The car would come in handy as a means of escaping her father's endless diatribes. At some point she met the Alexis Mdivanis and the Serts at San Sebastián, across the border in Spain, a luxury resort with its own clutch of vacationing cosmopolites and resident aristocrats. In San Sebastián attending the bullfights was *de rigueur;* Barbara enjoyed the color, crowds and fanfare, but found the kill and bloodspill distasteful.

The next meeting took place at Palamós on the Costa Brava of Spain, not far from Barcelona, where the Serts owned a spectacular castle called Mas Juny. To celebrate its recent renovation, the Serts gave a series of at-homes for friends and family. Barbara received an invitation. When she arrived, accompanied by Ticki, Clinton Gardiner (her chauffeur) and a footman, she was greeted by Alexis and Louise Mdivani, who were staying in the same quarters as the Serts. The others, including Barbara, were placed in guest cottages, not far from the main house.

For the first time there was an air of open hostility between Barbara and Louise, whose incredible patience had finally worn down. Louise took every opportunity to make Barbara feel ill at ease. But Barbara was quick on the uptake. During one reputed exchange Louise asked Barbara whether she had difficulty finding clothes that fit. "You're unfashionably big-busted," Louise pointed out. Barbara, who was sensitive about her figure, lashed back at Louise. "Better big than concave," she said, referring to her adversary's cadaver-thin body.

For the remainder of her stay Barbara steered clear of Louise. She would either go off swimming by herself or join the other guests on trips into Barcelona. She thought about leaving Mas Juny and taking up the battle at a later date, but it was Roussie who convinced her to stay, a decision that was to play a major role in Barbara's future.

Late in the afternoon a few days later, a number of Roussie's guests, including an Italian count and countess named Vespucci and a French baron and baroness named D'Antoine, decided to go into town for a bite to eat. Somebody remarked that Barbara might want to accompany them, so they strolled over to her cottage to ask. They barged in and found Barbara and Alexis in the middle of making love.

Not even Alexis could hope to talk his way out of this predicament. Barbara, who was desperate to avoid a full-blown scandal, packed her bags and returned at once to Biarritz and then to Paris. Alexis, always the gallant and accommodating warrior, did the only thing he could do under the circumstances—he offered his wife a divorce. At this strategic point Roussie Sert re-entered the picture, convincing Louise that Alexis was an incorrigible scoundrel whose propensity for women was a failing shared by all her brothers. Louise needed little prompting. She had already hoisted the white flag, and by the time the lawyer Charles Huberich made his expected appearance in Spain, Louise was ready to sign any and all papers. Pola Negri and Serge Mdivani had been divorced at The Hague, a site that seemed to everyone as convenient as any. Thus by the end of November 1932 the eighteen-month marriage of Louise and Alexis Mdivani was legally terminated.

⁊❧

"The saga of Mas Juny," as Barbara later dubbed the devastating Palamós episode, eventually became part of her permanent repertoire, a tale she repeated *ad infinitum* to anyone who would listen. Long after the event Barbara concluded that she had been duped, that it had been Roussie Sert's idea on that forelorn summer day to drive into Barcelona and her idea as well to take Barbara along, knowing full well what explicit scene awaited the party of intruders as they barged into the unlocked guest cottage. The irony of the situation was that prior to the day in question there had been little or no physical contact between Barbara and Alexis. There were hugs and kisses but nothing of serious consequence. Barbara had successfully thwarted Mdivani's sexual advances by reminding him of the sanctity with which she held marriage. That argument had begun to sound distressingly hollow, particularly after Barbara's arrival in Spain and the dissolution of any pretense of friendship that had previously existed between Barbara and Louise.

In the autumn of 1932 Barbara was in London and was seen dining with Prince George (the younger brother of the Prince of Wales), Lady Portarlington, and Major the Honorable Piers Legh. She sported an impressive looking ruby on her left hand and gossip columnists speculated that the announcement of her engagement to Prince Alexis Mdivani would be forthcoming any day.

The columnists were wrong. Not only was there no announcement, but Barbara was currently seeing another man, the future actor David Niven, for the moment a commissioned officer in the British Army. In his 1972 memoir, *The Moon's a Balloon*, Niven describes young Barbara as "a petite snubnosed blond, very pretty American girl with the smallest feet I had ever seen....She was a gay and sparkling creature, full of life and laughter." This description did her only partial justice. Her European travels and independent cast of mind had helped make her a woman of charm, sensitivity and wit; she possessed dignity and taste; she was supremely well-mannered and gave at least the impression of being completely in control of herself. Only a few close friends realized that she was not as much in control as she appeared to be; fewer still were aware that she was not at all in control and in addition suffered from an intense lack of self-esteem, a commodity she would never display in great quantity.

Before Barbara left England for the United States on November 25, 1932, aboard the *Bremen*, she invited Niven to visit her in New York on his next furlough. The opportunity soon presented itself during a four-week Christmas leave, and Niven took Barbara up on her invitation, docking in New York the last week of December on what was to be his first stateside visit.

Barbara was waiting for him at the dock and had brought along several carloads of friends. After a rousing welcome, Niven was driven to the Hotel Pierre, at Sixty-first Street and Fifth Avenue, where Barbara and her family were staying in several large suites while their two apartments at 1020 Fifth Avenue underwent renovation. "I was given a very nice room in one of the suites," Niven writes, "and Barbara, the perfect hostess, made it clear that she hoped I would spend as long as I liked there but to feel perfectly free to come and go as I wished and not to feel bound to her or her family." In this way Barbara was also letting Niven know that their friendship was to remain platonic.

The following evening Barbara threw a party for Niven at the Central Park Casino, transporting her guests to the Casino's entrance at Seventy-second Street and Fifth Avenue in two dozen hansom cabs. "It may have been Prohibition but no one seemed to notice." Niven says. "A vague pretense was made to keep bottles out of sight, and many people made extra trips to the John or to their cars."

Christmas morning was spent with Barbara's family, and there were presents for Niven "of hair-raising generosity." He was not the only lucky recipient. On Barbara's Christmas list that year were no fewer than five of New York's most eligible young bachelors: Tony Biddle,

Bobby La Branche, Jimmy Blakely, Raymond and Winston Guest. Then, according to Niven, the entire group boarded a private railroad coach that went to Princeton, New Jersey, to watch the Princeton football team play for the Ivy League championship.

The remainder of Niven's stay consisted of parties, parties and more parties, interspersed with sporting events at Madison Square Garden, Broadway shows, dinner and drinks at the 21 Club, in those days a fashionable speakeasy. Another haunt visited by Niven was Harlem's Cotton Club, well known for its fine jazz bands and lively dance floor. Barbara and her gang went there frequently, usually late at night.

One of the more memorable members of Barbara's group was a wealthy Texan named Howard Hughes. "Always with the prettiest woman," writes Niven, "Hughes was a tall, shy, silent, slightly deaf, and compared to the rest of us, very serious-minded citizen." Niven gives the impression in his memoir that Hughes, for all his wealth, rarely picked up the tab. His lack of charity was evidently of little consequence to Barbara, whose friendship with Hughes continued off and on until the late 1930s when, for one brief and bewitching moment, it would explode into something quite unexpected.

About the time Niven returned to England (his passage financed by Barbara's cousin, Woolworth Donahue, and with a case of champagne provided by Barbara), Alexis Mdivani was on his way to New York, his passage paid for by Louise Van Alen, who had stubbornly ignored her family's warning to close out their joint checking account. Alexis had promptly emptied the account and was using the money to pursue Barbara. On the same boat as Alexis, also on their way to visit Barbara, were Jean and Morley Kennerley. En route Alexis made it plain to them that he had every intention of pursuing Barbara all the way to the altar.

The Kennerleys were met at the pier by Rosemary O'Malley Keyes, a houseguest of Barbara's. Mdivani was met by the press. He insisted he had no intention of courting Barbara Hutton and then took a cab to the Savoy Plaza, where he had booked a room.

Barbara and her family, having vacated the Pierre, were back at 1020 Fifth Avenue. When Mdivani called on Barbara the next day, he received a chilly reception, not just from Franklyn Hutton, but from Barbara as well. Of the members of her family only Jimmy Donahue, with his customary good cheer and careless chatter, treated him well. Barbara redeemed herself somewhat a few days later by throwing a party for Alexis at the Central Park Casino.

But Barbara's family made it impossible for her to do much more than that. Her father, stepmother, aunts and uncles took turns trying to talk Barbara out of her interest in the fortune-seeking foreigner. "It's hard to say how Barbara felt," remarks Jean Kennerley. "She blew hot and cold, and her father did his best to keep Mdivani away from her—with some degree of success, I might add."

A reporter in search of a story went over to the Savoy Plaza and caught Mdivani as he was packing to leave.

"Are you engaged to Miss Hutton?" he asked the prince.

"I have nothing to say," Alexis replied glumly.

"Is it true that her family is opposed to your friendship with her?"

"That's something you'll have to ask them," he snapped.

Further investigation revealed that Barbara's family wanted her to find herself an attractive young American rather than risk her future on the uncertainty of a foreign title. Franklyn Hutton's idea of a suitable match was a Payne marrying a Whitney, a Biddle marrying a Duke, a Mellon marrying a Carnegie, or a Cabot marrying a Lodge—the dynastic alliances of wealth with wealth.

When Barbara's despondent prince finally left town, everyone in the Hutton camp cheered. They apparently didn't know the Mdivanis. The durability of their resolve and the brilliance of their tactical gamesmanship were two factors not to be denied. The Huttons were also up against an unexpected foe, Louise Van Alen, whose bitterness had at long last reached its saturation point. Convinced that Barbara had destroyed her marriage out of pure spite, and dismayed by Barbara's seeming indifference, Louise went into uncharacteristic action. Roussie Sert had managed to persuade Louise that Barbara had encouraged the divorce without the least intention of marrying Alexis. Confronting Barbara, Louise threatened to spread the story of the "Mas Juny affair" all over New York unless Barbara went through with the marriage. It was a strange twist of logic, but it represented a potent threat to Barbara's reputation, especially considering the tenor of the times and the antagonism that already existed among the general populace toward the fabulously rich in general and Barbara Hutton in particular.

"My main weakness," as Barbara said later, "is my inability to cope with responsibility. Faced with the need to make decisions, my first impulse is always to run. I turn into a child again, a quirky, spoiled, rebellious child."

Her natural bent was enhanced in this case by a fortuitous occasion: following Mdivani's departure, Barbara and Jean Kennerley went to the movies and saw a film about Bali. When it was over, Barbara announced, "I'm going to Bali. You and Morley must come." Barbara, of course, offered to pay their way.

"Barbara," says Jean Kennerley, "was famous for deciding on a change of scene at the last moment. She didn't need a reason to pack her bags and go, though in this instance she had a reason—to get as far away as possible from Louise Van Alen."

Barbara, Jean, Morley and Ticki boarded the Curleyhut and traveled cross-country to Los Angeles, where they were joined by still another of Barbara's suitors, Count Manolo Borromeo-d'Atta, without question one of the most attractive yet impecunious of all the Italian bluebloods. Borromeo accompanied the group to San Francisco, and it was there that he purportedly popped the question. Barbara planted a passionate kiss on the count's lips, promised to consider his proposal, and left him behind as she joined her companions aboard the steamer *Lurline*, bound for Hawaii, New Zealand, Australia, Malaya, Fiji, Samoa, Bali, Java and Siam.

On January 28, 1933, the date of Barbara's sailing, the San Francisco *Chronicle* ran an article outlining the various complexities of what had become a virtual track event. Alexis Mdivani was cast as an improbable outsider. Others in the field included Count Borromeo as well as Prince Girolamo Rospigliosi, who had already taken the liberty of announcing his engagement to Barbara in the Italian press. Another highly regarded Italian nobleman often mentioned in connection with Barbara was Count Carlo Gaetani, of the ancient, once wealthy Gaetani family of Naples. Carlo had been Barbara's guest in New York on several occasions and had received numerous presents, including an all-expense-paid world cruise. There was also Carlo's cousin, Count Loffrado Gaetani-Lovatelli (otherwise known as Lolo), whose marital pursuit of Barbara was no more successful than any of the other Italian aristocrats.

To add to Barbara's dilemma there was an unresolved question in her mind regarding Raymond Guest, the younger brother of Winston Guest. Tall, rugged and darkly handsome, Raymond Guest had dated Barbara off and on during his senior year at Yale. She found him sensitive and gentle; he found her uncommonly attractive but too rich for her own good and too much in the news. He once described her as "a gossip columnist's dream." When the *Lurline* docked in Hawaii she sent off a telegram to Palm Beach inviting Guest to join her group for the duration of the cruise. When no answer arrived they left without him.

"If she was disappointed," says Jean Kennerley, "it didn't show. The pleasure Barbara derived from being on the high seas overshadowed everything. She had good sea legs. She loved to travel. Every detail of the trip interested her. She wasn't spoiled or afraid to soil her hands. She used to eat tuna fish and salmon straight out of the can. She did her own hair, her own ironing, her own nails, There wasn't much choice actually, because our ladies' maid went dotty and had to be sent home."

The real purpose of the trip had been to visit Bali, and Barbara found there everything she had hoped to find: beaches, volcanoes, gardens, dusky village lanes, terraced paddy fields, Hindu temples and shrines. It was remote and exotic. "No one had really gone to Bali," says Jean Kennerley. "There were no tourists. There was no electricity. The natives told time by the position of the sun. Everywhere were these beautiful, smiling, barebreasted native girls in sarongs. Morley's favorite part of the voyage was when Barbara and I went native. Barbara joined them in their ceremonial dances and quickly mastered the subtle, precise movements of the eyes and hands performed to the music of the gamelan, an ensemble of bamboo xylophones.

"In the village of Ubud we befriended a painter and teacher, Walter Spies, who, following Gauguin's example, had emigrated from Europe. Spies lived in one of the loveliest homes on the island. It was primitive but very elegant. You washed by pouring well water into a canvas bag and you read by kerosene latern. Spies had enormous talent and was much loved by the natives, and he was a highly entertaining storyteller."

Just as Barbara and her small group were leaving Bali for adjacent Java, Alexis Mdivani was leaving Paris for the same destination, the money for his not inconsiderable excursion provided by Roussie Sert, whose expectations for her brother's success were high. After his long voyage Alexis trapped his quarry in the lobby of her Javanese hotel. The setting was right: he proposed and she accepted. The party resumed its trip. A week later a stunned Franklyn Hutton, vacationing with his wife in Palm Beach, received a radio-telephone call from the American consul's office in Bangkok.

"Sorry to trouble you, sir," the diplomat started, "but your daughter is here and wants me to marry her to a Prince Alexis Mdivani. She is still underage and needs your consent."

Hutton was furious. He asked for his daughter, but Alexis came on the line instead and immediately presented his demands. Barbara, he said, had agreed to marry him. He would marry her at once, with or without anybody's permission, unless Hutton consented to make public the news of their engagement.

Franklyn cajoled, shouted, threatened, and finally accused Mdivani of blackmail. When he realized that Alexis was impetuous enough to carry out his threat, he tried to stall for time. He would go along with their engagement provided they postpone the marriage until a proper site could be selected. Mdivani agreed, and that night they celebrated.

"Alexis bought every flower in Bangkok," recalls Jean Kennerley. "Whenever we passed a flower merchant on the street he would jump out of the car, buy out the merchant, and throw the flowers into the back seat. Later that night he brought the entire orchestra back from a night club to play in our hotel suite. And the next day he bought hundreds of baby ducks and put them in everybody's bathtub. It was childish stuff, but it didn't hurt anyone."

To cap the frivolity Alexis sent Roussie Sert a telegram: BANGKOK. APRIL 14, 1933. HAVE WON THE PRIZE. ANNOUNCE BETROTHAL.

When the wire services approached Franklyn Hutton for confirmation of the story, he hemmed and hawed. "I don't think Barbara has any plans to marry," he said. "I have been in constant communication with my daughter, who is on a trip around the world, and she has said nothing to me to indicate that she wants to marry. When she does marry I think her father will be right by her side, at least I hope so."

This statement was followed a few weeks later by the announcement that the Franklyn Huttons were aboard the *Europa* on their way to Paris for a showdown with Barbara, who was returning from Bangkok with Alexis and the Kennerleys aboard the *Chitral*. Whatever faint glimmer of hope Hutton retained of changing his daughter's mind dissolved the moment he saw the determined glint in her eye.

The engagement was formally announced on May 21, and if any doubts remained they were erased by Barbara's latest petition to Surrogate Court:

> I did not anticipate that I would marry before coming of age. I am, however, engaged to Prince Alexis Mdivani, who resides in Paris, France, and our marriage will take place there on or about June 20, 1933. My marriage to Prince Mdivani, and the plans which have been made in connection with the intervening months before I come of age, will necessarily entail heavy additional expenditures, which were not anticipated by me or my father.
>
> I have discussed the amount of these necessary expenditures with my father, and both he and I estimate that they will amount to at least $100,000.
>
> Even with this additional allowance I will still be spending, in the year preceding my majority, only a fraction of my income, and my fortune is so large that I see no necessity why, upon my marriage, I should not immediately enjoy the luxuries which a fortune such as mine will enable me to have when I enter into possession of it.

Court approval was immediately forthcoming. Another petition was filed a few weeks later for an additional $156,000 to cover the cost and operating expenses of three new custom-built Rolls-Royces, one of them a gift to her father. Added to her current annual allowance of

$300,000, the two petitions brought her expenditures for the year to $556,000—a small fraction of her total next egg, then worth more than $42 million and climbing at the rate of $2 million a year.

For those who like statistics, here is the actual year-by-year increase of Barbara's fortune as indicated in the annual accountings rendered by her father:

1926	$26,703,309.96
1927	$26,892,753.60
1928	$34,266,540.22
1929	$38,309,222.25
1930	$39,022,034.18
1931	$40,352,995.42
1932	$41,739,079.09
1933	$42,077,328.53

It was precisely because Barbara had so much money and was willing to spend it so frivolously that her ongoing saga aroused such intense interest. The details of her existence provided a momentarily diverting excursion for the less fortunate into a cosmos they could only dream or read about. Despite their avowed distaste for the spectacle of such a lifestyle, people were endlessly fascinated by Barbara Hutton. There was evidently something irresistible about the knowledge that stupendous wealth did not in and of itself necessarily imply stupendous joy.

Barbara Hutton became as well known as any celebrity of her day. Even the men in her life, by virtue of their association with her, attained the status of public personalities. Dale Carnegie found the legend of "the marrying Mdivanis" so intriguing that he attempted to analyze the secret to their success in the pages of his best-selling *How to Win Friends and Influence People:*

> Flattery seldom works with discerning people. True, some people are so hungry, so thirsty for appreciation that they will swallow anything. Why, for example, were the much-married Mdivani brothers such flaming successes in the matrimonial market? Why were these so-called "Princes" able to marry beautiful and famous screen stars, and a world famous prima donna and Barbara Hutton with her five-and-ten cent store millions?

While flattery may have helped to conquer Barbara Hutton, it did nothing to assuage her father. He made his feelings known in a newspaper interview conducted from his suite at the Paris Ritz.

"There's an old saying," he commented, "that you don't always get to choose your in-laws. But Barbara's face is radiant and that is enough."

"Is Mdivani after your daughter's inheritance?" asked a reporter.

"I don't read minds," said Hutton, "I hope not. Maybe at the beginning that counted. But now? I look at the two of them and I can only think that they're in love."

With little time remaining, Hutton was apprised of one very disquieting fact: there was a French law which ordained that if the wife hadn't yet reached the age of majority (twenty-one in France), her property would come under the absolute control of her husband. To circumvent this ordinance Hutton immediately set the family lawyers to work on a prenuptial agreement that would protect Barbara's financial interests. There was some haggling between William S. Pauling-Emrich, who was helping to draw up the contract, and Charles Huberich, who represented Mdivani. Pauling-Emerich eventually convinced Alexis of the necessity of safeguarding the marriage from the charge of fortune-hunting by waiving any rights that the French law might otherwise give him to the Woolworth millions. It was arranged and publicly announced that on signing the agreement Alexis would receive a dowry of $1 million plus a substantial annual allowance. Supplemented by a million-dollar divorce settlement recently negotiated in his favor with Louise Van Alen, Alexis was rapidly attaining a reputation as not only the best-looking but the cleverest member of his clan.

The selection of a site for the marriage ceremony proved somewhat problematic. Franklyn Hutton insisted on a religious ceremony for his daughter, while Alexis wanted only a simple civil ceremony. Eventually Alexis agreed to both, provided that the religious rite take place in a Russian Orthodox church. "My daughter isn't affiliated with that religion," Hutton remarked. Neither, apparently, were the Mdivanis. Alexis had to be formally baptized into the Russian Orthodox faith before the church would agree to sanction the marriage.

On the legal forms that he signed to qualify for a marriage certificate, Alexis described his profession as "Secretary to the Georgian Legation" in Paris. His responsibility there seemed to consist almost entirely of answering questions regarding the authenticity of the Mdivani title. The only advantage derived from the post was that it enabled him to travel on a diplomatic passport; in addition, his Rolls bore the emblem "CD" (for Corps Diplomatique), which gave him special parking privileges. He informed the press that the Georgian legation was the headquarters of the counterrevolutionary movement. Asked by a reporter what he meant by "counterrevolutionary," he mumbled something about reinstating the Czar. To Franklyn Hutton he spoke more than once of his "work" on behalf of the legation, never specifying exactly what that work entailed. His diplomatic passport was revoked late in 1933 after the signing of a Franco-Russian nonaggression pact that once and for all put to rest the absurd myth that Georgia was anything but a southerly and minuscule division of the Soviet Union.

Meanwhile, Barbara set to work preparing her trousseau. She transformed her suite at the Ritz into a veritable bazaar where salesmen and representatives of sundry Parisian fashion houses displayed their latest wares—gowns, jewelry, handbags and other accessories. From Jean Patou she ordered thirty-five outfits, including the wedding gown to be worn for the religious segment of the ceremony. Pictures of the gown appeared in newspapers around the world: it was of ivory satin, with sleeves puffed at the shoulders, a shawl of lace draped from the head, held by a blond shell comb encrusted with a flower spray of diamonds reproducing the motifs in the lace pattern. Before she was finished, Barbara had bought some eighty ensembles, all from the finest couturiers of Paris.

Most of the world's press was outraged by the excessiveness of the occasion. The New York *Daily News* published a scathing attack on the would-be princess:

> Our felicitations and whatever else may be appropriate to Miss Barbara Hutton, who is spending nobody knows how many millions of American nickels and dimes collected from poor people in America in anticipation of her marriage to a foreigner whose name has slipped our mind.
>
> Miss Hutton is handing over nickels and dimes to French racketeers of fashion.... The eighty outfits she has bought with American nickels and dimes will all be out of fashion within a few weeks. If Miss Hutton really does need all those clothes, being an American one would think she would distribute those nickels and dimes in America, where desperate efforts are being made to get money in circulation. The same can be said for her choice of a husband.

Defending her choice of a "foreign" husband on the grounds that she was marrying an individual and not a country, Barbara issued a statement that received wide circulation. "Alexis is kind and gentle. He listens to all my hurts and problems. When I try to explain to him all my bewildered thoughts, all the hurts and fears, he doesn't seem bored about it at all the way other people are. He doesn't dismiss my fears with a laugh and just tell me that anybody who has as much money as I do shouldn't worry about anything."

The civil ceremony took place June 20, 1933, in the city hall of the exclusive Passy district, the sixteenth arrondissement. Barbara had chosen a conservative pearl-gray print dress, designed by Chanel, with a waist-length cape of the same material, a wide-brimmed picture hat of gray organdy and a sable stole. She wore a necklace of uncut diamonds, a gold ankle bracelet and a black pearl engagement ring set in platinum that Alexis had purchased with money from the Louise Van Alen divorce settlement.

Two hundred reporters and twenty photographers jammed the press section. A cordon of police held back a rowdy mass of spectators that had gathered outside the city hall. Barbara was escorted by her father and her aunt, Jessie Donahue; Alexis chose as his seconds José Maria Sert and Akaki Tchenkeli, the chief diplomat of the Georgian legation.

The photographs show Alexis, in formal attire, napping through the wedding speech by the deputy mayor of Paris, Daniel Maran, while Maran extolled the "prince and princess," expressing his delight that Paris had been chosen for this momentous union and then launching into a lengthy discussion of the enduring nature of the bonds of matrimony. He wound up by wishing the newlyweds happiness, *bonne chance*, and many children, and thanked Mr. Franklyn Hutton for his "substantial donation of funds to be distributed among the poor, as occasion should arise." Hutton's donation of 20,000 francs was then worth roughly $1,000, hardly an earth-shattering sum by anybody's standards.

The religious portion of the two-part wedding ceremony, held two days later, was by comparison a De Mille production. It took place in the Russian Cathedral of St. Alexander Nevsky on the Rue Daru, the home (as Alexis claimed) "of all Georgian, anti-Bolshevik exiles." From the appearance of the vast crowd gathered outside the cathedral it seemed as though Paris had decided to take a holiday.

The New York *Times* reported that while the church was packed with eight hundred guests, including social and diplomatic leaders, "it was not so congested as the little Rue Daru outside, where 8,000 uninvited guests struggled for nearly two hours, and finally overpowered the gendarmes, in their efforts to crowd around the entrance to see the lovely bride in her splendid ivory satin gown and old ivory lace veil." A sizable proportion of these gate-crashers were young Frenchwomen and shopgirls. Many of them, impelled by curiosity and forgetful of gentleness or of ordinary delicacy, pushed, hauled, mauled and powered their way to the front lines.

On the arrival of the bride in her limousine there was a new surge of screaming and shoving. A canopy and a red carpet had been installed for the event. The church interior was blanketed with chrysanthemums and lilies that spilled yellow and white along the walls, backed by long fronds of emerald palm; the aisle was carpeted in brilliant scarlet; the altar was illuminated by a thousand white candles in tall bronze candelabra.

Alexis preceded his bride to the altar, passing between church attendants wearing breeches, with gold chains around their necks. A choir of thirty was chanting the wedding anthem. The guests remained standing throughout the hour-long service, for, by tradition, there are no pews in Russian Orthodox cathedrals. And in accordance with Russian Orthodox custom, there were no bridesmaids. Barbara was attended only by a beadle in full regalia who held her eight-foot train. The guests crowded close to the couple as the bearded high priest in golden vestments, surrounded by five other priests, conducted the rites in Russian.

Barbara and the groom, led by the high priest, circled the altar twice while ushers in morning coats and striped trousers held heavily jeweled crowns over the heads of the bridal pair, signifying that they had been crowned with the highest earthly happiness. Among the ushers, who took turns holding the crowns, were Barbara's cousins, Jimmy and Woolworth Donahue, and Frazier McCann; Count Renault St. Croix; Victor Grandpierre; Prince Theodore of Russia (another unlikely Georgian title); Morley Kennerley; the Maharajah of Kapurthala (in purple turban); and the Russian-born *premier danseur* Serge Lifar.

The ceremony swirled to dramatic conclusion as the couple sipped sacred wine out of ornamental goblets, bowed before ikons (a departure from the usual practice of kissing them), exchanged rings, walked about holding candles, knelt before the altar, inhaled the aroma of incense, and exchanged vows. At one point a priest asked, "Has either of you promised your love to anyone else before?" Alexis unhesitatingly replied, "No," conceivably invalidating the entire ceremony. The ritual ended when deacons placed a ceremonial pink rug on the floor and then retreated. According to an ancient Russian tradition, the person who treads on the rug first will dominate the marriage. Alexis went for it with his usual gusto, but he wasn't as fast as Barbara, whose two tiny feet touched down an instant before his.

With the completion of the service, ineffectual efforts were made to clear the street outside the church. The crowd, anxious for one more peek at the bride, held its ground and for twenty minutes it was impossible for the newlyweds to reach their limousine. Finally, by maneuvering the car through the crowd to first one entrance, then to the other, a temporary path was cleared, and the bride and bridegroom disappeared into the back seat. As the car pulled away, the crowd cheered and Barbara waved. Arriving a few minutes later for a luncheon reception at the Ritz, the couple was again mobbed, this time by a throng that had gathered in the Place Vendôme.

There were so many wedding presents that Barbara was forced to rent an extra suite at the Ritz just to store them. Prince David Mdivani gave the couple a Cartier clock encrusted with diamonds; Serge's gift was a gold vanity case for Barbara studded with rubies, and gold cuff links for his brother; Nina Huberich presented Barbara with several Georgian ceremonial gowns embroidered with gold thread and pearls; Sert painted them a large landscape of the Spanish seacoast. In addition, there were diamond-and-ruby earrings, diamond bracelets, the inevitable gold toilet sets and silver tea services, heavy boxes of George III silver flatware, sets of Baccarat crystal and porcelain from Limoges. Franklyn Hutton gave Barbara a costly jade necklace, and his son-in-law a high-powered motor launch fifty-eight feet in length named the *Ali Baba* ("Ali" for Alexis, "Baba" for Barbara), which was delivered to the Lido in Venice, where the couple planned on spending part of their honeymoon.

The bride's presents to the groom were a string of Argentinian polo ponies and pearl shirt studs from the Orient. When Barbara learned that Louise Van Alen had given him similar gifts, she proceeded to buy him a second string of polo ponies. Alexis gave Barbara a rope of pearls and several months later a jade necklace for which he paid $40,000, all of it Barbara's money, and which turned out to be worth considerably less. The E. F. Huttons gave Barbara a diamond brooch in the shape of a polo pony. This was perhaps the most appropriate gift she would receive, for polo and polo ponies were soon to become an integral feature of her life. A year into their marriage, Barbara would tell a friend, "I didn't expect polo to take up every moment of my husband's waking life. It seems I ought to have been born a polo pony." Many years later she made the rueful comment: "We would have been happier as Mr. and Mrs. Alexis Mdivani, but Alexis would never drop his title."

Six

THEY HAD seventy pieces of honeymoon luggage between them, each trunk and suitcase embossed with a crown and the Mdivani family initials. A police escort drove interference as the caravan of Rolls-Royces carrying the newlyweds and their personal retainers made its way to the Gare St. Lazare, where reporters and the midnight express awaited them. Barbara's brief commentary— "It's going to be fun being a princess" —kicked up a dust storm of bad press. Henry Cabot Lodge, the senator from Massachusetts, had Barbara in mind when he wrote in a Boston newspaper that "every pork-baron's daughter will try to buy a European title, because she comprehends that the title has value as a trademark and a trademark is something she understands." Another American newspaper accused Barbara of "having spent thousands on a meaningless, ritualistic wedding."

Not even Franklyn Hutton escaped the wrath of the press. An article in the Paris edition of the *Herald Tribune* reported that Hutton, the father of the bride, had neglected to pay his bills for the use of the Russian cathedral where Alexis and Barbara were married. The article mentioned that while the choir and the thousands of flowers used in the ceremony had been paid for, the bill for the rental of the cathedral and for the services of the priests remained unpaid. Hutton took exception to the article and responded with a letter of protest: "I owe nothing to the Russian Church, nor did I, by any inference, suggest in any way to any of its members that I would make payment or give any

sum by way of gift or otherwise, and I naturally resent any suggestion
to the contrary." The letter was subsequently printed, but the newspaper refused to publish a retraction.

The only aspects of Barbara's life the press neglected to mine were
the private events of her wedding night, although in time these too
became known. As their train breezed through the night on its way to
Lake Como, the first stop on their itinerary, Barbara put on one of her
fetching silk-and-lace nightgowns while Alexis sat watching her. It was
at this point that he blurted out a comment he would later come to
regret. "Barbara," he said, "you're too fat!"

She was five feet four and weighed 148 pounds. She was pleasantly
plump but had stunning legs and a memorable face, some said a
beautiful face. Her breasts were well-shaped but too large, a physical
trait of all the Woolworth women. "Barbara was top-heavy in an age
when men and women were busy shedding the excesses of the
Victorian age," comments Louis Ehret. "Thin was chic, a sign of pure-
bred puritanism. Barbara was luscious-looking but a trifle Rubenesque.
Chanel's ensemble for the civil ceremony was prim and appropriate,
but Patou's creation for the religious service did Barbara a disservice.
Patou's clothes were for women with dainty figures. Barbara was more
voluptuous than dainty and the result was disastrous."

Her awareness of the problem did little to ameliorate the pain
inflicted by her husband's remark. Barbara went on a crash diet that
consisted of nothing but three cups of black coffee a day—no solids of
any kind. Maintaining this excruciating pace for three weeks at a
stretch, she managed to lose nearly forty pounds within the first few
months. In jest she called it her "Mahatma Gandhi diet—it either kills
you or you lose weight." It nearly killed Barbara.

Despite the diet and the slight of her wedding night, Barbara enjoyed
Lake Como, finding its tranquillity an almost meditative experience.
They stayed at the Villa d'Este in Cernobbio, surrounded by mountain
peaks and overlooking the silken waters of the lake. From Cernobbio
they headed for Venice, stopping overnight at Lake Garda to call on the
Italian poet-playwright-politician Gabriele d'Annunzio at the Vit-
toriale, his mountaintop retreat. D'Annunzio's wedding gift to Barbara
was Arthur Waley's 1929 English translation of *The Tale of Genji*, a
volume of eleventh-century court writings by the Heian period courtesan Murasaki Shikibu. This collection, together with Tagore's
poems, was to prove influential in Barbara's later development.

Barbara and Alexis arrived in Venice at the height of tourist season,
having booked the royal suite at the Excelsior Hotel on the Lido, that
seven-mile-long sand bar on the Adriatic where the rich gathered in

blue-and-white candy-striped cabanas to escape the summer heat. Awaiting the couple on their arrival was the high-powered Chris-Craft that Franklyn Hutton had ordered as a wedding present for Alexis. Alexis loved the boat, and Barbara loved being in Venice.

Her notebooks for this period are crammed with fragmentary notations of sights seen: "A dark church, illuminated in an unexpected corner by a masterpiece; an arched bridge over a canal; the rose-orange-lavender façades of faded, still regal palazzos; the Viennese waltzes played at Quadri's; a white wicker table at a quayside café; a courtyard rose garden in the Campo San Barnaba; the tolling of bells in the Campanile at dusk." And parties attended: "A brilliant whirl thrown by Coco Chanel at the Grand Hotel des Bains; a dinner party...in a 16th-century villa half-hidden beneath a bower of umbrella pines; cocktails at Baron and Baroness Rudi d'Erlanger."

Of all the social connections that Barbara established in Venice, none was to prove more valuable than her friendship with Princess Jane di San Faustino, the American-born Jane Campbell, a seventyish widow who after her marriage to Prince Carlo di San Faustino had become one of the most imposing leaders in Italian society. Anyone who had ever attended her salon at the Palazzo Barberini in Rome could attest to the vigor of her scrutiny. Sir Oswald Mosley recalled her salon as "a university of charm, where a young man could encounter a refinement of sophistication whose acquisition could be some permanent passport in a varied and variable world. If he could stand up to the salon of Princess Jane, he could face much." In Venice she was regarded as the first and last word on who rated and who did not, and her judgments in such matters were not only final but frequently cruel.

At first Barbara found the princess an almost frightening apparition. "She would sit in her cabana," wrote Barbara in her notebooks, "and play backgammon for hours on end, sipping Amaretto and cream, talking a mile a minute about any subject that popped into her mind, interrupting herself to screech at servants and complain that the Italians were the slowest, dumbest, laziest people on earth. A moment later she would proclaim the Italians the true master race, the greatest artists, the most noble civilization.

"She was a wonderful juggler. She could keep numerous activities going at once, planning a dinner party while listening to a conversation while playing backgammon while reading a book while knitting a sweater while berating the cabana boy while recounting the latest gossip—in the middle of it all she insisted I tell her my life story: '...And don't leave out any intimate details.' She loved unsavory details, loved dirt. If you paused, she grew impatient. 'Go on, go on, I'm listening!' The instant you picked up the thread, she returned to her torrid pace of activity. But she took it all in, because when we were alone she asked pertinent questions about certain very minor details I had mentioned in passing. When asked how she did it, she said she had peripheral hearing and more than a one-track mind."

Princess Jane soon became one of Barbara's most loyal patrons and supporters, introducing her to everyone, paving the way for her continued emergence as a leading figure on the international social stage. One reason for Barbara's meteoric rise was her ability to transform herself physically from a pretty girl with money into a luminous beauty with money. She had chic and style and already the cool polished elegance of a grande dame. Her grinding diet gave her a sleek, varnished look, which she refined by regular visits to the hairdresser, daily exercise sessions and constant shopping for new designer's fashions, although she admitted that she hated the false flattery lavished by the couturiers and the time it took to accumulate her wardrobe.

She became on of those women every other woman wanted to look like, the Condé Nast type—svelte and smooth-skinned, her nails long and sharp, her hair thick and glossy. She cultivated the kind of remote, blond beauty whose unblemished perfection of feature, creamy pink-and-white coloring, and dainty lips and candid eyes caused many a man to curse the falseness of the sweet exterior that concealed a temperament and a will worthy of Marie Antoinette. For the first time Barbara also learned to play the role of hostess, giving frequent luncheons at the Lido, served outside her cabana by liveried footmen. She adopted a new carefree attitude, acquiring her husband's taste for spontaneity and wild living. She became more impulsive and less self-conscious, sexually as well as psychologically, returning her husband's frequent amorous attentions. Alexis had "fallen in love" with his reborn wife. The newest couple became the gayest couple, driving off to the Salzburg Music Festival, boarding the Orient Express, or going to Tangier, a city whose deep mystery bewitched Barbara.

Barbara and Alexis carried on like nineteenth-century royalty. One of Mdivani's great pleasures was to go tearing up and down the sinuous Grand Canal and the Giudecca in his multihorsepowered Chris-Craft with its crew of three. He and Barbara surrounded themselves with titled friends, the wealthier the better, and a phalanx of retainers, secretaries, maids and chauffeurs, as well as Ticki Tocquet, who was den mother to the entire group. They gave a big party in Venice, and a caravan of gondolas transported a hundred couples to the lavishly decorated ballroom of the Grand Hotel. Barbara spent $20,000 on party favors for her appreciative guests.

After Venice the couple and their servants sojourned south to Florence and Rome, always reserving the largest hotel suites and palazzos, and then to Capri, where they leased a forty-room villa. Colorful and fragrant flowers blossomed in all their bedrooms and sitting rooms. Messengers and delivery boys were forever darting about, running errands, carrying clothes, jewels and messages for either Barbara or Alexis, lending their traveling side show an air of self-importance.

Following Capri they journeyed to Biarritz, where Alexis rode on Lord Louis Mountbatten's team in the Prince of Wales Cup polo competition; Mountbatten's crew took top honors. The Mdivanis went on to Paris, where they encountered Elsa Maxwell. Her impression of the divine twosome found its way into her New York newspaper column: "Barbara has become an incredible exotic beauty. Her husband, however, is still the same queer, ambitious, reckless character he was while married to his first wife, Louise Van Alen."

Elsa proceeded to blame Mdivani for developing in Barbara the dangerous trait of extravagance, pointing out that the underage heiress, still awaiting her inheritance, was using her unlimited credit to buy everything in sight: "Barbara has no idea of the value of money, but she still hesitates whenever the price of something she wants to buy seems prohibitive. Alexis laughs. 'Buy it,' he urges, aided by the merchant, who eagerly protests that Her Highness can have anything in his shop and pay for it at her leisure."

Alexis never forgave Elsa her cutting remarks. When she invited the Mdivanis to attend the Folies-Bergère, he declined. Barbara went alone with Elsa to watch Josephine Baker, "the Black Goddess of Cabaret," parade across the stage clad in nothing more than a pink flamingo feather. She danced the Charleston with a string of bananas tied around her waist. She changed into a sequined bodysuit, an ostrich-feather cape and a four-foot-high plumed headdress to dance the Bunny Hug, Castle Walk and Turkey Trot. Afterward Barbara and Elsa went backstage, and Barbara gave Elsa some more material for her column by removing a diamond ring she was wearing and presenting it to Miss Baker in appreciation of her brilliant performance.

The day after her evening at the Folies, Barbara and Alexis made a reservation on the *Bremen* to return to New York. It was mid-October and Paris was turning cold. New York was also turning cold, but

Barbara was about to celebrate her twenty-first birthday and had good reason to celebrate it in the United States. She was going home to pick up her birthday gift, a check worth more than $42 million.

The birthday party, held in her father's apartment on the evening of November 14, 1933, created the kind of commotion to which everyone associated with Barbara was rapidly growing accustomed. A dozen policemen stood guard outside 1020 Fifth Avenue as a surly mob began to congregate. Reporters and photographers were out in force. Upstairs in the apartment a fire blazed in the walk-in fireplace as the slimmed-down birthday girl stood in the foyer greeting her fifty guests. The celebration had a pleasant flavor to it. Waiters dressed as Cossacks offered hors d'oeuvres and champagne, while drinks were served at two stationary bars. The apartment was festooned with branches from the rowan tree, whose bright red berries, prolific in winter, signify life after death in Russia. In one room guests were entertained by a gypsy band playing Russian folk tunes, and in another room they watched a performance by Russian sword dancers and acrobats. Dinner was served at small round café tables decorated with evergreen and assorted winter flowers. There was also a large pink birthday cake with twenty-one candles.

After supper Franklyn Hutton took the entire group to a night club for dancing. The following day there was a smaller gathering in his apartment solely for members of the immediate family. And on November 16, two days after attaining her majority, Barbara filed what would be the last of her many petitions to the Surrogate Court of Suffolk County:

> I am the former Barbara Hutton. I was married to Alexis Mdivani in Paris, France, on the 22nd day of June, 1933, and since my marriage have, of course, been known as Barbara Hutton Mdivani. I became 21 years of age on November 14, 1933, and as I have attained my majority I am entitled to the possession of all the property which my father and general guardian now holds for me.
>
> In the spring of 1932 I had my father's transactions as general guardian, as shown by the accounts he filed with this court, checked by independent special counsel retained by me. As a result of this check-up they have reported to me that my father and his counsel had displayed conservatism and wisdom in the management of my property, and that I was very fortunate that it was then in this situation, not withstanding the vicissitudes of the past few years. I have agreed with my father that his

account as general guardian be settled out of court, and upon the delivery
to me of the principal and income belonging to me, which my father now
holds in his hands, I am prepared to deliver to him a general release
releasing him, his heirs, executors, administrators and assigns from all
liability and responsibility whatsoever.

Franklyn Hutton was thus released from his high-priced bond, and
the one-third share of F. W. Woolworth's vast estate was turned over to
Barbara Hutton Mdivani. At the time of transfer her inheritance
amounted to $42,077,328.53. According to the U.S. Treasury Depart-
ment more than $32 million of this sum was invested in tax-exempt
securities of the U.S. Government. Added to the income and holdings
she had already derived from her inheritance, plus the inheritance from
her mother's estate, her net worth at age twenty-one exceeded $50
million—approximately $750 million at current market prices.

Her first act on receiving the money was to present her father with a
gift of $5 million—his reward for nearly doubling her original inheri-
tance. Her second act was an anonymous donation of $1 million to
charity. She then added another $1.25 million to the previous million
settled on her husband. "She must be pleased with her husband," read
an editorial in the New York *Times.* "Apparently she has no intention
of turning him into a hardworking American businessman."

Ed Sullivan in his pretelevision newspaper days printed an "open
letter" to Barbara in the *Daily News:* "The unreality of your existence
must be boring, Princess. You have a husband who has little or no
relation to everyday life... Here we are, face to face with stark realities,
stark distress, and your Prince is spending American dollars on toys
that gratify his own vanity." Sullivan suggested that the heiress
establish an annual "Princess Barbara Christmas dinner" by contributing 1000 Christmas baskets to the poor: "The whole thing wouldn't
amount to $5,000, and out of it you'd get $50,000 worth of honest-to-
God happiness."

She complied and Sullivan cheered: "Princess Barbara is the tops.
You're a swell person—just swell!" Unfortunately Sullivan's exuber-
ance was quickly buried beneath an avalanche of negative publicity,
resulting from the disclosure of a new scandal involving "the marrying
Mdivanis." In 1932 Serge and David Mdivani and their wives, Mary
McCormick and Mae Murray, pooled more than $200,000 to found the
Pacific Oil Company. Most of the capital was supplied by the two
women and a gaggle of second- and third-rate actors and writers. An oil
strike was soon made in Venice, California, on property belonging to
Mae Murray, marking the opening of the famous Venice oil fields. By

June 1933 Mae and Mary, both in the process of divorcing their husbands, discovered evidence of company mismanagement on the part of their spouses. It appeared that the two brothers had diverted a substantial portion of company funds to their own use, falsifying accounting records to justify expenditures they had made in their official capacities as officers and directors. Another accusation levied against them involved their illegally drawing large sums of money from company profits that should have been paid out as earnings to investors.

An investigation ensued, and on December 16, 1933, David and Serge Mdivani were indicted by a grand jury on fourteen counts of grand larceny. Bonds for Serge and David were set at $10,000 each; the money was posted by none other than Barbara Hutton Mdivani. The trial date was set for mid-January 1934. Matters became even messier with the disclosure of certain events surrounding the divorce cases of the brothers Mdivani. On the witness stand in Superior Court, County of Los Angeles, Mae Murray accused her husband of "using both fists on me. He socked me and locked me in my room. On another occasion he broke into my dressing room and raped me." Mae Murray's career all but ended and at another hearing, much later, she testified that David had cleaned her out financially: "He took my stocks, bonds and money. He left me penniless. I have no property, no income. Because of him I haven't been able to perform in a film for years." Worth $3 million when she married David, she was now down to nothing; she had been evicted from a sleazy midtown Manhattan hotel for nonpayment of her bill: "I packed an old hatbox with the things I needed to maintain myself and went to Central Park, where I stayed for three days and nights without a nickel to my name. I sat on a bench with my little hatbox. I walked out on my marriage with the clothes on my back."

Mary McCormick's divorce saga was more of the same. Having once described Serge as "the world's greatest lover," she now called him "the world's worst gigolo." In response to his complaint in court that she had scratched and hit him, she said, "Why deny it? They ought to give me the Congressional Medal of Honor for it." She entertained the court by reeling off a long list of her husband's indiscretions, adding that he had never once made an effort to support her: "It was left to me to take care of the household bills. And he refused to let me have any friends. He said that I must remember that I was a princess and I could no longer associate with common people. At the same time, he made it obvious that he felt he was associating with a common person by being married to me. He told my friends that I was beneath his station in life." To this litany she added one final complaint: she had lent her husband

$40,000 for "business investments" and he had made no effort to repay her. Serge's response: "Ridiculous! How can a man borrow money from his wife? If one has money, the other uses it." As for the adultery, he accused Mary of being the unfaithful partner: "But I'm too polite to name names."

Serge and his opera singer were legally divorced the day before Barbara's twenty-first birthday. Several days later Barbara read in a gossip column that Serge had become involved with Louise Van Alen, Alexis Mdivani's former wife and her own arch nemesis. She also chanced upon an interview with Mary McCormick in the *Daily Mirror*. "The Mdivanis are suave and cosmopolitan," the singer observed, "but they are Georgians, and Georgians are Asiatics. The Asiatic male regards himself above all as a male and his wife as a slave. When I married Serge the continental veneer soon came off and I knew I was hooked. Once he stormed at me: 'I hate work and I hate you because you want me to work.' He told a simple truth and it was so obvious I actually sympathized with him. But not in the same way I can sympathize with a girl who is married to one of them."

Fed up with the mudslinging and not wanting to be drawn into the forthcoming trial, Barbara and Alexis embarked on what she and Alexis called their "second honeymoon" —an extended voyage to the Orient. On January 5, 1934, they were "smuggled" into New York's Grand Central Station, where the Curleyhut had been attached to the train bound for California. What with sixty trunks and their usual entourage of retainers, it was hardly a clandestine operation. And if all the commotion caused by a phalanx of overworked porters didn't attract attention, there was always Barbara's nineteen-year-old cousin, Jimmy Donahue, who was also making the trip.

The train had barely pulled out of Grand Central when Alexis opened the newspaper to read that he had just been subpoenaed by the Los Angeles District Attorney's office to appear at his brothers' trial. An examination of the oil company's books revealed that he had plunged $12,000 of his own money into the company's operating budget, making him a material witness in the case.

The next morning as the Curleyhut rolled into the Chicago station, fifty reporters were on hand to interview the fugitive couple. Nancy Allard, Barbara's social secretary, roused Jimmy Donahue out of his sleep to get up and appease the press. A born exhibitionist, he appeared on the observation platform a few minutes later, clad in blue silk pajamas, a loud yellow silk robe, bright red cravat and alligator slippers.

"What're you doing on Barbara's honeymoon?" one reporter asked, recognizing the lanky blond playboy.

"Why, I'm here for my brilliant wit," Jimmy responded. "I'm the court clown without a court. They tried to get Ed Wynn, but he couldn't make it. Actually I'm Barbara's bodyguard." Reaching into the side pocket of his robe he pulled out a small handgun and waved it at the crowd. "Anybody care to argue the point?"

Jimmy Donahue was in high spirits. He was where he belonged: in front of an audience. He entertained the reporters with dramatic tales of his prep school days at Choate and then launched into a set piece on his short-lived show-business career. "I'm sure you all saw and loved me in the chorus line of *Hot and Bothered.** It was a ten-day wonder, a royal flop. Flops run in the family. My old man knew all about them. How many of you remember my old man?"

"Seriously, Jimmy, what're you doing on this trip?" interjected a reporter. "Is this really Barbara's honeymoon?"

"Well, boys, I'll be earnest for a change, just like Oscar Wilde," said Jimmy. "I'm here because I want to be here. I've never been to the Far East, and this is as good a chance as any. And no, this isn't a honeymoon. They've been married eight months and already went on a honeymoon."

"They're getting along all right then?" the same reporter asked.

"They get along beautifully," said Jimmy. "They never quarrel, and that's no lie. They're made for each other."

"What about the subpoena?"

"Well, what about it? Alexis hasn't been served yet. And if he is, I'm sure he'll do whatever he has to do."

The interview terminated with photographers snapping pictures of Jimmy, while he obliged a few autograph hunters by signing his name on scraps of paper.

Despite Jimmy's assurances, Alexis had not the slightest intention of testifying in court. When the train stopped in Reno, he found Charles Huberich at the station; the lawyer had just arrived from Sacramento with news that a process server intended to board the train in Los Angeles.

The race was on. Alexis took the first flight out of Reno, landing in Salt Lake City, and several hours later flew to Portland, where he promptly registered in a hotel under the conspicuous alias of G. R. Gonsome. The next day he rented a car and drove to Seattle, booking passage on a Japanese liner, *Hikawa Maru*, bound for Yokohama out of Vancouver. Barbara continued in the Curleyhut from Reno to San

---

*At eighteen, using the stage name Jimmy Dugan, Donahue had danced in the chorus of a musical comedy *Hot and Bothered*, which opened at a theater in Jackson Heights, about five miles from Broadway, and closed ten days later.

Francisco, checking into the Mark Hopkins Hotel. In anticipation of her visit to the Orient, Barbara went to Gump's, the store she had first started visiting as a child. There she spent $50,000 on a pair of Ch'ien Lung (eighteenth century) beakers, at that time the most valuable and expensive jade items ever purchased outside China. A day later, she, Jimmy Donahue, Ticki Tocquet and Nancy Allard boarded the Japanese steamship *Tatsuta Maru* and sailed off.

Alexis was the first to reach Japan, arriving on January 24. He learned at once that there had been a hung jury at his brothers' trial and that while new indictments would be issued, the theft charges had been dropped. The brothers would subsequently plead guilty to the reduced charge of conspiracy to commit a crime, a misdemeanor requiring only the payment of a fine.

Mdivani was pleased with the outcome of the trial, less pleased with the reception he was accorded by Japanese immigration officials. The Georgian passport he presented for disembarkation was declared invalid. Alexis was detained aboard ship for twenty-four hours until French consular representatives could be contacted. While reaffirming that Georgia had indeed been annexed by Russia, the French representatives informed the Japanese officials that the prince was married to Barbara Hutton, one of the wealthiest women in the world, whose arrival in Tokyo was imminently expected and whose capacity for spending was infinite. To a chorus of deeply apologetic bows, Alexis was practically carried off the ship, trundled aboard a train and transported to Tokyo in time to meet his wife at the dock.

Reunited, the couple spent their first night in Tokyo at the theater. *Hochi*, the city's largest-circulation newspaper, quoted Barbara as saying, "I'm so happy to be with Alexis again that I can hardly watch the show. His expertise in wise spending and in gaining access to the choicest circles is one of the reasons I married him." Alexis demonstrated his expertise the next day by purchasing a diamond pin to wear on his lapel, a mere trifle at $10,000. Not to be outdone, Barbara bought herself an ornamental dragonfly with "plaque à jour" enamel wings (giving a stained-glass effect), large diamond tail and an enameled gold and rose diamond head. The price was $20,000.

Even in Tokyo, Barbara had trouble avoiding the press. After considerable pressure she consented to a news conference during which she announced that she and Alexis wanted to adopt a Chinese infant because "the Chinese have such a long and honorable civilization." The remark, of course, offended her Japanese hosts.

After a week the Mdivanis moved on to the ancient imperial city of Kyoto. They stayed at the Hiiragiya Ryokan, an inn noted for its distinguished clientele of prime ministers, movie stars and millionaires. From Kyoto they went to Kobe and caught a small steamer, the *Choku Maru*, bound for Shanghai. Accompanied by a homburg-topped Jimmy Donahue, the Mdivanis paid $200 a day for the Royal Suite plus ten additional rooms at the Grand Hotel. When not sightseeing or partying at one or another of the city's many tightly packed night clubs, the couple could be found at the race track hobnobbing with local dignitaries and playing the horses. During the day they went shopping, picking up anything and everything that caught Barbara's eye, from jewelry and vases to screens and carpets.

Finally they went to Peking and stayed in a Chinese palace made ready for their comfort. They were attended by twenty household servants and a Mandarin chef, whose specialties Barbara refused for fear of gaining weight.

Peking was more sedate and residential than bustling, tourist-saturated Shanghai and therefore much less to Mdivani's taste. Alexis thrived on night life, the giddy swirl of night clubs, dinner parties and midnight balls. Barbara was content to immerse herself in the cultural life of the capital, avidly pursuing her latest enthusiasm, the collection of seventeenth- and eighteenth-century (early Ch'ing Dynasty) porcelains, of which she gradually amassed one of the best privately owned collections.

While staying in Peking, Barbara hired a skilled tutor of Chinese. Her name was Princess Der Ling, the wife of T. C. White, a former American ambassador to China. The princess had been lady-in-waiting to the famous Dowager Empress Tz'u Hsi, whose death in 1908 preceded by four years the end of the Ch'ing Dynasty, the last imperial Chinese court. Princess Der Ling's recollections of the dowager empress fired Barbara's imagination, but while Barbara luxuriated in Peking's age-old splendor and historic tradition, Alexis retreated into a shell. It was as if he had arbitrarily decided to dislike everything that his wife liked. On a tour of the Imperial Palace he reclined on a bench in the lotus gardens and promptly dozed off. He was bored and distracted during their visit to a Buddhist monastery on the outskirts of Peking. The very sights that aroused Barbara—long-robed merchants hawking their wares; tiny shops crammed with antiques and curios; rickshaws and coolies scurrying about in madcap confusion—seemed only to alienate Alexis. His mood darkened by the day, inflamed still further by Barbara's mounting infatuation with every rite and ritual she happened to see. Alexis began to have what Barbara later characterized as "temper tantrums," hurling himself on the floor and screaming every time Barbara decided to prolong their stay.

After two months in Peking the group moved on, arriving a few days later in Bombay. According to newspaper clippings as well as Philip Van Rensselaer's *Million Dollar Baby*, Alexis clearly preferred the carnival atmosphere of India's busiest port to the ascetic atmosphere that enveloped Peking. Bombay bustled with night life, with sporting emporiums, with gaming houses, where one mixed with the maharajahs, princes and nabobs of royal India. There they came across their wedding guest, the Maharajah of Kapurthala, who introduced them to other maharajahs, including the polo-playing Sawai Man Singh of Jaipur. "Jai" had his own polo stadium in Jaipur, which immediately endeared him to Alexis. He also owned a ski chalet at St. Moritz, mansions outside London and Paris, a summer residence in Cannes, another in Nice. His proudest possession was his two-hundred-room pink palace at Amber, a towering structure of balconies, portals, roofs, arches, stone elephants guarding entranceways, enormous silver urns filled with the sacred waters of the Ganges, and his own game reserve.

When Barbara and Alexis visited the palace at Amber, Jai explained the customs of his principality, of how each Maharajah of Jaipur once in his life was led blindfolded to a fort behind the palace and from its trove of treasures was allowed to take one piece back with him. Jai's father had chosen a solid-gold macaw studded with volcanic rubies and emeralds, which still stood in one of the rooms of the palace. One of the galleries was filled with solid-gold trunks filled with raw uncut diamonds. Another gallery contained hundreds of painted miniatures and illuminated manuscripts from Jai's collection.

This extraordinary display of wealth was to be found in other palaces visited by the Mdivanis. The Maharajah and Maharanee of Cooch Behar lived in a mammoth turreted palace filled with Louis XV furniture and Rembrandt portraits. After dinner hundreds of nautch girls would be brought out to perform exotic dances for the guests. Alexis and Barbara were given lessons in riding an elephant and later joined the maharajah on a *khedda*, an elephant hunt, in which elephants were rounded up to be trained and put to work.

After a point the excessive wealth of the maharajahs seemed to blot out the extreme poverty to be found everywhere outside the palaces. The Maharajah of Baroda threw a feast in their honor and appeared weighted down—head, neck, chest and arms, fingers and toes—with such a sight and wonder of vast diamonds, emeralds, rubies and pearls that he could barely move. Barbara was almost relieved when the Maharanee of Baroda took her along on a tour of the hospitals and medical clinics in and around Delhi to deliver parcels of food and clothing to the children on the wards.

"There was one hospital for orphans in Delhi I shall never forget," wrote Barbara. "When we arrived we were led down a dark and dingy corridor to a long and narrow room filled with row upon row of sickly, emaciated children on broken cots and torn mattresses. One little boy, maybe eight or nine, lay naked beneath a soiled sheet, his face bloated and his belly grossly distended. Despite his misery he wore an angelic smile and his eyes shined brightly. I sat next to him on the floor. A small gold religious medallion I was wearing caught his eye. I removed it and placed it around his neck. I took a hand mirror I had in my purse and held it up for him to see. He studied his reflection as if for the first time. He had barely the strength to lift his head, but he seemed to be pleased with his new acquisition. The next day when we returned to the same ward the little boy was no longer there. When I asked the nurse about him, she shook her head. He had died during the night."

Philip Van Renesselaer, in tracing the travels of the Mdivanis through India, reports that by May they were once again with the Cooch-Behars en route to the northern province of Kashmir in an effort to outrace the hot sun. In the middle of the trip the travelers—Barbara, Alexis and Jimmy Donahue—came down with what seemed bad cases of amoebic dysentery and were forced to return to Europe. Even without the illness it was clear that Barbara wanted to return. For reasons she couldn't quite express, she felt terribly depressed and embittered. "I feel bored," she wrote in her notebooks. "I feel bored with Alexis. I feel tired. I feel tired of Alexis. I want to go to sleep." By the end of May the Mdivanis were back in London, sharing the same suite at Claridge's but sleeping in separate rooms. Barbara's constant refrain these days was a plea for "more space and more privacy." Her rejection of Alexis came as a blow to his brittle ego. Reflecting on the course of recent events, Barbara wrote in her notebooks: "For all my speculations about Alexis, for all the satisfaction I derived from his extravagant courtship, there is no tenderness in what I now feel for him, and while this probably puts me in the minority among the women of this world, there's nothing I can do about it." There was no compelling reason or single explanation for Barbara's reversal of feeling toward Alexis. In a way she had outgrown him. She would say later that she had never really loved him, that their marriage was a convenient way for her to get out from under her father's thumb. The challenge, if there ever was one for Barbara, had been met at Mas Juny when she took Alexis away from Louise Van Alen. Alexis was too boyish and self-centered. She tended to dominate him in a way that now made her feel unwomanly. Her physical attachment to him had ended during their trip, so that now she felt only a vague sense of security in his companionship, as one might feel in the company of a friend or distant relation.

For Alexis this was to be a difficult period. He had begun to drink heavily, but drinking only aggravated his frustrations. He looked for outside diversion and found it where he always had—on the polo field. At night he often went to the Embassy Club in Bond Street, an overcrowded, smoke-filled night club made famous a decade earlier when it was a favorite haunt of the Prince of Wales. The Embassy was no more than a long, dark underground basement, noisy and poorly ventilated. But it had become the most popular nightspot in London.

Alexis could usually be found alone at the bar, drinking himself into an even fouler mood and deeper stupor. One evening he engaged in a shouting and shoving match with the Embassy's owner, a former maitre d'hotel named Luigi. Charged with disorderly conduct, Alexis spent the night sobering up in the holding pen of the nearest police station. By the next morning the story of his arrest was all over town. To avoid the publicity caused by the incident, Barbara fled to a West End nursing home, thereby establishing a pattern of escape she would use more than once in the coming years. To add to the mystery of her "hospitalization" came news that Franklyn and Irene Hutton were on their way to England. On June 1, 1934, when the *Bremen* arrived at Southampton, Barbara's parents found themselves besieged by the press. Asked whether his daughter was contemplating a divorce from Mdivani, Hutton was the model of ambivalence. "I doubt it," he said. "Alexis is a straight shooter and a straight fellow. I was at my daughter's wedding and as far as I'm concerned I have no reason to believe such rumors. Of course, women are notoriously fickle and Barbara is more fickle than most."

Hutton went to the nursing home to see his daughter the following day and was taken aback by how pale and worn-out she looked. After conferring with her physician, Dr. John Slesinger, Hutton announced that he was taking Barbara on an enforced rest cure to Carlsbad—alone. Before leaving for the Czech spa, she went to Roehampton to watch Alexis and his polo team engage an American squad captained by Winston Guest. The Americans won. Barbara kissed Winston on the cheek and then posed with her husband for the press to show the world that all was well.

The Huttons left London on June 17. Mdivani stayed behind to play out the polo season and reflect on the tattered remains of his marriage. He must have given it a good deal of thought because a month later he joined the Huttons in Carlsbad on his way to India to engage in still another round of polo matches. He implored Barbara to join him, insisting that a wife's place was by her mate's side. When she refused, he went off without her. She demonstrated her own independent spirit by traveling with Silvia de Castellane first to Biarritz and then to Nice. In both resorts she put down sizable deposits on a pair of summer villas—$60,000 and $65,000, respectively—that she later decided she didn't want. Only one half of the $125,000 was refundable— "but at least I proved I can spend my own money without Alexis breathing down my neck," she wrote to her stepmother.

Alexis returned from India, and by late August, after their summer apart, they were together again in Venice, staying at the Gritti Palace Hotel, situated in the fifteenth-century former abbey that had belonged to the Doge Andrea Gritti, an ideal spot for Barbara to write poetry. She wrote so many poems over the years that she began carrying them around in their own Vuitton suitcase. Her outflow was based for the most part on the personal events that informed her day. If a main theme emerged, it centered around the failure of her marital expectations; "I Had Dreamt," written during her stay at the Gritti Palace, was characteristic:

> *I had dreamt your love would be*
> *A simple lovely thing.*
> *Unfraught by savage words*
> *That lead to suffering*
>
> *I had dreamt your love would be*
> *As a blossom-laden May,*
> *Fragrant for the mind to store*
> *In melodies of yesterday.*
>
> *But derision scorns my dreams,*
> *Has turned it ashen cold and gray,*
> *For love was dead within your heart*
> *When leaving me today.*

She turned increasingly to poetry as a means of self-expression, encouraged in part by Morley Kennerley, who frequently sent Barbara books of verse, particularly by women poets such as Emily Dickinson and Edna St. Vincent Millay. "She enjoyed talking to my wife, Jean, about poetry," Kennerley remarks, "so I developed the habit of sending her whatever I thought she might like. She reciprocated by sending us samples of her work. She produced in spurts, penning reams of the stuff whenever she felt depressed or cut off from the world. It was not great or even very good poetry, but some of it was quite moving—at least it moved me.

"At first Barbara seemed rather shy about showing her work. Her poems meant a great deal to her and she labored at them. When we finally saw some of them, my wife and I suggested that it might give her satisfaction to have a limited number privately printed for herself and her friends. I had expected her to reject the idea totally, but as a matter of fact she was delighted by the prospect, and since I was with Faber and Faber, it was not difficult to arrange for a small edition to be produced of about two hundred copies.... On the whole Barbara was very definite about her poems, their construction and selection, and wrote without particularly wanting advice. She wrote what I would call primitive verse—unsophisticated and unschooled but full of feeling."

Barbara's first volume, *The Enchanted*, which she published under the name Barbara Mdivani, ran a hundred pages and contained seventy-nine poems. Dedicated to Morley Kennerley, it appeared in October 1934, shortly before her twenty-second birthday. The limited edition, printed by R. Maclehose & Co., a press unofficially affiliated with the University of Glasgow, had a title-page color illustration by the English artist Rex Whistler of four contrasting landscapes: New York, Venice, Peking and Bali. Beyond its charting of the downward slope of her failing marriage, the volume renders descriptions of these and other locations, including Paris, Rome, Honolulu and Fez. In "Grand Canal: Morning," a typical poem, Barbara depicts Venice's central waterway as seen early in the day: "Rose palaces rise/Like drowsy mermaids,/With tender eyes,/and from their hair/Confusion of flowers/Fall over balconies/In coloured showers..." But the main thrust of the poem is love's labour's lost:

> *Yet alas! no marriage can ever be*
> *No blending of earth and worshipful sky*
> *For the whole of eternity between*
> *Me and my beautiful love doth lie.*

Perhaps, as author Dean Jennings has suggested, *The Disenchanted* might have made a more appropriate title. Disenchantment was the motivating force behind Barbara's emotional reaction to Alexis in Venice during the fall of 1934. It was clear to both parties that their marriage was beyond repair. While Barbara remained hidden behind locked doors, her frustrated and confused spouse attempted to dissipate his anger by taking wild rides up and down the Grand Canal in the *Ali Baba*, occasionally adorning the boat with attractive first mates. On September 15 he won the first trial heat for the Duke of Genoa's Cup in the annual Venetian motorboat races; he placed second overall. Barbara wasn't impressed. Accompanied by Jean Kennerley, she left on a two-week trip to visit her friend Count Carlo Gaetani in Naples.

A few days before her departure she gave Alexis a personal check for 3 million lire (then roughly $90,000) with instructions to buy an ancient palazzo in Venice called the Abbazia San Gregorio. It was a small but typically ornate fourteenth-century structure overlooking the Grand Canal with thick stone walls and a thousand hidden nooks and crannies. After she left, Alexis attended to the details of the purchase, exceeding Barbara's directives slightly by placing the deed to the property in his own name. As it turned out, the Abbazia San Gregorio was Barbara's going-away present to Alexis.

A less subtle farewell was tendered on November 14, at Barbara's twenty-second birthday party, held at the Hotel Ritz in Paris, a celebration arranged by Alexis but subsidized by Barbara. It started with a sit-down dinner for 150 guests and was followed by a ball for 2,200 guests that spread through the hotel's tea room, banquet halls and huge Regency ballroom, which had been transformed for the occasion into a street in Casablanca called La Koutabia.

Alexis spared his wife no expense, chartering three airplanes to fly their friends and the Jack Harris orchestra over from London. The Yacht Club Boys, a quartet of American entertainers, were engaged to play and sing during the orchestra's breaks. In 1938, when Marie Louise Ritz published her biography of César Ritz, the hotel's colorful Swiss-born owner, she described the soirée as one of the greatest triumphs in the history of the Ritz. "Every possible whim of a rich young modern was indulged in the creation of this party," she wrote. The guest list featured such formidable names as Princess Natalie Paley (the Russian expatriate whose haunting waiflike features made her one of the most enticing women in Paris); Vicomtesse Marie-Laure de Noailles (a poetess, and the demimonde's favorite beauty); Jean Patou; Elsa Maxwell; Daisy Fellowes; Señor Antenor Patiño (son of the Bolivian tin king); Prince Aly Khan; Elsie Lady Mendl; Coco Chanel and the Duke of Westminster; British Cabinet Minister Leslie Hore-Belisha; Noël Coward; Adele Astaire (Fred's sister) and her husband, Lord Charles Cavendish; ballet dancer Serge Lifar; and the Marquis de Portago (one of the wealthiest men in Europe).

There was another guest in attendance that night not mentioned by Mme. Ritz, Count Court Haugwitz-Reventlow, a Prussian-born Dane not much given to the international party circuit. He and Barbara had met for the first time in a London movie house when they were introducd by Alexis Mdivani, who was an acquaintance of Reventlow's. They had met a second time at Carlsbad when Barbara was there with her parents. A third encounter took place in London shortly before Barbara's twenty-second birthday party, when both were staying at Claridge's.

From the first, Barbara was immensely attracted to the thirty-nine-year-old Reventlow. He was tall and dapper with sharply defined features, muscular physique and impeccable manners. He spoke five languages fluently, was an accomplished skier and mountain climber, and a highly eligible bachelor. When she met him in London again she had invited him to her birthday party.

On arriving at the Ritz, Reventlow was surprised to find himself seated at the table of honor, directly to Barbara's right. His presence caused an instant stir that spread from guest to guest and table to table. The music started and Barbara and the count took to the dance floor while Alexis looked on with mild annoyance. As the orchestra played on, and the couple continued to dance, Mdivani became more and more agitated. He prowled the sidelines like a caged panther, deep lines of worry creasing his usually smooth features.

Barbara and her guest danced on through the night and into the misty dawn. At party's end they stood in the middle of an empty ballroom floor while busboys swept away the debris from the night before. Alexis had gone to bed hours earlier. "We were alone," Barbara would write. "Alone but together. It was the nicest birthday party a girl ever had."

Seven

Wɪᴛʜɪɴ twenty-four hours of the birthday party, the gossip columnists were unanimous in predicting a quick end to the Barbara Hutton–Alexis Mdivani marriage. Barbara vehemently denied the rumor. As the gossip continued to mount, she boarded the *Europa* in Southampton and sailed for New York. Alexis said goodbye in London and Reventlow saw her off in Southampton. The press had a field day. A reporter in New York asked Barbara if she thought the prince devoted too much time to polo. The princess responded, "Well, he's got to do something with his time." She divulged their plans: Alexis would go to India to play polo "or something," and she would spend Christmas and New Year's with family and friends. She expected to rejoin him in six weeks' time in Cairo—"if all goes well."

Things went very poorly at first. In a country still wracked by the Great Depression, the papers were full of sensational muckraking speculations on the private lives of public figures, the richer and more powerful the better. The big newspaper story for the fall of 1934, for example, was the traumatic custody battle that raged over the tiny person of ten-year-old Gloria Vanderbilt. New Yorkers paying two and three cents for their daily newspaper found that the *Matter of Vanderbilt* shared headlines with another story, namely the arrest and arraignment of Bruno Richard Hauptmann for the kidnapping and murder two years earlier of the infant son of Charles and Anne Morrow Lindbergh. There was a third story in the press that happened to coincide with Barbara Hutton's return to the United States. A Canadian parliamentary commission was established in Vancouver to conduct investigations into the operation of chain discount stores in the Dominion. Among those subpoenaed to testify was Leslie Harrington, managing director of all Worthworth stores in Canada. Under oath Harrington admitted that employee wages in the five-and-dime operation in Canada had dropped by 10 percent over the year, while net profits for the same period rose by 20 percent. He went on to explain that wage policy for all Woolworth stores was determined entirely by Woolworth's New York-based board of directors.

At the same time that the press covered the Canadian hearings, the New York *Times* published a scorching editorial condemning Barbara Hutton for her vast expenditures abroad, singling out her twenty-second birthday celebration at the Paris Ritz, variously estimated to have cost between $10,000 and $50,000. "And all this," preached the *Times*, "for a young lady whose nail polish is purportedly changed three times a day to match the color of her latest change of clothes." The implication, however unfair or farfetched, was that there was a direct correlation between the low wages in the Woolworth company stores and the opprobrious wealth of Miss Hutton.

The prevailing sentiment among her friends was that she had become a detested symbol in her homeland for everything that was wrong with it, the victim of a vicious press campaign designed to pander to the reading tastes of an audience that lived vicariously through the tragedies, successes and luxuries of the country's leading celebrities. If the Lindbergh kidnapping case and the Little Gloria custody battle confirmed for the man-on-the-street that money didn't always inspire pleasure, then the Barbara Hutton story confirmed the public's conviction that most people with money were moral degenerates.

The year 1934 also saw the release of an RKO film comedy, *The Richest Girl in the World*, loosely based on the early life of Barbara Hutton. Starring Miriam Hopkins in the featured role of Dorothy Hunter, the movie is basically the story of an orphaned heiress of enormous wealth who invents various devices, some less hackneyed than others, to reassure herself that she is desired by men for her personal allure and not for her money. Harmless enough, the bubbly spoof nevertheless drew attention to Barbara and added to the overall effect of the newspaper coverage.

The reception that Barbara received in New York in 1934 led her to describe herself as "the most hated girl in America." Whatever she did, wherever she went, there was trouble. She was snubbed by waiters and salesgirls, ignored by doormen, cursed by cab drivers and abused by the press. One reporter constantly on Barbara's back during this period was Maury Paul, the powerful society columnist and chronicler of the lives of the rich, who wrote under the penname Cholly Knickerbocker for the Hearst newspaper syndicate and under a half-dozen additional monikers for a number of other publications. Paul, coiner of the phrases "Old Guard" and "Café Society," was an admitted homosexual who lived at home with his mother, wore solid-gold garter clasps, a corset, a pink carnation in his lapel, and so much rouge and eau de cologne that he was banished for life from the New York Athletic Club. His success as a gossip columnist was mainly the result of his psychological insight into this highly restricted "community," coupled with an ability to charm some of its influential citizens into befriending and even confiding in him.

In the vernacular of the trade, he was what is commonly known as "a walker" —an entertaining male escort who is usually sexually un-threatening to the husbands of the women they "walk" to social events. Maury Paul made himself available for lunch dates, doctor appoint-ments, trips to the hairdresser, shopping sprees. He advised the women on what to wear, where to shop, what to eat, what to do, how to have their hair styled. His perseverance reaped its inevitable reward. But as Old Guard slowly merged with Café Nouveau, Maury Paul revised his view of society—of who and what belonged. He began to concentrate on the new—new people, new faces, new money. Among his most famous celebrity "creations," as he labeled them, were Mrs. Harrison Williams, Mrs. William Rhinelander Stewart, Barbara Cushing (later "Babe" Paley), Adele Astaire, Brenda Frazier and Gloria ("Mimi") Baker. Whenever he introduced a new face in his column Paul served notice to his readers that "the newcomers of today are the Old Guard of tomorrow" —not that he necessarily subscribed to this dictum.

Because of the commercial pressures to keep his column "lively," Paul developed one feature he called "Great Tragedies of Society" — features that bore titles such as "Suicides Stalk the Joneses of Long Island," "Cup That Cheers Wrecks Laura Biddle," "Polo Fall Drove Socialite Arthur Scott Burden Violently Insane," "Ernest Simpson: The Unimportance of Being Ernest." In 1934 he drew a bead on Barbara Hutton. "Huttontot Drops Prince for Count" was the title of this latest and greatest of societal tragedies:

> ...That's Barbara Hutton as in Huttontot, late of Peking, Paris, and New Delhi, back at last to grace our humdrum shores. Word of mouth has it that America's version of Catherine the Great is ready to dump her princely spouse, trade him in for a bigger and better model. What better

way to spend all those jillions and trillions? At age 22 Huttontot has already amassed one of the largest jewelry collections in the world and proved it by wearing her million-dollar diamond necklace to a party thrown by her cousin Jimmy Donahue the other night at his mother's quaint Fifth Ave. duplex. Isn't it nice to have money these days? Seriously, folks—What does it all mean? It means that crass, brash Babs Hutton has done more in a few short years to kill off Society than any six American heiresses combined. And then we come to the touchy question of charity. Has Huttontot donated as much to the Salvation Army as she has to her phony Russian prince? Lest you forget, this is the same Huttontot who spent $25,000 in Paris a few short weeks ago to commemorate the anniversary of her birth. But not to worry: there's plenty more where that came from. For the rest of us, my dears, Christmas comes but once a year.

Maury Paul was never one to worry very much about the veracity of his statements. He ought to have worried more than he did, because more often than not the facts were erroneous. His latest diatribe was no exception, particularly with respect to Barbara Hutton and "the touchy question of charity."

A cursory examination of Barbara's financial statements indicates that she did, in fact, make substantial contributions to charity. In 1934, for example, she donated $25,000 to a fund in support of the archeological expeditions of Roy Chapman Andrews; she donated $250,000 to the New York City Mission Society and gave a matching grant to the American Red Cross; she gave $10,000 to the Musicians Emergency Fund, headed by Doris Duke. The New York Foundling Hospital, the Metropolitan Museum of Art, the Whitney Museum, the Julliard School of Music, the San Francisco Opera Company, the New York Philharmonic and the New York City Restoration Fund were only a few of the organizations she helped to support.

❧

When Ambassador T. C. White and his wife, Princess Der Ling, arrived in New York late in 1934, Barbara gave a Chinese dinner party for them on Christmas eve in her apartment at 1020 Fifth Avenue. Prepared by a Mandarin chef borrowed for the evening from the Hotel Pierre, the meal was served on authentic Chinese porcelain and eaten with the correct Chinese utensils. With her keen knowledge and appreciation of fine Chinese wares and art, Princess Der Ling was to become Barbara's private curator, assisting her in the accumulation of her peerless collection of Oriental artifacts. Another guest at the dinner party was

Lawrence Tibbett, a leading baritone with the Metropolitan Opera. Barbara had sent Tibbett a copy of *The Enchanted,* and finding her poems "charming," Tibbett suggested that she consider rendering several of them into songs to be performed at his next public recital. Tibbett's suggestion pleased Barbara. Her friends were mostly indifferent to her creative efforts; nobody, save the Kennerleys, offered any real encouragement.

Barbara set to work and decided to choose three poems about Peking. The only poem in the volume that seemed appropriate, however, was "In a Peking Street," which she retitled "Lantern Street (Teng Chieh)." She then wrote two new poems, "The Temple of Heaven" and "Chu-lu-mai," and gave the triad the collective title *Pieking Pictures.* Elsa Maxwell, aided by Noël Coward, set the three poems to music. Tibbett performed them in March 1935 on the Packard Motors Radio Hour from New York. G. Schirmer, Inc., the sheet-music publisher, released 2,000 copies of *Peking Pictures* ("for voice and piano") at $1.25 per folio set. But only a few hundred were sold, and Barbara's earnings from royalties came to $125.50. The significance of this figure is that it represented practically the only independent income she ever earned on her own. (One other time she earned $25 for granting scholar John Goette use of her poem "Bowl of Jade" from *The Enchanted* in his book, *History of Chinese Jade.*)

Barbara spent New Year's with her father and stepmother at Prospect Hill, their plantation outside Charleston. The purpose of the visit was to discuss her marital difficulties and to disclose her growing interest in Count Court Haugwitz-Reventlow. Franklyn Hutton's extensive network of spies had already apprised him of Reventlow, whom he had met only briefly at Carlsbad the year before. This time Hutton was leaving nothing to chance. He hired Harold Munro, a private investigator in London, to do some background checking for him.

Munro's report arrived shortly before Barbara did. The investigation was noteworthy for revealing that there were no Reventlow files to speak of in any of the various newspaper or tabloid morgues, no record of the count's having plundered the beachfronts and watering holes of Europe in search of young, helpless heiresses, no vicious gossip in the columns or mummified skeletons in the closet. The count's birth certificate gave his full name as Court Heinrich Eberhard Erdman Georg Haugwitz-Hardenberg-Reventlow, born 1895 in Charlottenburg, Germany. His mother's side of the family was Austro-Danish; his father, the late Count Georg Haugwitz-Reventlow, was of Polish-Saxon descent and had owned a successful cement factory in Germany.

The Reventlows moved to Denmark when Court was still a boy, but during World War I he became a commissioned officer and fought for Germany, earning an Iron Cross, first class, for valor. After the war he and his elder brother, Heinrich, returned to work the family farms on the island of Lolland, off Denmark's southeast coast. The farmland, comprising 16,000 acres, included the baronial manor house of Hardenberg Castle and a considerable staff of servants and farmhands.

Court Reventlow, having become a Danish subject, was an active, diligent, progressive dairy farmer, up at dawn for his long tours of inspection. He was a first-class stock breeder. His Danish bacon was second to none. There was a private railway on the property at Lolland to transport the milk to the bottling plant. Both Reventlow boys maintained a low profile, subscribing to a credo of hard work, simplicity of lifestyle, solitude and sobriety, broken by occasional bursts of gaiety during vacations in Berlin, London, Paris and Rome.

Summarizing his findings, Munro noted that "the Reventlows trace their lineage to a brother of Queen Adelaide of Germany and are distantly related to the current Queen of Roumania. The family farms are self-supporting but not profit-making. Count Court Reventlow is highly respected among his peers. He is considered worldly, competent, courteous, and a man of position, although it must be borne in mind that as the younger brother he is not considered by Danish law to be the owner of the family seat. Yet he is on excellent terms with his brother and is said to strongly desire a family life. He seems able to shoulder responsibility and should be fully capable of keeping your daughter in check."

Despite the optimistic tone of Munro's report, natural caution made Franklyn Hutton hesitate. He reminded Barbara that she barely knew the man, whereas her husband, for all his shortcomings, was at least a known quantity. Hutton was also hesitant because of a recent slew of well-publicized divorce proceedings involving other members of the family circle. Still fresh in the public's mind was the hotly contested divorce case between Marjorie Merriweather Post and E. F. Hutton, in which the lurid details of Ned Hutton's frequent infidelities had been laid out in the press.

At the same time that Aunt Marjorie was realigning her personal commitments, her two eldest daughters were realigning theirs. Adelaide Post Hutton (née Adelaide Close, but adopted by E. F. Hutton) divorced Tim Durant, a frustrated character actor and film producer whom Marjorie had set up with a seat on the New York Stock Exchange; it later turned out that he had played hard and fast with his wife's personal bankroll. Eleanor Post Hutton (also adopted by Ned) divorced screen writer-director Preston Sturges, whose artistic interests had long alienated him from the rest of the Hutton clan. Only Barbara Hutton approved of Sturges and expressed disappointment when the marriage dissolved.

This sequence of marital calamities convinced Barbara to reconsider her own options. She needed more time to make a decision and agreed to meet her husband in Cairo as originally planned. What she didn't tell him was that she was arriving in Egypt two weeks early and that her traveling companion on this leg of the journey would be Court Reventlow. Also in the entourage was Jean Kennerley, who recalled: "Barbara and I stayed in one room, Reventlow in the other. He resented my presence on the trip, and the disenchantment was mutual. Barbara found him frightfully good-looking, but I thought he had a cruel face. He relished ordering people around, including Barbara's servants. 'Do this, do that, do the other.' He was a man of ungovernable temper, and easily and often and without the slightest provocation would have a fit. One day a little Arab boy in rags asked us for some coppers. Reventlow gave the poor child a box on the ear. When we were alone I said to Barbara, 'You're not serious about marrying this man, are you?' But she was ga-ga about him and had already made up her mind. Finally poor Alexis arrived, and Reventlow did his Houdini act. Alexis knew about Reventlow. Barbara wasn't behaving well. She was transparent. The rest of the trip was torture, and I was relieved when we returned to London."

By late March 1935 the stage was set for a final confrontation. The Mdivanis were in their suite at Claridge's, while Court Reventlow was staying in a penthouse apartment atop the Berkeley Hotel. Barbara spent an afternoon talking with Court and that evening returned to Claridge's to have it out with Alexis. She must have made short work of it, because a few hours later Alexis was on the phone with Roussie Sert in Paris. He had just had a talk with Barbara, and she had told him that it was finally, completely, irretrievably over between them, and that she would never come back to him.

"Where's Barbara now?" asked Roussie.

"She took her bags and cleared out," said Alexis. "She's probably at the Berkeley with Reventlow."

"Do you want her back?"

"Certainly, I want her back."

"Then don't do anything until I get there," Roussie warned. "I'll be there tomorrow. I'll have a talk with Barbara. She always listens to me."

Recording the latest developments in a hurried letter to Serge Mdivani, Roussie left for London the next morning, March 23. When she arrived she went straight to the front desk of the Berkeley and asked for Barbara. The desk clerk said he was sorry but the princess and her party had checked out earlier in the day.

"Did she leave a forwarding address?" asked Roussie.

"Yes," said the desk clerk. "We're to send her mail to 1020 Fifth Avenue in New York. She boarded the *Bremen* this afternoon. She should be in New York in a few days."

As the next day's London *Times* attested, Barbara had indeed boarded the *Bremen*, accompanied by a sizable entourage that included her friend Jane Alcott, Jimmy Donahue, Ticki Tocquet, her chauffeur Clinton Gardiner and his wife, Lilian, her Swedish masseuse Karen Gustafson, and her French maid, Simone Chibleur.

There was the usual hubbub and commotion among newsmen as Barbara disembarked in New York. Anticipating the worst, Franklyn Hutton had hired a half-dozen security guards to meet Barbara at the pier. While Jimmy Donahue pranced and mugged for the press, Barbara was wedged into a waiting limousine and driven to Jessie Donahue's duplex at 834 Fifth Avenue to spend the night. Early the next morning she was taken to Newark Airport, where a chartered United Airlines Mainliner waited to fly her and her New York Attorney, Willard Thompkins, Jr., to Reno, Nevada, the divorce capital of the world.

In Reno she was housed at the estate of George Thatcher, a prominent local attorney retained to represent Barbara in Nevada. Her security guards worked in round-the-clock shifts. Clinton Gardiner was also drafted into the palace guard and trailed along whenever Barbara left the house.

Gardiner protected his mistress even when she wasn't around. The chauffeur was drinking in a downtown Reno tavern one night when the man next to him began mouthing off about the Woolworth heiress. Gardiner decked the fellow with a roundhouse right and the knockout was recorded in every newspaper from coast to coast.

He also accompanied Barbara the day she paid an unannounced visit to the Woolworth store in Reno. In glittering jewels she walked up and down the aisles, inspecting the merchandise, smiling at the sales personnel, signing autographs, and then departed without spending a nickel. It was the first and last time she ever set foot in one of her grandfather's stores.

While Barbara sweated it out in Nevada, Count Reventlow was in Copenhagen arranging an audience with His Majesty King Christian X. Like other feudal landowners under the jurisdiction of the Danish crown, he was expected to procure the monarch's consent before entering into a matrimonial contract. The king gave his official sanction and Court, accompanied by his German valet, Paul Wiser, sailed for New York. He was emphatic in his denials that he would not—no, never, never, never—marry Barbara. "I've been a bachelor for forty years and don't intend to change," he said. He bet one newsreel photographer $25 to that effect, proving himself as formidable a fabulist as any of the Mdivanis. Within twenty-four hours he and Wiser boarded a train for Reno. They were scheduled to arrive on May 13, the same day as Barbara's divorce hearing.

In Reno, at a few minutes before eleven in the morning on the appointed day, a gray Rolls-Royce stopped at the side entrance of the Washoe District County Courthouse. A dozen deputies and Barbara's team of security guards, already positioned outside the courthouse, linked arms to keep a throng of reporters, photographers and tourists at a safe distance. The chauffeur and a private detective emerged first and helped Barbara out of the back seat; George Thatcher and Willard Thompkins, Jr., followed. Barbara wore a crisp navy blue suit, navy blue pumps and a matching felt hat with a tiny brim; she carried a mink furpiece thrown over one shoulder. She took Thompkins' arm as they moved through the crowd toward the rear of the building, up a flight of stairs into the courthouse, and down a long corridor glutted with another mass of journalists. The flashbulbs began to explode, and Barbara managed a half smile, as a line of guards cleared a narrow path through the crowded hallway.

A marshal locked the courtroom door behind Barbara, forcing reporters to press their faces against a small window in the door. It was a closed hearing, with only a handful of courtroom personnel in attendance: the clerk of the court, a court stenographer, a bailiff, a deputy sheriff, two city marshals and the presiding district judge, Thomas Moran. Alexis Mdivani was represented in absentia by attorney George S. Brown, whose sole contribution to the proceeding was a broad smile, presumably in anticipation of his $10,000 legal fee. Barbara was spoken for by her two attorneys and Ticki Tocquet, whose testimony was needed to establish the fact that Barbara had been a legal resident of Reno "for no less than six weeks." From start to finish the hearing lasted less than twenty minuts and cost Barbara an estimated $250,000 in legal fees and personal expenses. Following Ticki's brief testimony, Barbara took the stand and answered several perfunctory questions before offering a fuller statement on the failings of her marriage:

> When I got married I had no conception of love. A strong desire for
> independence from my family was the main reason I married Prince

Mdivani. I realized it was a mistake even before the wedding, but things had gone too far to stop. Yet in reality I was more prepared for marriage than my husband. The Prince was totally unaware of the burdens and responsibilities that such a bond entailed, and I am now convinced that he married me only for my money.

The divorce was granted and Barbara was hurried out of the court-house. Following the hearing, Judge Moran, no stranger to society divorce proceedings, held a five-minute press conference in his private chambers, informing reporters that the Hutton-Mdivani case "is no different than a thousand others I've adjudicated in the course of my career on the bench. It's true that Miss Hutton has more money than most folks, but in the eyes of the law everyone is considered equal."

Barbara had been divorced only hours when Court Reventlow's train pulled into the town of Verdi, thirteen miles from Reno. There he was met by Willard Thompkins, Jr., and driven off toward Lake Tahoe. That evening when Barbara and Court walked arm in arm into the Tahoe Tavern, a resort lodge overlooking the lake, the world took note. Wooster Taylor, a roving reporter for the San Francisco *Examiner*, broke the story the next morning under the bold headline: THE PRINCE IS DEAD. LONG LIVE THE COUNT!

This unofficial announcement of Barbara's second marriage un-leashed a flood of public speculation on what was evidently the question of the day. Even Will Rogers ventured into the fray. In his syndicated newspaper column he examined both sides of the proverbial coin:

> Well, a big headline today says Barbara is marrying a count, or a duke or something, and we get all excited and start criticising as though she was a ward of the people. It's her money. It's her life. She must pay a tremendous lot of taxes to our government. She deserves some right. Her fortune was made from five-and-ten-cent purchases, so nobody got stuck very much. So, if she wants to pick up where the United States Government left off and finance all Europe it's her own business.

Despite Will Rogers, Barbara's public image was hardly enhanced by her decision to remarry less than twenty-four hours after her divorce. To her credit, she kept the wedding ceremony short and simple and as private as her celebrity would permit, holding it in the home of Dr. A. J. Bart Hood, a physician who was a neighbor of George Thatcher's. Barbara wore a plain yellow print dress and straw hat to match; Reventlow wore a business suit and presented his bride with a nosegay of wild flowers. The Reverend William Moll Case of the Presbyterian Church in Reno performed the ten-minute service. George Thatcher and Willard Thompkins, Jr., signed the marriage certificate as co-witnesses. The guests included Judge and Mrs. Bartlett (friends of the Hoods'), Princess Der Ling and Ambassador White (then living in California), Jimmy Blakely (also living in California), Ticki Tocquet, Mr. and Mrs. Franklyn Hutton, Jimmy Donahue and Reventlow's valet.

Following the ceremony Mrs. Hood served a filling country breakfast, and then the newlyweds stepped out on the front porch for a picture-taking session with the other members of the small wedding party. No fewer than two dozen special deputies, bodyguards and private detectives, among them Reno Sheriff Ray Root and Chief of Police J. M. Kirkley, both attired in cowboy boots, fringed Western leather jackets, and new ten-gallon hats, ringed the Hood estate. There was good reason for their presence. A large crowd of gawkers and newsmen had flocked to the site to catch a glimpse of the newlyweds. They perched atop their cars or sat in the high cottonwood trees to get a better view. They brought binoculars, telescopes and cameras with telephoto lenses. One news photographer scaled a neighbor's house and established a makeshift crow's nest on the roof.

By early afternoon a honeymoon caravan of fifteen cars bound for San Francisco climbed the Sierra Nevada Mountains. The caravan consisted mostly of police cars deployed to see the newlyweds safely to their destination. The journey was not without incident. Soon after leaving Reno, one of the deputy sheriffs drove his police car into Jimmy Blakely's Rolls-Royce and both vehicles had to be towed off for repairs. Another police car broke down and had to be abandoned. But by evening the Reventlows were safe in their suite at the Mark Hopkins Hotel, the same seventeenth-floor suite Barbara always reserved for herself when visiting San Francisco.

"On our first night in San Francisco we were both as nervous as hens. We wanted everything to be perfect," writes Barbara. "The occasion lacked spontaneity. There was something cold about it. Court felt it too because after a few minutes of nothing happening he complained of exhaustion. We awoke early the next morning, and in the half sleep of dawn made love."

That morning, as word spread of their arrival, the hotel lobby quickly filled with all manner of voyeurs, some actually bearing gifts for the couple. One man in particular, carrying an illuminated dime-store goldfish bowl he insisted would go nicely in Barbara's boudoir, had spent the night on a couch in the lounge, refusing to budge until he could give Barbara her wedding present.

They had wanted to make a day of it in San Francisco, a city that Court had never seen before. But from the minute they left their suite, they were followed wherever they went. Reporters and photographers smothered the newlyweds with requests for interviews, while spectators shouted at them from behind police barricades. When they returned to their hotel after a morning of sightseeing they found the bedroom banked with dozens of bouquets of flowers. Three telephones were going at once. Invitations to appear here and there were hand-delivered all afternoon by a medley of exhausted bellhops. Valets, butlers and maids were in and out of the suite every minute, carrying the latest reports to the newspaper people in the lobby: the kinds of foods the Reventlows ordered, the color of Court's pajamas (sky-blue), the outfit Barbara planned on wearing to the party they were throwing that evening in the hotel's main ballroom.

Is it going to be like this from now on? Reventlow must have wondered as they danced and mingled with their five hundred guests, most of whom he had never seen before and would never see again. He felt out of place among so many new and strange faces. And he was agitated by the eternal flux of reporters and newspaper columnists. A hundred times in the course of the evening he was asked how he was enjoying San Francisco, and a hundred times he responded with a chilly "It's a wonderful town!" Later that night after the last stragglers had gone, the newlyweds engaged in their first disagreement. Court wanted to leave San Francisco, Barbara wanted to stay. Barbara finally gave in.

About noon the following day they made their escape through the hotel's underground garage. A police escort led them to the Oakland railroad station, where the Curleyhut sat waiting, the last car on a New York-bound express. If Reventlow's feathers were ruffled by the mob in San Francisco, he was to find New York's baying throng all but repulsive. They were waiting for the Curleyhut when the train pulled into Pennsylvania Station—an irate gathering of Woolworth Company clerks armed with placards and banners calling for higher wages and more generous benefits. Bearing their homemade billboards the protesters followed Barbara uptown to 1020 Fifth Avenue. There they formed a picket line, handing out leaflets and gathering signatures on a petition supporting their demands. Whenever Court or Barbara emerged from the apartment building they were greeted by a chorus of catcalls and an unmelodious rendition of a parody on a familiar tune.

Barbara Hutton's got the dough, parlay voo;
We know where she got it, too, parlay voo;
We share at Woolworth's five-and-dime,
The pay we get is sure a crime,
Hinky dinky, parlay voo.

Soon after their New York arrival something strange happened. A shabbily dressed woman arrived in the lobby of 1020 Fifth Avenue and insisted she was the Countess Anna Reventlow, a cousin of Count Court Reventlow. She wore a shawl wrapped around her head and carried a large shopping bag, which she claimed contained a present for the newlyweds.

Without first verifying the woman's story, the doorman sent her upstairs. She rang the Hutton doorbell and informed the servant who soon stood before her that she was the count's cousin and had brought a wedding present, a valuable porcelain that had once belonged to the Romanov czars. She wanted to give it directly to her cousin or his bride, and she wondered if they were available. Reventlow, who was resting in a bedroom at the time, sent word that he had no cousin named Anna but that the woman could leave the gift if she wanted. She did and when the valet opened it he found a cheap crock pot filled with a yellow rubber chicken. The woman, it turned out, was an unemployed cook, and the rubber chicken was her idea of a practical joke.

The incident was forgotten and on May 30 the Reventlows sailed for Europe aboard the *Bremen*. Although delighted to be returning to the Continent, Reventlow had already experienced some serious misgivings concerning his bride. In the two weeks since their marriage, he had reached the inescapable conclusion that Barbara was an absolute glutton for publicity. For somebody who claimed to detest the savagery of the press, she behaved in a most extraordinary manner, granting interviews, news conferences and photo sessions, and making herself generally accessible to any and all comers. This was not to say that she went out of her way to cultivate a public image or to establish ties with the press, but at the same time she did little to thwart their repeated advances. She followed what was written about her with a close eye, perusing the daily newspapers, weekly tabloids and monthly fashion magazines from first line to last, paying rapt attention to the columns and the society page, tossing the periodical angrily aside on those days her name failed to appear, and complaining to Ticki Tocquet that she was already a has-been.

Another major problem faced by Reventlow had to do with Barbara's dietary practices, her panic every time the scale showed the slightest gain in weight. At the beginning, when she refused to eat anything but an occasional vegetable dish, he thought she was merely trying to shed a few pounds. On learning that her diet was routine, the count became concerned and began asking questions. Had she ever consulted a diet doctor? he wanted to know. Barbara shook her head. She knew no diet doctors, she said, and added that her unwillingness to eat was her own problem, not Court's, and she was perfectly content to continue as her own nutritionist.

Reventlow was deeply distressed. Each meal became a struggle, an exercise in self-control. It reached the point where he felt guilty for every morsel he swallowed. After their divorce he discussed the ritual with a reporter, observing that in time he found it more and more difficult to enjoy his meals. At the table he felt her ravenous eyes watching every move his fork made, until he started eating faster and faster, or else eating as lightly as she. After four years of marriage, Reventlow's weight had dropped from 200 to 160 pounds.

During their first summer together Reventlow somehow succeeded in convincing Barbara to visit a famed dietary clinic in Freiburg, Germany, operated by two English physicians, Drs. Martin and Peters, neither of whom made much headway with their stubborn patient. Dr. Martin eventually diagnosed her ailment as anorexia nervosa, in those days a rare psychosomatic disorder. He advised her to consult with a psychoanalyst.

Barbara was glad to leave Freiburg. The swastikas and anti-Semitic slogans on the sides of buildings terrified one of her servants, an American girl named Leah Efros, who was Jewish. When a restaurant in Freiburg refused to serve Leah, Barbara decided she had seen enough. They went briefly to a health spa in Carlsbad, the town where they had first met. Reventlow convinced his wife that if she exercised regularly she could afford to eat without gaining weight. The scheme worked as long as they remained at the spa. But by the time they arrived in Egypt she was fasting again. They stayed with Baron Jean Empain, a wealthy Belgian, at a palace he owned outside Cairo. They then went to Jerusalem. In Jerusalem, Barbara developed a vaginal infection and went to see a gynecologist. After examining her, the doctor confirmed that she had a mild yeast infection. He also informed her that she was at least two months pregnant.

❧

Prince Alexis Mdivani, meanwhile, had begun a new life for himself on the harvest of his two years with Barbara. Besides two very generous trust funds, his speedboat (the *Ali Baba*), a string of polo ponies, a

Rolls-Royce and a collection of valuable jewelry, there was also the house in Venice, the Abbazia San Gregorio, completely refurbished by Alexis following the divorce. José Sert added to the Abbazia's value by painting a large mural of an old Venetian canal scene on one of the walls and a second mural on the domed ceiling of the living room. Roussie also helped with the decorating by selecting the furniture and fabrics.

In Paris Alexis acquired another residence, an apartment on the Place de Palais Bourbon, decorating it with soft white satin divans, overstuffed throw pillows and floor cushions from India, and bright Indian silks. He hired two Indian man-servants, dressed them in white silk tunics with scarlet sashes, and bought a coal-black Great Dane. Just as the apartment was completed, he met a woman who captured his fancy. She was Baroness Maud von Thyssen, the estranged wife of Baron Heinrich von Thyssen, a steel magnate whose family was the leading developer of the mining and industrial Ruhr district in Germany.

In July 1935 Alexis and Maud paid a visit to the Serts at Mas Juny in Spain. On Roussie's recommendation Alexis bought an old estate not far from Mas Juny, part of a larger plot that had once belonged to Peter III of Aragon. The property included a small, crumbling chapel, which Alexis intended to restore. It was here that he planned to marry Maud, the ceremony to take place the moment her divorce from Baron von Thyssen became final. To expedite the proceedings she decided to return to Paris to confer with her attorney while Alexis remained with his sister at Mas Juny.

On the evening of August 1, Alexis began the seventy-mile drive with Maud from Palamós to Perpignan, France, where she would catch the train for Paris. They were late, and Alexis, always a fast driver, was doing ninety on the narrow country road. Halfway there, near the Spanish village of Albona, his Rolls struck a culvert on the side of the road, careened off a tree and flipped over five times before comiing to a rest upside down in a ditch. The occupants of a passing automobile pulled the two passengers from beneath the smoldering wreck. The baroness was severely injured but still breathing. Alexis was dead.

José Sert had gone off for the day, leaving his wife with their houseguests, Gaston and Bettina Bergery, the popular French Leftist leader and his American wife, and dancer Serge Lifar. When word of the accident reached Mas Juny, Roussie rushed to the site of the crash, arriving just as her brother's body was being carried off on a wooden donkey cart. The death of Alexis was a shock from which Roussie never fully recovered. Bettina Bergery stayed with Roussie for the rest of the summer. She later told a friend that she had never seen anyone suffer such agony. Following her brother's death, Roussie no longer seemed interested in partaking of the social scene that had played such a vital function in her life. Influenced by Misia Sert, of all people, she entered the netherworld of drugs—morphine, opium, barbiturates—in a futile effort to block out her painful loss. Drugs gradually washed away what remained of her youth and beauty and in the end only compounded the intensity of her despair. "Losing Alexis," she wrote to Barbara Hutton, "is like losing part of my own life. We buried him by the small chapel of Peter III that he liked so much. The horror of visiting his grave prevents me from going very often. Alexis was only twenty-six and had his whole life before him."

Six months after the death of Alexis, his former spouse Louise Van Alen stunned society by becoming Mrs. Serge Mdivani. Louise thus achieved the dubious distinction of becoming the first person to brave two of "the marrying Mdivanis," a feat one columnist likened to jumping off the top of the Empire State Building and surviving—not once but twice.

Disaster was, however, about to strike the Mdivani clan a second time in less than a year. Serge and Louise honeymooned in the Caribbean and in Palm Beach, where Serge, also a polo enthusiast, entered an international tournament, riding for a team called The Georgians, made up of several other Russian émigrés. In the course of the tournament The Georgians tackled a team from Texas, captained by Cecil Smith, America's premier polo star. Halfway through the second chukker, on a wet and slippery field, Cecil Smith's horse accidentally collided with Mdivani's mount. Serge was thrown, and as he fell to the ground his startled horse reared and kicked, striking him in the head and killing him instantly. Louise Van Alen was again dragged through the gossip columns, this time as a widow rather than a divorcée.

Eight

N EWS OF Alexis Mdivani's fatal automobile accident reached Barbara as she, Court Reventlow and Jimmy Donahue were arriving at Hardenberg Castle on the Danish isle of Lolland for their first visit with Reventlow's family. Traumatized by the death of Alexis, Barbara went into a severe depression. Locking herself in her room, she could soon be heard playing a stack of Bing Crosby records she had brought along on the trip. Court Reventlow, more Prussian than Danish in his staid outlook on life and women, couldn't understand how Barbara could be broken up by the sudden death of a man she no longer loved. Nor could he comprehend how Bing Crosby could make her feel better.

Reventlow later claimed that Barbara had a tremendous affinity for Denmark—and apparently he thought she did. In reality she detested the stark, lonely island of Lolland with its one small village of Saxkøbing and its damp and misty climate. Before their arrival there had been bonfires in the public square in anticipation of the American bride who would like Denmark so well that she would remain there. If she remained, then perhaps she would pay the taxes for the villagers near the castle and on the lands owned by the Haugwitz-Reventlows.

Court's older brother, Heinrich, who used only a few rooms of the castle, reopened the main part, renovated fifteen rooms and moved his own apartments to another section of the mansion, which, according to legend, was haunted.

(It was at Castle Hardenberg, said the natives, that Count Struensee, paramour of Queen Carolyn Matilda, won the enmity of eighteenth-century Danish nobles by plotting the improvement of social conditions in Denmark. Before he was beheaded, Count Struensee cursed the Danish noblemen responsible for his doom and for the imprisonment of Queen Carolyn. The "curse of Struensee" was still supposed to hang over the heads of noblemen who visited the castle.)

When the Danish press corps invaded Hardenberg to interview the visitors, Jimmy Donahue injected a touch of humor by claiming that Reventlow had actually rented the castle for their stay and planned to terminate the lease the moment they left. Jimmy, unhappy because he had been relegated to a guest cottage on the property rather than being allowed to stay in the castle itself, widened the growing breach between himself and Reventlow by imitating the count's clipped manner of speech and stiff Germanic mannerisms. At night in the cold cottage he would start a fire in the furnace by igniting pieces of furniture—tables, chairs, stools—and throwing them in with logs and tinder. Barbara, despite herself, couldn't help but laugh at her cousin's antics.

The only other occasion she remembered with any degree of fondness was a dinner party at Hardenberg, with Court's brother Heinrich as host, attended by a group of titled neighbors and several important European diplomats. After a splendid Danish feast, Court's brother presented Barbara with a bracelet of flashing heirloom emeralds in a modern setting, made by Tiffany's of New York. She was utterly touched. "It's the first time," she said, "I've ever really been given a present I didn't have to pay for myself."

By early September the Reventlows were back in Paris, living in a suite at the Ritz. A letter arrived advising Barbara that Alexis Mdivani's will had been filed for probate. The estate consisted of the two trust funds set up by Barbara and various pieces of property, including the real estate in Spain, the apartment in Paris and the palace in Venice. Barbara was named as one of the beneficiaries along with Mdivani's four siblings. The document specified that the heirs should gather at a meeting in Paris and work out a friendly and equitable division of the estate.

The bequest put Barbara in an awkward position. She had no intention of dickering for her part of the estate (which increased with the death of Serge Mdivani), and she had no intention of sitting around a conference table discussing the fine points of estate law. Barbara settled the matter by requesting that her share of the estate be donated to charity. The Venetian palazzo she had once wanted went to Roussie Sert.

The decision to remove herself from the proceedings eased her mind. For the first time in weeks she began to enjoy herself. She rose early each morning for a rousing match of tennis with her husband and friends at a nearby racquet club. Siliva de Castellane remembers Barbara dressed in tailored white tennis shorts, matching blouse and cardigan, tennis shoes, no make-up, no jewelry save earrings. "She had a kind of glazed perfect beauty, polished, a trifle icy. She looked fantastic on the tennis court. And she played a good game, much better than Reventlow."

Photographs of Barbara in her skimpy tennis whites graced the front pages of every major European newspaper. Her re-entry with a new husband into the Parisian stratosphere created excitement for a public generally fed up with news of economic distress and political backstabbing. Eric Hawkins, the editor of the Paris *Herald Tribune*, recognized at once the advantages of featuring Barbara regularly in the pages of his newspaper. When Barbara talked, no matter how commonplace her utterance, people listened. Her face sold papers. Hawkins assigned one of his crack reporters to Hutton. Readers were treated to minutely detailed, daily accounts of what struck many as a life of wanton excess, yet which made for compelling reading. Her days were taken up by hairdresser appointments with Alexandre; photo sessions for *Vogue* and *Harper's Bazaar* with society photographers like Horst P. Horst and George Hoyningen-Huene; shopping sprees in the fashionable Rue Faubourg St. Honoré (one companion noted that the shopkeepers practically washed their hands with invisible soap when they saw her entering their establishment); lunch at Maxim's; solitary strolls through the Bois de Boulogne, or across Place Vendôme and up the Rue de la Paix; visits to museums, art galleries or the book stalls along the Left Bank of the Seine. Her nights were reserved for the opera, the theater, ballet, dancing at Pré Catelan, small dinner parties, and large sublime balls.

The grand social rite of any Paris season in the 1930s had to be the annual mid-September fête at Elsie de Wolfe Lady Mendl's Villa Trianon, a Versailles château with its own aviary, topiary gardens and outdoor music pavilion. The house was built in the Louis Philippe period, and filled by Elsie, an interior decorator of renown, with wonderful eighteenth-century furniture and *boiserie* and modern murals that reflected its owner's enchanting taste. The entrance was on the Boulevard St. Antoine, but there was a little gate in the *potager* on the far side of the house that led right onto the grounds of the Palace of Versailles. Elsie shared the house (and a Paris apartment on the Avenue d'Iéna) with her urbane, charming husband, Sir Charles Mendl, press attaché at the British embassy in Paris. Their *mariage de raison*, like that of Cole and Linda Porter (who introduced them), was amiably chaste.

Everyone wanted to visit the Villa Trianon to see the celebrated Lady Mendl and especially to take a peek at her private bath, a chamber twice the size of her bedroom, with leopard-skin upholstered banquettes, a tub painted in *faux marbre*, the walls hung with a valuable set of Chinese mirror paintings, the room illuminated by a one-of-a-kind Venetian crystal chandelier, and the toilet disguised by a cane-seated chair. This room was her nest, her sanctum sanctorum, where she practiced her daily yoga and deep-breathing exercises, read the newspaper (often while standing on her head), played gin rummy, drank her favorite self-concocted cocktail (grapefruit juice, gin and Cointreau) and occasionally held court. It was in her bathroom that Elsie once lectured Barbara Hutton on French society—its traps and pitfalls.

Elsie loved having people around her and her parties were always a compelling mixture of artists, beautiful women, high society and young climbers on their way up. What made her such an attractive hostess, apart from her warmth and open manner, was her imaginative and sophisticated palate. She made up her own culinary rules, among them: "Never start your meal on a lake!"—by which she meant, never serve soup for a first course. Her latest party—attended by a lively crowd that included the Reventlows, Prince Jean-Louis Faucingy-Lucinge, Diana Vreeland, the novelist Colette, the fashion designer Elsa Schiaparelli, Lord and Lady Milford Haven, Cecil Beaton, Tallulah Bankhead and Bébé Bérard—featured a menu with champagne and steamed clams, followed by cold filet of sole and loin of veal Prince Orloff, accompanied by an array of choice dinner wines, and for dessert, pistachio bombe. When the guests gathered for after-dinner coffee in the long gallery overlooking the garden, Elsie announced that she was introducing a new cabaret singer whose voice would bowl over the kingpins of Paris. To great applause and laughter the familiar figure of Elsa Maxwell appeared. Clad in a tuxedo, she took a seat at the grand piano and launched into a medley of Cole Porter's songs. The prank was Elsie's idea and it evidently went over, because a dozen years later the Duchess of Windsor would repeat the scene at one of her parties in Paris.

The day after Elsie's soirée, Barbara visited the Rue Cambon salon of Coco Chanel, across the street from the Ritz, to be fitted for a maternity wardrobe. She was accompanied by a friend, Janet Montagu, the daughter of Lord Beaverbrook and the wife of the Honorable James Drogo Montagu, the second son of the Earl of Sandwich. After the fitting, the ladies followed Coco up two flights of winding stairs to the couturiere's daytime apartment above the salon. In this sumptuous shrine to beauty, with its many-mirrored entrance, Coco rested, ate, contemplated and entertained, spending her nights in a small sleeping suite at the Ritz. But the daytime apartment was her real dwelling, for here she kept her most meaningful treasures; the apartment was filled with screens, mother-of-pearl, ebony, ivory, gold and crystal, silver and bronze, ornamental deer and lions, African masks, richly bound first editions and a sprawling collection of Chinese *objets d'art*. "We sat in the rosy glow of a room glutted with all manner of furniture and ornaments," remarked Barbara in her notebooks. "Coco reclined on an endless doeskin-covered divan, sipping Scotch and water brought to her by a formally attired waiter wearing white gloves. 'I've been thinking about your pregnancy,' Coco said. 'I ask myself sometimes—how is it that a pine tree knows to be a pine tree? Or a maple a maple? Why does a maple tree never grow the leaves of an oak tree? How does a cherry know to have a cherry pit? And how does the human fetus know to come out looking like a human being and not a horse, although I must say I know several people with the most remarkable equine features. But that's the magic for me, not to know, simply to wonder...'"

Barbara's doctor in Paris, a distinguished society physician named Dr. Robert de Gennes, felt she was overexerting herself and recommended a temporary change of venue. Weighing the likely alternatives, the Reventlows decided on Rome, and once again Barbara invited Jimmy Donahue along, assuring her reluctant spouse that her cousin would be on his best behavior. They arrived in Rome at the end of September and checked into the royal suite of the Grand Hotel in the Via Vittorio Emanuele Orlando. It was the most elegant and expensive of the city's hotels, and well known for its conservative clientele.

Rome had long been a place where existence for the rich was festive, a city whose elegance of style was unmatched by any other European capital, with the possible exception of Paris. But the Rome that awaited the Reventlows was hardly the Rome of previous decades, its streets overrun by Mussolini's Black Shirts and unruly mobs bent on stopping traffic, setting cars afire, looting stores, attacking innocent pedestrians. Wealth and its accouterments were no longer a welcome part of the landscape.

At the beginning of October the Fascist mob staged a political rally in the plaza outside the Grand Hotel to celebrate the recent invasion of Ethiopia. As the hours passed, the crowd grew in size and became increasingly ugly, brandishing clubs and lead pipes, shrieking Fascist slogans, carrying huge posters plastered with pictures of Il Duce's glum face. In their suite on the third floor the Reventlows tried to block out the noise, but it rocked the very foundations of the building and rose like smoke.

Jimmy Donahue, having already downed his daily fill of Scotch, decided to quiet the mob in his own fashion. Stepping out on the balcony he lifted a potted rose bush and dropped it on the crowd below. As the rose bush crashed to the pavement, narrowly missing a group of legionnaries, he began shouting "Viva Ethiopia! Long live Haile Selassie!" Donahue then unbuttoned his pants and proceeded to urinate over the side of the balcony.

His prank might have had serious consequences had it not been for the Italian police, whose timely intervention prevented the hot-tempered demonstrators from storming the hotel. But Donahue was now seen as a potential catalyst whose continued presence in Rome could only encourage further violence. The following day a police captain returned to the hotel with an expulsion order, giving Jimmy twenty-four hours to get out of Italy. At the same time the Reventlows were informed by the hotel management that they would have to vacate their suite to make room for the former monarch of Spain. When King Alfonso arrived he insisted that Barbara stay, but the hotel had already taken steps to move her to a smaller suite. The Reventlows took the hint, and the next day, with Jimmy Donahue in tow, they returned to Paris.

In Paris, Barbara ran into an acquaintance, the Australian-born wife of Sir John Milbanke, director of an investments banking firm in London. Always helpful and brimming with advice, Sheila Lady Milbanke encouraged Barbara to have her baby in London, where she would be out of the harsh glare of the public spotlight. Sheila had a friend in London, Mrs. Wakefield-Saunders, whose handsomely appointed Regency-style house at 2 Hyde Park Gardens was available as a rental. Barbara was grateful for Sheila's recommendation and subsequently signed a one-year lease on the property.

In London the expectant mother went into seclusion, placing herself under the care of Dr. Cedric Sydney Lane-Roberts, the chief of obstetrics at the Royal Northern Hospital. After examining Barbara he prescribed liver and iron pills for a mild case of anemia. Otherwise she appeared to be in good health. By the middle of February 1936 she had gained a considerable amount of weight and approved of her doctor's suggestion that the baby be delivered at home. A bedroom was stripped and scoured and filled with the most modern equipment borrowed from the Royal Northern Hospital. Operating-room lights were hooked up to a portable generator. Four large bedrooms on the fourth floor of the house became a nursery. A nursemaid and a full-time baby nurse were hired. The baby nurse, Margaret Latimer (called "Sister" or "Sissy" by Barbara, because she had been a "sister" —or nurse—on a hospital ward), was given her own suite of rooms adjacent to the nursery. Born in Frampton, near Carlisle, in the north of England, Sister was a model of strict efficiency and devotion. She would become as indispensable and permanent a fixture in Barbara's entourage as Ticki Tocquet.

On February 23, with the onset of labor imminent, Dr. Lane-Roberts came over for a last-minute examination. Finding everything in order, he was about to leave when Barbara (according to author Dean Jennings) stopped him in his tracks.

"I want a Caesarean section," she told him.

"I don't think a Caesarean is indicated," said the doctor.

"Maybe not," said Barbara. "But I want one anyway."

The physician looked at Court Reventlow, who returned his confused, silent gaze.

"Is there any particular reason you want a section?" asked the doctor.

"No," said Barbara. "I'd just feel more comfortable doing it that way."

Dr. Lane-Roberts saw that it was useless to argue the point. Caesareans were becoming increasingly popular among those women of patrician background who felt uneasy about facing the pain usually associated with childbirth. He agreed to perform the section on Barbara and scheduled the operation for the next morning.

The delivery went smoothly. Dr. Lane-Roberts was assisted in the makeshift operating room by two attending physicians. The result was a robust, perfectly formed, full-term baby boy with blond hair and blue eyes— "a wonderfully handsome baby," according to his godmother, Silvia de Castellane. Front-page prominence of the event was given in all London evening newspapers. Under a page-wide banner headline (WORLD'S RICHEST BABY!), the normally reticent *Times* of London for February 25 reported that "A 7½ pound boy was born to the former Barbara Hutton yesterday, and began life with the assets of a European title and the prospect of inheriting a Woolworth fortune." The New York *Times* ran a front-page story announcing that the Reventlows had decided to raise their child in England. The piece went on to say:

> The Count and Countess are terrified that in the United States their baby may be kidnapped. They will make their permanent home in London. The Haugwitz-Reventlow child has not yet been named. According to the infant's father, "In Denmark it is considered bad luck to think of naming the child before the mother is fully recovered from the ordeal of giving birth. The Countess and I will select a name for the child within the next week. The christening will probably take place the week after."

With the mother are her father and stepmother, Mr. and Mrs. Franklyn Hutton of New York, who arrived in London expecially for the event. "They are very happy and almost as excited as the child's parents," exclaimed the Count. Also present are the mother's aunt and cousin, Jessie Donahue and her son, Jimmy, who is one of Barbara's closest family relations.

Barbara's joy over the success of the birth was short-lived. The next day she developed nausea, severe abdominal cramps, high fever, low blood pressure, hemorrhaging. When the fever failed to respond to medication, Dr. Lane-Roberts began to worry. He called in his former colleague, Lord Horder, physician in ordinary to the Prince of Wales. By the time Lord Horder arrived, Barbara's condition was serious. Dr. Horder examined the patient and determined that there was a ruptured blood vessel somewhere in the lower abdominal cavity. Unless immediate surgery was performed, Barbara could die.

The operation to locate and tie off the ruptured vessel took place on February 27 and involved the removal of one of Barbara's ovaries. But the bleeding did not stop. Barbara's fever rose to 106 degrees, and the doctors considered still another operation to remove the second ovary. Barbara was comatose, and while the doctors huddled to decide on a course of action her vital signs continued to slip. At one point a priest was summoned; obituaries were hurriedly scrawled and appropriate photographs were dug out of old newspaper files. Additional medical equipment was wheeled into the house by a team of hospital orderlies. Finally, on the fourth day of the crisis, her fever began to drop. She regained consciousness. The hemorrhaging was under control.

Barbara quickly regained her strength, and ten days after giving birth she was back on her feet. While recuperating she came across the name "Lance" in some trashy novel she was reading. The name, which means "straight and true" (it is a shortening of Lancelot, the valorous knight-errant at King Arthur's court), appealed to Barbara and she chose it for her son. Sister Latimer pronounced it"Lawnce," an intonation that never failed to amuse Barbara.

Lance's first press photograph appeared when he was just over a month old in connection with an article announcing Barbara's donation of $200,000 to several British hopsital funds as a token of gratitude for the health care that saved her life. It was one of the few occasions that a donation by Barbara was made public. The accompanying snapshot, taken by a photographer from outside the walls of the compound, showed Sister wheeling the infant in a shiny black perambulator through a private garden adjoining the property. Every possible precaution had been taken to protect Lance. A number of security guards and a sentry posted in a sentry box overlooking the front door to the house kept away all reporters, photographers and other unauthorized personnel. A highly sensitive burglar-alarm system was installed. There was good reason for such exacting safety measures. Two weeks after Lance's birth, on March 9, just as life at Hyde Park Gardens was returning to normal, a handwritten note arrived addressed to Barbara; the anonymous letter confirmed her worst fears:

Dear Countess:
I have read of your having a charming little son. Now don't get panicky. You should know that two men have left Manchester to kidnap this son, and you would be surprised to hear what elaborate plans have been made for his confinement, while they wait for the ransom they intend to demand of you. If you would like to learn of these plans, please send someone to meet me in Manchester at once, and I will let you know all that I know.
Don't get the police or I shan't talk. Please be sure to bring £200 in Treasury notes. Let your messenger be outside the long bar at the Gaumont Picture Theater on March 14 at 7 P.M. and let him have a red silk handkerchief in his left hand. He will be asked "Daily?" and he must reply: "No, weekly." If you intend to heed this, put an answer in the personals column of the Evening Chronicle of Manchester on March 12. I am helping you for revenge. The money is secondary.

The letter was immediately turned over to William M. Mitchell, the family's attorney in London, and Mitchell went with it to Scotland Yard. There the case was assigned to Reginald Clair, a senior inspector who had been with the Yard for thirty years. Clair drove out to Hyde Park Gardens, and after consulting with the Reventlows, advised them to place the advertisement as directed. On the appointed day Clair, Mitchell, Count Reventlow and a dozen special agents arrived in Manchester.

At exactly seven o'clock, with a red silk handkerchief dangling from his left hand, Inspector Clair appeared before the theater and walked slowly down the dark, deserted street. It was a damp, chilly evening and the cold wind stung his face. He turned up the collar of his overcoat and plunged his free hand into his pocket. He had walked less than a block when a shadowy form came up alongside him. Neither man said anything as they continued to walk. Then Clair heard a rasping voice whisper, "Looking for someone, mister?"

The inspector stopped short and with only a sideward glance said, "Yes, I'm looking for someone who writes letters to me."

"Daily?" said the stranger.

"No, weekly," the inspector replied.

They walked another block in silence, and finally the inspector said, "I guess you're the man."

"Did you bring the money?"

"It's all here." The inspector reached into his left pocket and pulled out a brown envelope. "Do you want to count it?"

"I believe you," the stranger replied, jamming the envelope into his jacket.

At that instant, before the man could utter a sound, a swarm of special agents descended from all sides, pinning his arms behind his back and placing handcuffs on his wrists before taking him away. The entire operation took no more than a minute.*

At the station house he identified himself as Alfred Molyneux, thirty-one, a textile fitter who lived in Middleton, a village outside Manchester, with his wife and two children. He glumly admitted that he had fabricated the kidnapping story only as a means of laying his hands on some ready cash. He had meant no harm and regretted any inconvenience he had caused the family. Molyneux was charged with attempted larceny, aggravated assault and extortion, and at his trial in a Manchester courthouse a month later was sentenced to four months in prison.

The foiled caper succeeded, however, in delaying the baby's christening until June 11. The baptismal rites were performed in the private chapel of Marlborough House in London. About seventy-five persons saw the three-and-a-half-month-old infant carried into the church by his nurse, accompanied by his mother and father. The service, which was conducted in Danish, was attended by the Danish minister to England and by several other members of the Danish nobility dressed in high-morning formal wear, as were all the other guests. The infant was transported to and from the chapel in a gray-and-silver family limousine surrounded by a cortege of police on motorcycle.

The kidnapping scare forced Barbara to vacate the house in Hyde Park Gardens and search out larger and easier-to-secure quarters elsewhere, even if it meant buying land and building her own house. She and Court toured the countryside of Cornwall, Surrey, and Northumberland in search of an appropriate site. Nothing they saw appealed to them. Then they heard about an elegant estate located in the center of London, off the outer circle of Regent's Park, once a royal hunting

*In the Dean Jennings version of this anecdote, it was Court Reventlow (not Reginald Clair) who carried the money and acted as bait. The present account derives from material provided by Scotland Yard in England.

ground. Situated on 12.5 acres leased from the British crown, the estate was the second largest private residence in London; the largest was Buckingham Palace.

Named St. Dunstan's Lodge, the cream-colored Regency mansion was designed by Decimus Burton in 1825 for the third Marquis of Hertford, who, it is said, used it as a harem. The American banker Otto Kahn acquired it in 1914, but with the outbreak of World War I, he donated it to the British government. It was used by a British charity for the rehabilitation of servicemen blinded in the war. The charity later moved its headquarters and the lodge was taken over by Lord Rothermere, the influential newspaper and publishing magnate. After a fire earlier in 1936 the property was put on the auction block.

One afternoon Barbara and Court drove to Regent's Park to see the house. An endless driveway, oceanic lawns and great lime, ash and chestnut trees gave it the sense of being far from the life of the city. Barbara bought the house and made the necessary arrangements to have it rebuilt. In place of a burned-out St.Dunstan's they erected a Georgian-style, three-story pink brick mansion containing thirty-five rooms, topped by a reinforced slate roof. Barbara named it Winfield House after her grandfather.

On the recommendation of Lord Louis Mountbatten, Barbara retained the architectural firm of Wimperis, Simpson and Guthrie to help with the project. Sheila Lady Milbanke earned a handsome fee by assisting with the interior decoration. Sheila and Barbara, working together, selected the wallpaper patterns, furnishings, fabrics and color schemes. "Everything was running smoothly," commented Barbara in her notebooks, "until Uncle Hans happened along."

Uncle Hans was Hans Sieben, a native German who studied furniture design in Berlin before emigrating to New York after World War I to work for the interior decoration firm of William Baumgarten. Sieben's first assignment was the redecoration of the Woolworth town houses on East Eightieth Street. He moved to London in the late 1920s to start his own firm, and when news of Barbara's building plans reached him, he got in touch. Hired as a consultant, Sieben took advantage of Barbara's generous nature and within days was orchestrating the entire project.

His first strategy was to construct a second dining room and enlarge the existing kitchen facility. He installed a new music room, library, billiards parlor, gymnasium, indoor and outdoor swimming pools, wardrobe and storage closets and ten modernized bathrooms. Barbara's bathroom featured heated towel racks, a Turkish bath, $10,000 worth of green and ivory marble, mirror-glass walls, crystal shelves, gold fixtures and fittings. Outdoors he built three greenhouses, a clay tennis court, a stable for horses. There was a wine cellar in the basement, two ten-car garages, a duck-filled pond, a boathouse, a private lake, a Gold Room (decorated throughout with 24-karat ornaments), a garden room, a breakfast room, five guest suites, lavish quarters for the servants. The third floor housed a six-room calfskin-lined pink nursery suite for Lance.

Having spent $4.5 million on the mansion and grounds and half again as much on furniture and furnishings, Sieben allocated another $250,000 for a security system consisting of a ten-foot-high spiked steel fence surrounding the entire property, electronically controlled gates, gatehouses, remote-control cameras, custom-made concealed wall safes, a walk-in cold-storage vault for furs, strong rooms for silverware and other valuables, police locks, high-intensity floodlights, an automatic fire-prevention sprinkler system, emergency generator and boiler unit, bulletproof windows, anti-kidnap alarms, direct police tie-in telephone lines, solid steel gates that slid across each window at the touch of a button, an underground tunnel system, fire doors, and numerous other devices and mechanisms guaranteed to ensure the safety of Winfield House and its residents.

The final results were most impressive in those areas of the mansion where Barbara was able to impose her own discerning taste, such as the garden room, Winfield's principal entertaining space, notable for its hand-painted yellow and blue-green eighteenth-century Chinese wallpaper. The room contained hundreds of pieces of rare porcelain from China, including a pair of invaluable six-foot temple vases. Barbara's world-famous collection of Chinese jade was on display in specially designed and illuminated wall-attached cases located both in her bedroom and throughout the downstairs hallway. Oriental embroideries were encased behind glass panels in the wide corridors on the second floor. Also on prominent display in the downstairs corridor was a group of paintings by the Italian master Canaletto, and several by a follower of Canaletto, Michiel Marieschi. In 1945 Barbara gave two of the Canalettos— "The Quay of the Piazzetta" and "The Square of St. Mark's"—and two of the Marieschis—"A Fête Day, Venice" and "The Courtyard of the Ducal Palace" —to the National Gallery of Art in Washington, D.C.

Another object of interest was a life-size statue of Barbara by a young Italian sculptor, Antonio Berti, which was kept in the mansion's Tudor garden. A photograph of this statue, a good likeness of Barbara wearing richly embroidered Oriental beach pajamas, appeared in a July 1938 issue of *Life*. The magazine ran an accompanying article, which portrayed Barbara in the worst possible light, reporting that when she went through her medical crisis following the birth of Lance, she had been saved by blood transfusions from Red Cross donors and not the blood of her society-oriented friends and relatives. Barbara's troubled life, said the periodical, proved that real happiness cannot be bought. She "should forget counts who spend her money and remember the Woolworth counter girls who earn it. It's unjust that girls in the five-and-ten stores are getting fifteen to twenty dollars a week when the heiress to the Woolworth fortune is living abroad spending her money lavishly in foreign countries and on husbands who are devoutly anti-American."

Whether or not her first two husbands were "devoutly anti-American" is open to debate. That they preferred Europe to America did not of necessity make them anti anything. The fact remains that Barbara was spending money with such reckless disregard for the times that it was bound to affect the way the media perceived her. Besides the mansion, she had recently paid $1.2 million for opera singer Ganna Walska's Leeds-McCormick emerald collection—consisting of diadem, double necklace, earrings and twin bracelets—considered by connoisseurs to be the most valuable single set of emeralds in Europe. Originally a gift from Napoleon III to Countess Verasis de Castiglione, the iridescent stones in their silver claw mountings were purchased for Mme. Walska by her husband, Harold Fowler McCormick—son of Chicago's "Reaper King," Cyrus Hall McCormick—and then sold, following their divorce, to Cartier of Paris. Jules Glaenzer, Cartier's adroit sales director, approached Barbara with the emeralds after learning of her interest in the stones. A few years earlier Glaenzer had sold her an emerald-and-diamond tiara that once belonged to Catherine the Great, and a ruby collection designed for Amalia von Solme, a seventeenth-century queen of Holland.

"Monsieur Glaenzer developed the habit of carrying the jewels around in his pocket," Barbara marvels in her notebooks. "No security guards, no fancy jewelry cases. He would come around and turn his pockets inside out on a coffee table or bed. There was none of that razzle dazzle with magic wands, kidskin gloves, and stronghold boxes that characterized some of the other stores. That's because Glaenzer had the merchandise. You either bought it or you didn't."

If living well was "the best revenge," it was also a dangerous one. Barbara's reputation as a spender hurt the commercial prospects and public relations efforts of the various Woolworth branch stores to the point where the individual managers shuddered whenever her name appeared in print. The more conservative elements in the executive offices on lower Broadway in New York also considered her a liability.

When the employees of the prosperous megacompany threatened to strike in 1938, the executive board blamed Barbara for their troubles.*

The immediate demands of the workers included a forty-hour work week, a minimum weekly wage of $20, and the right to a representative union shop. The board balked at these requests and the employees took to the streets. On March 17, St. Patrick's Day, the angry pickets in Detroit, Chicago, Milwaukee, Boston and New York broke into the Woolworth stores with blankets and cots while private security guards and local police looked on with idle indifference.

The strikers were further aggravated by daily newspaper accounts placing Barbara and Count Reventlow in Cairo, Egypt. They had just returned from a camel-back sightseeing tour into the Sahara led by Tolba Fadallah, a famous Egyptian guide, and were now staying at the Mena House Hotel, within eyeshot of the pyramids. Barbara was studying Arabic, while Court was busy posing—in white fez and red trousers—for an oil portrait by the English painter Sir Oswald Birley. The Reventlows were keeping good company, entertaining the Italian and Turkish ministers to King Farouk's court, the Begum Aga Khan (who gave Barbara a watercolor she had done of a red Egyptian sunset), and the sixth Earl of Carnarvon, whose father had funded and begun the excavation of Tutankhamen's tomb. Barbara threw a party for the young earl at the very British Chezira Sporting Club, and the earl reciprocated by giving a brunch in Barbara's honor inside Tut's burial chamber, of all places, the food served out of heavy golden vessels on top of Tut's manificent sarcophagus.

In an effort to capitalize on Barbara's notoriety, the strike committee in New York sent a telegram asking her to intervene in their behalf:

COUNTESS BARBARA HUTTON
MENA HOUSE
CAIRO, EGYPT

WOOLWORTH STRIKERS IN NEW YORK ASK YOUR INTERVENTION.

LOCAL 1250
DEPARTMENT STORE
WOOLWORTH AND CO.

---

*In 1937 the American division of the Woolworth Corporation had over 58,000 stockholders. Yet of its 9,704,000 shares outstanding, the heirs and executive board controlled sufficient stock to make the management a self-perpetuating body. Because of the sale by her attorneys and business advisers of large blocks of holdings in the United States, Barbara Hutton owned far less company stock than other members of her family, a fact that she reiterated at every opportunity. Until 1947, however, she owned substantial shares in the British division of the company, where working conditions were apparently somewhat better.

Whether or not Barbara could or would have intervened in behalf of the Woolworth employees was strictly a theoretical question. When Court Reventlow was handed the telegram meant for his wife, he slipped it into a pocket and conveniently forgot to give it to her. She had no idea of the strike or the telegram until weeks later when they were back at Winfield House, by which time the strike had ended. In any event, a new problem had arisen. During their absence the press reported that Barbara had filed a petition with the U.S. Board of Tax Appeals for relief from a deficiency tax assessment of $25,108. The appeal stipulated that the government had disallowed certain operating costs for services rendered prior to 1933 in the management of Barbara's trust fund. In view of her vast personal expenditures, the story gave the impression that she was a disgraceful Scrooge, miserly as well as unpatriotic. What the press failed to report was that Barbara had absolutely nothing to do with the appeal. It had been filed in her name, without her knowledge, by White & Case, the Wall Street law firm retained by Franklyn Hutton to look after Barbara's finances. Nor did the press bother to report the eventual settlement of the case, whereby Barbara reimbursed the government for $20,086 of her total claim.

To set the record straight on these and several other questions, Barbara agreed to an interview with Hearst newspaper columnist Adela Rogers St. John, who was in England on another assignment. The interview was arranged by a Hollywood press agent named Steve Hannagan, whose promotions of Sun Valley, Miami Beach and the Indianapolis "500" had established his reputation. Hannagan was anxious to add Barbara Hutton to his illustrious list of clients and felt that a favorable portrait of the heiress would increase his chances.

The hour-long tête-à-tête between Adela and Barbara resulted in an intriguing narrative, which, while predominantly positive, was not entirely uncritical. At its outset Adela writes: "There had always been something fantastic and a little useless and stupid about Barbara Hutton. Somehow I resented her and her millions, and the way she lived and played." As the interview progressed, Adela began to see Barbara in a more sympathetic light, less a victim of her own passions, which seemed at times scarcely to exist, than of the society around her. The common assumption was that if you had money you couldn't possibly understand the plight of the ordinary citizen. Thus the tendency among the wealthy was to feel guilty and apologetic merely for walking down the street.

"'Somebody once said the rich are different,'" Barbara told her interviewer. "'And maybe the rich are different. But for myself I'm only one generation removed from the women of my family who washed their own dishes and made their own clothes. I have a hunch that if I had to go back to the dishpan, I could do it. I'm not saying I'd like it, but I believe I could do it. I'm not under any illusions about myself. I like my friends, but I don't give a hoot for social position. We haven't any, really—how could we? If we didn't have all this money we wouldn't even be in the *Social Register*. And what is the *Social Register* anyway, if not a glorified telephone directory?'"

Coming from Marjorie Merriweather Post or Jessie Donahue, such an explanation would have elicited laughter; coming from Barbara Hutton, it sounded almost earnest. Her serious demeanor and straightforward gaze convinced Adela that she meant what she said. The journalist made a reasonable case for Barbara as the granddaughter not just of the multimillionaire Frank W. Woolworth but of the poor young man who started out as a $3-a-week clerk and conquered the financial world with hard work and perseverance. "She wasn't just the five-and-ten-cent-store heiress," wrote Adela. "She was heiress as well to the determination and dogged persistence and ability that made those millions....I found her gracious, intelligent and mellow. I knew that she'd never known some of the troubles you and I have had, about the first of the month's bills and the rent, and I knew her money had helped her...But I knew, too, that she had faced tragedy and heart-hunger and fears that you and I can know nothing about."

All in all, Barbara was pleased with Adela's efforts. She sent the journalist a letter expressing gratitude and a copy of her book of poety, *The Enchanted*. A few years later, when Adela needed money for an ailing and indigent aunt in Los Angeles, Barbara gave her a check for $5,000. It was one of those acts of generosity for which she almost never received recognition.

Nine

T HE BIG NEWS STORY out of England for much of 1936-1937 was the abdication of King Edward VIII in order to marry "the woman I love," the ubiquitous Mrs. Wallis Warfield Simpson. Randolph Churchill, the son of Winston, attended the ceremony at the Château de Candé in Monts, France, as one of only sixteen invited guests. A friend of Barbara's since her teenage years, he described the event to her as "a farce, definitely the darkest day in the history of the Empire."

Barbara, however, defended the marriage. At least publicly. She told one reporter that she had often socialized with Wallis and believed that "every woman has the inalienable right to a life of her own." It was a diplomatic statement, completely at odds with how she really felt. In her notebooks Barbara expressed a conflicting view, observing that a woman who was American-born, twice-divorced, and who had been branded "an adventuress" by the Queen Mother, could scarcely expect to attain the throne of England. Wallis was "too hard-edged to fit into English society, among whose members money is rarely mentioned and for whom social ambition, like social insecurity, is too degrading to even consider."

The Duke of Windsor was also given short shrift by Barbara: "David possesses neither the nature nor the spirit of a successful monarch. After the somber beards and mannerisms of his grandfather, Edward VII, and his father, George V, his clean-shaven, lounge-suited appearance does have the look of the new century to it. But he knows nothing of politics or humanity and is interested only in gardening and fashion. England is better off without him."

What is strange about her assessment is that she had fallen into as much disfavor with English society as the Windsors. Barbara's description of Wallis Simpson as a social misfit in England was equally applicable to her own situation and was one of the main reasons she never quite adjusted to London's high life.

Douglas Fairbanks, Jr., a friend since Barbara's New York debut, uses the term "million-dollar misunderstanding" to describe her relations with British society. "The ultraconservative upper classes of England never understood her," claims Fairbanks. "With her ceaseless globetrotting, her divorce scandals, the dubious titles of her husbands, the frequent appearance of her name in the news, she clearly upset their Edwardian sense of decorum. They understood the harmlessness of a minor fling or a one-night affair, but their flings and affairs didn't appear on the front page of the London *Times*, and Barbara's did. She was an item of curiosity, rather than 'one of them.' She was invited everywhere, attended all the right functions, but she was never on the *inside* of British society. She certainly wasn't happy in London, but she made the best of it."

The best of it in the spring of 1937 was the Coronation of King George VI and Queen Elizabeth, followed by a week of parties and balls capped by the Queen's Ball at Buckingham Palace, to which Barbara wore a flowing white gown and enormous, blindingly beautiful diamond earrings. The Queen made her first official appearance at the Chelsea Flower Show, a staggering display of blooms arranged in a series of pink tea tents on the Royal Hospital grounds. "True to her calling," Barbara observed, "Her Majesty, surrounded by sober-faced drones in morning coats and cutaways, flitted from bud to bud, sniffing and smiling, but mostly smiling as she wound her way through the stately ranks, pausing only for a dainty cup of tea. Curtsies and bows. Yellow picture hats. Satin dresses. Tradition. The English live so much in the past, the present is never real-seeming."

Next up was a Covent Garden Mozart Festival, which the Reventlows attended with Emerald Cunard (born Maud Burke in California, she ruled London society with an iron hand for more than three decades), and Garrett and Joan Moore (the Earl and Countess of Drogheda). Lord Drogheda and Barbara had met for the first time at Biarritz in the summer of 1926. "She was my dream girl," he remarks. "She was very attractive, with a beautiful head, enormous blue eyes, dark brows, not very tall. She had lovely hands and feet, which were so small she had to have shoes made to order. She was top-heavy, which gave her a complex. She thought she was hideous and ugly. That was the reason for the strenuous diet in later years. My infatuation was very innocent. We played tennis and went dancing in night clubs or at parties. She was shy and didn't care for parties. She went because it was the thing to do. Once you got her there she always enjoyed herself. There were many attractive girls in Biarritz in those days but Barbara stood out. She was not only exquisite-looking but had loads of money—an unusual combination. She remained a good friend of my wife, Joan, who was a classical pianist, and myself long after the period of adolescence."

Although Barbara never danced her way into the royal circle, she had other smart friends in English society, among them Patsy Latham, the sister of Garrett Moore, who had married Sir Paul Latham at about the same time Barbara married Alexis Mdivani: the two young couples spent part of their honeymoon together in Venice. She was also on good terms with the Honorable Whitney and Daphne Straight. He was a grandson of the late William Whitney, the nephew of the late Payne Whitney, and the son-in-law of the Countess of Winchelsea and Nottingham.

There was enough social activity in London to keep the most restless of souls occupied. The Reventlows attended Royal Ascot, horse racing's premier event, as the guests of the Aga Khan, arriving in a heavy antique carriage drawn by horses, attended by footmen and announced by a shrill coach horn. Top hats and tails were *de rigueur* for the gentlemen; ladies wore their most elegant gowns, with wide-brimmed hats and elbow-length gloves. It was customary to wear something yellow for Royal Cup Day, an event attended each year by the King and Queen. Barbara wore a yellow rose pinned to a black Mainbocher and froze in the damp chill of the day, too self-conscious to wear her fur coat.

Toward the end of June the Reventlows attended the finals at Wimbledon and were photographed courtside chatting with German tennis ace Baron Gottfried von Cramm, whom they had befriended on their last tour of Egypt. Von Cramm was scheduled to play the American, Donald Budge, for the men's championship. During the intense five-set match, in which Budge ultimately prevailed, Barbara cheered exuberantly for Von Cramm, applauding wildly whenever he won a point or made a graceful shot. Her favoritism did not go unnoticed. It began to unnerve Reventlow, who sat quietly and watched, saying nothing but taking mental stock of his wife's behavior. By the time the couple stepped into their Rolls to be driven back to Winfield House, Reventlow was livid. After engaging in a one-sided shouting match with Barbara, he took on Clinton Gardiner, her chauffeur. There was an exchange of unpleasantries, followed by the chauffeur's apology for speaking out of turn, and the incident seemed to be forgotten. But it wasn't—not by Reventlow, in any case.

The following day Barbara drove off by herself in her own car, a Lancia, to visit Daisy Fellowes, the French-born Singer Sewing Machine heiress then married to the Hon. Reginald Fellowes. Daisy, a woman of considerably clout in the word of *haute couture*, was both famous and feared for the aptness (and ruthlessness) of her social judgments, no less devastating for being habitually delivered in a small, thin, squeaky voice.

It was while Barbara was at Daisy's town house that Reventlow concluded his discussion with Clinton Gardiner. An argument broke out and Reventlow gave the chauffeur an hour to pack up and leave.

When Barbara returned later that afternoon, Court informed her of Gardiner's dismissal. Barbara was beside herself. What possible right had he to terminate *her* employee?

"He doesn't know his place," said Reventlow.

"Know his place?" Barbara laughed. "I feel sorry for you, Court. You're still living in the Dark Ages."

"Am I?" said Reventlow. "Perhaps. In any case you should learn to appreciate the status you've attained, thanks to your title."

"Status?"

"Yes. Today you're the Countess Haugwitz-Reventlow because of me."

"Who cares?" cried Barbara. "Who cares about such tripe as titles. Do you think I care a jot about your silly title?"[*]

Reventlow gave his wife a hard push. Enraged, she marched to her bedroom, threw a few belongings into a suitcase and stormed out of the house. She returned to the same West End nursing home where she had sought refuge during the waning days of her marriage to Alexis Mdivani.

Court learned of his wife's whereabouts from Ticki Tocquet, and then tried desperately to reach her at the home. The switchboard operator informed him that Barbara wasn't taking calls. Then he tried bribing Barbara with gifts that were returned unopened. Eventually he went to the nursing home to see her in person, but found two hulking security guards posted outside her door. In desperation he dispatched Ticki to the home with a written apology. Ticki was the one person

---

[*]Variations of this altercation have been reported by a number of Barbara's acquaintances, including Jean Kennerley and Frederick Brisson. Other versions appear in the Dean Jennings biography as well as the one by Philip Van Rensselaer.

who seemed able to influence Barbara, and that evening when she returned to Winfield House she brought Barbara along.

By the middle of July, Barbara and Court made their way to Venice. They took a suite at the Grand Hotel but spent their afternoons on the Lido at Barbara's cabana in front of the Excelsior. The 1937 season started earlier and lasted longer than any season Barbara could remember, the probable result of growing concern among the habitués over the increasing possibility of war. There seemed to be parties every night—in hotels, on yachts, within the great and ancient palazzos that lined the Grand Canal. The Reventlows attended a dinner party at the Palazzo Polignac given by Prince and Princess George Chavchavadze, whom Barbara had known since her marriage to Alexis Mdivani. Prince Chavchavadze, a member of an ancient Georgian Russian family, was a gifted professional pianist. The Princess, born Elizabeth Ridgeway, was an American heiress noted for her discriminating but generous abilities as a hostess. The night after the Chavchavadze affair, they went to a party at the home of Simone and Cino del Duca, a wealthy Franco-Italian couple whose cabana on the Lido was located next to theirs. On another evening it was a ball at the Excelsior hosted by Marion Davies and William Randolph Hearst. "After a while," wrote Barbara, "you feel like a locomotive chugging from station to station, everything blurring into one."

No Venetian season was complete without Elsa Maxwell's annual masquerade party, held in 1937 at the Palazzo Vendramin. The Reventlows attended in company with a few of Barbara's friends—the Volpi Sisters (Anna Maria and Marina), Countess Dorothy di Frasso, the Patiños, and Charles-Roux (French ambassador to the Vatican). To enliven the rather formal and stodgy interior of the fifteenth-century palace, Elsa decided to incorporate sound effects, and from a beekeeper she procured several beehives, which were then hidden behind the thick velvet draperies. The guests would gaze at the wood carvings of Donatello and the melodramatic and grandiose paintings of Titian while listening to the harmonious drone of bees. What at first struck everyone as a novel idea backfired when one of the hives mysteriously toppled over and the bees escaped, creating a mass exodus as a thousand guests streamed for the exits, many of them leaping into the canal to escape the enraged swarm.

Surely the social highlight of that summer was the arrival in Venice of the newly wed Duke and Duchess of Windsor. Like other honeymooners they fed the pigeons in St. Mark's and rode in a gondola as hundreds of tourists on the quay applauded and waved to them. Whatever they did, even when the Duke tossed a match over the side of the gondola after lighting his pipe, the crowds roared their approval.

The Reventlows hosted a small dinner party for the Windsors on the terrace of their hotel, inviting three other couples to join them: the Maharajah and Maharanee of Jaipur,* Gilbert and Kathryn Bache Miller (he was a Broadway producer; "Kitty" Miller, the daughter of investment banker Jules Bache, was a childhood acquaintance of Barbara's), and Count and Countess Galeazzo and Edda Ciano (Ciano, Italy's Minister of Foreign Affairs, was the son-in-law of Benito Mussolini).

The following morning Barbara took Wallis to Olga Asta, a store that specialized in handmade lace and outrageously expensive bed linens and pillowcases. An hour and $25,000 later, the two ladies moved on to Harry's Bar for lunch and then attended the Biennale art exhibit. That evening the Windsors again joined the Reventlows for dinner, and afterward they attended a screening at the Venice Film Exposition of George Cukor's *Romeo and Juliet,* starring Leslie Howard and Norma Shearer. Then they went night clubbing at Martini's and ended the long night over drinks in the Reventlow hotel suite.

After two days with the Windsors, Barbara was relieved to see them off. She was tired of having to listen to Wallis bark orders at her husband on everything from what to say to what to eat. It was equally frustrating to listen to the Duke's endless monologues on behalf of Fascism. In front of photographers the newlyweds were showered with flowers, and the Duke responded by giving the Fascist salute, a gesture that Barbara personally found offensive. "He was eager to do whatever he could to annoy and embarrass the British government," she wrote in her notebooks.

The Windsors left just as the Earl and Countess of Drogheda were arriving. The Earl of Drogheda recalls a strange series of happenings that started with a charity tennis tournament organized by Princess Jane di San Faustino. Baron Gottfried von Cramm had been invited to participate, and as if to demonstrate his indifference to the German tennis champion, Reventlow insisted on accompanying Barbara to the matches and to a post-tournament cocktail party also attended by von Cramm. Somehow Reventlow managed to maintain his composure at both events.

"The next day," recalls Lord Drogheda, "we decided to take a power launch out on the Lido. Reventlow was water-skiing while the rest of us remained on board. After he got back in the boat, a squall crept up suddenly from a clear blue sky. The skipper had tied the skis down to the top of the boat, but one of them slipped loose and was lost at sea. Reventlow discovered the loss just as we reached the pier. He ordered

*The Maharanee of Jaipur, a close friend of Barbara's, was named Ayisha. She was the daughter of the Maharajah of Cooch-Behar.

the skipper to turn the boat around and find the ski. It was teeming, and when the skipper refused, Reventlow became very abusive. Finally, Barbara intervened. She tried to calm Reventlow by promising to buy him another pair of water skis. At this point he suddenly exploded. 'How dare you contradict me!' he shouted at her. 'I want the man to find that water ski!' And with that he turned and stomped off the boat, beet-red and raging."

"With one stroke of the pen I alienated an entire nation...." This notebook entry made by Barbara in 1970 refers to a document signed in a federal courthouse in New York in 1937, an "Oath of Renunciation," by which she relinquished her American citizenship "and all rights and privileges thereunto pertaining." The entry doesn't begin to touch on the prolonged negotiations that preceded the ill-timed signing of the document. Nor does it allude to the behind-the-scenes manipulations that induced her to go through with the unfortunate act.

The plan was launched sometime in the late spring or early summer of 1937 when Barbara and Court Reventlow held a number of meetings with Clifford Turner, a London investment counselor, and Raymond Needham, a lawyer and financial adviser to the Bank of England. Turner and Needham discussed a proposition with the Reventlows that would virtually eliminate Barbara's annual tax plight—$100,000 in English residency taxes and $300,000 in American income taxes.

The facts and figures concerning Barbara's finances were undeniable. Although Barbara's annual income from investments totaled roughly $2 million, she was spending far more than she was taking in. During 1936-1937 she had spent in excess of $2 million on jewelry alone. She had put millions into Winfield House. She had purchased two new Rolls-Royces, a Packard and a bright-yellow Buick convertible. She had spent $250,000 on a yacht, the 157-foot *Troubadour* (later renamed the S.S. *Barbara*), a twin-screw, diesel-electric craft with nine baths and two elevators that she kept moored on the Lido. Her other expenses— servants (thirty-one retainers at Winfield House alone), clothing, entertainment, travel—were also staggering. At her current pace she would almost certainly succeed in depleting her fortune. There was another point to consider: under existing U.S. government inheritance-tax regulations, Barbara's estate would be reduced by as much as two-thirds in the event of her death, leaving her heir or heirs with a fraction of what she herself had inherited.

A solution to her escalating financial problems was first suggested to her by Court Reventlow and seconded by Barbara's legal advisors at

White & Case, who were able to work out a plan only because when she married Reventlow she automatically acquired Danish nationality. One of the principals instrumental in formulating the scheme was Graham D. Mattison, a thirty-two-year-old Harvard Law School graduate whose knowledge of tax regulations and estate management far exceeded his years. Mattison had joined White & Case in September of 1929 and in the mid-1930s was serving in the firm's Paris office, where he first came to Barbara's attention. Mattison had been present at the preliminary meetings in London with Turner and Needham, and then proposed a follow-up session in New York to work out the final details. What the plan amounted to was for Barbara to renounce her American citizenship and then gradually transfer her funds from the United States to England. The British Treasury (this was where Clifford Turner and Raymond Needham came in) had agreed to waive not only her residency taxes but her income taxes as well. In order to accomplish this financial hocus-pocus, Barbara's monies would be placed in a special fund, a kind of private, long-term loan to the British government, which would enable her to draw an annual income and save roughly $400,000 a year in taxes. And in the event of her death, her estate would be governed by the more reasonable inheritance-tax laws of Denmark.

Barbara remained apprehensive about the prospect of signing away her American citizenship but was ultimately convinced that it was the only way Lance would ever see a fair share of his inheritance. At a later date Barbara would tell a judge that her husband's desire for money was paramount with him to the exclusion of all other ideas and sentiments. Shattering as this discovery must have been for Barbara, it was one she ought probably to have made sooner. Reventlow—shrewd, cold-blooded, disciplined—wanted a nest egg not only for his son but for himself, and he had planned ahead carefully to get it. He had a nasty, imperious temperament and with it—coupled with Barbara's lack of knowledge of money affairs—he bludgeoned her into making a decision she would come to regret. Her willingness to go along with the idea was primarily an act of appeasement, reinforced by a battery of lawyers who seemed very much in favor of the plan. And so on September 3 the Reventlows boarded the *Queen Mary* and sailed for New York.

There they met with Henry Mannix and Joseph M. Hartfield of White & Case; Raymond Needham and Graham Mattison likewise attended the meeting. Mattison expressed the firm belief that the operation could be pulled off smoothly and efficiently with a minimum of publicity if Barbara returned to New York by herself sometime in mid-December, announced her intention to spend the holidays with her family, then signed the appropriate legal documents in court, and returned to England on the same boat the next day.

There was one catch to the plan. Before Barbara could execute her Oath of Renunciation, Court Reventlow would have to take an oath of his own. He would have to sign a document waiving any and all rights to Barbara's inheritance. Graham Mattison, well aware of the difficulties that had arisen in the marriage, had also concocted this aspect of the scheme. Mattison's proposition caught Reventlow off guard and placed him in an impossible situation. If he refused to sign the document, he would be accused of having designs on Barbara's fortune; if he signed, he forfeited his rights. Mattison was about to outmaneuver not just the U.S. Treasury Department but the wily Court Reventlow. To make it difficult for Reventlow to refuse the offer, the attorney advised him that the agreement called for him to receive $1 million in the event of a divorce and twice that sum should Barbara predecease him—a miniscule amount considering the extent of Barbara's wealth. Court sheepishly signed the document, and the Reventlows returned to England.

On December 8 Barbara boarded the *Europa* in Southampton and returned to the United States as planned. Arriving at Pier 58 on Manhattan's West Side a week later, she was spotted by news photographers as she leaned against a rail waiting to disembark. "I'm here to spend Christmas with my father," she told reporters. "I have no intention of spending the rest of my life in Europe. We'll buy a place here someday, maybe on Long Island." It was sheer fabrication, but it sufficed to throw the bloodhounds temporarily off her trail.

The next day, December 16, accompanied by Graham Mattison and Henry Mannix, Barbara arrived at the Federal Courthouse on Foley Square. It was the lunch hour and the fifth-floor courtroom of Justice William Mondy was deserted, except for the judge, a deputy clerk and a clerk of the court. The deputy clerk handed Barbara several papers with instructions on how to fill them out. In her nervousness she erroneously identified her husband's birthplace as Berlin and gave her own birth date as November 12, instead of November 14. Nobody seemed to notice. Barbara was then asked to read aloud the Oath of Renunciation: "I hereby absolutely and entirely renounce my United States citizenship and all rights and privileges thereunto pertaining, and abjure all allegiance and fidelity to the United States of America." Her voice never rose above a whisper, and her hand shook as she affixed her signature to the document.

Thirty-six hours after her arrival she was back at the pier. She boarded the *Europa* by one of the lower gangplanks at a few minutes of midnight and remained out of sight until the liner sailed an hour later. The following day, with the *Europa* safely out at sea, her attorneys at White & Case summoned the press, handed out a formal announcement and followed it up with a great salvo of silence. The countess, the release declared, had automatically become a Danish subject when she married Count Court Haugwitz-Reventlow in May of 1935. Her consequent American-Danish nationality presented "various legal complications." As a result, Barbara had been forced, by circumstances beyond her control, to renounce her American citizenship. She had done so, and was at present en route to Europe.

Graham Mattison, it would turn out, had made only one miscalculation: he had failed to anticipate the incredible reaction that followed in the wake of the announcement. There was nothing to compare it to, except maybe the outcry that followed William Waldorf Astor's abandonment of his American citizenship in 1899 to become a British subject. The basic objection to Barbara's *bon voyage* to America was that the United States had given the heiress her fabulous fortune; America received scant advantage from her wealth; now she had "robbed" the country of $45 million and absconded with it to distant shores. Her escape was termed a betrayal and it provided the country, said one commentator, with "a modern moral lesson." The lesson varied from sector to sector. It proved useful to the adherents of President Roosevelt's New Deal policies for whom Barbara became a quick symbol of American economic injustice. Reporters and clergymen and statesmen portrayed her as the devil reincarnate, an object lesson in avarice and greed. Walter Winchell took to the airwaves to tell his devoted radio flock of the improprieties inflicted upon the nation by "Society's most outrageous child."* "The absentee landlord has never been a beloved figure," crowed the New York *Daily News.* "Good riddance!" clamored the *Journal-American.* "Despicable!" proclaimed the New York *Times.*

Scripps-Howard columnist Westbrook Pegler provided the most zealous and prolonged attack, devoting no less than a week's worth of columns to the controversy. As he wrote: "In a way it was none of the shopgirls' business whom Miss Babbie married, but in a sort of way it may be at that. Because even shopgirls have dreams of love on $10 a week....And furthermore, these shopgirls...had been contributing their mites toward the income of $2,000,000 a year without which their own 'princes's' might never have aroused the love of her ideal. Now she has betrayed them for all time."

---

*Several months later when Winchell learned that Barbara had been coerced into the act, he went on the radio and placed the blame where it belonged—on Court Reventlow. He was the only commentator to revise his original stance.

Such talk helped incite a new rash of Woolworth employee strikes. Within two days of Barbara's departure, three New York stores were closed completely and thirty-six others were on the verge of shutting their doors. the placards and sandwich boards shot up all over town. BABS RENOUNCES CITIZENSHIP BUT NOT PROFITS was one *cri du coeur;* WHILE WE STRIKE FOR HIGHER PAY, BABS TAKES HER MONEY AND RUNS AWAY was another. The demonstrators again resorted to Western Union as a mode of communication; a wireless reached Barbara while she was still at sea: URGE THAT YOU ORDER MANAGEMENT TO CONCEDE A LIVING WAGE TO THOUSANDS NOW EXISTING ON STARVATION WAGES. Barbara offered nothing in the way of a response. And when confronted by reporters in Southampton, she maintained her silence.

Having renounced her American citizenship, Barbara was now thinking of renouncing Court. It was January of 1938 and the Reventlows were vacationing at the Palace Hotel in St. Moritz. The realization that the marriage was over was accompanied by all the now familiar trappings. For eighteen months or so, it appeared that she had made a mature adjustment to married life. She was devoted to her child and gave frequent expression of desire for a domestic lifestyle. But she had married Reventlow on the rebound, and now she was bored with him and fed up with his unaccountable bursts of anger, his jealousy, his lack of levity and tenderness. Court was as staid and stiff as an old English clubman, happiest maintaining a strictly enforced schedule, reading the same newspapers, sitting in the same chair, following the same routine day in and day out. Barbara was the direct opposite. She abjured the clock, turned night into day, was motivated by the currents of her swiftly changing moods, and enjoyed living for the moment. Under normal circumstances such differences might have been surmountable; in the case of Barbara Hutton they became the focus of her entire being, an obstacle impossible to overcome.

Theater producer Frederick Brisson knew Barbara during her years with Reventlow. "She was unable to communicate with him on anything but the most superficial level," says Brisson. "He lacked sensitivity, and she lived on a knife edge. I saw them together both in London and Paris. He was giving her the business. He was pushy, always telling her what to do with her money. He struck me as a typical German landowner of the sort that disappeared with Otto von Bismarck. But the supreme irony is that the land his family owned in Denmark wasn't worth hay. He was one of the coldest fish I've ever met."

The general feeling was that Reventlow was extremely manipulative. One by one he managed to alienate and ostracize each of Barbara's confederates, especially those he suspected of trying to undermine his influence over Barbara, the Jimmy Donahues and Graham Mattisons whose advice to Barbara on a variety of issues conflicted with his own. For many months it was the Milbankes—Sir John and Lady Sheila— who bore the brunt of his rage. He had used them at first to gain a foothold into the ranks of Mayfair society, but when Sir John began counseling Barbara on financial affairs, Reventlow accused him of overstepping his bounds. Barbara was in the middle, and when she took Milbanke's counsel over that offered by her husband, the row that had been smoldering for months came to a head—and offered Barbara, at long last, an opportunity to "tell off" her husband and set in motion the machinery that would lead to the termination of their marriage.

The end was precipitated by a series of raucous exchanges. In February the Reventlows were back at Winfield House when Roussie Sert, while visiting London, paid an unannounced call on Barbara. Staggeringly drunk and filled with drugs, she looked wraithlike and bedraggled and could talk about nothing but the death of her brother Alexis. Nothing Barbara said or did lessened her despair. Barbara finally tried to induce Roussie to eat, but the distraught visitor pushed aside the food in favor of a half-dozen Seconals and a quart of vodka.

That evening, back from an afternoon tennis lesson, Reventlow became enraged when he learned of Roussie's visit. He began yelling at Barbara as he always did when the name Mdivani came up. He told his wife that he didn't want Roussie in *his* house. Barbara reminded him that it was her house, not his.

"Don't you know that Roussie Sert is a morphine addict?" said Reventlow.

"I don't care if she's a murderess," said Barbara. "She's a friend and she's welcome here whenever she wants to visit."*

By the first week in March their latest altercation had been temporarily forgotten as the Reventlows departed on a prearranged boat trip to India, arriving in Bombay two weeks later. There they attended a round of parties given in their honor by local dignitaries. At one of these Barbara met somebody who was to play a key role in the eventual breakup of her marriage. Prince Muassam Jah was the twenty-one-year-old grand-

---

*Barbara apparently repeated the details of Roussie's visit and the ensuing argument with Court Reventlow to a number of acquaintances. Philip Van Rensselaer records his version in *Million Dollar Baby*, pps. 136-41.

son of Nir Usman Ali, the tenth Nizam of Hyderabad, one of the world's wealthiest men. The Nizam's estimated fortune of $2 billion was highly visible, piled up in his palace in the form of gold bricks, chests of diamonds and pearls, mountains of silver rupees. People talked about his three hundred Rolls-Royces, Daimlers and Cadillacs, to say nothing of a thousand personal servants and five hundred dancing girls. He had three wives, forty-two concubines, and so many children that he had lost count.

Just as extraordinary as his wealth was the Nizam's parsimony. Visitors to tea were reputedly rationed one biscuit each, while the Nizam smoked only the cheapest of cigarettes, eschewed his three hundred luxury roadsters for a battered Ford, and wore the same shabby clothes for weeks on end. His attire was such that the uninitiated frequently mistook him for one of the servants. He slept not in his palace, which was one of the largest in India, but in a small white-washed room in a nearby cottage. A pet white goat was his closest companion for many years, and the animal always stood near him munching turnips while the Nizam sat on his cottage veranda chewing betel nuts, smoking opium and writing exquisite poetry in Persian.

Prince Muassam shared his grandfather's interest in poetry. It was, in fact, Muassam's literary sensibility that first turned Barbara's head. Over the following weeks she saw a good deal of him, first in Bombay and later at Falaknuma, the royal palace in Hyderabad with its famous library of twenty thousand volumes, including one of the earliest editions of the Koran. Muassam read Barbara his poems on India; she read him hers on China. While the poetry readings went on, Reventlow took up the sport of pigsticking, a gory spectacle in which a single man on horseback with a long spear was pitted against a wild boar or buffalo. The carnage often entailed numerous passes as the rider gouged countless holes in the hide of the defenseless prey. Pigsticking must have afforded the count an ideal outlet for his pent-up hostility.

Many years later Reventlow recalled his visit to India for journalist Dean Jennings, remarking that his wife had shown "an unusual interest in the prince, though I thought it was one of those innocuous crushes that would be forgotten by the time we returned to England. What I didn't count on was Barbara being again seized with the poetical urge and then thinking of no better pen pal than Prince Muassam."

The inevitable confrontation between Barbara and Court over the Indian prince took place a month after their return to London when Reventlow appeared suddenly in his wife's bedroom and noticed a wallet-sized photograph of Muassam on Barbara's night table. Next to it was a thick parchment envelope embossed with Muassam's regal seal.

"Where did you get that?" Reventlow asked.

"It's from a friend," said Barbara.

"May I see it?" Reventlow asked.

Without waiting for a response the count grabbed the envelope and pulled out a sheet of paper. As he read it his face became rigid. In the letter Prince Muassam declared his love for Barbara, and insisted that his life was meaningless without her. He said that their correspondence meant everything to him. At the end, he asked her to return to India as his personal houseguest.

"How long has this been going on?" Reventlow demanded.

"Not long...a few weeks," said Barbara.

"We've only been back a few weeks," Reventlow reminded her.

"Well, what of it? What's wrong with having a pen pal? I don't even understand what Muassam is trying to say."

"You don't? Well, I happen to understand him very well. And I'm telling you to write him at once and ask him to stop sending his letters here and also to return those you've sent him."

"And if I refuse?"

"If you refuse, I may have to write to him myself. And what I have to say isn't going to make for very pleasant reading."

When he saw that Barbara had no intention of complying, he took the prince's letter and rushed out of the room. Although it occurred to Barbara that Court could use the letter for blackmail purposes, there was nothing she could do about it.*

"The final humiliation," as Barbara termed it, took place in Paris on the next-to-last night of a four-day visit in late May, when Reventlow made her accompany him to a sex exhibition in a run-down fire trap that housed a bar on the first floor. Reventlow pushed her through the bar to a steel door at the rear, then up a staircase to the next landing which opened into a large room bathed in red and blue light, walls and ceiling lined with mirrors, a small stage at one end of the room surrounded on three sides by tiered benches and on the fourth by a red velvet drop curtain. An overstuffed divan partially covered by an old sheet was the only prop on stage.†

Barbara recounts the rest: "An obese woman with a wide, salacious grin and sunken cheeks took Court's money and pushed us toward the grandstand, which was filled mostly with old and decrepit men. The sorrowful audience had ten to fifteen minutes to ponder what sordid act would take place on that tiny stage. Finally a scratchy phonograph record came on and from behind the curtain emerged a buxom woman

*See Dean Jennings, *Barbara Hutton*, pps. 119-20.

†A similar, though less detailed description of this scene is offered in Philip Van Rensselaer's *Million Dollar Baby*, pps. 147-48.

in her twenties dressed in a transparent tunic and high heels. She threw herself into her performance, removing the tunic, flaunting her nakedness, leaning forward and holding her breasts out to the audience—a sacrificial offering. She was presently joined by a young child of twelve at most, whose large flirtatious eyes glittered below spit-curls coquettishly stuck to her forehead. Her glistening lips smiled as she threw her head back, closing her eyelids and imitating the gyrations of big sister, the tip of her tongue snaking out of her half-open mouth and licking her lips...

"Shortly a gargantuan Negro appeared and took his place on the couch. Lying on his back, naked as a jaybird, his immense paunch flopping over on either side, he commenced to twitch and kick, his legs in the air, family jewels in the middle, like an oversized baby being powdered after his bath.

"What was 'naughty' and maybe just a bit silly had turned sleazy as the threesome proceeded to cannibalize each other—a breast here, a limb there, glands and orifices everywhere. The walls and ceiling were covered with mirrors set slightly askew, making the twisted bodies visible from every angle. Multiplying the image of an embrace, the mirrors gave the impression of a multitude of bodies imprisoned in rock crystal, struggling and locked together in positions that left nothing to the imagination. Once the prurient interest of this sickening exhibition had worn off there was nothing left—just the depressing actions of three individuals being paid to humiliate themselves in front of a sad gathering of cripples."

Reventlow was evidently stimulated by the spectacle. When they returned to their suite at the Ritz later that night he tried wrestling Barbara into bed. She resisted; they toppled to the floor, Reventlow on top, pressing his full weight down on his struggling wife. With a free hand she tried to scratch at his face. Reventlow pinned her flailing arms to her side and began to take her by force.

"The fact that he had physical control over me, simply because of his unearned muscular strength, seemed deeply unfair," she later wrote. "I submitted but refused to give of myself. Court no longer entered my fantasy: I was indifferent to him. When he finished with me he dragged me by the hair into the bathroom. 'You've always had an interest in scatology, Barbara. Now's your big chance to experience it.' He forced me to sit in his lap while he excreted into the toilet. Then he locked me in the bathroom overnight."

The Reventlow-Hutton psychodrama was about to reach its zenith. Several days after their return to London, on May 27, Barbara and Court attended a supper dance at the Chesterfield Street home of Sir Adrian and Lady Baillie. It was there that Barbara met a very blond young German with whom she repeatedly danced, while Court regarded them restlessly from his table, perhaps recalling a night several years earlier when he had been the intruding stranger and another husband, Alexis Mdivani, had watched hopelessly from the side.

If titles meant anything to Barbara, she had finally hit the jackpot. Her dance partner was Prince Friedrich of Prussia, the fourth son of former Crown Prince Wilhelm and Princess Cecile of Germany, grandson of Kaiser Wilhelm II, great-great-grandson of Queen Victoria, godson of King George V, whose funeral he had attended as official German emissary early in 1936. Friedrich was twenty-six years old and was in London to learn English by working at Schroeder's Bank. Barbara found him attractive, intelligent, personable—and most convenient. He was the perfect foil to help her rid herself of Court. The fact that he was from the most aristocratic German family of all would have the effect of annoying Reventlow even more. She invited the prince to her home the next day for lunch and a game of tennis.

Reventlow left the house in a huff before the prince arrived. Barbara and her guest lunched on the terrace and played three sets of tennis, followed by a dip in the swimming pool. As he climbed out of the pool Friedrich stumbled and twisted his ankle. Barbara helped him into the house and up the stairs into her husband's darkened bedroom. She asked a servant to bring a bucket of ice and an Ace bandage. When Court returned he found the prince on top of his bed and Barbara next to him, still ministering to the injured ankle.

During the next four weeks Prince Friedrich's black Mercedes was parked so frequently at Winfield House that some of the servants suspected that its owner had moved in with the Reventlows. And in a way he had. Wherever Court looked there were annoying traces of the prince's presence. Barbara made no attempt to hide her intentions. One morning over breakfast she said, "Imagine, Court. I could marry the man who might one day rule Germany."*

Reventlow finally took the hint and moved into the nearby Bath Club. He soon received a visit there from William Mitchell, who had been the family solicitor, but was now apparently representing Barbara. He had brought a message. The message was that Barbara wanted a divorce. She would retain custody of Lance until a more permanent arrangement could be made. She had also authorized Mitchell to inform Court that she was prepared to offer him a check for two million

*Both this and other snippets of conversation in this section are taken from depositions provided by Barbara and Court during their Bow Street trial in London. See also Dean Jennings, pps. 122-26.

dollars, a million more than he had bargained for. And all he had to do in return was sign a few legal papers.

Reventlow wouldn't be bought off. He still cared for his wife very much, despite everything. He informed Mitchell that he had made plans to vacation in France. While he was away he hoped Barbara would come to her senses and see her "ridiculous German prince" for what he really was—"a big Nazi nothing."

Before his departure, Reventlow went to Winfield House to pick up some more belongings. While there, he had a chat with Barbara's new houseboy, Robert Hawkes. He asked Hawkes to keep an eye on his wife over the next two weeks and to send occasional reports to him in Divonne, France. He assured Hawkes that he would be well remunerated. Reventlow had barely checked into his hotel when the first report arrived:

> I commenced at 7:50 P.M., and I noticed that the motor car owned by Prince Frederick was standing in the drive opposite the main entrance. The cook then entered the Servants' Hall and I asked her if she had a busy day. She replied: "Prince Frederick has been here all day with the Countess. I served them lunch, tea, and dinner." At 9 P.M. I was told they had gone for a short drive. They were back by 10:30 P.M. Shortly after 11 P.M. I noticed that the drawing room half door was open, but the room was in semi-darkness. I could discern two people with lighted cigarettes on the settee near the fireplace. At midnight, they came out. Prince Frederick got in his car and drove away. On returning to the Servants' Hall, the first footman said to me: "They seem to be getting very chummy. I think it's serious."

Five days later Reventlow received his second dispatch:

> Late last night when I went out to lock up the garage I noticed Prince Frederick's car still parked in its usual place. It was after midnight. It was still there at 2:30 A.M. This morning one of the maids said the Prince had stayed the night in one of the guest rooms. A second maid verified the story.

The final communiqué from Hawkes came as a shock to Court. The houseboy reported that he was in the house when Ticki Tocquet handed him an envelope. The envelope contained a week's advance in cash. William Mitchell then arrived and told him they were aware he was spying on Barbara. He was asked to leave at once.

Reventlow was furious but his fury was tempered by a sense of loss, the feeling that without Barbara his life lacked meaning. From Divonne he wrote his wife asking her to consider the possibility of a reconciliation, assuring her that he was still in love and had every intention of making the marriage work.

When she failed to respond he telephoned her and in a fit of jealousy repeated everything he had heard from Hawkes. Barbara freely admitted she had spent time with Friedrich and then angrily accused Court of spying on her.

"It isn't necessary to spy on you," he retorted. "People can see and people are talking all over London."

"And what do you propose to do?"

"I am returning to London in a few days," he said, "and if I see Prince Friedrich anywhere near the house I'll shoot him like a dog."

The threat, theatrical as it sounded, was not to be taken lightly. For one thing, Reventlow had taken to carrying around a loaded pistol— "for self-protection," he claimed. For another, he had a notoriously bad temper and was capable of almost anything if provoked. Or so Barbara believed. She informed William Mitchell of their conversation, and the next day the attorney arrived in Divonne bearing the following letter from Barbara:

Dear Court:

I have received your letter, which makes it even more difficult to say what I have to say. Now that I have had time to think things over I feel more strongly than before that your attitude last year and especially during the last few weeks has made it impossible for me to go on living with you.

I don't wish in this letter to go into details and recriminations which must be hurtful to you. We have had all that out already. Rather I want to say that I hope you are well and that I want you to have a happy life, just as I want it for myself. Together that is impossible...I shall have no hard feelings about you, and I don't want you to have any about me, and I send you all my good wishes.

There is just one thing I am going to ask you, and I know you will honor my wish: Please do not ask to try to see me again. At first sight you will think this unkind of me but on reflection you will realize that I am right, as any further meeting would only make things more difficult.

There is also this I want to say. My decision is my own, and I have not been influenced by anyone in coming to it. As regards the details, I am leaving all those to Mr. Mitchell whom I have asked to give you this letter. I wish to be reasonable, and I know that you will be too.

With all my best wishes, always affectionately,

Barbara*

Reventlow's first reaction on reading the letter was to break down and cry. He then proceeded verbally to abuse both his wife and Prince Friedrich, remarking that someone in English society had written him stating that unless he challenged the prince to a duel he would never again be allowed to show his face in public. "But dueling," he said to Mitchell, "is too good for that bastard. If I lose this battle, I might as well take my own life. If I blow my brains out, everyone will know that Barbara drove me to it. The tragedy will haunt her all her life and no one will ever speak to her again."

Before the end of the day Mitchell managed to calm Reventlow by promising to do everything in his power to bring about a reconciliation, but by the next morning when the two men met for breakfast Court's mood had changed. He said he no longer wanted a reconciliation, but that he wanted a large sum of money and custody of the child. His decision was to return to London and take Lance, which was his absolute right. "Tell Barbara," he said, "I shall behave like a gentleman, and I expect her to behave like a lady. If there is any monkey business or attempt to interfere with me in any way, I will not be responsible for my actions. All I can say is, 'God help her and God help me.'"

"Is that a threat?" inquired Mitchell.

"You may take it any way you wish," replied the count.

Mitchell took it as a threat. When he returned to London, he and Barbara went before Magistrate T. W. Fry of the Bow Street Police Court and on June 20 swore out a warrant for Reventlow's arrest. The charge against him stipulated that "having used certain threats against his wife, she apprehends she goes in danger of her life or of some bodily harm that he will do or cause to be done unto her." The charge was not one which fell under the rubric of "extraditable offenses," and if Reventlow had elected to remain in France, there would have been no legal process to compel his appearance in an English court of law. Reventlow reasoned that his wife's strategy was designed to keep him out of England, thereby jeopardizing his rights to any future negotia-

---

*Both this letter and the communiqués from Barbara's housekeeper, Robert Hawkes, to Court Reventlow, were admitted as evidence at the subsequent Bow Street trial of Reventlow, which is described in forthcoming pages.

tions involving custody of their child. On the advice of his Paris attorneys he agreed to return to England and turn himself in.

On July 2 Reventlow and his valet Paul Wiser arrived at Dover, where they were met by Court's British attorneys, Norman Birkett and Vernon Cattie (who were the lawyers for Wallis Simpson in her divorce action against Ernest Simpson). Also present were several gentlemen from Scotland Yard. Reventlow was placed under arrest and taken directly to the Bow Street Police Court in London to be arraigned. Chief Magistrate Sir Rollo Graham-Campbell set July 5 for the trial and released Reventlow on £2,000 bail.

On the day of the trial more than two hundred reporters squeezed into the courtroom. Barbara, dressed in black, sat between Sir Patrick Hastings and Arthur Winn, attorneys with the same firm (Clifford Turner & Co.) as William Mitchell. Reventlow sat in the dock a few yards away.

William Mitchell was the first to take the stand as a material witness and he dutifully outlined the case against the count. He presented the details of his visit to Divonne, recounting Reventlow's belligerent plans for his German rival—identified by stipulation only as "a certain gentleman in London"—and implied that the count threatened similar punishment for Barbara, "forcing her to barricade herself in Winfield House and hire extra security guards to patrol the grounds."

"Do you recall the terms used by Count Reventlow to describe his wife?" asked Sir Patrick Hastings.

"It was strange," said Mitchell. "At one moment he would abuse her in obscene language and at the next he would indicate that nothing was too good for her."

"Would you say that Count Reventlow was very emotional that day?"

"As I say, his demeanor varied from temper to emotion to self-commiseration, and there were moods in which he was cold and what I should describe as calculating. One second he wanted me to effect a reconciliation and in the next breath he was ready to consign his wife to three years of hell with headlines."

"During the years you have known him as family counsel, did you ever see him in that state before?"

"I don't think I would describe myself as the family counsel. My connection was essentially with the Countess. But yes, I had known him to have tempers and emotional storms. On the other hand, I had never been with him that length of time before."

"But you took the threat seriously?" asked Hastings.

"Certainly, I did," said Mitchell. "He seemed very distraught. He showed me a pistol he carried around and threatened to start shooting people's heads off. At another point he announced his intention of taking Lance away from his mother forever. Why shouldn't I believe him? He was in deadly earnest."

Now that the dirty linen had been exposed, there was nothing to prevent Norman Birkett, Reventlow's attorney, from getting to the bottom of the grimy bundle. Birkett's first point during his cross-examination of the witness was that Mitchell had indeed acted the role of family attorney in the past and had therefore misrepresented himself by betraying a client's confidence.

"Isn't it a fact, Mr. Mitchell, that you were secretly working against the Count in your Divonne conversation and deliberately obtained information which caused the Countess to sign the arrest warrant?" said Birkett.

"I think it was perfectly clear that I no longer represented Count Reventlow," responded Mitchell.

"Isn't it true, Mr. Mitchell, that you had a hand in composing the letter from the Countess which you then hand-delivered to the Count in France?"

"I did not compose the letter, but helped with the drafting of it. The Countess altered it and I knew only the substance of the final draft."

"Did you inform the Count that you had a role in drafting the letter?"

"No, that point never arose. Nor do I think it mattered."

Birkett now turned his attention to Mitchell's meeting with Reventlow at the Bath Club in London, prior to his departure for France.

"When you saw him at that time did he not show you a letter addressed to the Countess from a Prince Muassam Jah of India, which was one of the matters that grieved him very much?" asked Birkett.

"Yes, he showed me the letter."

"Did you express sympathy with him?"

"I don't think so," said Mitchell. "My feeling when he showed me that letter was that it was an infamous thing to have taken his wife's letter."

"Did the Count not say, 'I love my wife very much indeed, and despite everything I still love her and always will?"

"Yes. He said words to that effect."

"Did he say, 'I would rather do anything in the world than lose her'"?

"I don't recollect exactly. But that was probably the substance of it."

"Was there any talk of money between you at that time?"

"Yes, there was. I told the Count that his wife was willing to pay a sizable settlement provided the entire mess could be worked out in a peaceful manner. I told him he would receive $2 million, a million above and beyond what he was supposed to get. He said he had no intention of being bought off and that the figure was laughable. His wife could give him $5 million without making the slightest dent in her bank account. And since she had put him through the wringer, he felt he was entitled to at least that much."

"But isn't it a fact that when you met him in France you offered the Count only £50,000?"

"Yes, as a gesture of good will. He had already threatened his wife, invalidating the previous offer. Just before I left I told him to reconsider. I told him he had blown the $2 million, but that he would get £50,000 if he signed the divorce agreement. Under the circumstances, the offer was generous. The Count called it 'an insult.'"

"Was the offer made with your client's consent, Mr. Mitchell?"

"To the extent that I was empowered to represent her to the best of my ability—yes, it was made with her consent. I did not phone her at that instant and ask for her consent. We had a prior agreement that I would simply attempt to resolve the situation as quickly as possible."

"But isn't it true, Mr. Mitchell, that you also threatened the Count by saying that if he didn't go along with the divorce, his name would be smeared all over Europe?"

"Those were not my words. When I saw him while he was still in London I told him it would be best if he would agree to a divorce. I said I understood there had been some ugly incidents with his wife. 'Like what?' he said. 'Like forcing her to attend a lewd sexual exhibition,' I said. 'Like rape. Like locking her in a powder room overnight.' 'I did not rape my wife,' he said. 'I made love to her.' I had no desire to belabor the point, so I let the matter drop."

"And you don't consider then, Mr. Mitchell, that you threatened the Count?"

"Absolutely not. My intention was to work out an amicable settlement."

Birkett then raised the specter of Prince Friedrich of Prussia.

"It is plain, is it not, Mr. Mitchell, that one of the chief features of the case is that this matter of 'the gentleman in London' upset the Count profoundly?"

"Yes, Mr. Birkett, and in my view, childishly."

"Never mind your view," said Birkett. "Husbands are not like solicitors. I've known husbands who've killed their wives for far less than sleeping around."

"Sleeping around, Mr. Birkett, is not the appropriate term in this instance. According to the Countess, her husband is a wife-beater, a sexual deviate, and a sado-masochist. Under such conditions adultery is hardly a luxury; it is a necessity."

"Your characterization of the Count is not only biased, it is libelous. I can assure you that whatever was said by the Count in the heat of the moment, it was never his intention to threaten the safety of his wife. My client's only object in these proceedings is to refute the allegations. He is naturally also concerned for the welfare of his son. Under the present circumstances he feels that Winfield House is not the proper environment for the child. But that is a matter for another day."

Sir Rollo Graham-Campbell concurred. He brought down his gavel and adjourned the case until July 13. "The developments of the past twenty-four hours," stated the next day's *Times* of London, "have given England its greatest sensation since King Edward VIII renounced the throne eighteen months ago for love of Mrs. Wallis Warfield Simpson."

Sensation was the last thing Barbara wanted. Back in her barred and gilded cage, she had time to consider the matter. By her actions she had already done enough harm to her reputation; whatever hope she might have had of ever redeeming a place for herself at the helm of English society was now totally shattered. She dreaded having to take the witness stand to be grilled before an open court about her deepest, most private feelings. "I just want to live happily," she told her attorney, Sir Patrick Hastings. On July 13 Hastings stood before the magistrate and asked that his client's complaint be withdrawn; she no longer felt Court Reventlow was out to do her harm. The charges were officially dropped. Reventlow was free to go.

It was a limited victory for the count, because it marked the end of his union with Barbara and the beginning of a lifelong feud. Their stormy future dealings were prefigured by a visit Reventlow paid to Winfield House to clear out his few remaining possessions. In his absence, as he soon learned, a private safe in his bedroom had been cracked and its contents removed. Included in the take were several joint bank accounts he held with his wife and the treasured letter from Prince Muassam that he had placed in the safe before leaving for France.

At Reventlow's instigation, Norman Birkett went to the British Law Society and demanded that William Mitchell be censured for his duplicitous role in the Hutton-Reventlow case. Following an investigation of the proceedings, the society found Mitchell "deserving of grave censure" for "using confidential information secured from Count Reventlow for the benefit of his client, failing to advise Count Reventlow that the information could be used against him and failing to properly advise the Count that he [Mitchell] no longer represented him as family attorney." The society ordered Mitchell to pay all of Reventlow's legal fees. Worst of all for Mitchell, Barbara belatedly saw the justice of her husband's claim and dismissed him as her personal counsel.

On July 28 Barbara and Court and their legal representatives went to the Royal Danish Legation in London and signed a deed of separation valid in accordance with Danish as well as English law. The agreement stipulated that while their child was still "of tender age" he would spend the greater part of each year with his mother, and that when he reached "school age" he would divide his school holidays evenly between both parents. Reventlow was to retain jurisdiction over the boy's education and have the right to approve governesses, doctors, religious training and extensive travel. To help enforce these points Lance had been made a ward in chancery—a ward of the English court—which meant that until he reached the age of majority, neither parent could make a ruling affecting his future without the consent of the Surrogate Court.*

The separation agreement gave Count Reventlow no alimony or financial settlement of any kind beyond the $1 million previously agreed upon by Court with White & Case, but did make him trustee of a $1.5 million fund established by Barbara in her son's name. As trustee of the fund Court derived benefit of its income, a portion of which he used to finance Lance's upbringing and education. Barbara's father, convinced that Reventlow had possessed the right combination of qualities to deal with Barbara, still felt kindly toward him. As a final gesture of good will he gave the count a gift—the keys to a custom-built Hispano-Suiza sedan. It served handily as a second car. Barbara's birthday present to Court the year before had been a tan Duesenberg.

*The writ making Lance a ward of the English court was nullified by Barbara's attorneys in 1941, following her divorce from Court Reventlow.

Ten

P EOPLE perpetually warned me that Barbara Hutton would try to take away my husband," remarks Jean Kennerley. "I didn't believe it. Morley and Barbara were like brother and sister. And Barbara was loyal to her friends. But it was difficult to forget the Alexis Mdivani-Louise Van Alen breakup. The truth of the matter is that Barbara did try to seduce Morley. It took place years later, long after her personality was distorted by drugs and alcohol. It ended our long friendship. But I still give her the benefit of the doubt. It was something that couldn't have happened under more normal circumstances."

Barbara's reputation as a home wrecker originated with the press, which in its eagerness to invent a life for the heiress accused her of a series of romantic interludes that were largely fictional. Each week she was linked with some other happily married, well-established member of British society. The most preposterous rumors involved the Honorable Drogo Montagu, which reached the point where Barbara refused to see Janet Montagu, if only to discourage the ridiculous coupling of her name with that of the husband of a friend. Janet Montagu had for several years spent her winter vacations with Barbara at St. Moritz, but when Barbara refused to see her she took it as a snub and thereafter would have nothing to do with Hutton.

If such rumors disturbed Barbara, they were even more distressing for Court Reventlow, who was currently residing at the Ritz in Paris. Having lost home, wife and child, he would gratefully be spared the pain of seeing Prince Friedrich of Germany make off with Barbara. The prince, whose family disapproved of the relationship, soon faded into permanent oblivion. But there were other whisperings in the air. One persistent rumor, which did prove to be true, concerned Barbara's relations with her old friend Howard Hughes, whom she had known in New York in the early 1930s. The reclusive Texan was staying at the Savoy Hotel in London, completing plans for a three-day, round-the-world airplane flight he intended to make later that year. Frederick Brisson saw Barbara and Howard together at a dinner party, "looking very sweet, holding hands, misty-eyed."

Barbara's frank notebook appraisal of the Hughes affair testifies to a lack of sexual compatibility: "He sees that I have difficulty reaching orgasm, tries desperately to make me do so the first time, thereafter pleases himself and tells me I won't have one anyway. If I touch myself, he brushes my hand away with an angry snort. He can't take it when a woman loses herself in pleasure. Howard feels he has to be able to control a situation. When he doesn't, panic sets in."

And yet, Barbara always defended Hughes against his loudest critics, gave him sisterly affection, and on a few occasions procured him entrée to places where he might othewise never have gained admission. "Howard," she was to write, "had a talent for making enemies. People think of him as a half-deaf, stuttering billionaire whose only interest in life is money. For myself, I've never met a less materialistic man. He owns two suits and no tuxedo—if he needs one he borrows it. He usually wears tennis sneakers, the result of bad feet, and when he travels he packs a cardboard box with a few shirts and pairs of unmatched socks. He eats nothing but salads and would sooner sleep on a cot than in a comfortable bed. That is, when he sleeps at all. He is an easy person to be with. Doesn't bombard you with a barrage of ideas, doesn't pry, never argues. The charming thing about Howard is that he isn't charming."

Another of Barbara's flings during this period was with David Pleydell-Bouverie, a talented and successful English architect, a cousin of the extraordinarily rich Lord Radnor, of Longford Castle, Salisbury. Bouverie, who was later married to the heiress Alice Astor, thinks of Barbara today as the tragic case of a self-destructive woman who went to extremes to plot her own ruin and was incapable of enjoying those gifts good fortune had bestowed upon her. "When she was younger she was full of hope and humor. She was intelligent enough and compassionate enough and rich enough to have lived a rewarding and useful existence. But she was dogged from the start by chronic ill health and pursued by unmanageable compulsions. We met again in the summer of 1952 when we were both free of entanglements, and we gave each other a few more weeks of happiness."

In August of 1938 Sister took Lance Reventlow with her on vacation to Yorkshire while Barbara and Ticki checked into the Excelsior Hotel on the Lido. Venice was unusually quiet considering the time of year, but Barbara was content to pass her days lounging on the beach with Countess Edda Ciano. She occasionally joined American heiresses Millicent Rogers and Audrey Emery at Harry's Bar, where they exchanged gossip and small talk about ex-husbands. She accompanied Daisy Fellowes on a three-day cruise aboard her yacht, the *Sister Anne*. Barbara picked up two pointers from Daisy: First, that all men, regardless of their station or success, enjoyed being mistreated, especially by women. Second, that the secret to everlasting youth was a diet of caviar, smoked salmon and vodka.

Toward the middle of the month a letter came from Court Reventlow in Paris. He was about to leave for Vienna but had "important business" to discuss with Barbara and felt that personal contact was preferable to a meaningless correspondence. He wondered, therefore, if she would mind his detouring by way of Venice. Barbara had no desire to see Court and her first impulse was to follow the advice of Daisy Fellowes. In the end, however, she agreed to the visit.

He arrived a day ahead of schedule and found Barbara on the Lido promenade. As they sat talking over coffee, Court showed her some photographs of Lance he had taken in St. Moritz the winter before. Although the word "reconciliation" never crossed his lips, there was no doubt that this was the motive behind his visit—the photographs, after all, could have been sent through the mail. Later that day Reventlow in an interview with an English journalist expressed his hope for a reconciliation with his wife:

> Marriage in my country is considered sacred. There hasn't been a divorce in my family for 800 years. Barbara is still my wife. I love her as much as ever. She's so delicate, so precious. She has such tiny, exquisite wrists. Our child is too young at the moment to know what's happening. But later, what sort of life is it going to be for him if he's dragged from pillar to post, forced to spend part of his time with me, part with his mother? He should have a consistent home life. Every child deserves that much.

The futility of Court's mission became apparent the following morning when he met Barbara in the lobby of her hotel. The hotel was swarming with reporters, and Barbara asked Court not to make any statements that could be interpreted as unfriendly. They crossed the lobby to the hotel bar, where they each had a drink and exchanged vacant words and stares. When they were finished Barbara accompanied Court to the entrance doors of the hotel. He kissed her hand and left his wife for the last time.

Elsa Maxwell arrived in Venice just as Reventlow was departing. Barbara had agreed to an interview for a series Elsa was preparing for *International-Cosmopolitan* to be called "The Truth About Barbara Hutton." But the literary collaboration only added to Barbara's problems: the "truth" as Elsa Maxwell perceived it did not necessarily mesh with Court Reventlow's version.

In the second installment, published in November 1938, Miss Maxwell attacked Reventlow for "giving psychologically damaging" evidence at the time that Barbara abandoned her American citizenship. The article went on to say: "Court Reventlow must have pretended at first...because only after months of marriage did Barbara begin to discover he was literally not the man she thought he was. Discovery of the sort of man he really was came as a great shock."

The same article implied that Reventlow married Barbara not only for mercenary reasons, but also as a means of gaining access to English society. According to Elsa, when Court and Barbara moved into Winfield House they had to collect an entourage for entertaining, and Court busied himself looking for important people. He dragged Barbara from one boring house party to another, from one country estate to the next in a hopeless search for the ultimate in grandeur. On the few occasions that Barbara happened to cross paths with someone she liked—the Milbankes, for example—her contentious husband did everything he could to short-circuit the relationship. To gain his approval, their friends had to be inferior as well as subservient to Reventlow.

After reading an advance copy of the article, Reventlow—through his attorneys—notified the pubisher of his intention to file a suit for libel, as well as an injunction to keep the magazine off the newsstands. Simultaneously Court communicated with Graham Mattison, who was now handling most of Barbara's business dealings, and threatened to write his own account of life with Barbara. "If the Maxwell references to me are not withdrawn," he wrote to Mattison, "I will feel compelled to protect myself by publishing my version of things."

The interview had been a mistake. Instead of being rid of Reventlow as she had wished, Barbara provided him with an opportunity to reenter the picture, if only through the threat of further litigation. She finally agreed to pay the magazine a flat sum of $50,000 to cover the cost of excising the third and final installment of the story from the already printed but not yet distributed periodical.

Toward the end of October, Barbara returned to London to have an impacted wisdom tooth removed. Waiting for her at home was a letter from Count Heinrich Haugwitz-Reventlow requesting the return of the emerald bracelet she had received as a wedding present in Denmark from Court's family. "The emeralds are family stones," said Heinrich, "and since you are no longer in the family I think they should be returned." The letter was a reflection of the count's reaction to Barbara's dealings with Court—the separation, Court's arrest, the divorce agreement, Barbara's purported romances with other men, and of course the Elsa Maxwell articles.

Barbara may have understood the motive behind the letter, but she was deeply wounded by the manner of Heinrich's approach. "If it is a family heirloom as you say," she wrote back, "then it will be Lance's one day. And in any event I would not have minded if you asked me nicely to return it. As is, I am shocked."

Barbara was again shocked, this time in a pleasant way, when on her twenty-sixth birthday she received a telegram and a spray of red roses from Court Reventlow. Always grateful for the smallest token of affection, she wrote him a warm and gracious note of appreciation, apologized for the Elsa Maxwell mix-up, and in a postscript recommended a movie she had recently seen and enjoyed.

Court dear,

How terribly sweet of you to send me such glorious red roses with such a dear note for my birthday. It made me very happy. I am leaving for Paris soon to see about my clothes and will be away about a week....

I hope you're content with the settlement regarding the Elsa Maxwell business. It was the very best I could do. I want to say how dreadfully sorry I am about it all, and to beg you to forgive my gross stupidity. I thought I was doing Elsa a favor by giving her an interview, but once in print it never comes out quite the way it should.

With all my heart I thank you again, dear Court, for my lovely birthday greeting of roses.

With much love,
Barbara

P.S. Weren't you glad to see Snooky [Barbara's pet dachshund] again? She got fat, didn't she? By the way, have you seen *Marie Antoinette*? It's marvelous, and I'm sure you'll adore it. The hero reminds me so much of you. Do see it if you haven't.*

Reventlow never saw the film, although he later commented to a reporter, "Maybe I should have, though I doubt it would have saved our marriage."

On November 16, as planned, Barbara arrived in Paris. She was accompanied by her latest admirer, the golfer Robert Sweeny. Robert and his brother Charles had been dazzling London society for some time with their Irish-American good looks and urbane charm. They were both brilliant golfers. Charlie captained the Oxford University team in the early 1930s, and Bobby (also an Oxford graduate) captured the British amateur cup at Sandwich in 1937. California-born Bobby Sweeny was a member of several of London's leading sporting clubs and a frequent guest at the largest estates in England. Tall and sleek, with a countenance that revealed his droll, playful personality through twinkling eyes and the trace of a smile, Bobby was particularly attractive to women. Relaxed and informal, he laughed easily and often and had a soft and soothing voice that immediately appealed to Barbara. "He is the smoothest dancer in London," she commented in her notebooks. "The first time we met I realized two things—I was undoubtedly attracted to him, and he to me."

Barbara threw herself into the romance with her usual abandon and for the first time in her life found herself with a man who could satisfy her completely. Sweeny was an accomplished and considerate lover whose unabashed openness and gentle, easygoing manner helped liberate Barbara sexually. They were together constantly, whether in London, Paris, Corinth, or Le Touquet, the French beach resort on the Channel where they spent part of the fall. They went horseback riding together, played backgammon, danced, laughed, loved. In December 1938 they visited Greece, and in January, while Lance was taken by his father to Switzerland, Barbara and Bobby traveled to Egypt. Jean Kennerley went with them. "After the brutality of Court Reventlow," she remarks, "Bobby Sweeny was a breath of fresh air. It was like pulling up the blinds and letting in the light."

In April, Sweeny returned to England, while Barbara retrieved Lance and took him by boat on his first visit to the United States. They spent

---

*An inaccurate and abbreviated version of this and several other letters from Barbara to Court Reventlow are quoted in *Barbara Hutton* by Dean Jennings.

a month in Palm Beach with Barbara's father and stepmother and then returned to New York for the opening of the World's Fair.

In mid-June Barbara and Lance boarded the *Normandie* to return to Europe. On their second day out Barbara sat down to dinner and found herself staring at a man she thought she recognized. She recognized him, it turned out, only as a giant image on the celluloid screen. The man was Cary Grant, and the familiar face was staring back at her. The next evening they dined together and found they both knew Dorothy di Frasso and Frederick Brisson. Grant amused his dinner companion with anecdotes of his early experiences in Hollywood. Barbara found him witty, warm and gracious, not at all stuffy and stuck-up as she might have imagined him to be. He was equally impressed. Before disembarking in Cherbourg, they exchanged addresses and telephone numbers and promised to keep in touch.

Just as she arrived back in England, Barbara learned that the American embassy in London was sending out alarming letters to all U.S. citizens residing in Great Britain advising them of the strong possibility of war and urging them to pack up and return to the United States. Instead of a letter, Barbara received a telephone call from the office of Ambassador Joseph P. Kennedy. He wanted to see her in person and his secretary arranged an appointment.

Joe Kennedy and his wife, Rose, were friends of the family, especially of Marjorie Merriweather Post and her third husband, Joseph E. Davies, the American ambassador to the Soviet Union from 1937 to 1938. Barbara also knew the Kennedys and was well aware of Joe Kennedy's reputation as a ladies' man. Yet in the past Kennedy had always been kind to Barbara, almost fatherly. When they met they often discussed the latest adventures of Barbara's Aunt Marjorie, and one of Kennedy's favorite anecdotes was the way in which she had arrived in Russia in 1937, her monstrous yacht laden with a cargo that included specially prepared foods as well as furniture, iceboxes, electric fans and other paraphernalia she would be unlikely to find in Moscow. Several thousand pints of frozen cream were also brought along, shocking a number of Soviet officials who pointed out that the country still had cows.*

When Barbara arrived at Grosvenor Square to see Kennedy at the American embassy, she found him in a more serious frame of mind. He had called her in, he maintained, because of the urgent political situation and because she was no longer an American citizen. Never-

---

*The information on Marjorie Merriweather Post comes from William Wright's *Heiress*. The Kennedy-Hutton anecdote appears in a somewhat different form in Philip Van Rensselaer's *Million Dollar Baby*, pps. 236-37.

theless, he had taken the liberty of conferring with the U.S. State Department and they had agreed that she could re-enter the country on the strength of her Danish passport. She would have to make arrangements to leave Britain as soon as possible.

As they continued to talk, the tenor of their conversation gradually turned. Kennedy became less earnest and more playful. He offered Barbara a drink. She declined. He poured himself one instead and leaned against the edge of his desk. Barbara, sensing a difficult situation, wanted to leave, but didn't know how to extricate herself without insulting Kennedy. Yet as he talked on, he became more flirtatious, more direct, more threatening. Within minutes Kennedy was propositioning Barbara, offering to make her his mistress, chasing her around his desk.

Barbara was aghast. She subsequently related the incident to Lady Diana Cooper, whose husband, Alfred Duff Cooper, was later to become the British ambassador to France. Diana, in turn, with a ribald, iconoclastic wit, wrote about it to Conrad Russell, a cousin to the Duke of Bedford: "Kennedy was eager to help, but the help was to consist mainly of setting Barbara up as his mistress. I gather some pouncing accompanied these propositions. How amusing, and how little I would have thought of it! Mr. Asquith and Lord Wimbourne, to think of only two old gentlemen, both put forward more or less the same plan to me, and I thought it so flattering. While poor Barbara feels she can never look Kennedy in the face again. She is probably right and I am wrong."*

It was Lady Diana who suggested that Barbara hire the international transport and storage firm of Pitt & Scott to help with the closing down of Winfield House. It fell to the company's director, W. J. Sutton, and his young secretary, Mrs. Hazel Dews, to pack up the vast inventory of valuables and furniture that filled the house. According to Mrs. Dews, "This meant visits to the mansion for many weeks to make sure that every item was numbered and in a huge leatherbound volume and always in the careful charge of Miss Hutton's valuer, Mr. William L. Williams, a gentleman well into his seventies, very pedantic and meticulous and courteous, reminding me of a character out of Dickens.

"The contents of Winfield House included a considerable amount of French antique furniture, very large and ornate, mostly of the Louis XIV and XV periods, as well as a good deal of fine English pieces. And then, of course, there were the endless sets of Meissen dinnerware, gilded crystalware, gold and silver centerpieces and serving trays,

*See Philip Ziegler, *Diana Cooper*, p. 195.

silverware, leatherbound books from the library and beautiful soft furnishings and Miss Hutton's priceless jade collection. There were many Oriental objects as well—intricately carved Chinese panels, jade screens, silk tapestry, and so forth. There were valuable paintings everywhere and there were countless *objets d'art*—cigarette boxes, ornamental gold boxes, snuff boxes—which had to be packed away, to say nothing of mirrors, rugs and carpets, fine linens, and several rooms of nursery furniture. The valuable Meissen, jade, and art objects were relegated for storage in Worcester because of risk from enemy action during the coming war...

"Being on the spot as it were and in the thick of all that activity amidst so much that was precious and fragile was somehow very unnerving, as if an age of splendor was on the verge of ending. Even the furniture and furnishings of the servants' quarters were of great value. A final note: during the preparations prior to the removal, I recall the astonishing sight of a huge pile of shoes left in a corner of the main bedroom, all size 4, all specially made and belonging to Miss Hutton— no less than 300 pairs of shoes."

At the beginning of August 1939 Barbara and Bob Sweeny were staying in a villa near the Piccola Marina bathing beach on the island of Capri; they were joined by Sheila Lady Milbanke, Gilbert and Kitty Miller, Elsie Mendl, and others hopeful of reaching the United States. Six weeks later, with the war already under way, Barbara and Bobby went to Biarritz to wait for Count Reventlow to release Lance so that his mother could take him with her to New York. Reventlow, who had been vacationing with the boy in the north of France, suddenly decided he was opposed to the idea of sending Lance off with Barbara, and it took all of Graham Mattison's considerable negotiating skill (by telephone from New York) plus a check from Barbara for $250,000 to convince Court to surrender his son.

After Lance's return the entourage went to Genoa, where Count Galeazzo Ciano personally arranged their exit visas and passage aboard the Italian liner *Conte di Savoia*. Barbara's ship party included Sweeny, Lance, Sister, Ticki, six servants, two dogs and a Persian cat. On October 22, Barbara was greeted in New York by the usual reception committee of hissing, rowdy women with placards and pamphlets.

Barbara's eyes flashed with indignation as one of the demonstrators thrust a brochure titled "Consider the Woolworth Workers" in her face. As she stepped into a waiting limousine a cascade of rocks slammed into the side of the car. When they reached the Hotel Pierre on Fifth

Avenue, the Hutton group found itself the object of a second demonstration, also organized by Woolworth employees.

There was no surcease to Barbara's troubles. The press was filled with items, stories and articles about her, mostly fabricated or founded on hearsay. Shortly after her return, outside a Broadway theater on Forty-fourth Street, she was accosted by another angry crowd. One woman threatened to throw acid in her face. At the Pierre she was inundated by a hundred poison-pen letters a day. She attended a Hawaiian-motif birthday party for Doris Duke, hosted by her first husband, James H. R. Cromwell, in the Duke mansion, at 1 East Seventy-eighth Street. When she left the party with Bobby Sweeny and Tallulah Bankhead, a mob awaited them armed with ripe tomatoes and rotten eggs. The three were bombarded as a limousine pulled up to take them away.

It took little prodding on Jessie Donahue's part to convince Barbara to make an appointment with press agent Steve Hannagan, whose public relations firm had recently opened a New York office. Hannagan was a logical choice. He had helped Barbara once before, and he was an authority in the field.

"Whenever you deny a story that appears in the press," he told her, "you reinforce your vulnerability. When you refute a libel, you give the newspaper and gossip-sheet editors license to publish your denial but also to repeat the libel. It's counterproductive. What you need to be selling is humility, not self-indulgence."

"And how do I do that, Mr. Hannagan?" asked Barbara.

"Well, for one thing," he began, pointing to an enormous diamond ring on her right ring finger, "by not wearing rings like that one. In times like these it doesn't take much to turn people against you. All it takes is an expensive diamond, a mink coat, a big car, an impudent remark to a newspaperman—any or all of the above."

Hannagan's agency billing for a year was $60,000 plus expenses. Barbara signed. In addition she agreed to follow his directives to the letter. "If you don't," he said, "you're wasting your money."

The public relations campaign to improve Barbara's image was under way. Its first major test came with the disclosure that Franklyn and Irene Hutton were about to dissolve their marriage. Franklyn moved out of his Fifth Avenue apartment and headed for his plantation in the South while Irene remained in New York and consulted with an attorney. Hutton apparently did the same because a nonliability notice appeared in a New York newspaper, whereby Hutton renounced all responsibility for his wife's past and future debts. A week after separating the couple resolved their differences and reconciled. On November 23, under the headline "Dime Heiress Reconciles Parents," the *Herald Tribune* ran a three-column story that began: "Barbara Woolworth Hutton, who herself has experienced two marital shipwrecks, was credited by friends today with effecting a reconciliation between her father and stepmother." Her "friends" in this instance were none other than Steve Hannagan and Ned Moss, the adroit and energetic Hannagan agency employee assigned to handle her account.

The publicity machine of Hannagan and Moss began churning out an endless inventory of Barbara's magnanimous deeds—her financial support of some fifteen needy American families; the donation of her yacht to the British Auxiliary Navy; her gift of ten fully equipped ambulances to the British Red Cross; her contribution of $50,000 to the British War Relief Fund; her purchase of $100,000 worth of defense bonds; her establishment of scholarship funds at Bryn Mawr and Vassar; her "private" charities, especially for women with neither funds nor family.

Pictures of Barbara knitting sweaters and socks to raise money for the rehabilitation of disabled French soldiers appeared in every big-city newspaper. The public read reports of Barbara's cash deposits in a Toronto bank account to be used in the recruitment of "volunteers" for an American Escadrille to fly war missions for England against the relentless German war machine. They read about her donation to a wildlife fund and about the new medical pavilion that was going up in her name at New York's Wickersham Hospital.

They didn't read about the Christmas check for $10,000 in Barbara's name that Steve Hannagan sent to Maury Paul, with written instructions to donate the check to the charity of his choice. Maury reciprocated by writing in his column that Barbara's pending marriage to American-born Bobby Sweeny proved her abrogation of European titles: "She's terribly pro-American these days. And humble as pie. Never mind that she was named for the fourth year running to the Best Dressed Women in the World list. Appointed, one should say, by the *grands couturiers*, the owners of *les maisons de grand luxe*, in appreciation of the grand sums she has doled out on fashion over the years, never less than a hundred thousand big ones per annum. But that's all behind her now. From now on she'll go in rags and give her money to the poor."

Hannagan's next brainstorm was to have Ned Moss take Barbara to a meeting at the Waldorf-Astoria of the ladies' committee of the United Hospital Fund, on which many socially prominent young women served. Though some of the ladies resented Barbara's reputation, they were pleased when she was asked to appear in a Movietone newsreel to publicize their charity. The committee's chairwoman, Mrs. Vincent

Astor, presented Barbara with a special citation honoring her contributions and fund-raising abilities. Another of the committee's members, Mrs. Charles Payson,* formerly Joan Whitney, became friendly with Barbara and invited her to join the Board of Trustees of the American Red Cross. Barbara declined but gave generously to the organization. For the most part Barbara's relations with the charity ladies remained cordial—that is to say, she made frequent donations without attending their functions. Yet the publicity she derived from her contributions helped restore her image, at least temporarily.

T. Dennie Boardman, an affable and long-time Palm Beach realtor, received a telephone call in late November from Graham Mattison concerning the availability of a winter rental for Barbara and her entourage. Boardman asked around and learned that the Spanish-style mansion of Harrison and Mona Williams, previously leased by the Duke and Duchess of Windsor, was empty for the season. Mattison reserved the house for Barbara and asked Boardman to rent a separate cottage at the Everglades Club for Robert Sweeny. Although registered at the Everglades, Sweeny stayed with Barbara in the Williams house and used the club only for golf. Another member of the group was Ned Moss, who stayed at The Breakers Hotel.

To avoid reporters, photographers and striking Woolworth employees, Boardman arranged for Barbara's train to discharge her party five miles north of West Palm Beach. "You can't imagine the magnitude of her star appeal," says the realtor. "As soon as word spread that she was in the area, all of Worth Avenue poured out for a closer look. The shoppers and the shopkeepers alike would line the streets."

Barbara tried to maintain a low profile that winter, giving and going only to small informal parties. The one major affair she attended was the Palm Beach wedding of her cousin Woolworth Donahue to Mrs. Gretchen Wilson Hearst, granddaughter of Stonewall Jackson and the former wife of John Randolph Hearst, son of the newspaper publisher. At the reception Barbara got into a small tiff with Charles James, the clothing designer, whose recent reference to the five-and-dime stores as "Barbara Hutton's boutiques" appeared in an interview in *Vogue*. Otherwise she restricted herself to seeing people she knew: Countess Dorothy di Frasso, Prince Serge Obolensky, the Charlie Munns and the Laddie Sanfords.

*Joan Payson was best known in later years as the colorful owner of the New York Mets baseball team.

The Munns—Charles A. ("Mr. Palm Beach") and his wife, Dorothy—could always be counted on for interesting, newsworthy dinner guests and good party lists. Munn detested the notoriety he had achieved as the patent holder of the Totalizator, an apparatus for registering and indicating the number of tickets sold to betters on each horse in a race. Munn's name appeared on the back of every parimutuel racetrack ticket, and his Palm Beach villa Amado was often in the news. Elsa Maxwell wrote a particularly distressing article, "Palm Beach is All Munn's Land," which induced Charlie to declare Amado out of news bounds for more than a year. Munn's dinner parties, kept small that year for Barbara's sake, were usually followed by private screenings of the latest Hollywood films, a ritual Barbara loved.

It was through the Munns that she met the Sanfords. Steven "Laddie" Sanford, the carpet heir, was a leading international polo competitor with residences in Palm Beach, Saratoga and Old Westbury, on Long Island. His wife was the former stage actress Mary Duncan. Society at first took a dim view of the marriage, especially the snobbish editors of the *Social Register*, who opposed the inclusion of performers in their directory. When the editors voted to drop Laddie from the *Register*, his father, John Sanford, became so enraged that he forced the editors to take his whole family out. *

Mary Sanford found Barbara "highly insecure but very sweet and likable—almost girlish. She seemed lonely and isolated, as if nobody would take her seriously. She could sit for hours in the same position and not say a word or move a muscle. She practiced yoga and read. She didn't go out much, although she and Sweeny sometimes went dancing at the Everglades or Bath and Tennis, or they would dine out. Barbara would pick at her food. She never ate. Bobby Sweeny was pleasant-looking but a bit mellowed out. Barbara completely dominated him, as she dominated most of her men."

Ned Moss kept a circumspect eye on Barbara, controlling all press releases and establishing himself as chief censor of all photographs given out to the press. A mysterious breakdown in communications led to the embarrassing publication in the Palm Beach *Daily News* (known locally as "The Shiny Sheet") of a snapshot of Barbara smooching with Alfred Gwynne Vanderbilt at the Patio Club. Moss promptly phoned Emelie Keyes, society columnist for the paper, and the next shot to appear in The Shiny Sheet showed Barbara and Bobby Sweeny as spectators at an Everglades Club tennis tournament, a black poodle (Sweeny's birthday present to Barbara) nestled in her lap.

---

*Barbara Hutton was officially dropped from the *Social Register* in 1938, presumably because she was so often in the news.

By the end of January 1940 Ned Moss was back in New York, while Steve Hannagan was out on the West Coast attending to several new clients. In Palm Beach, Barbara received a visit from Duff and Diana Cooper. The Coopers were in the middle of an American lecture tour designed to draw attention to the British war effort, and had just come from President Franklin D. Roosevelt and a White House dinner party. But the wealthy and ultraconservative elements of Palm Beach were predominantly anti-war and anti-British and wanted no part of the war in Europe.

As an outspoken advocate of American intervention in the war, Barbara did her utmost to aid the Coopers. Besides conducting an active telephone campaign, she took out newspaper advertisements soliciting contributions to the British war chest. She also helped Duff Cooper tailor his speech to appeal to the interests of an audience whose needs and aspirations she felt she understood.

It proved to be largely an exercise in futility. The talk, given at the Everglades Club, was sparsely attended and poorly received by those who did attend. The following week an editorial in one of the local papers labeled Barbara "a war-mongering Anglophile, a swaggering dollar princess with no sense and no concept of political reality."

The attack upset Barbara. Without a word to anyone, she and Sweeny and their retinue returned to New York and checked back into the Pierre. The city was bursting with social activity, much of it centered around the international set that had drifted to the United States following the outbreak of war in Europe. Emerald Cunard was staying at the Ritz-Carlton in a suite adjoining that of her paramour, the distinguished conductor Sir Thomas Beecham. Interior decorator Syrie Maugham (former wife of W. Somerset Maugham) had an apartment at the Dakota on Central Park West. Cole and Linda Porter occupied a suite of rooms at the Waldorf Towers. Gilbert and Kitty Miller were back and forth between their Park Avenue apartment in New York and a house in Beverley Hills. Arturo Lopez-Wilshaw, the Chilean millionaire art collector, had taken over an entire floor of the St. Regis Hotel with his cousin-wife, Patricia, his intimate companion Baron Alexis de Rédé (an Austrian businessman) and some twenty retainers. The St. Regis was also home to its acting manager, Serge Obolensky, whose black-tie champagne dinner dances atop the pink lighted St. Regis roof brought together many of the wealthy sheep of this wandering herd.

Although she felt more comfortable within the bounds of international high society than in the company of the supercilious winter colonists of Palm Beach, the first signs of spring set Barbara's mind in motion. She thought seriously of taking a long trip to California as well as Hawaii, if for no other reason than to show Lance off to some of her old West Coast friends, many of whom she hadn't seen in years. Ned Moss had already joined his employer on the Coast; the responsibility for getting Barbara safely to California was thus relegated to a young Hannagan agency trainee named Charles McCabe. McCabe, who in later years became a columnist for the San Francisco *Chronicle*, wrote and spoke about the difficulty they had in trying to avoid the media.

"The trip had to be by railway, because reporters covered airport arrivals like a shroud. And you had to avoid the terminals of the railways, because they had their spies.

"My job was to accompany the titled personage until I turned her over to our man on the coast. I met Barbara, which I soon learned to call her, in a small apartment she was hiding in on the Upper East Side.

"We were driven to Pleasantville, about 20 miles up the Hudson, where we boarded the 20th Century Limited, a great old train. Pleasantville is where the *Reader's Digest* is published. There are no reporters meeting trains there.

"Our journey cross country is easily recorded. The lady taught me gin rummy in her sitting room. She always seemed to have a towel on her head. The game, which had been as obscure as Egyptian papyrus to me, came easily. She was either a good teacher, or I had good hands.

"Her entourage included her son, her traveling companion [Ticki], her son's nanny [Sister], a French governess [Hilly Duchamps], a social secretary [Helen Livingston], a personal maid [Simone Chibleur], a chauffeur [Harry Leach], several housekeepers, and a burly bodyguard in pale-gray flannel, growing fat and flabby in middle age, aptly dubbed 'Mr. Big' by the little boy. When we reached San Francisco I turned them over to Ned Moss. Moss took me aside. 'Where's Sweeny?' he asked. I gave him a blank stare and he repeated himself. 'Bob Sweeny, the golfer, Barbara's sweetheart. Didn't he make the trip?' 'Doesn't ring a bell,' I said. Moss rolled his eyes. I eventually found out what happened to Sweeny. Barbara gave him $350,000 and the royal screw. He returned to England and ended up with the RAF. And I went back to New York and never saw or heard from the lady again."

Barbara and her troupe, including Ned Moss, moved into her old quarters at the Mark Hopkins. Barbara's behavior over the next few weeks was more erratic than usual. In Palm Beach she had gotten hold of a prescription for Seconal and was taking the barbiturate three tablets at a time with brimming glasses of champagne, claiming that it calmed her nerves. Moss found that it had the opposite effect. He never knew whether she would be up or down. "Which is it today," he would chide her, "—Jekyll or Hyde?"

According to Dean Jennings, Moss escorted Barbara to the Chinese Theater in San Francisco's Chinatown and took her and Lance to the Aquarium. They then visited a men's clothing store and Barbara chose a luxurious oriental blue-green silk robe, which she later gave to Moss, as well as a gold watch from Van Cleef & Arpels.

During her last week in San Francisco Barbara visited her old friends Harrie Hill Page and Susan Smith. She spent time with Nini Martin and attended a dinner party at the home of Jane Christienson, a childhood acquaintance who had wed Count Mark de Tristan of France. Another person she saw was her father's cousin Curtis Hutton, a less affluent member of the family. In 1941 Barbara gave Curtis a gift of $1 million.

Before leaving California on her long-awaited trip to Hawaii, she had a last-minute confrontation with the press. Finding herself short of change one morning, Barbara asked one of the bellboys to run down to the nearest bank and break a bill for her. The bill was in an envelope and when the bellboy presented it to the teller he heard a loud gasp: Barbara had given him a $10,000 bill.

Herb Caen, a gossip columnist for the San Francisco *Chronicle*, ran a story pointing out that while most people couldn't scrape together $10,000 over a lifetime, here was someone using it for small change. "She has no perspective on money," wrote Caen. "Her view is distorted simply because she has too much of it. The possession of a ten-thousand-dollar bill is as natural to Miss Hutton as a five or ten is to you and me."

Nobody was more pleased than Ned Moss when Barbara finally sailed for Hawaii. She had been given free run of an estate called Windward Island, a tiny private atoll an hour from Honolulu, with its own manor house, playhouse, shooting gallery, bowling alley and white sand lagoon beach. The three-mile-square island belonged to Santa Barbara millionaire Chris R. Holmes, a friend of Doris Duke's.

Arriving on May 8 in a group that included her friend Dorothy di Frasso, Barbara was immediately disappointed. Granted Windward Island was an idyllic spot if one wanted to get away from prying eyes, but nothing else about it lived up to expectations. The so-called playhouse, located in the hull of an old, anchored yacht, was dank and musty-smelling; there were hundreds of eels squirming about the ship's bow. The shooting gallery was of the amusement-park variety. You pushed a button and a row of ducklings went bobbling by. The bowling alley was located in a dilapidated barn that also housed slot machines, pool tables, ping pong and other arcade amusements. Here you pushed a button, and model airplanes raced back and forth across the ceiling. But none of the other games worked, and in addition the barn was infested with giant red ants. The main lodge was only a slight improvement. The furniture, most of it of Oriental design, appealed to Barbara, but the sharpened native spears and the shrunken heads left something to be desired. Two weeks after arriving in Hawaii, the party returned to California.

Barbara's re-emergence, this time in Los Angeles, was covered by Harrison Carroll of the Los Angeles *Examiner*, who reported seeing Barbara in a Beverly Hills restaurant with none other than Cary Grant. Steve Hannagan and Ned Moss were as surprised as everyone else to read about this unlikely coupling. At least the news helped explain the sudden, unceremonious dismissal by Barbara of her previous beau, Bob Sweeny. Insofar as it was possible to reconstruct the order of events, it appeared that the golfer had simply been swept aside to make room for his glamorous successor.

In sorting the facts, Hannagan and Moss learned of Barbara's fateful first encounter with Grant in 1939 aboard the *Normandie*, and their second meeting a few weeks later at a party in London given by Dorothy di Frasso. Thereafter they saw each other periodically; their paths happened to cross at social gatherings in London, Paris, New York and Palm Beach. During Barbara's stay in Palm Beach she and Grant spoke frequently by telephone. The frequency and manner of their meetings soon began to change, particularly after Barbara's arrival in San Francisco. Hannagan and Moss were chagrined to hear that during Barbara's stay at the Mark Hopkins in San Francisco, she had gone off to see Grant in private.

Veteran Hollywood drumbeaters Hedda Hopper and Louella Parsons agreed that the Grant-Hutton liaison had little foundation for a promising future. They may have seemed the perfect match, and though they looked wonderful together and appeared to get along, beneath the surface there were some rather striking discrepancies in their respective beliefs and backgrounds.

Cary Grant had the advantage of having known from the start what it was he wanted to become. He made his choice in England when, as thirteen-year-old Archibald Alec Leach (born in Bristol on January 18, 1904), he ran away from home to join the Pender Boys, a troupe of wandering music hall acrobats. He had good reason for leaving his row-house home. His father, an impoverished pants presser in a garment factory, was an alcoholic. His mother, with an early history of mental illness, was institutionalized shortly after his birth. The first time Archie left home his father went after him and put him back in school. He finished the term before setting out again, this time for good.

Rejoining the Pender Boys, Leach accompanied them in 1920 on their first tour of the United States, including a stint at New York's

Hippodrome Theater. When the group later returned to England, Archie and several of the others decided to stay. Over the next few years he struggled to find work as an actor while subsisting on a variety of part-time jobs, everything from peddling hand-painted neckties to walking the Coney Island boardwalk on stilts to advertise Steeplechase Park. In 1927 he succeeded in landing a small role in the Otto Harbach-Oscar Hammerstein II musical comedy *Golden Dawn*, which opened on Broadway. He spent three more years as a contract player in Hammerstein musicals and operettas before moving to Hollywood and a new career in feature films.

It was in Hollywood that Archie Leach became Cary Grant, destined for stardom in a succession of films opposite many of the leading ladies of the day, from Carole Lombard and Rosalind Russell to Marlene Dietrich and Mae West (who chose Grant out of a group of young Paramount hopefuls to co-star with her in the 1933 film *She Done Him Wrong*). Grant's major breakthrough did not come until 1936, when he appeared with Katharine Hepburn in *Sylvia Scarlett*, where he played a petty English crook with a cockney accent, the type of role he needed to solidify his reputation. *Topper*, *The Awful Truth* and *Bringing Up Baby* soon followed, catapulting him to the top of the Hollywood heap.

By the time Barbara Hutton met him, Grant was one of the industry's highest paid stars, in a league with Clark Gable, Spencer Tracy, John Wayne, Gary Cooper and maybe one or two others. In 1937 Grant helped smash the autonomous control that the major studios exerted over actors by becoming the first freelance performer in Hollywood. "It didn't turn out too badly, either," he claimed. "Without being tied down to a studio contract, I soon pushed my salary up to three hundred thousand dollars a picture."

Grant was earning considerably less in 1934, the year he married his first wife, Virginia Cherrill, the enticing blonde who played the blind girl in Charlie Chaplin's *City Lights*. The marriage, which took place in England, lasted seven months. For a man of Grant's ambitions, failure of any kind must have been difficult. Although he was romantically linked with a number of attractive actresses—among them Mary Brian, Ginger Rogers, Phyllis Brooks—it was not until he met Barbara Hutton that he considered the possibility of a second marriage.

In 1940 Grant was living in the same oceanfront Santa Monica beach house he had once shared with actor Randolph Scott, a comfortable dwelling with a view and a bathtub-warm swimming pool. Barbara, following her return from Hawaii, took a year's sublet on Buster Keaton's former estate, located behind the Beverly Hills Hotel at 1004 Hartford Way. Modeled after an Italian villa of the Renaissance, the thirty-room mansion stood atop a steeply landscaped terrace overlooking a Roman-bath swimming pool, a trout-filled brook (which turned on and off at the flip of a switch), tennis courts and acres of rolling lawn. When Buster Keaton used to give visitors the royal tour, he'd tell them, "It took a lot of pratfalls, my friends, to build this dump."

Now that Barbara was back in public view, Steve Hannagan found himself burdened with the difficult task of neutralizing the flood of publicity that accompanied the announcement of her romance with Cary Grant. Hannagan considered it fortunate that Grant had a deep-seated aversion to publicity and would go to almost any lengths to avoid it. "We're absolutely stupid to be embarked in a business where our face is connected with our accomplishments," Grant had once said. "When you get it from morning to night, it's no longer wonderful. No dear public ever did anything for me, and a few people in our industry have the courage to say: 'Oh, my dear public, I'd kick 'em if I could!'"

This was the man who on one occasion told Hedda Hopper, considered by many in the colony to possess the power of life and death, that what he did when he wasn't making films or public appearances was "nobody's goddamned business," least of all hers. Grant's "never complain, never explain" attitude revived again the perennial debate as to whether a person in his position would have attained the success he did without benefit of publicity—unsolicited or otherwise.

Grant and Barbara took every precaution to avoid public exposure, restricting themselves to meetings at his place—or hers. They ventured forth to restaurants and nightspots only occasionally, and only after Grant elicited an advance guarantee from the management that there would be no publicity and no reporters. Once or twice they went dancing at the Catalina casino, accessible only by boat. Tommy Dorsey's orchestra played the casino, and he had his new singer, Frank Sinatra, who at that time looked all of twelve years old but was causing a sensation. Grant and Sinatra eventually became great pals. Barbara resisted Sinatra's charms, describing him as "an egomaniac with a beautiful voice."

For the most part Cary preferred small dinner parties at home or at the homes of friends. The size of Barbara's Italian villa made it convenient for Grant to throw his own Sunday night gatherings. The regulars at these weekly functions were David Niven; Jimmy Stewart; Rosalind Russell and Frederick Brisson;* English playwright Frederick Lonsdale; actress-singer Constance Moore and her Hollywood agent

---

*Frederick Brisson met Rosalind Russell through Cary Grant. They were married October 25, 1941, at Solvang, a Danish community in the Santa Ynez Mountains, north of Santa Barbara. Barbara Hutton and Cary Grant attended the ceremony. Grant was best man.

husband, Johnny Maschio; Merle Oberon and her husband, Sir Alexander Korda; Marlene Dietrich; "Prince" Mike Romanoff (the restaurateur); character actor Hugh Fenwich; and a character named Bill Robertson, a top-seeded amateur tennis player, who later became Barbara's resident manager, a position she created for him out of gratitude for his devotion.

"We chose Sunday evenings because Barbara's household staff had the night off," explains Grant. "The guests did their own cooking, such as it was, and washed their own dishes. After dinner we gathered in the drawing room and played charades or clustered around the piano and sang." Grant, say his friends, demonstrated his impudent wit by singing popular songs with his own revised, suggestive lyrics.

Barbara, according to Grant, was shy at first. She knew only a few in the group and felt uncomfortable. "Then one evening," he says, "Connie and Johnny Maschio came to dinner alone and after dinner went to Barbara's room to look at a Chinese table lamp she had bought from a local antiques dealer. Barbara suddenly put some Chinese music on the record player and on an impulse kicked off her shoes and started dancing in time to the music. None of us knew what we were looking at, but she explained the significance of each step and hand movement. It was delightful, and the next time we met as a group, Johnny encouraged Barbara to repeat her performance. After a few feeble excuses she dimmed the lights and put on the music before launching into an intricate pattern of movements. It broke the ice between Barbara and the group.

"Years later, long after our divorce, I recognized Barbara's interest in dance and poetry as a need for a kind of expression that her life didn't provide. She wasn't your run-of-the-mill society belle, the sort who, as she lolls down the boulevard, peers into every shop window to ascertain whether her reflection is still there. She was intelligent and sensitive but lacked a suitable means of self-expression, a medium of communication that would allow her to vent her frustrations. And I had no understanding of either dance or poetry and I didn't encourage her in that direction, and I think few people did. The lack of encouragement was as much responsible for her unhappiness as anything.*

*Cary Grant's comments in this and other chapters of the book are derived primarily from the following sources: Grant interview with Theresa Stanton (researcher), June '79; Grant interview with author (telephone), Aug. '79; articles by Grant in Ladies' Home Journal, Jan. and April '63; author interview with Frederick Brisson; Dudley Walker interview (telephone) with Kathleen O'Brien (researcher); 1968 biography of Barbara Hutton, by Dean Jennings; biographies of Cary Grant, by Lionel Godfrey and Albert Govoni (see bibliography); assorted newspaper and magazine clippings.

During October 1940, while Grant embarked on a new film project, Barbara went to San Francisco to visit friends. She returned the first week of November to pose for the Russian portrait artist Savely Sorine, who had known Barbara in Paris during her marriage to Alexis Mdivani. Stella Hanania of the I. Magnin store in Beverly Hills designed a blue velvet gown and matching headdress with a flowing white feather for the sitting. Just as Sorine was putting the final touches on the portrait, word arrived that Franklyn Hutton had taken ill on his plantation in South Carolina. Barbara made immediate plans to fly to Charleston.

Irene Hutton, Jessie Donahue, Uncle Ned (E.F. Hutton), and Aunt Grace were already there by the time Barbara arrived. If her father was aware of her presence at his bedside, he lacked the strength to express the thought in words. He died on December 2, aged sixty-three. The official cause of death, according to his death certificate, was cirrhosis, or liver failure.

The obituary notices commented on Franklyn's fiscal sagacity, his hail-fellow sportsmanship, his reputation as a genial host. His will, a document of considerable length, mentioned his daughter only once: "I realize that my beloved daughter Barbara is possessed in her own right of worldly goods ample for her future comfort, as well as for the future comfort for those who may be or become dear to her, and that any bequest of a monetary nature that I could make would be quite inconsequential. Therefore, I will to her a loving father's blessing for her future happiness."

Barbara reacted to the will by suing her father's estate for $530,000, plus 5 percent accrued interest, to recover monies lent him over the years. Irene Hutton, sole executrix of her late husband's $5 million estate, repaid the debt in full, observing in the press that it was simply "a private arrangement between a father and his daughter." After Franklyn's death, Barbara and Irene remained on cordial terms. They saw each other at regular intervals and Barbara was always generous with her stepmother on Christmas and birthdays.*

❧

As more than one historian has noted, America's gradual involvement in the European war effort had a noticeable effect on the social patterns of Hollywood's hyperactive gentry. Premieres, tent parties, studio galas, once held to promote motion pictures, were now given under the guise of fund-raisers and bond drives. Hollywood's fashionable restaurants and nightspots—the Trocadero, Mocambo, Ciro's, Romanoff's, Player's

---

*A year after Franklyn Hutton's death, Irene married New York businessman James A. Moffett, who died in 1953. Irene passed away in 1965.

(owned by Barbara Hutton's former relation-by-marriage, writer-director Preston Sturges)—were all doing a brisk business. Even in the high-priced specialty shops along Rodeo Drive in Beverly Hills, sales had picked up. One reason for this sudden upsurge was the arrival in Los Angeles of a new contingent, an international assemblage of social climbers, publicity seekers, heiresses, socialites, dethroned royalty and plain old-fashioned aristocrats whose permanent vacations abroad had been disrupted by the war.

The advent of these adventurers gave Hollywood's flagging social scene a much-needed boost. Formal wear forged back into style, jewelry was removed from safety deposit boxes and combination wall safes, expensive fur coats came out of storage. William Randolph Hearst set the social Risorgimento in motion. His fêtes at San Simeon and at Marion Davies' Santa Monica beach house were not just grand but grandiose. Mammoth circus tents were raised over the sweeping lawns and gardens. Swimming pools were boarded over to serve as dance floors. Orchestras were flown in from New York. Fireworks showered the sky. Parties were attended by casts of thousands.

Others followed Hearst's example. Darryl F. Zanuck threw a majestic beach bash for silver-mining heiress Dolly O'Brien; Louis B. Mayer gave a glittering reception for the Earl of Warwick; Samuel and Frances Goldwyn hosted a giant lawn party for British statesman Leslie Hore-Belisha; King and Elizabeth Vidor gave a Romanov costume ball for Grand Duchess Marie of Russia; Dorothy di Frasso, whose latest companion was the darkly attractive mobster Benjamin "Bugsy" Siegel, threw prodigious parties for the Eric de Rothschilds, Baroness Renée de Becker, Baron Hubert von Pantz and the authors Ludwig Bemelmans and Erich Maria Remarque. At one of her Bedford Drive social affairs Dorothy di Frasso, a regular Friday-night fight fan at the Hollywood Legion Arena, had a boxing ring erected on her front lawn, and guests were "entertained" with three bloody bouts in which the gladiators were old battered pros.

As bizarre as Dorothy's boxing shindig was Elsa Maxwell's dinner for Richard Gulley, an English bon vivant and cousin of Sir Anthony Eden. Elsa, sharing a house in Beverly Hills with Evalyn Walsh McLean, owner of the Hope Diamond, found herself shorthanded in the kitchen the night of the party and instead of canceling decided to improvise by giving paper plates and crayons to her guests and awarding a prize for the most originally decorated paper plate. First prize was a china dinner setting, the only one permitted that evening. The other guests had to eat their meals from paper plates of their own design.

"The problem with these parties," observes Cary Grant, "was that people would meet Barbara Hutton for the first time and immediately become tongue-tied. They couldn't treat her normally. People who were usually bright became absolute nitwits in her presence. They said absurd things. They said, 'Why, you know, you're quite a nice gal even with all that money,' which connotes that because she had money she wasn't supposed to be nice. They would ask whether her fortune was a bore, a trial, or a pleasure. Or they would say, 'For all that money, by God, you're quite normal.' They probably expected her to be a raving maniac."

Grant recalls one incident at a Hollywood dinner party, an affair brightened by some of the top names in the industry: "Barbara was sitting opposite one of the better-known directors in Hollywood. I won't mention his name because he's still around. Anyway, at some point during dinner he looked over at Barbara and blurted, 'Tell me, how does it feel to have so much money?' Conversation at the table stopped as twenty-five pairs of eyes focused in Barbara's direction. Barbara slowly lowered a fork that was halfway to her lips, gave the director a bright smile, and replied, 'It's wonderful.' I wanted to raise her hand and shout, 'The Winnah!'"

The gentleman in question was not invited to a party Barbara herself threw in mid-January 1941. Herb Stein, writing for the *Hollywood Reporter*, noted that "hundreds of yards of white satin decorated with tiny white feathers draped the walls and ceilings of the house, and covered the café tables out by the pool that were centered with red roses in crystal vases. The waiters wore red-and-white color-coordinated uniforms. Two silver-stringed orchestras played until dawn. The hostess wore a shimmering gold Oriental gown and glimmering emeralds. Cary Grant wore his rosewood sun tan and familiar smile. They make a smashing couple, even by Hollywood standards. And they seem to know it."

Among the countless partygoers who drifted in and out of the vortex that evening were Jean Kennerley, Joan Moore (Lady Drogheda) and Patsy Latham (the sister of Lord Drogheda). This gracious trio and their three offspring were in the United States only because Barbara had persisted in her efforts to bring them over from England. Always extremely concerned, she had sent a succession of telegrams and other messages imploring them to escape London and come by the fastest means to America, to be her guests in California and to stay for as long as they liked.*

---

*During the war Barbara sent monthly checks to a number of friends residing in Europe, including Silvia de Castellane, who was then living in France. Cary Grant sent food packages and $100 a month to his mother in England, the maximum figure allowable by law.

Derry Moore, Joan's son, today a professional photographer in England, was a four-year-old when his mother took him to California in 1941. The trip was long and exhausting, and on first arriving, he took one look at Barbara and said, "I hate you!" With her customary sense of humor, Barbara responded, "I hate you, too!"

As things developed, Jean Kennerley remained with Barbara until 1942, when she rejoined her husband in England, leaving her daughter Diana with Morley's parents in Ohio. Joan Moore and Patsy Latham, finding it difficult to adjust to California's freewheeling lifestyle, settled in New York, where through Barbara's kindness and with the aid of small concert earnings by Joan, they and their sons (Derry Moore and Richard Latham) managed to outlast the war. The only mishap during this period occurred when Joan lost a $25,000 blue-mink coat Barbara had lent her for the winter. The coat, designed by Maximilian of New York, disappeared from a restaurant cloakroom, and the insurance company refused to reimburse Barbara on the grounds that it was not in her possession at the time of loss. "I only hope," said Barabara, refusing Joan's offer to make good on the coat, "that it fits its new owner."

On March 6, 1941, after untold delays, King Christian of Denmark sanctioned the divorce decree that officially terminated the marriage of Barbara Hutton and Court Reventlow. Barbara and Cary traveled to New York to celebrate the event with a small "victory dinner" at El Morocco. And that summer they vacationed together in Mexico. Cary drove down first, accompanied by Bert Taylor (Dorothy di Frasso's brother) and another friend, Danny Hunter. They stayed at Dorothy's newly leased hacienda in Mexico City. Barbara and Mrs. Hunter followed a week later and caught up with the group at the Hotel La Riviera in Acapulco. Barbara and Cary then went off by themselves to explore the Mexican countryside, unmolested for once by the press. But from the first day of Barbara's arrival in Mexico, neither she nor Grant made a move without being observed, and while they appear to have been unaware of this fact, they were trailed wherever providence took them by special agents of the Federal Bureau of Investigation.

The FBI investigation of Barbara Hutton (code named "Red Rose") originated with Dorothy di Frasso, whose connections to Mussolini and other influential members of the Italian Fascist high command aroused the Bureau's suspicions and gave them reason for concern. Mexico City, at the time a haven for international spy rings, smugglers and black-market operators, was considered a crucial listening post by the FBI because of its proximity to the United States. Dorothy di Frasso was of special interest to the Bureau not just because of her Italian connections but because she also had access to the leaders of the Hollywood film community. The initial report on Dorothy, filed from Los Angeles on September 9, 1941, contained at least one serious allegation and several of a more scurrilous nature:

> Subject reportedly now living in Mexico City, D.F. with ____ and ____, and from another source reportedly building a pretentious villa at Acapulco, Mexico, where she is often in company with ____. Subject has been out of the limelight in Hollywood society since May. She is notorious for her nymphomaniac propensities, lecherous parties, and publicity seeking; also for being close to MUSSOLINI. ____, together with subject, reportedly friendly with CARY GRANT and BARBARA HUTTON, and GRANT and HUTTON recently in Mexico City and presumed to have been subject's guests. Theory advanced by one informant that DI FRASSO may be financed by Mexican Government to draw Hollywood film stars to Mexico City....

While none of these charges was ever substantiated, Bureau operatives needed only to know that Dorothy di Frasso and Barbara Hutton were friends in order to launch an all-out investigation into Barbara's activities. A few weeks later a second "confidential" report was filed, again examining the Hutton-Di Frasso connection:

> ...It is reported that on or about December 15, 1940, COUNTESS DI FRASSO telephoned the Crown Prince of Italy in Rome at the request of BARBARA HUTTON. HUTTON's first cousin, JIMMY DONAHUE, arrested for petty fraud, was in an Italian prison. According to informant, King and Queen of Italy are permitted twenty releases of prisoners each New Year's Day, and DI FRASSO called Crown Prince on phone to request that he intercede in behalf of HUTTON's cousin. DONAHUE released on New Year's Day as favor to King upon payment by BARBARA HUTTON of a seventeen thousand dollar fine.*

Piecing together several hundred FBI documents released under the Freedom of Information Act, it appears that the Bureau used every means at its disposal to pursue the Hutton case. When Barbara and Cary stayed at the Hotel Reforma in Mexico City, their rooms were wired and the entire staff of the hotel was conscripted by the FBI to

---

*Jimmy Donahue was imprisoned in Milan for bouncing checks against a bank account he had previously closed. Such actions on his part were obviously not mandated by financial need.

keep an eye on the couple. Everyone Barbara and Cary saw or contacted in Mexico, including the fiery actress Lupe Velez (who happened to be a close friend of Jimmy Donahue's), was also open to scrutiny. Considering the time, energy and money expended by the FBI, very little in the way of meaningful information seems to have emerged. A summation of the Bureau's findings went to FBI director J. Edgar Hoover:

> ...The Bureau is aware of the fact that over the past six months BARBARA HUTTON has made several trips to Mexico City, staying at the Hotel Reforma. According to information developed by SIS [Secret Intelligence Service], subject has placed a number of radio-telephone calls from Mexico City to BARON VON CRAMM in Germany. VON CRAMM, a former Davis Cup tennis player and a close friend of the subject, was previously imprisoned in Germany for alleged homosexual acts. Information developed through censorship reveals that HUTTON was instrumental in gaining release of VON CRAMM through DR. H. FLEIRSCHBROTH, a cousin of VON CRAMM and a German diplomat stationed in Switzerland until last year. VON CRAMM now in German army. Information obtained by SIS is that HUTTON vacations in Mexico but now living in Beverly Hills and associates considerably with CARY GRANT and RICHARD GULLEY, a cousin of ANTHONY EDEN. Bureau could look into possibility of using VON CRAMM connection to discredit subject in press.

None of this proved anything beyond the fact that Barbara had twice intervened in cases involving people she knew—once on behalf of her cousin Jimmy Donahue, once on behalf of a friend, Baron Gottfried von Cramm. Even though the Bureau had no practical use for this information, someone decided to feed it surreptitiously to select members of the press. The purpose of the smear campaign against Barbara was never very clear—not even to the FBI. On July 7, 1942, exactly twenty-four hours before Barbara's marriage to Cary Grant, Washington correspondent Drew Pearson wrote a syndicated column drawing heavily on the FBI's files:

> Renowned Woolworth heiress Barbara Hutton has been trailed by Federal agents for months now because of secret transatlantic telephone calls she has placed to a certain "German Baron." Barbara, apparently deeply in love with this German sportsman, and not interested in his Nazi views, has made a practice of taking a private plane from Hollywood to Mexico, where she has made her calls. Barbara must not have known that every word she ever said or wrote to the Baron was being intercepted or recorded by Federal censors. But not long ago she either cooled off on the Nazi Baron or learned that he worked for the German government, for

she sent him a cable instructing him not to communicate with her anymore....

The actual events surrounding the Von Cramm affair bore little resemblance to Drew Pearson's rendition. The most glaring error in the Pearson story concerned Von Cramm's purported political alliances. The German sportsman, a national tennis hero in Germany at a time when tennis was being played on the front page, had been arrested by the Gestapo on March 15, 1938, following his return from a tennis tournament in Japan. He was charged with "pederasty" (for allegedly engaging in sexual relations with another male member of the German Davis Cup team). It was evident, however, that both the charge and arrest were politically motivated. Earlier in the year while playing tennis in Australia, Von Cramm had made derogatory comments about the Third Reich. His status as Germany's best tennis player lent weight and credence to his views, and it became necessary for Nazi officials to discredit him.

At his trial Von Cramm made a formal confession to the charges, blaming his homosexuality on an unhappy former marriage to a German noblewoman who undermined his self-esteem by engaging in extramarital affairs. Despite his admission he insisted that the sexual charge against him was mere subterfuge, that he was being persecuted not for his sexual leanings but for his avowed opposition to Adolf Hitler.

In rejecting Von Cramm's defense, the German court found him guilty as charged and sentenced him to a three-year prison term. The proceedings, according to an internationally renowned contingent of athletes, including Donald Budge and Joe DiMaggio, constituted nothing more than a kangaroo court. Released after serving a year of his term, Von Cramm was ordered to the Russian front as an enlisted man and later served in North Africa under Field Marshal Rommel, a fate he considered almost worse than death.

Angered by Pearson's irresponsible attack and the FBI's lamentable attempt to embarrass Barbara, Cary Grant went on record to say that he knew of Barbara's telephone calls and didn't question them: "The Baron is a very dear and old friend, and he is not a Nazi. Nor did Barbara instruct him not to communicate with her. In short, Mr. Pearson's story is a piece of Swiss cheese without the cheese."*

---

*It was Dr. H. Fleirschbroth, the German diplomat and a cousin of Gottfried von Cramm, with whom Barbara severed communications. Aware by then that she was being scrutinized by the FBI, she correctly reasoned that further correspondence with a German official could only be misconstrued as complicity with the enemy. She continued to write to Von Cramm throughout the war, getting her letters to him via the International Red Cross.

The Grant-Hutton marriage took place on July 8, 1942, at the Lake Arrowhead summer home of Frank W. Vincent, Cary's agent and business manager. A week before the ceremony the bridegroom changed his legal name from Archibald Leach to Cary Grant, and concurrently went through the final formality, initiated five years earlier, of becoming an American citizen. At his own instigation, he also signed a waiver relinquishing all future claims on Barbara's fortune in the event of a divorce.

The Reverend R. Paul Romeis, pastor of the English Lutheran Church in San Bernadino, conducted the marriage ceremony. It was held on a patio overlooking the lake. Madeleine Haseltine, a friend of Barbara's and the wife of the sculptor Herbert Haseltine, was matron of honor, while Frank Vincent attended the groom. Bill Robertson and Frank Horn, Cary's secretary, stood alongside. The compact wedding party was rounded out by Ticki Tocquet.

Barbara wore a navy-blue silk suit and cyclamen blouse designed by Stella Hanania; she held a bouquet of pink roses. Grant was attired in a gray-blue business suit and dark-blue tie; he wore a large pearl stick pin from Cartier, Barbara's wedding present.

There were no members of the press. John Miehle, an RKO staff photographer, took pictures; these were distributed to the media through RKO's publicity department. At the end of the ceremony, when the thirty-eight-year-old groom carried his twenty-nine-year-old bride over the threshold and into Frank Vincent's living room, Miehle captured the moment on film. The widely reproduced photograph led reporters to dub the pair "Cash 'n' Cary."

This was not the only newspaper reference to Barbara's wealth. Louella Parsons, less impressed by the romantic than by the economic implications of the union, began her next column: "In a marriage made in a bank, Cary Grant and Barbara Hutton, the first or second richest girl in the world, were wed yesterday in a secret ceremony at Lake Arrowhead."

In London a reporter for the *Daily Mail* interviewed one of Cary's Bristol relations and elicited an even more bitter commentary. "Now we can go into Woolworth's and have anything we like," said the relation, "provided we pay for it!"

Eleven

THE GRANT-HUTTON Hollywood connection pitted two subcultures of equal stature against each other: the motion picture celebrity versus international high society. Cary Grant summed up the dichotomy: "She preferred royalty—Prince Such-and-such, Countess So-and-so— while I preferred the movie buffs—David Niven, Jimmy Stewart, Rosalind Russell, Frederick Brisson." Still, for all its difficulties and disparities, Barbara's marriage to Grant provided her with a fleeting moment when the aimlessness of her life seemed to dissolve and her self-destructive urges seemed to dissipate. If Cary Grant was not the ultimate love object of Barbara's dreams, he nevertheless gave her the kind of unselfish guardianship that neither of her previous spouses had been able to provide.

"I was able to help in certain areas," Grant has said, "and not in others. I protected her from publicity during the time she was married to me, or tried. It was my idea to dismiss Steve Hannagan as her public relations expert. Hannagan was fine up to a point, but he had served his purpose and I felt that any future trouble could be easily handled."

Dispensing with Hannagan's services may have been a tactical blunder. Grant became so immersed in his role as Barbara's public defender that he tended to overlook his own coverage in the press. The Hollywood news corps, with a long-standing vendetta against Grant, had waited for years to nail him to the wall. His cool detachment, his persistent refusal to give extended interviews or sit still for photographers had never endeared him to the purveyors of trivia. Hollywood's golden boy was fair game, and with his marriage to "Miss Moneybags" (as one columnist described Barbara) the opportunity for revenge presented itself.

Albert Govoni, an early Grant biographer, points out that the actor was charged with a wide array of misdemeanors, the least of which were social climbing and fortune hunting. Some of the character assassins wondered in print whether Grant's "eagerness" to become an American citizen might not have been prompted by his desire to escape military service in his beleaguered homeland. The two most persistent rumors portrayed Grant as a miserable tightwad, and as a homosexual (or at least a bisexual).*

Had he elected to respond, Grant could no doubt have dispelled many, if not all, of these allegations. He might have pointed out, for example, that as early as 1940, following England's entry into the war, he and Sir Cedric Hardwicke, as representatives of the British Film colony in Hollywood, flew to Washington, D.C., for a meeting with Lord Lothian, the British ambassador, to solicit his advice on how best to serve the war effort. The ambassador felt that British stars like Grant and Hardwicke should remain in Hollywood, continue making films, and give their time and money to projects that would promote the British cause. Grant resumed his work in Hollywood and began making huge donations, ranging from $25,000 to $125,000, to British and, later, to American war relief organizations. In 1941, after the death of an uncle, aunt and cousin in a Bristol air raid, Grant turned over a check for $125,000 to the British War Relief Society, a substantial portion of his earnings from *The Philadelphia Story*. When he made *Arsenic and Old Lace* in 1944, he again gave a check to the society, this time for $100,000. Grant served on the Los Angeles committee of the British War Relief Society, which took the extremely practical step of sending over thousands of packets of seeds to the National Allotments Society for distribution in Great Britain, where, throughout the war, the population was encouraged to grow its own fruits and vegetables.

After the Japanese attack on Pearl Harbor and America's declaration of war, Grant volunteered for the Army Air Corps but was rejected because of his age. He continued his behind-the-scenes participation, performing in a Warner Bros. ten-minute short called "Road to Victory" to help promote the war drive. He toured GI service camps. He joined other Hollywood stars at war bond rallies and went on a three-week

*The only time Grant has publicly addressed himself to the gay rumor was in a 1977 *New York Times Magazine* profile by Warren Hoge. "It's ridiculous," said Grant, "but they say it about all of us."

whistle-stop entertainment tour to raise funds for the war. Bert Lahr had a renowned "Income Tax" sketch in which he used Grant as his straight man. It was said to be the troupe's most popular act.

Barbara did her part as well. She was the sole financial source for a U.S. Army medical clinic in San Francisco and another in Santa Barbara. She supported the Naval Aid Auxiliary canteen in San Pedro. She sent large sums of money to France Forever, an organization that helped arm the French underground. Her single most generous contribution was an anonymous check for $1 million to General Charles de Gaulle's Free French movement.

While the couple's acts of generosity received little publicity, there was no scarcity of talk about the luxurious lifestyle they chose to lead at a time when the rest of the nation was buckling under the oppressive weight of wartime austerity. The Grants had moved into Westridge, Douglas Fairbanks, Jr.'s, twelve-acre estate at 1515 Amalfi Drive in Pacific Palisades, overlooking the ocean bluffs of the Pacific on one side and Will Rogers' ranch on the other. The house, leased to the Grants when its owner went on active duty in the Naval Reserves, boasted the usual combination of comforts: swimming pool, tennis courts, sauna, five master-bedroom suites (the Grants slept in separate but adjoining bedrooms) and an impressive collection of signed eighteenth-century French furniture. Yet Fairbanks' pride and joy had been a Japanese-style garden of exotic and rare plants that he personally had spent hours cultivating. There was also a guest cottage on the property that the Grants used as quarters for their servants. But since they had more servants than space, they were forced to rent three additional houses in the surrounding area to accommodate them all. The Grants employed three in the pantry, three in the kitchen, one butler, one footman, one houseman, two in the laundry, four in the nursery, two chauffeurs, a valet, two personal maids, two chambermaids, a secretary/bookkeeper, two security guards, a gardener, a gardener's helper, a masseur/exercise boy and Barbara's companion Ticki Tocquet: twenty-nine in all.

The large staff consumed vast supplies and cost an enormous amount of money to support. Cary was convinced that the household could be kept afloat with fewer personnel. "The servants had so many shifts to feed at mealtime," he complained, "that Barbara and I were lucky to get a sandwich." Cary constantly nagged about the backstairs overhead: the "staggering" bills for their electricity, gasoline, food— even for such items as soap and toiletries. Although Barbara assumed the brunt of the household expenses, the costs brought out Grant's

The Source: Woolworth window displays attracted
customers in droves and made F.W. Woolworth one
of the wealthiest men of his time.

Mr. and Mrs. F.W.
Woolworth at Palm Beach,
1913. At far right is their
younger daughter, Jessie.
(UPI)

"Hutton-tots"—Brothers E.F. Hutton (left) and Franklyn Laws Hutton (Barbara's father) attend a Roaring Twenties costume party. Between them stands Barbara's aunt Marjorie Merriweather Post. *(UPI)*

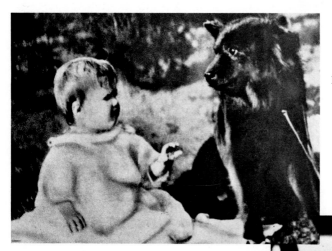

Barbara at one.

At the age of three, Barbara Hutton would clench a chubby fist and keep a firm grip on her possessions. *(UPI)*

Barbara, still unfashionably plump, in the south of France, 1929.

Elsa Maxwell, whose unconventional parties were all the rage, arrives in New York in 1937 aboard the S.S. *Bremen*. With her is Saga, her boxer dog. *(Wide World)*

The Woolworth Building, designed by Cass Gilbert and built in 1913, was F.W. Woolworth's pride and joy. For many years it was the world's tallest building and it remains a prestigious address.

Barbara Hutton, age twenty-three, through the
camera of George Hoyningen-Heune. *(Courtesy
Lilian K. Gardiner)*

Barbara with first husband, Prince Alexis Mdivani,
at Roehampton Polo Club near London. The
marriage was already on the verge of collapse.
(Wide World)

Barbara in the gown she wore at her
marriage to Alexis Mdivani.

Barbara in Egypt, 1935. *(Courtesy Lilian K. Gardiner)*

Jimmy Donahue dancing in the Sahara, 1935. *(Courtesy Lilian K. Gardiner)*

Princess Barbara Mdivani receives a handshake from her father, as she arrives from Europe aboard the S.S. *Europa* in 1934. On either side of her stand her stepmother, Irene Hutton, and her cousin Jimmy Donahue. *(Bettmann Archive)*

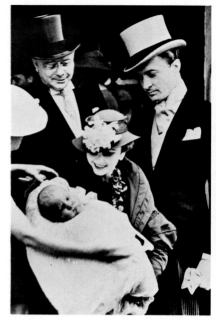

Count and Countess Haugwitz-Reventlow with their fifteen-week-old son, Lance, leaving their home in London for the baptism at the chapel of Marlborough. *(UPI)*

Count and Countess Haugwitz-Reventlow. *(U*

Woolworth sales girls haunted and taunted Barbara throughout her life. Here they carry placards following her renunciation of American citizenship in 1937. *(UPI)*

A portrait of Barbara by Russian artist Savely Sorine, Beverly Hills, 1940.

At the beginning of the custody battle between Barbara and Count Reventlow over Lance, Barbara hired security guards and private detectives to protect the child. He is shown here arriving in Palm Beach at the age of three. *(UPI)*

Barbara and Bobby Sweeny at the Everglades Club in Palm Beach, January 1940. *(UPI)*

Barbara's short-lived affair with billionaire Howard Hughes led her to write, "I've never met a less materialistic man." *(Wide World)*

Cary Grant and Barbara on their wedding day, July 10, 1942. At right is Ticki Tocquet, Barbara's longtime companion. *(UPI)*

Barbara knitting sweaters and socks to raise money for the Allied cause during World War II. *(UPI)*

Code letter from Lance to Barbara showing how he was supposedly being turned against his father. First lines read: "To hell with my father. I hope he drops dead." *(Wide World)*

Barbara in St. Moritz with husband number four, Prince Igor Troubetzkoy. *(Bettmann Archive)*

Playboy-diplomat Porfirio Rubirosa gives Barbara a peck as her son, Lance, looks on during a press conference in New York, December 30, 1953. Their marriage—her fifth, his fourth—lasted just fifty-three days and netted the groom millions. *(UPI)*

Zsa Zsa Gabor sports an eye-patch to cover the black eye Rubirosa gave her. She holds a photograph of Rubi and Barbara on their wedding day. "Barbara looks like she's on a death march," she commented. "Maybe she should have worn white." *(UPI)*

A somewhat polluted Barbara on the Lido with sixth husband, former German tennis ace Baron Gottfried von Cramm (standing). She had good reason to be drunk: the marriage was never consummated. *(Bettmann Archive)*

Barbara dances with Cecil Beaton at Charlie Bestegui's masked ball at the Palazzo Labia in Venice. The press called it "the party of the century." *(Wide World)*

Lance Reventlow, right, with his best friend, Bruce Kessler. *(Courtesy Nina Kessler)*

James Dean once spent a night with Barbara at the Beverly Hills Hotel. "It seemed the right and natural thing to do," she wrote in her notebooks. *(Wide World)*

At many of Barbara's parties in Tangier the guests dressed in drag. Here she dances with David Herbert, second son of the Earl of Pembroke, who is dressed as Ira Belline. The real Ira Belline is in background. *(Courtesy David Herbert)*

Maurice Doan, Barbara, and Raymond Doan, her seventh and last husband, pose in ceremonial costume at Sidi Hosni, Barbara's palace in the Kasbah. *(Courtesy Jean Mendiboure.)*

ot long after her forty-ninth irthday, Barbara posed for a friend, med British photographer Cecil eaton *(Forbes Magazine ollection)*

"Sumiya"—translation: "little house on the
corner"—was Barbara's $3.5 million Japanese-style
mansion in Cuernavaca, Mexico. *(Courtesy James
Douglas)*

Barbara Hutton (wearing tiara) and he
formally attired guests watch a belly
dancer perform at Sidi Hosni. Graham
Mattison, Barbara's business advisor,
is seated at her feet. Behind him, in
white dinner jacket, is Lloyd Frankli
the love of Barbara's life. *(Courtesy
David Herbert)*

James Douglas, eighteen years Barbara's
junior, was her constant traveling companion
from 1957 to 1960. (*Courtesy James Douglas*)

Haggard-looking sixty-year-old Barbara
Hutton with her latest beau, twenty-
four-year-old Spanish matador, Angel
Teruel. 1972. (*Wide World*)

Barbara's Australian bodyguard, Colin Frazer, carries her out of the Plaza Athénée in Paris into a waiting limousine. The ailing heiress is about to leave Europe for the last time. *(Wide World)*

The Woolworth mausoleum in Woodlawn Memorial Cemetery, New York City, where Barbara's body was interred.

worst fears and furies—fear of poverty, and fury over the staff's extravagance.

When they weren't squabbling over the number of employees at Westridge, the Grants seemed to enjoy themselves. They became more social, attending parties, visiting friends, going to the theater and the movies. They went to the benefit premier of *The Talk of the Town*, starring Grant, Jean Arthur, Ronald Colman and Edgar Buchanan. They attended a musical benefit at the Los Angeles Philharmonic Auditorium featuring Arthur Rubinstein and Joseph Szigeti performing selections from Mozart. They were invited to a tenth-anniversary dinner party for the Arthur Rubinsteins and were frequent guests at the home of Charles and Elsie Mendl. There were also a number of outings with Lance—tours of the old Hollywood movie lots, the San Diego Zoo, the Farmer's Market and occasional drives in the country.

When she was in good form Barbara could be great fun. She loved word games and code names and often invented her own. The word "Wiebo," for example, meant "Will it ever be over?" One of her patented phrases was the name "Eddie Koch," which was a signal she used on the telephone to alert the other party that people were present and she couldn't speak freely. She might answer the phone and say, "Oh, so you say you saw Eddie Koch yesterday?"—and that was the tip-off. She identified days of the week not by name but by color. Monday was mauve, Tuesday was green, Wednesday was red, and so on. "I feel so mauve today," she would say at the beginning of the week, dressing and behaving accordingly.

"Barbara had a wonderful word for anything that lacked taste," recalls Grant. "'My God, isn't that *ig*,' she'd say. We were once guests in an Italian villa in Hollywood. The house was in good taste except for one thing—there was a huge pink bar that stretched across one whole end of the living room. The owner was exceptionally proud of it, and she finally said, 'Don't you just love the bar?' There was a pause, and then I said, 'Yes, it's so wonderfully *ig*.' Well, I tell you, Barbara went ape. She staggered around the room shrieking with delight and she was still doubled up with laughter when we reached the car."*

After a while the Grants began talking about having children. Several months of unsuccessful attempts convinced them to seek professional counsel. They went to a Hollywood specialist, a leading internist

---

*One version of this anecdote is related in *Notorious Divorces* (1976), by Edward Z. Epstein.

named Jack Hollins.* Dr. Hollins ran a battery of tests to determine whether the removal of her right ovary following the birth of Lance had anything to do with the problem. The test results were inconclusive and Hollins recommended that the couple try artificial insemination. He also put Barbara on estrogen, advised her to give up smoking and alcohol, and to do regular exercises. She complied with his instructions but was unable to conceive, and in time they stopped trying.

Those who knew Cary Grant could attest to his utter dejection. He placed the blame not on Barbara, but rather on the medical profession. It was Grant's contention that his wife "had been cut to ribbons" long before he knew her. In Grant's opinion, Barbara's money was incentive enough for doctors to want to perform surgery at once. They would take one look at her and immediately wheel her into the operating room.

Count Court Haugwitz-Reventlow had arrived in the United States on July 31, 1940, and spent most of his first year at Sun Valley, Idaho. Graham Mattison paid Court a courtesy call to assure him that Barbara had every intention of remaining on friendly terms. As a demonstration of good will she sent Lance to Sun Valley, and father and son spent several months getting reacquainted.

On July 30, 1942, three weeks after Barbara became Mrs. Cary Grant, Reventlow married Margaret (Peggy) Astor Drayton, a slim and vivacious artist whose great-grandmother was the very social and rich Mrs. William Astor (her Astor family ties made Peggy a second cousin of Louise Van Alen). Following their marriage, Court and Peggy rented a cottage on the grounds of the Huntington Hotel in Pasadena, California. Lance was enrolled by Barbara in an elementary school in Westwood and lived half the year at Westridge, half the year at the Huntington Hotel.

Peggy Reventlow (today Mrs. Peggy Brent) recalls how spoiled the boy was by his mother. "His luggage was always filled with tailored suits

*Dr. Jack Hollins is a pseudonym. It should be noted, however, that in the original version of *Poor Little Rich Girl* (1983), the author inadvertently referred here (and elsewhere in the book) to a California-based physician named Dr. Edward A. Kantor, Dr. Kantor, born in 1929 and graduated from the Univ. of Nebraska Medical School in 1954, maintains that he treated Barbara Hutton only between 1969 and 1975, and that "numerous other doctors attended her during that time as well." Other references were made in the original edition describing Dr. Kantor as having prescribed excessive drugs for Ms. Hutton, which Dr. Kantor insists was not the case. Another reference in the original edition notes that Dr. Kantor gave an interview concerning details of his confidential medical treatment of Ms. Hutton to Dean Jennings for use in his 1968 biography of Barbara. Dr. Kantor insists that he has never given an interview about the confidential medical treatment of any patient of his.

and frilly imported shirts." Lance had a gold jewelry case that contained solid gold cuff links and tie clasps from Cartier. At the bottom of one of his suitcases she found a wad of currency, totaling several thousand dollars. To her dismay, she also discovered a name tag sewn into each article of clothing that read "LANCE GRANT."

"My husband was insulted," she says, "because Lance was *his* son, not Cary Grant's." The Reventlows detected a number of telltale signs that Lance was being affected by the constant shifting to and fro. He was more moody than usual and was given to using foul language much of the time. He also suffered severe bouts of asthma and was thus absent from school far more than he should have been.

When Court Reventlow complained to Barbara over the telephone that Lance was missing too much school, she laughed it off. She blamed his use of foul language on Lance's youth and attributed the faulty laundry tags to a printer's error.

"The truth of the matter," according to Peggy, "is that Barbara blew hot and cold. One day she cared about her son, the next day she didn't. She spent time with him only when it suited her. I remember the first time I bathed him. He said, 'Why are you bathing me, Mommy? My real mother never does. The governess does it.'"

One day when Lance was staying with his father, Court picked up an extension telephone and heard the boy conferring with his mother. They were discussing a "secret code" that Lance had devised to be used in future letters home.

Barbara inquired whether Lance had told Binky* about the code, and when he said he hadn't, she responded, "Well, don't. We'll keep it to ourselves."

Several days later while tidying Lance's bedroom, Peggy Reventlow found a copy of the code and showed it to her husband. It was a simple code, consisting mostly of dots, dashes and circles. The next time Lance wrote to his mother, Court opened the letter. The first two coded lines read: "To hell with my father. I hope he dies."

After making a copy of the note, Reventlow posted the original and awaited Barbara's response. When it came he again intercepted it. "Darling Lance," it began. "Thank you for your very nice letter which I

---

*Binky was the nickname of Court's stepdaughter Alida, Peggy Reventlow's child by her first husband, Pierre VanLaer. Binky was eighteen months younger than Lance, and after Lance joined the household they shared a succession of governesses, including a Miss Gapen, a Mme. Malnuit and a Miss Grant. Miss Grant later became a governess to Hope Cooke, who married the Crown Prince of Sikkim. Miss Grant had a habit of stripping Lance bare, standing him in the bathtub and beating him with a coat hanger when he couldn't remember the words to the Lord's Prayer.

enjoyed a lot. I got a good laugh out of your coded message! You must write me some more like that..." Barbara ended with news of the family dog and the notation: "General [Cary Grant] sends his best love."* As a postscript she included her own coded message in the form of a limerick: "There once was a fellow named Court Who was a most peculiar sort He wanted a wife and he wanted a son But lost them both and bought a gun And that seems pretty dumb."

The situation was further aggravated by the appearance in *Photoplay* of a profile of Barbara by Louella Parsons, quoting her as saying that her son wanted to be known as Lance Grant, which helped explain the nametag confusion. Reventlow took the article and the letters to a Los Angeles attorney, Joseph L. Lewinson, who examined the material and then wrote to Barbara on behalf of his client:

Dear Madam:

Court Reventlow has submitted evidence to us as his counsel, showing that while Lance Reventlow was in your household you neglected his health, education and religious instruction, and undertook to poison his mind against his father. Also that when Lance was living in his father's home you endeavored to prejudice the child against Mrs. Peggy Reventlow and to undermine his respect for his father. Included in the materials submitted to us are copies of correspondence partially written in code and containing harsh language. It appears, from an examination of this material, that you encouraged your son to continue such correspondence.

Count Reventlow has also submitted a recent article from *Photoplay*, written by Louella Parsons, in which you are quoted as saying that Lance is devoted to your present husband and wishes to be known as Lance Grant, that you bought your divorce from Count Reventlow for several million dollars and that at the time of your marriage Count Reventlow took advantage of the love you then bore him to renounce your American citizenship.

We have been instructed to notify you that Count Reventlow will not suffer you to go on prejudicing...and undermining your son's respect for his father. We have also been instructed to notify you that Count Reventlow demands you retract the untrue and libelous statements above referred to, and, inasmuch as this is not the first time you have published

---

*In addition to the family dog, Barbara also had a large Mexican myna bird. According to one visitor, the bird did a mean imitation of Cary Grant and knew the beginning of an old Cockney ballad Grant used to sing: "Good bye-ee, don't cry-ee, wipe a tear, baby dear, from your eye-ee ..." When Barbara moved away from California after the war, she gave the bird to Merle Oberon. It was Barbara who gave Cary Grant his nickname (General), a play on General Ulysses S. Grant.

or inspired untrue and libelous statements, demand is further made that you give assurances against repetition of such statements and charges....*

When Barbara failed to answer Lewinson's brief, he wrote again and elicited a similar response. He finally advised Reventlow to sue Barbara, claiming that she was an unfit mother and therefore demanding that Lance be left permanently in his father's care.

This time Barbara acted, hiring the celebrated Hollywood attorney Jerry Giesler to represent her. Giesler countersued, charging Reventlow with malicious harassment and asking the court to terminate his income from the $1.5 million trust fund established by Barbara for Lance's maintenance. Giesler wrote separately to Lewinson proposing a dramatic out-of-court settlement: "My client is prepared to pay Count Haugwitz-Reventlow the sum of $3 million to abrogate the original custody agreement and to step out of Lance's life forever." The offer was brusquely rejected.

Reventlow, however, was unnerved by the vastness of Barbara's wealth and the knowledge that when she set her mind to it, she was capable of almost anything. He began to consider seriously the consequences of facing her in a court of law, with Lance's fate hanging in the balance. Mulling the matter over, he decided to take matters into his own hands. On June 27, 1944, a few days before Lance was slated to be returned to his mother, Court Reventlow piled his wife, his eight-year-old son, and his stepdaughter into a station wagon and drove to Canada, stopping only when he reached Vancouver.

News of Reventlow's departure spread quickly. Barbara shut off her telephone and said nothing, while Giesler went out of his way to make noise. Following an abrasive press conference at which he branded Reventlow "a child stealer," he approached California District Attorney Fred Howser and asked that a warrant be issued for Reventlow's arrest. "What's the charge?" asked Howser. "Kidnapping," said Giesler. Howser reminded the attorney that a parent couldn't be charged with kidnapping his own child. The matter was out of his hands, and he advised Giesler to pursue the case through the Canadian courts.

₰

Even without the added strain of the post-divorce tug of war over Lance, it was evident that the romance between Barbara and Cary was beginning to lose much of its initial glitter. There was arguing and

*Photocopies of Lewinson's letter, as well as those of Barbara and Lance, were provided to the author by Wide World Photos.

bitterness in the rented estate on Amalfi Drive, some of it the result of an almost daily barrage of news-provoking events, of which the custody battle was only one small part.

Two other incidents created a stir. The first occurred while the Grants were away in San Francisco. In their absence Barbara's butler, Eric Gosta, while tending bar at an Errol Flynn party, became involved in a fist fight with James Fleming, Flynn's movie stand-in. When the Grants returned to Los Angeles they found Gosta in the hospital with a fractured skull. It seems that in the course of the fight somebody had hit Gosta over the head with a hammer. The fact that the victim was Barbara's employee was reason enough for the press to give the incident front-page attention.

The second event brought the Grants face to face with their old nemesis, the FBI. It came to light that a loquacious young Latin visitor to California was given a responsible position in a Los Angeles bank because he had been recommended by the Grants and had in his possession a glowing letter from Barbara. He turned out to be a German agent, and when the FBI bearded him the Grants admitted that they had been taken in. He had been sent to them by a friend in Mexico. The friend, who also claimed to have been duped, was none other than Dorothy di Frasso.

Such episodes frustrated Grant, who gradually came to believe that his wife purposely sought publicity, that she enjoyed the notoriety. He feared that further coverage of this sort would have a deleterious effect on his film career, and he began to understand that as long as he was married to Barbara he would be a meal ticket for every gossip-minded reporter in Hollywood. Yet there were other problems in the marriage, and many of these were of his own making.

Dudley Walker, Cary's valet during these years, provides ample testimony to some of the internal struggles that were slowly pulling the couple apart; in general, Walker's views echo those held by many other members of the household staff. "I don't care how many six-figure donations Grant made to the war effort, he was stingy as hell," claims Walker. "Here's somebody who never in his life picked up a tab in a restaurant, if he could help it. And if he did, he'd spend an hour recalculating the waiter's figures. He ran around the house turning off lights to save electricity. When he discarded his shirts, he cut off the buttons first. He claimed it was because his shirts were made with a particular kind of button and he wanted to save them to replace buttons that fell off of other shirts. The truth is that he was too cheap to enjoy his own wealth.

"He had these four silver-veined crystal liquor bottles, and he used to put little marks on the bottle to see if anyone was knocking it off behind his back. It was all Barbara's liquor, anyway. She was paying ten dollars for tea and ten dollars for bacon and ten dollars for chicken from some guy out here on the Strip who was black market. The pantry bill alone, what with help, came to thirty-five hundred dollars a month, and all that was being paid by her. But Grant was still worrying about it. He begrudged the help every bottle of Coke they took from the pantry. His rule was no soda between meals, only with your meal. If he caught you drinking a soda, he docked it out of your pay.

"Then there were the newspapers. Grant would come home from the studio at night, park his car in the garage, and on the patio he'd wade through five copies each of the *Herald-Examiner* and the New York *Times*. He'd be cussing before he even stepped into the house. 'Now, why in hell does each servant have to have his own copy of the paper?' Well, in those days you were paying something like two dollars a month for home delivery. There was one copy for Barbara, one for Grant, one for Ticki, one for the nursery, and one for the help. In big houses in England or on Long Island there was always a paper for the help. But Grant wouldn't hear of it. 'If the help want a newspaper, they can bloody well buy their own.' And with that, he went ahead and canceled our one subscription.

"Half of it with Grant was a question of appearance. It didn't look right for Barbara to be driving around in a Rolls during the war. It didn't look right to live in such luxury. When he was living at 1038 Ocean Drive—this was before he and Barbara were married—he'd go down to the nearest Army canteen and shake everyone's hand, and when he met someone down there, some young officers or something, he'd say, 'Oh yes, come and see me, come and see me at my house.' And when they came around he'd lock himself in his bedroom. 'Could we see Mr. Grant?' they'd ask. And I'd have to say, 'I'm sorry, he isn't here just now.' And I couldn't even offer the poor fellow a bottle of beer.

"But Barbara was extraordinarily generous—about everything. She's the only reason the help stayed. She made a point of giving beautiful Christmas boxes every year, also at Easter and on your birthday. Four-hundred-dollar watches for all the help, and she'd say, 'Don't put them in the drawer, wear them.' She gave the maids and pantry girls dresses and jewelry. It was all designer stuff. She'd let them have her dresses from the party the night before. She wasn't at all stuffy that way. She once gave me some very special heavy gold cuff links from Gump's in San Francisco. Grant saw them and said, 'You don't have to do that,

Barbara. You don't have to give Dudley anything. He's my man. I will give Dudley something.' So he collared my links and gave me an old cheap pair that Bugsy Siegel once gave him as a gift. Can you beat that? You were lucky with Grant if he gave you a five-dollar bottle of men's cologne once a year for Christmas. Barbara thought it was disgraceful. She sent us to the best restaurants on our days off and let us sign the checks over to her.

"She was entirely out of his class. He would sit at dinner and eat and put his fingers in his mouth and suck his fingers. He would eat very heavily, and Barbara would barely touch her food. And he was a bad drinker. He would get real nasty and cold. He would become sadistic. He could be a terrible bastard, that one."

By the end of 1943, with his marriage eroding, Grant threw himself into his work. Over the next year he appeared in five major motion pictures: *Mr. Lucky, Destination Tokyo; Once Upon a Time; None But the Lonely Heart; Arsenic and Old Lace.* The first of these, *Mr. Lucky,* was written by Milton Holmes, a former instructor at the Beverly Hills Tennis Club. Bill Robertson, who knew both Barbara and Holmes, apparently suggested that he show the script to Grant. What Grant saw in it was an opportunity to play a draft-dodging gangster who loads the dice against a war relief agency until a determined heiress educates him in the ways of righteousness and the war effort. The story appealed not only to Grant but to RKO, which bought the script and then set out to produce it.

Charles Turner, an RKO executive, immediately hit upon the idea of casting Barbara Hutton in the role of the regal heiress. In Turner's opinion Barbara was a natural—attractive, sensitive, a person with the ability to create dramatic tension. Whether she could act or not seemed secondary; it was her name and image that Turner hoped to utilize.

Barbara, recalling her performance ten years earlier as "The Spirit of Adventure" at Madison Square Garden, was enthusiastic. Cary was not. "I can't see it," he told Turner. "She doesn't need the work, and frankly, I don't need the aggravation." The heiress role in *Mr. Lucky* went to Laraine Day, the future Mrs. Leo Durocher.

"While Cary was at the studio all day, Barbara had nothing to do," says Frederick Brisson. "She began saying that the marriage would never last. She wanted someone to be at home all the time. It was a shame, because Cary loved her. And he was a good influence. Barbara blossomed at the beginning of their marriage. She gained confidence. She no longer felt pangs of guilt because she had money and others didn't. He gave her perhaps the best time she ever had. He was absolutely sweet to her. Until Cary came along, I don't think Barbara was ever exposed to the real world. In the real world every marriage has its ups and downs. In the real world people go out and earn a living. But for some reason she rejected the real world. She wanted to inhabit a world of her own creation, a world of unicorns and winged white horses."

Barbara's friends had initially believed that being married to a serious and hardworking actor would have a stabilizing effect. But Barbara was bored by the discipline required to maintain her husband's career. In the past and in the future she always settled money on the men she married to relieve them of the tedium of honest labor. It was possible, even probable, that she preferred a nonworking husband. Grant was the one notable exception, the only husband she ever had who earned his own keep. He didn't need his wife's financial support, which eliminated the possibility that she could ever rule him merely by dint of her money.

Out of boredom as much as frustration Barbara suddenly became a heavy drinker. Frederick Brisson recalls that one day she would have straight tomato juice for lunch, and the next day straight gin or vodka. On one occasion when she could find nothing else in the house, she downed half a bottle of white vinegar. "I don't know if she can accurately be described as an alcoholic," says Brisson, "but in ordinary social terms she drank too much. And because she had difficulty sleeping she was on tranquilizers. The two together screwed her up. Cary said that she hadn't slept with him in months. And when they had made love, she didn't want her hair messed up."

In the middle of her latest troubles Barbara became involved in what one journalist described as a "warm human-interest story." When Simone Chibleur, her devoted personal maid, and Harry Leach, her chauffeur, decided to marry, it was Barbara who made the arrangements, including a lavish reception at Westridge with herself and her friend Renée de Becker as co-hostesses. The guests were maids and second maids, butlers and chauffeurs and other servants from the great estates of Hollywood, four hundred of them to be exact, and Barbara and Renée walked around serving caviar and champagne. Her wedding present to the couple was a check for $10,000, and when they left on their honeymoon she and Renée rolled up their sleeves, donned aprons and washed most of the dishes themselves, claiming that it wouldn't be fair to have the staff go into the kitchen after their own party.

This wasn't the only gala held at Westridge. Shortly after the wedding reception, Barbara began giving nightly dinner parties of an inordinately elaborate nature. One of Cary Grant's friends says of these formal affairs, "What was on the table was sometimes different, but what was on the chairs was always the same. Barbara surrounded herself with a consortium of fawning parasites—European titles, broken-down Hollywood types, a maharajah or two, a sheik, the military, several English peers, a few tennis bums and a throng of faggots. Barbara developed a reputation as a 'fag hag.' She was fascinated and perplexed by homosexuality, and it became a constant theme in her life. It was an ego trip to have them groveling at her feet. Cary didn't care for Barbara's crowd because he knew she was keeping most of them. She fed them, clothed them, gave them money. Grant has been quoted as saying, "If one more phony earl had entered the house, I'd have suffocated."

At the Grant-Hutton divorce trial in 1945, Barbara testified that "Mr. Grant and I did not have the same friends. Mr. Grant did not like my home, and on more than one occasion when I had a dinner party and invited friends, he refused to come down because he was too bored. He had his food sent up to his room with the excuse that he had to learn his lines for the next day's shooting, or had to work on his scrapbooks. My friends at dinner would ask where he was, and I would have to make some excuse, which was very embarrassing. When he did come down, he obviously didn't look amused, and they could see it, and I could see it. That was embarrassing too. It made me nervous, and I had to get treatment from a physician."

Barbara spared the court some of the more explicit details. But there was one dinner party at which each foreign guest was served the dish most popular in his or her homeland. This banquet irked Grant; at the start of the meal he purportedly entered the room, and in his loudest Cockney blared, "Now, Hi comes from Lime'ouse, and Hi's just a bloody Cockney. Where's me fish 'n' chips?"

Another story has it that he attended one of his wife's affairs on a pair of stilts, thumping into the drawing room and announcing to the upper-crust gathering, "Hm—cold as a witch's tit down there, ain't it?"

Dean Jennings reports both incidents and though Grant claims to remember neither of them, he has admitted being fed up with his wife's dinner parties. He was up early and at the studio all day, and when he returned home in the evening he was in no mood to host a formal dinner. He wanted to relax with his wife and maybe listen to the radio. But by the time he arrived home, Barbara was ready for her evening's entertainment.

One of the more distinguished guests at Barbara's gatherings was the French-born fashion designer Oleg Cassini, at the time a second lieutenant in the U.S. Cavalry and the husband of actress Gene Tierney.

Arriving in the United States from Italy in 1937, Oleg—possessing the title of count—was briefly married to cough-drop heiress Merry "Madcap" Fahrney. When that marriage ended, he gravitated to Hollywood for a short-lived career as a movie costume designer.*

Tall, gaunt, ascetic-looking, with high cheekbones and a drooping mustache, Cassini cut an impressive figure in his military uniform with his gold-braided parade jacket, riding breeches and knee-high boots. He wore his uniform to one of Barbara's parties, prompting her to introduce him to another guest, a three-star general, as "Leftenant Count Cassini," in the British fashion, because she considered it chic.

Barbara's conversation that evening was jumpy, a constant flitting from one topic to another: Paris, polo ponies, the war. At one point she drew Oleg aside and proceeded to shower him with compliments. She saw in him all the qualities she admired in a man: intelligence, sensitivity, breeding. "American men don't understand me," she said. "Europeans are more sophisticated, more aware. And Englishmen are like American men—they have a childish mentality, they're completely self-absorbed."

Cassini had no inkling what Barbara was driving at, or where the conversation was going.

"What I'm about to say," she continued, "I mean not as a pleasantry, but to be taken seriously. You and I understand each other. We share the same philosophy and ideas. For too long I've been involved with all the wrong people. You could make me happy, Oli. Why don't you marry me?" She said it as though she were inviting him for a cup of coffee. He was shocked.

"You look surprised," said Barbara. "But I mean it. I've never been more serious."

"I believe you," said Cassini, slowly regaining his composure. "But it's so sudden. I hardly know what to say."

"Then don't say anything," said Barbara. "We'll discuss it another day."

When it was time for Oleg to leave, Barbara waited with him for his car. He heard nothing more for the next three weeks. Then one afternoon she called and asked him to meet her that evening at an address in Beverly Hills. When he arrived he found himself in a cozy, candlelit *pied-à-terre*, a high-ceilinged flat with things draped and dripping and sparkling darkly in the flickering light. Needlework cushions, inlaid tapestries, embroidered fabrics covered furniture and

---

*Oleg's younger brother, Igor Cassini, was Maury Paul's successor as the Hearst newspaper syndicate's new Cholly Knickerbocker.

walls. On the marble mantle over the fireplace were precious Chinese ceramics. A tangle of plants, flowers, reeds, were arranged in the bays formed by a series of tall windows.

Before taking a seat, Barbara lit a stick of sandalwood incense and slipped it into a holder on the mantle. She placed a stack of records on the record player. For the next hour, with a dulcimer chiming discreetly in the background, she read to Oleg from a thick sheaf of her own poetry. When she was done she set out a quiche and a bottle of Moët for her guest, and a glass of mineral water for herself. She was curled into a couch now and was talking about poetry and how she had found solace in the work of certain poets like Tagore. At some point it occurred to Cassini that the evening was passing and nothing was coming of it. Then there was a lull in the conversation and Cassini reached for her hand. He held it and stared into her eyes. She stared back. As he leaned forward to embrace her she suddenly began talking again, this time about marriage. She had everything figured out. First she and Cary would get divorced; then she would give Gene Tierney $1 million; Gene and Oleg would get divorced; finally Barbara and Oleg would ride off into the sunset together.

Although nothing came of the fantasy, Oleg thought he understood the motivation behind it. "Most of us, when we need a lift," reflects Cassini, "go out and buy a new suit, a new car—or we might even redecorate the den. But this didn't work for Barbara, for when you can buy anything, buying is no fun unless perhaps you buy the ultimate— another person.

"Men were the chief stimulus in Barbara's life. She bought and sold them, bartered them or replaced them in much the same way a stockbroker operates on the Exchange. She was always 'in love' with several men, but real love to her was that greatest of rarities, a true romantic friendship that somehow transcended sexuality. She divided men into two groups—those she loved and those she took to bed. Her marriages were essentially sexless, and her affairs were bereft of love. Her inability to combine the two forces in one man was what kept her going from husband to husband. By some miracle of fate she hoped to find her knight in shining armor, he was always just beyond reach."

What the Grants had once shared and mutually enjoyed was now carefully divided into "his" and "hers." It was as though the Great Wall of China ran through their house, cutting it down the middle. They existed separately, dined separately, entertained separately, slept separately. Finally in April 1944, Grant gathered his bags and moved into a guest cottage owned by the Brissons. It was to be an abbreviated estrangement. After two days Rosalind Russell invited Barbara over for dinner, Barbara and Cary wound up spending the night in Frederick Brisson's bedroom, while he moved in with Rosalind. The next morning when Brisson went to his room to get a pair of socks, he found Barbara alone in bed. Then he went into the bathroom and there was Grant asleep on the floor. Stepping over the sleeping body, Brisson picked up a toothbrush and returned to his wife's room. "I think we're in trouble again," he told her.*

But the Grants returned to Westridge, and Barbara rewarded Rosalind Russell's efforts in reconciling them by giving her a gold bracelet, three inches wide and covered with diamonds, priced at $40,000. The most famous couple in Hollywood resumed their erratic relationship. They were seen together at several parties, including Elsa Maxwell's spectacular bash celebrating the liberation of Paris. Party-goers were shocked by Barbara's appearance. She was grossly underweight and worn-out looking. During the entire party she and Grant barely spoke two words to each other.

"In general," recalls Frederick Brisson, "Barbara and Cary appeared to have a real love-hate thing going. When he was around; she hated him. When he was away, she couldn't bear to be without him."

🐚

Barbara spent the afternoon of August 14 rearranging some living-room furniture with the help of Dudley Walker. They were hanging paintings when Grant walked in. He took one look at the wall and snarled, "No Barbara, that is not what I want. I don't like that." Then he stalked out.

Barbara put her arms around Dudley and started to cry. The valet tried to console her. "Oh, don't cry. Don't take any notice of him," he said, patting her head.

An hour later she was sitting at the piano. Grant was in his study drinking rum and looking over a film script. When Dudley saw the houseman come down the stairs carrying one of Barbara's suitcases, he went to find his employer.. "Mr. Grant, sir, your wife is crying and has packed a bag," he said. "Why don't you put your arms all around her and be nice to her?"

Grant slowly lifted his head. "Why don't you mind your own goddamn business!" he growled.

*Rosalind Russell related this anecdote in her autobiography, *Life Is a Banquet* (1977).

"All right, all right," said Dudley. "I was only trying to help."

By the time the valet returned to the living room Barbara and her suitcase were gone. Without telling anyone where she was going, she moved into Bill Robertson's house on Magnolia Drive in Beverly Hills, recently refurnished by Barbara with rare Chinese and Japanese antiques. When the press finally tracked her down, she made no effort to hide the fact that she had walked out on Grant, blaming herself for most of their marital difficulties. To gain some perspective, she flew to Washington, D.C., to visit with Aunt Marjorie.

Marjorie Post and her husband, Joseph E. Davies, had returned from Russia and had settled in an estate on Embassy Row. Davies was named Special Assistant to the Secretary of State and had written his memoirs, *Mission to Moscow,* about his years as ambassador. Marjorie, according to her biographer William Wright, was busy cataloguing the vast collection of Russian art treasures she had brought back from the Soviet Union.

A conversation between Barbara and Aunt Marjorie that has been recounted by several people in several different ways had to do with Barbara's complaints about the collapse of her latest marriage.*

"You're too impetuous," Marjorie told her. "You should try to patch things up with Cary."

Barbara looked discouraged as they discussed the Grant situation. Eventually Barbara said, "Maybe I just haven't met the right man yet."

"Nonsense," snapped Marjorie. "You've already had too many husbands. You must be doing something wrong."

"Like what?" asked Barbara.

Marjorie thought for a moment, then said, "Have you tried rotating your hips? I'm told it makes it much better for the man."

❧

By the end of September Barbara was back on the Coast, staying at the Mark Hopkins Hotel in San Francisco. Jerry Giesler called to say that the Reventlows had fled Vancouver and were now living in Boston. Lance was attending school in Brookline. Giesler had served new legal papers on Court Reventlow in an effort to terminate the endless custody struggle.

Barbara received a second call, this one from Cary Grant. He implored her to see him again. She accepted, and he flew to San Francisco to be with her. On October 4, seven weeks into their separation, the Grants announced their reconciliation.

---

*For one version of this anecdote, see William Wright, *Heiress,* p. 4.

They returned to Pacific Palisades and were greeted by a letter from Douglas Fairbanks, Jr., announcing his release from the Naval Reserves and plans to return to Westridge. Cary's aim in seeking new living quarters was to find a place where they could thrive with a smaller household staff. He felt particularly oppressed by the constant presence of Ticki Tocquet and Margaret Latimer. Ticki and Sister watched over Barbara like a pair of mother hens, coming to her defense at the slightest provocation, shielding her from everything they considered detrimental to her well-being, including her husband. While he could not fault their motive—they were completely dedicated to Barbara—he was eager to have them demoted to a less prominent position in the family hierarchy.

He soon found what he thought was an answer to their needs, a compact two-story house at 10615 Bellagio Drive, not far from the Bel Air Country Club. The house was comfortable but too small to accommodate more than three or four servants. The rest of the staff, Ticki and Sister included, lived elsewhere. The Grants were alone when they most needed to be alone. They stayed home nights, refused invitations, sent none out. They passed their weekends in Palm Springs. This new arrangement seemed to work for a while.

A mild disturbance occurred when Fairbanks arrived at Westridge and found his house in a state of disarray. In the first place, Barbara had uprooted his exquisite Japanese garden and replaced it with acres of potatoes, presumably to give to the wartime poor. To compound his agony, Fairbanks' French antique furniture had sustained considerable damage because Barbara had insisted on keeping the thermostat in parts of the house blazing at the constant hothouse temperature of 100 degrees. The heat had scorched the wood and caused the brittle furniture to come unglued. While there was no way to replicate the once glorious garden, Barbara agreed to have the furniture restored. When the work was done, she produced a legal binder for Fairbanks to sign absolving her from all future responsibility toward the house. Fairbanks was flabbergasted. "It was as if all the wily characteristics of her grandfather were finally emerging in Barbara," he observes. "I didn't mind the damage as much as the fact that she didn't seem to trust me."

There were other examples of bizarre behavior. Sir Michael Duff, a member of British society and Barbara's friend since the days of her English debut, remembered visiting Los Angeles about this time with Serge Obolensky. "We were in Hollywood and of course called Barbara and asked if we could see her. She replied that it wouldn't be possible for the next three days, but on the fourth day, Cary was going somewhere and we could come to the Bel Air house. We went, and we were laughing and talking with her, because we hadn't seen each other for a while, when we heard a commotion outside the door. Barbara excused herself. When she returned she looked shaken and frightened and asked us apologetically if we would mind going out the back door since Cary would be furious if he knew we were there. We left and the next day Barbara telephoned and explained that Cary loathed all her friends. I thought it rather peculiar because I had always known Cary to be a decent chap. But I asked her why, if that was the case, she would stay married to him. 'I'm not,' she said. 'We're getting a divorce.'"

Cary was practically the last to know. Barbara told him of her decision nearly a week later. Life, she said, was too short and fragile that hers should be extinguished so casually and randomly. She couldn't rationalize jeopardizing her life further to the service of his career. "It's time we stopped deceiving ourselves," she said. "We both knew it would never last."

On February 15, 1945, they separated again, this time for good. Barbara moved out of their house and, as before, moved in with Bill Robertson. On July 15 she filed for divorce, charging "grievous mental distress, suffering and anguish." Six weeks later, on August 30, she and Giesler stood before Superior Judge Thurmond Clarke in a Los Angeles courtroom. Barbara took the witness stand and fifteen minutes later emerged from the hearing with an interlocutary decree of divorce.

Cary Grant chose not to attend, but as Barbara was leaving she saw Frank Vincent, at whose Lake Arrowhead home they had been married a little more than three years before. Barbara and Frank kissed. Reporters at the hearing observed that she was wearing a black moiré suit, a black straw hat and white gloves. They also said her slip was showing.

Grant thus became another chapter in Barbara Hutton's perilous history of marriage and divorce, the only spouse who neither asked for nor received alimony of any kind. Yet he derived other benefits: a welcome education in gracious living, a group of paintings by Utrillo and Boudin, a first-rate collection of men's jewelry. Barbara left with a lesser legacy: on the sunny side of her thirty-third birthday—and already three times divorced—she seemed to understand that another door had clanged shut behind her. *

---

*Mrs. Norman Woolworth, the New York socialite whose late husband was a cousin of Barbara's, remarks that after the Grant divorce Barbara rarely socialized with members of the family: "She saw Jimmy Donahue and Aunt Jessie, and that was about it. Before 1945 she always paid us a visit when she came to New York. We often took her to the theater or out to dinner. After Grant we never saw her again. I think the Grant divorce was the beginning of the end for her. The real problem was her loveless childhood—no mother and an absentee father. That was the root of all her subsequent problems."

Barbara later reflected on the difficulty of being married to an actor: "Cary and I hardly went out when we were married. I almost never saw him. In many ways I loved him—I mean really. I wanted to build a life for him as well as for myself, to make a real home for Lance, to be loved and to love, to become a complete woman. It was a frustrating period. Cary is very sweet, but his life is his work. It's his wife, his mistress, his family."

Grant's only public utterance about their divorce was offered to the *Hollywood Reporter:* "I don't really know why the marriage failed. It could have been successful, but we just moved on, that's all. There's nothing very extraordinary about that if people have the courage to do it. ... I still have a great feeling for Barbara. We are great and good friends. I wish her well. I wish she could be supremely happy. I shall be so pleased when I see her smiling and happy with someone she loves or even smiling without anyone."

This statement was perhaps an example of Grant's tendency to say one thing while thinking something else. A short time after their final separation, Barbara attended a dinner party at the home of tennis player Francis X. Shields, whose wife was Donna Marina Torlonia, the daughter of Prince and Princess Torlonia of Italy, whom Barbara had frequently seen when she lived abroad. It was at the Shieldses' that she met a struggling actor named Philip Reed, who actually bore a striking resemblance to Grant. They started dating, and Grant reacted adversely. Reed later told biographer Dean Jennings that he and Barbara were in love, and Cary was exceedingly "difficult" about it. "Cary hated my guts and he thought I was breaking up his marriage, but it was already finished," claimed Reed.

Reed also claimed that Barbara was incapable of sustaining a relationship, that sooner or later she became bored and restless, and that when this occurred she couldn't run fast enough. Reed defined it as the eternal conflict between Barbara's yearning to be loved and her yearning to be free.

It was only after her romance with Reed had ended that Barbara and Grant established a strong bond of friendship. One way Cary showed affection for Barbara was through his ongoing relationship to Lance, for whom he continued to be a father figure. Throughout his school years the boy spent long stretches with Cary. And when Grant married actress Betsy Drake on Christmas Day 1949, Barbara sent Betsy a large selection of handwoven caftans. "Barbara had a gift for friendship," says Grant. "She maintained friendships all over the world. But even with all her friends, I doubt if anyone ever understood Barbara. In fact, I doubt if Barbara ever understood herself."

Part Three

The Wayfarer

Twelve

...These are then the wanderers,
The homeless, the unblessed,
Who by the grace of God
Find their refuge and their rest.

BARBARA HUTTON,
from "The Wayfarer" (1957)

ERROL FLYNN's sidekick for many years was an equally handsome character named Frederick Joseph McEvoy. Freddie had first known Flynn when both were growing up in Sydney, Australia. Educated at the Jesuit School of Stonyhurst in England, Freddie early turned his attention to athletics. He became an expert marksman, race-car driver, deep-sea diver and boxer. He captained the British bobsled team at the 1936 Winter Olympics in Garmisch-Partenkirchen, and a year later led the same team to victory in the World Cup Bobsledding Championship at St. Moritz.

McEvoy had an insatiable appetite for intrigue and adventure. He could number among his professions those of jewelry designer, public relations consultant, professional gambler, smuggler, black marketeer and gigolo. He was addicted to games of chance and over the years won and lost a fortune in the gambling casinos of Europe. He was one of those rare individuals whose actual life stories were as exciting as the ones invented by the press. He admitted to having once killed a man during a barroom brawl in Marseilles. He bet $10,000 that he could drive from Paris to Cannes in less than ten hours, and covered the distance in a Talbot racing car with nearly an hour to spare. One night he won $25,000 playing backgammon in Monte Carlo, and the next day he bought a Maserati with his winnings. Later on he placed third with it at the 1936 Vanderbilt Trophy races, held at Roosevelt Raceway on Long Island. Never one to let money burn a hole in his pocket, McEvoy usually risked his cash prizes on the horses; whenever he picked a winner he celebrated with pink champagne, boasting that he was drinking the blood of a wounded bookmaker.

By his own admission McEvoy was a rogue, a swindler, a con man who used guile, intelligence, charm and sociability to get his way. He also used his good looks. He stood six feet one, weighed 175 pounds, and had broad shoulders, narrow hips and waist, pencil-thin mustache, sensual full lips, muscular arms and legs and penetrating light-blue eyes. He bore an uncanny resemblance to his friend Errol Flynn, so much so that when he stood up for Flynn as a character witness during a statutory rape trial in Hollywood, not even the plaintiff could tell them apart.

Barbara Hutton remarked on their astounding resemblance the first time she met McEvoy in the mid-1930s in the south of France. Although attracted to him, she knew of his reputation and made every effort to keep him at a distance. In 1940 McEvoy married a woman twice his age, sixty-two-year-old Beatrice Cartwright, the Standard Oil heiress and a social butterfly. At one time a reigning beauty, she was overweight and somewhat battered by the time Freddie got hold of her. But she was rich and could afford to give him an annual stipend of $100,000 plus wardrobe allowance and a new car every other year.

He made it through one automobile. They were divorced in 1942, the same year McEvoy met and married Irene Wrightsman, the eighteen-year-old daughter of Charles B. Wrightsman, the president of Standard Oil of Kansas. Wrightsman promptly disowned his daughter and cut off her multimillion-dollar trust fund. Two years and one child later, Irene and Freddie separated. He spent most of 1944 shuttling back and forth between Mexico City and Beverly Hills, smuggling arms, jewelry, liquor and other valuable cargo in and out of the United States. He and Flynn formed a team operation. "We raised some hell and had some fun," McEvoy told Dorothy di Frasso, at whose Mexico City house he frequently stayed. Dorothy was one of Freddie's most generous patrons. His fame among her friends for his bedroom performances was worth more than money in the bank. Returning to Flynn's Hollywood home one day, Freddie found a message waiting for him. It read, "If you want me, call me," and was signed "Barbara Grant."

It marked the beginning of a clandestine affair with meetings at Barbara's Beverly Hills *pied-à-terre* that lasted from November 1944 to March 1945. Barbara was in complete agreement with Dorothy's assessment of Freddie's skills: he was a superb lover. But he was more than that. He had a firm understanding of the subtle and complex nuances of human nature. In Barbara's estimation, he understood women better than any man she had ever known. He was one of those rare individuals able to rally her spirits even when she was morbidly depressed.

By the fall of 1945 Barbara and Freddie were both living in New York—Barbara at Joseph Davies' town house at 16 East Seventy-second Street, Freddie at the Park Avenue penthouse apartment of John Perona, owner of El Morocco. Freddie had just undergone surgery for the removal of a duodenal ulcer and was still recuperating when Barbara arrived in New York and paid him a sick call. Apparently the operation didn't at all impair his sexual performance.

The only other person Barbara had dealings with at this time was Anya Lynn Sorine, the wife of Russian portraitist Savely Sorine. The Sorines lived on the East Side not far from Barbara, and she and Freddie were frequent dinner guests.

Freddie was well rewarded by Barbara for his generous companionship. During this period he reaped what seemed an illimitable payload of prizes: diamond watches, cabochon emeralds, a bright-red Ferrari, a check for $50,000. Over the Christmas holidays the couple drove up to New Hampshire to do some skiing. They rented a charming ski chalet in Franconia, which Barbara later bought for McEvoy.

On their return to New York, shortly after the New Year, Barbara heard from Graham Mattison, recently out of the service and back as a full partner with White & Case. Mattison had taken over the Lance Reventlow custody case from Jerry Giesler and was about to settle the matter out of court, reverting to the previous arrangement of co-visitation rights. Court Reventlow insisted on two conditions. First, Barbara's visitation would apply only as long as she remained in the United States. In the event she lived abroad she would have custody of Lance only during his summer vacations, since he could scarcely be sent from school to school simply to accommodate Barbara's travel plans. The second condition called for Barbara to increase Lance's trust fund from $1.5 million to $5 million, with Court Reventlow permitted to live on the trust's income; when Lance reached the age of majority the fund would revert to him. On Graham Mattison's recommendation, Barbara agreed to the new terms.

Lance was soon back with his mother. His asthma had become worse and a number of allergists were brought in, one of whom provided the boy with a thousand-dollar air purifier. Another suggested that Barbara consider sending him to Arizona or New Mexico, since both of these states had pollen-free climates.

If Lance's medical condition was troublesome for Barbara, the escapades of her cousin, Jimmy Donahue, were positively calamitous.

Jimmy's saucy and impudent manner, often humorous and light-hearted, also had its darker and more somber side. Although he was well known in international café society for his generosity, his blithe spirit and his incurable frivolity, he was also recognized as a wildly egocentric exhibitionist whose sexual habits more than once were the source of grave concern to the members of his family. The first instance was his dishonorable discharge after six months in the U.S. Army for "sexual impropriety." Jimmy Donahue was a renowned homosexual who thought nothing of removing his clothing in public and dancing nude on top of a bar counter. It was common gossip that Jimmy liked to cross-dress and entertain his mother's friends, including Francis Cardinal Spellman, while attired in petticoats, a dress, wig, falsies and high heels.

One of the more risqué stories had it that he once telephoned a muscular male hustler he knew and invited him over for the night. Previously engaged, the hustler sent his roommate, an obese and unattractive man. Jimmy was so incensed that when the man disrobed he seized his clothes and ordered his valet to see the fellow out of the house—in the nude.*

Another instance of gross sexual misconduct took place on the night of March 18, 1946, while Jimmy was making his usual rounds of New York's poshest watering holes. At some point he entered Cerutti's, a gay bar on Madison Avenue. Truman Capote, then working for *The New Yorker*, recalls what happened: "Cerutti's was a wonderful place. It was in two different rooms. The first room was all servicemen, and the second room had a marvelous pianist named Garland Wilson. It was there that Jimmy Donahue picked up this soldier. I was there that night. Jimmy was giving a party at his mother's apartment on Fifth Avenue and he came into Cerutti's with Fulco di Verdura, the jewelry designer, and they made a dragnet of the bar. They picked up all these servicemen. They had a fleet of taxis waiting outside. They got them all into the taxis and took them back to the party. One of the servicemen passed out in the middle of the party. They put him on a couch and took off his pants and then got out the shaving cream and a sharp razor and they were shaving off his pubic hair.

"They thought it hilarious. They were all drunk and stoned. He came to in the middle of it and someone accidentally cut off his prick. Anyway, they said it was an accident. When that happened there was a great panic and they wrapped this guy up in a blanket and put him in

*The last time this anecdote was reported in print was in Stephen Birmingham's *Duchess: The Story of Wallis Warfield Windsor*, 1981.

Jimmy's car and dumped him somewhere on the Fifty-ninth Street Bridge. When the police found him he was in shock. They got him to the hospital and managed to save his life. All he could remember a few days later was the name Cerutti's. The police went there. The bartender said yes, the guy had been there with Mr. Donahue. Fulco and Jimmy got into a lot of trouble over this. But Fulco had nothing to do with it. As I understand it, it was all Jimmy Donahue."*

Details of the story, often distorted in the telling, spread from one end of café society to the other. Mrs. Jessie Donahue paid the victim a flat sum of $200,000 not to press charges. The case never went to trial and went unreported by the press. Through her attorneys Mrs. Donahue let it be known that she would sue for libel any publication that so much as alluded to the case. But the amount of buzzing and whispering that went on made it imperative for Jimmy to leave town. His mother chartered a plane and flew him, and another friend also somehow involved in the incident, down to Mexico (where they remained for the next two years).

Graham Mattison regarded the Donahue affair with an eye to its potentially damaging effect on Barbara Hutton's public image. He didn't trust the press not to run the story and feared that Barbara would somehow be implicated. He suggested that now was as good a time as any to return to Europe. Barbara jumped at the opportunity. She made reservations aboard a Paris-bound TWA flight scheduled to leave New York on April 12. Lance was sent off to Tucson, Arizona, with Ticki, Sister and Leon Christen, his newest tutor. On April 5 Freddie McEvoy boarded an ocean liner, taking along thirty of Barbara's trunks. At the airport a week later, Barbara was asked by the press whether she thought she would prefer living in Europe again as opposed to staying in the United States. "It's not that I prefer Europe," she said. "It's that Europe prefers me more than America does." She then denied that her trip had anything to do with Freddie McEvoy: "I am going to Paris simply because I couldn't resist the temptation to see it again. I plan to visit London as well. But I definitely do not intend to marry again. You can't go on being a fool forever."

🦢

Nobody was more pleased to see Barbara again than Max Charrier, the bell captain at the Ritz, whose association with the hotel went back nearly forty years. Charrier was the eyes and ears of the Ritz, the

---

*Although Capote told this story to the present author, a rendition of it also appeared in an interview with Capote in *Interview* (January 1978).

unofficial hotel historian, the keeper of the flame. He had watched in stunned silence as the Nazis commandeered the Ritz and the wealth, financial and cultural of the defeated nation while making race hatred, torture and murder the rule of the day. He recounted the tragic period of the occupation for Barbara, told of how the Nazis had cut down the flowers in the Bois and of how Hermann Göring, while staying at the Ritz, had ordered pig's knuckles and dark beer for breakfast.

For what it was worth, Barbara was glad to be back in Europe, and especially Paris. In a strange way it seemed as though nothing had changed. Elsa Maxwell gave a party at Laurent, and there Barbara encountered many old friends: the Patiños, Noël Coward, Lady Diana and Duff Cooper, Daisy Fellowes, Randolph Churchill, Arturo Lopez and Baron Alexis de Rédé.

A week later Cordelia de Castellane, a cousin of Silvia's, gave a ball, and since Barbara had no escort, she was fixed up with a friend of Cordelia's, Count Jean de Baglion, a short, subdued nobleman who became one of Barbara's closest friends. "I remember her telling me that for the first time in her life she felt like a free woman," says Baglion. "'There is no one, but absolutely no one, to tell me what I must do or not do,' she said. 'All my life I've been bullied by men—first by my father, then by my husbands because unfortunately I'm the sort of person who can't stand scenes. When people start yelling I say yes as quickly as I can to make them keep quiet. At least that's how it was until a few weeks ago. But now I'm on my own. I wander around in the sun, without a hat, looking into shop windows, doing what I want, and nobody pays the slightest attention to me.'"

Following one of her daily peregrinations, Barbara returned to the Ritz to find the lobby glutted with statesmen and high government officials in tuxedos, all scurrying about in busy preparation for the arrival of the King of Cambodia. Barbara, wearing tennis shorts, bobby socks and penny loafers, was stopped at the entrance to the hotel by a security guard. Looking reproachfully at her attire, the guard suggested that she enter the lobby from the rear of the building.

Barbara did not take kindly to the suggestion and settled the dispute after her own fashion by telling the guard that she had the same rights as anyone else, including the King of Cambodia. She then walked boldly through the swinging doors of the Ritz. By chance a photographer from *Life* saw Miss Hutton and asked her to pose for the camera. The security guard later asked the photographer the name of the woman whose picture he had just taken. "That," said the man from

Life, "was Barbara Hutton, one of the richest and most famous women in the world."*

Although Freddie McEvoy was presently living in Paris, he had been gently cast aside in favor of Barbara's newest pursuer, a lean and bronzed French aristocrat named Count Alain d'Eudeville, whose family headed the prosperous champagne house of Moët et Chandon. Barbara and her latest escort were not only seen together in Paris but in Cannes. According to one newspaper, they showed up nightly in the casino at the Carlton Hotel.

In July Count d'Eudeville accompanied Barbara to London on her first visit since before the war. The main purpose of the trip was to decide on the fate of Winfield House, which had been used during the war as an RAF officers' club and later as a convalescent home for Canadian servicemen. When she saw it again, she was shocked. Everywhere in the house there were peeling walls, buckling floorboards, broken windows, wires dangling from ceilings and walls. Plaster had fallen in huge chunks and had been ground to dust in Lance's nursery on the third floor. The roof and parts of the exterior had been damaged by firebombs.

The next day Barbara telephoned Graham Mattison in New York and informed him that she wanted to make a present of Winfield House to the U.S. State Department. The mansion, she suggested, could be repaired and used as the official residence for the American ambassador to the Court of St. James's.

Mattison transmitted Barbara's offer to American government officials, and within days Ambassador Averell Harriman went to look the place over. His report on Winfield House raised several issues. For one thing, the budget for running an embassy wasn't nearly enough to encompass the cost of operating a residence of such mammoth proportions. There was also the problem of furniture and furnishings. Since most of the furniture owned by Barbara was Louis XV, it seemed unlikely that any great quantity of it would be appropriate in a Georgian residence in London occupied by an American ambassador. This meant that the State Department would have the added financial burden of having to refurbish the house.

Barbara received a personal letter from President Harry S. Truman acknowledging her "most generous and patriotic offer to give the

---

*A number of the details regarding Barbara's postwar return to France are derived from interviews with close friends and acquaintances of the subject. See also Dean Jennings, *Barbara Hutton*, pp. 187-200.

Government your fine property." The letter went on to say, "I wish that I could accept promptly the gift so generously and simply made, but there are, I am told, administrative steps which intervene, and I have therefore asked the Secretary of State to get in touch with you and discuss the matter further. ... It was most thoughtful of you to have in mind the needs of our Government for representation abroad and to give so generous an expression of your thought."

The letter struck Barbara as an administrative brush-off. When told by Mattison that the State Department was concerned about the size of the house, she angrily responded, "What do they want, a tepee?" She was on the verge of rescinding her offer when a second letter arrived from the White House. "After further consideration," wrote Truman, "it seems that we would be foolish not to accept your kind offer of Winfield House. The property will be restored to its former grandeur as soon as possible and will be used as a residence for all future American Ambassadors to the Court of St. James's. The country is deeply indebted to you...."

The one unforeseen problem was the acute shortage of building materials in England after the war, along with an ordinance prohibiting the use of existing materials on private residences while public struc- tures, such as hospitals, were still in need of repair. It was not until January 18, 1955, nearly nine years later, when Winthrop Aldrich was ambassador to England that Winfield House was first used as a full- time residence. Barbara declined an invitation that year to attend the opening ceremonies, which were presided over by Queen Elizabeth and Prince Philip. "In truth, I would feel uncomfortable on such an occasion," Barbara wrote to Ambassador Aldrich. "Winfield House represents a closed chapter in my life, and while I am grateful that the residence now has a new existence, there are too many memories in its walls—both good and bad—that I don't wish to rekindle."

While in London, Barbara was told of a palace for sale in the then internationally controlled Tangier Zone, in Northern Morocco, and that fall she and Count d'Eudeville went to Tangier and checked into El Minzah, the city's leading hotel. The palace of Sidi Hosni, as they soon learned, was named for a nineteenth-century Moslem holy man whose tomb stood nearby and whose family had once owned the property. It was a tall whitewashed structure with crenelated stone walls rising above the steep and narrow rue Ben Raisul in the oldest part of Tangier—the Upper Medina, or more properly, the Kasbah. Barbara was fascinated not only by the physical aspect of the palace but by its unique history.

The property, originally consisting of seven individual houses surrounding a large central structure of seven rooms, had been a prison for debtors and later a Moorish café before it was acquired in 1870 by Sidi Hosni. In 1925 his descendants sold the property to Walter B. Harris, foreign correspondent for the London *Times*, whose intention it was to connect the outer domiciles to one another and then to the inner central house. Harris died before completing the project. In 1933 the unfinished structure was acquired by Maxwell Blake, the U.S. minister to Tangier, who took the next ten years to complete the job, enhancing the palace with furniture and artifacts from all over the Orient. From Fez he brought the last of the great Moorish artisans in stone carving, an ancient tribesman with a single eye, whose maze of geometric arabesque designs, magically light and transparent, stretched from wall to wall and pillar to pillar. The completed palace resembled a honeycomb, a kind of Kasbah in miniature with corridors, chambers, rooms and terraces winding off in every direction and situated on many different levels connected by a series of ramps and staircases.

Early in 1946 Blake decided to sell the palace and retire from his diplomatic post in order to return with his wife to the United States. Generalissimo Franco, dictator of Spain, dispatched a team of specialists to have a look at the palace and then make a bid. His offer, in the neighborhood of $50,000, was the highest made on the palace. That is until Barbara Hutton came along.

After a twenty-minute tour of the residence she offered to double Franco's bid. Blake was more than satisfied and the papers were immediately drawn up. Barbara readily agreed to retain Blake's entire household staff, seven devoted Spanish servants and their families. Ruth and Reginald Hopwood, Blake's daughter and son-in-law, had also been living at Sidi Hosni, and Barbara invited them to stay. Most of the year they resided in the main suite of apartments. When Barbara visited, usually for several months in late summer, they moved temporarily into a guest wing.

Barbara embarked on a wild decorating spree of her own, making the mansion grander still by importing a fortune in furnishings from around the world. She had some of her own furniture flown in from warehouses in England and the United States, but had much of it custom-designed by Adolfo de Velasco, a furniture maker in Marrakech. She bought a number of antiques from Jacques Robert, a Swiss, whose shop in Tangier also sold jewelry, caftans and leather goods.

From the Maharajah of Tripura she acquired what became known as the Million-Dollar Tapestry, a fifteenth-century Indian wall hanging tied with gold threads and laden with diamonds, pearls, emeralds and rubies; it came with dozens of matching floor cushions also covered with rare jewels. For the main sitting room, Murano Glassware near Venice was commissioned to design a chandelier that came down massively in a cascade of milky white and pastel swans' necks. The same firm designed Barbara's Moroccan table setting. The set contained twenty blue-and-silver pieces per setting, and there were a hundred settings. James R. W. Thompson, the American-born founder of the Thai Silk Company in Bangkok, produced rolls of shimmering silk for the palace, complementing and enhancing the effect of the ornamental stone carving, the latticework tiles, the painted and carved panels of hard and soft woods. In every room and bath Barbara installed a signed gold mantel clock from Van Cleef & Arpels. There were thirty such clocks at Sidi Hosni, priced at $10,000 apiece. And there was an art collection that included works by Fragonard, Braque, Manet, Kandinsky, Klee, Dali, El Greco, Grandma Moses and Hassan el-Glaoui, the son of the Pasha of Marrakech.

Obsessed as she was with the beautification of Sidi Hosni, she was nonetheless aware of the conditions that prevailed elsewhere in Tangier. Her letters mention "whole families that cook, eat and sleep in wooden packing crates strewn by the sides of roads," and others who "live in tiny hovels without plumbing or cooking facilities, the ceilings so perilously low they have to crawl to get from room to room." In the frenetic lower depths of the medina—the market place—she found "so much heat, so many piled-up colors, such congestion," that it was impossible not to suffocate.

Determined to improve conditions in Tangier, Barbara approached Mohammed Omar Hajoui, the local delegate of the Moroccan Ministry of Tourism and president of the Tangier Royal Golf and Country Club, and asked him for a list of charitable and philanthropic organizations in the area. She then sent these groups dozens of anonymous checks in amounts ranging from $1,000 to $50,000. Each year she procured a revised list and repeated the process.

Over the years she developed two other projects. The first was the establishment of a soup kitchen to help feed the impoverished Rifians who had fled to Tangier late in 1945 as a result of a terrible famine in their native mountainous coastal region. Her generosity, which included gifts of clothing and toys for the young, fed more than a thousand tribesmen a day, many of them living in the wretched *bidonvilles* on the outskirts of town.

In the early 1960s she became involved with the American School, located on a thirty-one-acre tract of land overlooking the Rif Mountains. On her own initiative she started a fellowship program there for the children of the poorest families in Tangier. Each year a dozen children were selected for the program. They were clothed and housed by Barbara in a dormitory that was built on the campus at her expense. Books, learning materials, tutors, teachers and a dormitory supervisor were included. The students went all the way from the first to the twelfth grade, and those who showed academic promise went on to college. Of all her philanthropic endeavors, it was this program that gave her the most personal satisfaction.

It was in Tangier more than anywhere else that Barbara established a popular following. She was one of the first of a parade of wealthy Americans and Europeans to descend after the war, many of them acquiring property in the region known as the Mountain, a residential suburb of decorous villas and estates hidden behind massed shrubs and walls of trees. That Barbara by-passed the Mountain and chose instead to reside in the supposedly dangerous and seedy Kasbah helped eradicate the impression among tourists that Tangier was nothing more than a den of sin and iniquity. "Increasingly," remarks Mohammed Hajoui, "tourism appeared to be the lone answer to our economic prayers. What encouraging news then, when people heard that a figure of Barbara's stature had settled in the middle of the Kasbah. With her arrival Tangier became a boom town, one of the 'in' spots for café society, a mecca for those seeking a tax-free haven only a few hours from Spain. Because of its international sovereignty, Tangier imposed no taxes on its citizenry. Well-to-do people like industrialist Gerhard Voigt, Malcolm Forbes, Yves Vidal, who bought York Castle in the Kasbah, began to follow in Barbara's footsteps."*

Because of Barbara's importance to Tangier for propaganda purposes in attracting tourists, Hajoui did everything possible to accommodate her needs. Over the years his services took many different forms, not least of which were the introductions he provided her to Morocco's oldest, most aristocratic families. His help was also of a pragmatic nature. Barbara imported several Rolls-Royces from England and had a garage built behind Sidi Hosni, only to discover that the arches in the medina were too narrow for the cars. Hajoui took her case to the city council and an ordinance was passed requiring all arches in Tangier to

*By establishing herself as a legal resident of Tangier, Barbara boosted the value of her fortune. During the late 1940s and throughout the 1950s she had a tax-free income of roughly $3 million per year, not an excessive amount considering her exorbitant outlays and the increased cost of living.

be of sufficient width to permit the passage of automobiles as wide as the Rolls-Royce. Those arches that failed to meet these criteria were either torn down or reconstructed.

Barbara's parties at Sidi Hosni reaped world-wide press and publicity. At the beginning Hajoui helped Barbara by providing the names of possible Moroccan guests, arranging for caterers, lining up entertainment. Her personal favorites were the belly dancers, many of whom worked in the local night clubs, and the picturesque "Blue People," descendants of the nomadic Berbers who, wearing their distinctive blue robes, put on exuberant singing and dancing exhibitions.

"Every tourist to Tangier wanted an invitation to one of her parties," notes Hajoui. "There was a whole black-market operation, lots of invitation scalpers. If people couldn't get an invitation, they wanted to at least see her palace. It was one of our main tourist attractions—the house with the sentry box in front and the American flag flying overhead. The local guides included it on their itinerary: 'And this is Sidi Hosni, the palace of Her Serene Highness Barbara Hutton, the Queen of the Medina!'

"Her parties attracted the biggest names: Charlie and Oona, Greta and Cecil, Ari and Callas. Since she was always marrying and divorcing, the engraved invitations read: 'Mrs. Barbara Woolworth Hutton requests the pleasure of your company ...' When the parties were to be held on the roof, there was always a notation in the bottom right-hand corner of the invitation: 'In Case of Wind, Your Hostess Requests You To Indulge Her By Coming Another Night.' Two hundred guests on the average would be invited to the larger parties and a thousand would come. People brought their friends, which is customary in Morocco. Others came to watch. They would crowd the streets and climb the neighboring rooftops for a better view. It reached the point where the descendants of Ali Baba were gouging precious stones out of the tapestries and harem cushions. She had to hire discreetly armed plainsclothesmen to patrol the rooms during her parties. And when that became too much of a bother she began holding them outside Sidi Hosni—behind the walled gardens of Guitta's Restaurant and at the Parade Café or in large tents at the Caves of Hercules, the limestone quarries several miles outside Tangier."

The American author Paul Bowles, who moved permanently to Tangier in 1947 and who lived with his wife, Jane Bowles, also a writer, in a small apartment several houses distant from Sidi Hosni, describes Barbara's North Africa as "the Garden of Allah, where nightingales sang and fountains splashed and one clapped one's hands for the musicians to be brought."

In his autobiography, *Without Stopping,* Bowles writes: "She wanted everything around her to show an element of the unreal in it, and she took great pains to transform reality into a continuous fantasy which seemed to her sufficiently *feerique* to be taken seriously." The author then gives an example: "One summer when she gave a ball she brought thirty Reguibat camel drivers with their racing camels from the Sahara, a good thirty miles distant, merely to form a *garde d'honneur* through which the guests would pass at the entrance of the house. The camels and men stayed encamped in the Palace Sidi Hosni for many days after the party, apparently in no hurry to get back to the desert."

The largest and most memorable of Barbara's parties, it is true, reverberated with more than a tinge of the surreal. They were held in gilded Moroccan tents set up on the multitiered roof of the palace, which she would transform for the occasion into a stage setting with carefully arranged spotlights, cushions of Arabic design in brilliant shades, obelisks, balls and humanoid figures made out of marigolds, zinnias and sunflowers. Some of the parties were black tie, but the majority called for North African dress: traditional robes, caftans, *haiks, jalabahs* and *baboush* (slippers). The Honorable David Herbert (the second son of the Sixteenth Earl of Pembroke), who moved to Tangier about the same time as Barbara, recalls her at one party sitting on a red-and-gold throne wearing the famous emerald and diamond tiara that had belonged to Catherine the Great. Underfoot were priceless Oriental rugs and on both sides of her stood huge gold candelabras. The palace itself and half the Kasbah were floodlit.

Not all the parties, according to Herbert, were for the benefit of the idle rich. Each year she entertained the U.S. Sixth Fleet when it put into port, giving one party for the officers, another for the enlisted men. She threw an annual party for the local police department and another for her Moorish neighbors, most of them poor, who crowded onto her roof and sat clapping their hands in time to the movements of the belly dancers.

Parties aside, Barbara's visits to Tangier were undertaken primarily as a means of escape. Sidi Hosni was her magic palace, a refuge, a hideaway in which to evade the curiosity, the envy, the judgments of the outside world. The house was self-enclosed, an island of tranquillity hidden behind impenetrable walls, where the only sounds were the occasional cries of young Arab boys at play or the fireworks that were set off nightly during the holy month of Ramadan. Otherwise nothing, only the chanting voice of the *Fqih* and the children from the Kotab located next door, a Koranic training school attached to a mosque. One of her neighbors was a musician and she could sometimes hear him playing the guitarlike oud, at other times the guinbri, instruments whose soft, wistful sounds brought back images of her childhood.

Barbara would sit for hours on the shaded terrace beneath a lofty fig tree and contemplate the roll of the distant sea. She valued the languor of Tangier. She also loved the beaches and enjoyed swimming in the sea and walking along the strand. In the late afternoon she would sip mint tea at Madame Porte's, a quaint French pastry shop. She liked to drift among the crowds in the Grand Socco, listening to the hawkers peddle their wares—silks, jewelry, leathergoods. She learned enough Arabic to sit in the cafés and follow the tribal storytellers as they wove their intricate tales. In the evenings she and the Hopwoods would occasionally drive out to Robinson's Beach, not far from the Caves of Hercules, to build a fire and watch the sunset.

"When I first met Barbara," says Ruth Hopwood, "she weighed one hundred and sixteen pounds and looked wonderful. She kept saying she wanted to come down to a hundred pounds. 'I feel better,' she said, 'when I weigh about a hundred.' She was obsessed with losing weight, even though she liked to eat, especially rich foods like couscous, smoked salmon, pâté de foie gras. There were times when she would go on binges and eat everything. She was a person of extremes—extreme happiness, extreme sorrow. She hated to be told what to do. If you told her she was spending too much money, she'd say, 'Oh don't be a penny pincher.' Another favorite expression of hers was: 'Moderation is a bore.'

"When it came to men she oscillated between overidealization and overdevaluation—in love with somebody one minute, couldn't stand him the next. When she arrived in Tangier in 1946 she was crazy about Count d'Eudeville. After she lost interest in him she assured me she had no intention of ever marrying again. But, of course, the next I heard she was about to marry husband number four, Prince Igor Troubetzkoy."

Prince Igor Nikolaiewitsch Troubetzkoy, at thirty-five, had the sleek body of an athlete and the cherubic face of a choir boy. He had dimples, a high forehead, twinkling green eyes, butterscotch hair and a delicately formed mouth. His lithe frame was the result of a bicycle-racing career. For years he had practically lived for cycling, attaining his goal by winning the French amateur championship in 1931 and then turning professional, eking out a living on the basis of part-time employment.

His present employer was Freddie McEvoy, whose latest enterprise was a black-market operation specializing in U.S. Army surplus goods and equipment. If a prospective client wanted to buy a slightly used but reasonably priced jeep (repainted and reconditioned), McEvoy could arrange it. Freddie was also in the currency business, supplying French bank notes in exchange for American dollars and Swiss francs. Igor was McEvoy's bagman. His job was to meet customers in backwater bistros to collect money and make deliveries.

Before Barbara's departure for Tangier, McEvoy had introduced her to Troubetzkoy. It had been a brief meeting. Barbara had previously known Igor's older brother, Youka, a former contract player for Universal Studios in Hollywood. Youka was a large, blunt, outgoing man who was currently making a living as the star of a radio soap opera in New York. Both brothers possessed wit and charm.

The first person Barbara called upon her return from Tangier was Freddie McEvoy. She invited Freddie to the Ritz for a drink. Once he arrived she wasted little time. She wanted to know everything there was to know about Freddie's pal, Igor Troubetzkoy. Being a practical and adaptable man, Freddie must have decided on the spot that if he couldn't claim Barbara as his own, he could at least help a friend, and in so doing perhaps himself as well.

Prince Igor was born the same year as Barbara. His father was Prince Nicholas Troubetzkoy; his mother was Countess Catherine Moussine Pushkin. They were of Lithuanian descent. The family, with nothing more than its princely title in hand, fled Russia as early as 1905, arriving the same year in America, where they already had relatives. Youka was born in Los Angeles in 1906. Igor was born in Paris. The family eventually settled in Nice, and it was there that the boys went to school.

Whatever else there was to say about Prince Igor would have to come from his own lips. It was enough that he owned a legitimate title. Barbara asked for his telephone number and Freddie gave it to her. She called him up and invited him over for dinner the next evening. He arrived carrying a bouquet of flowers. Dinner was served in the suite. When they were finished Barbara led her visitor into her boudoir. Looking back on that particular night, Igor would say: "She phoned. We dined and—my word!—how fast!"

The prognosis was favorable. In New York Youka was telling the press that Barbara wasn't at all the kind of woman she seemed. She was highly intelligent, warm, sensitive, generous and funny. "People with money like that naturally do not have the same sense of values as we who have to work for a living," he added. "I have read that Miss Hutton said she would meet lots of nice young men only to find that something odd seemed to come over them sooner or later. They probably got to thinking about her money, or anyway she thought they were thinking about it.

"All that money is very pleasant to think of, and is enough to give an ambitious fellow buck fever when he sees the big opportunity in front of him. Igor does not think that way, however. His mind is clear enough to reject the idea that the money could be an obstacle. Now me, I would be sick bothering myself that she thought I wanted only her money and it would make both of us unhappy. But Igor will not think of that at all. I am very happy for Igor, and also for Miss Hutton. In Igor, she will have someone different from those she is accustomed to."

Youka was both right and wrong about his brother. Igor was certainly different from Barbara's other suitors—on the whole he was more innocent, less jaded—but, on the other hand, he couldn't help but be overwhelmed by the magnitude of Barbara's wealth. He made the rounds of the great fashion houses of Paris with Barbara—Balenciaga, Dior, Molyneux and Chanel—and gasped at the prices she paid for each new creation. She often took friends like Silvia de Castellane and Jean Kennerley* and their children along on these expeditions and outfitted the entire family. Igor walked around Barbara's second-story suite overlooking the Place Vendôme, the Ritz's most expensive suite at $800 a day. (The same suite today rents for $3,500 per night.) He was in awe of the art treasures that spilled through the apartment: antique gold snuff boxes, Chinese porcelains and jades, a Botticelli painting, a Cèzanne, an incomplete but very valuable Gutenberg Bible. She showed him her collection of jewels—parure after parure of diamonds, emeralds, rubies, sapphires, bijoux of inestimable monetary and historic worth.

He was no less amazed by her generosity, her support of indigent families and friends, her gift of $30,000 to a Parisian millinery shop that had nearly gone bankrupt, her check for $10,000 to a news vendor to start his own business, her donations and allotments to numerous funds, foundations and charities.

---

*Barbara frequently gave me her old clothes," says Jean Kennerley. "By this I mean dresses and gowns by the finest French designers she had worn maybe once or twice at most. People told me not to take them, that she ought to buy her close friends only new clothes. I didn't see any reason not to take them, so I did. Barbara was always giving somebody something, and people became very touchy about it. On our twenty-fifth wedding anniversary, she gave us a check for $25,000, with which we bought a used Bentley. Friends of ours said, 'Well, why didn't she just buy you a new Bentley?' Everybody was very quick to criticize her. It didn't matter what she did."

"Barbara was very delicate about giving money away," says Igor. "She didn't do it in such a way that people felt slighted. Also it didn't bother her particularly if a merchant or shopkeeper hiked his prices a little for her benefit. 'They have to make a living too,' she would say. She paid a lot of money to a furniture maker in Paris to design four wooden chairs for her suite at the Ritz. When some woman told her she had paid too much for the chairs because they were uncomfortable, Barbara shot back, 'Good. If they're uncomfortable, people like you won't sit around too long and bore me.'"* Although Barbara's wealth had an undeniable draw for Troubetzkoy, his initial attraction to her was physical in nature. "She wasn't tall," he says, "but she had long muscles, wonderful breasts, doll-like hands and feet, remarkable eyes and hair. She also had a quality called presence. Those who have it are people one is immediately aware of. They fill a room. The minute they enter all eyes follow. I don't know how else to describe it. It has nothing to do with wealth or beauty or even self-confidence. Maria Callas, Charles de Gaulle and Marilyn Monroe all had it. Greta Garbo and Jacqueline Kennedy Onassis have it. And Barbara Hutton had it. She didn't do much with it, but she had it. That's why for forty years, whenever you opened the newspaper, you found her name in it."

Barbara and Igor were together most of the winter, first in Paris and later at the Palace Hotel in St. Moritz, where they were joined by Freddie McEvoy and a comrade of Igor's, Baron Edward von Falz-Fein, a Russian who currently lived in the tiny country of Liechtenstein. Falz-Fein would spend hours talking with Barbara while Igor and Freddie tested the ski slopes.

Among the many subjects Barbara and Falz-Fein discussed was the question of Barbara's strange and unrelenting diet. The same topic came up over dinner one evening. Igor and Falz-Fein urged Barbara to give up her starvation diet for once. They kept at her until she agreed to sample the specialty of the canton, something called *Bundnerfleisch*— a cut of smoked, dried, thinly sliced beef—washed down with an abundance of champagne. Just as the last bite disappeared Barbara was overcome by a wave of nausea. She raced for the nearest powder room, where she resorted to the old Roman trick of thrusting her fingers down her throat.

She felt better a few days later when Anya and Savely Sorine flew in from New York. Their arrival tipped McEvoy off that some cataclysmic

*Igor Troubetzkoy's comments in this section of the book are derived primarily from the following sources: Troubetzkoy interview with Theresa Stanton (researcher), July '79; 1968 biography of Barbara Hutton, by Dean Jennings; assorted newspaper and magazine clippings.

event was about to take place. It didn't take him long to figure out what it was. He confronted Troubetzkoy with his suspicions. Igor hemmed and hawed for a few minutes before admitting that he and Barbara had indeed discussed marriage. "She wanted to surprise you with the news," said Freddie.

When he returned to his room that night McEvoy found an envelope sitting on top of his bed. Inside the envelope was a check from Barbara for $100,000, and a note: "To Freddie, for everything. But especially for Pixie. Love, Barbara." "Pixie" was Barbara's nickname for Igor.

Barbara had originally hoped to marry Igor in St. Moritz and had already sent invitations to a group of European dignitaries, including former King Peter II of Yugoslavia. But two weeks before the ceremony the news was leaked to the press and a thousand reporters descended on the Swiss resort.

A whole new set of tactics had to be devised. Following a brief news conference at which they announced their intention to marry in Paris instead of St. Moritz, the couple boarded a Paris-bound train. But when the train arrived in Zurich they sneaked off and quietly checked into the Dolder Grand Hotel, where they were soon joined by the Sorines. On March 1, 1947, the two couples stepped into a rented limousine and were driven to Chur, a picturesque village sixty miles from Zurich. They were married that afternoon by the mayor of Chur, Lucius Chiamara, in the local registry office.

The newlyweds returned to Zurich and spent another week there, appearing in public only once, taking lunch at the Café Huguenin, where waiters surrounded their table with screens to protect their privacy. From Zurich they were driven to the Bellevue Palace Hotel in Bern, of which Barbara was to see only the ceiling of her bedroom. She was bedridden with the flu and during their stay never left the suite.

The honeymoon ended on April 1 with their return to Paris. In an effort to sidestep the press they rushed off the train at the Gare St. Lazare, and in their haste left Barbara's jewelry case with its precious contents sitting on the luggage rack. It was still there when Igor retraced his steps several minutes later to retrieve it. The near catastrophe slowed them down sufficiently for the press to catch up. Barbara was caught in the crossfire and shot back with what had become her standard line of defense. "I've never been happier," she said. "We will be on our honeymoon for thirty or forty more years."

The sentiment behind this comment was as short-lived as the taxi ride from the railroad station to the Ritz. Once in her suite, Barbara laid down the law. They would occupy separate bedrooms and would entertain guests or step out only when Barbara felt up to it. The bedroom edict surprised Igor since on their honeymoon they had always shared the same bed. But he decided not to make a fuss about it.

His reward for being good-natured was an elaborate dinner party that Barbara threw for him a few weeks later in the Ritz Ballroom, inviting among others the Duke and Duchess of Windsor, Lady Diana and Duff Cooper, Elsie Mendl, Randolph Churchill, Mr. and Mrs. Antenor Patiño, Harrison and Mona Williams. "The cuisine was incredibly well prepared," said one of the guests, "but Barbara didn't touch a thing. She just drank black coffee and smoked cigarettes."

Barbara's dietary practices took the same gradual toll on Igor that they had taken on her previous husbands. Except for an occasional morsel, Barbara refused to eat. Troubetzkoy had to race to the nearest restaurant for a quick bite, because formal meals were rarely served in her suite.

In addition to the diet there was her insomnia. She absolutely couldn't sleep at night. From his bedroom Igor could hear his wife prowling back and forth in her room like a restless prisoner. Or she would leave the Ritz and take long solitary strolls, often not returning until the first light of dawn.

At other times when she couldn't sleep she would either write poetry or call up her friends on the telephone. She apparently thought nothing of calling New York or Los Angeles or London or Tangier. She would call whenever she felt the urge—two, three, four o'clock in the morning. It seemed that she was always on the telephone with Baron Gottfried von Cramm, the German tennis champion. They would talk for three, four hours at a clip. She also wrote to Von Cramm, and Von Cramm wrote back. What bothered Igor most about this friendship was Barbara's refusal to talk to him about it. She made occasional references to Von Cramm, even calling him "my tennis player," but she refused to answer questions. After a point Igor stopped asking.

Most difficult on Igor were Barbara's lightning changes of mood. In the span of an hour she would go from anger to depression to ecstacy and then back again. "She would sit in a room reading a book and suddenly tears would roll," explains Igor. "At other times she would start laughing for no reason whatsoever. A thought might pass through her mind that struck her as humorous and she would begin to laugh in a high-pitched girlish giggle."

Barbara's mind and opinions changed almost as rapidly as her moods. One day she would spend thousands of dollars on lingerie and the next day she would give it away or throw it away, only because she was too lazy to exchange it.

Examples of Barbara's unpredictable nature abound. "I once gave her a miniature dachshund," recalls Igor, "and for weeks she lavished affection on it, to the point where she would take the dog into the bathroom with her. She fed the dog only the finest filet mignon. The dog was never out of her sight. Then one day she grew tired of it. She summoned the maid and said, 'Here, give this thing back to Igor. I don't want it anymore.' The next day she took the dog back again. She acted the same way with people. One minute she wanted you around, the next minute you were dismissed. And you never knew in advance which of the two it would be."

One of Barbara's problems at this point was her growing dependence on various drugs and medications. She was taking appetite suppressants and was growing more manic by the minute. She came gradually to believe that drugs contained the answers to all her problems. To counter the effect of uppers she began to take downers. She took amphetamines in the morning, depressants in the afternoon. She went from one sleeping pill to another: Seconal, phenobarbital, Nembutal. There were more doctors in and out of Barbara's bedroom now than at any other time in her life. Each one had another remedy and a new pill to prescribe. "It killed everything," Igor would later tell Dean Jennings. "Her appetite, her sleep patterns, her sex drive."

Barbara was in bed and ailing when Joan Moore and her son Derry came from London to visit. Derry, then still a young boy, recalls being driven around Paris in Barbara's Rolls-Royce by her chauffeur and shown the sights. "Barbara never left her room," Derry recalls, "and every evening she ordered the same meal for us: lobster cocktail, steak, pommes soufflées, a salad and chocolate mousse."*

Igor Troubetzkoy struck Derry as "a sweet, shy chap, not at all your typical playboy. He went everywhere on his bicycle and was learning how to paint. He was very nice, too nice. Barbara was *exigeante*—overly demanding. She abused him."

By late May the Troubetzkoys and a staff of six left Paris and moved into a villa near Cannes, but after a week Barbara decided she preferred the mountains, and as a result they moved into a chalet overlooking the Lake of Thun high in the Swiss Alps. On July 1 Lance arrived from

---

*When Derry Moore attended Cambridge University some years later, he received a monthly allowance from Barbara. She was always extremely generous to the children of her friends, constantly buying them clothes, sending presents, paying for their education. She soon had more than a dozen godchildren, and in certain cases it became clear just why she was such a popular godparent.

Newport, where the Reventlows had recently acquired a house on Cliff Walk. His presence lifted Barbara's spirits and for the rest of the summer—the duration of Lance's stay—she again became active. But it was only a temporary recovery. By early September she was back in bed.

One evening toward the end of the month Barbara complained of an excruciating pain on her left side. Igor carried her to the car and drove her to the Salem Hospital in Bern. There she was examined by a leading urologist, Dr. Walter Hadorn, who determined that she was suffering from acute inflammation of the kidneys, a painful and in those days relatively dangerous condition.

Her condition became worse before it became better. At the height of the illness, when there was reasonable doubt as to her eventual recovery, Barbara asked Dr. Hadorn to telephone Gottfried von Cramm at Wispenstein Castle in Hanover. Von Cramm arrived in Bern the next day and remained at the hospital for nearly a week. Igor felt humiliated by the tennis star's presence and demoralized that his wife would turn to somebody else in her moment of need. Barbara got better and Von Cramm finally left Switzerland, taking with him a new wardrobe and a large check—gifts from Barbara.

By the end of the year she was out of the hospital and recuperating in Gstaad. She showed such rapid improvement that one morning she even went skiing with Igor. That same day, however, she was crippled by sharp pains in her abdomen. Igor returned with her to Bern and the soothing hands of Dr. Hadorn. After examining her, Hadorn called in two of his colleagues, Dr. Kurt Egger and Dr. Jules Mennet, both of them gynecologists. A series of X-rays revealed that Barbara was suffering from an intestinal blockage of some kind and a large ovarian tumor.

On January 20, 1948, Dr. Egger performed an intestinal section; he extracted the tumor, the left ovary and the left fallopian tube. There was no malignancy, and a week later he completed the operation by removing the intestinal blockage. The operation was proclaimed a success by everyone but Barbara. When she learned that they had removed her second ovary, rendering her permanently sterile, she went into an intense depression, accusing her physicians of performing surgery without her consent and without advising her of the consequences.

After a prolonged convalescence, Barbara returned to Paris and resumed many of the same habits that had marked her first year with Igor. Above all, she kept him at arm's length. She drank heavily and took an endless supply of medication. She read, listened to music (often playing the same record over and over again), and wrote poetry (a great deal of it).

"In her verse," says Igor, "she frequently described herself as a hollow seashell washed up on shore. She saw herself as a glittering trinket whose sole purpose was to amuse an occasional beachcomber, who would admire her briefly but would always cast her off and eventually grind her into the sand. She was haunted by a feeling of longing. The longing, although I doubt she knew it, was for a mother, any mother, to do the things for her she knew mothers did. Barbara was molded by her affectionless, insecure childhood, and nowhere was this more evident than in her poetry."

Igor, priding himself on being a student of graphology, spent hours trying to analyze his wife's handwriting, hoping thereby to find the missing link in her personality. "One practically had to be a François Champollion, who deciphered the Egyptian hieroglyphics on the Rosetta Stone, to decode her script," says Igor. "Once you cracked it, it was all there—the phobias, the fears, the extreme behavior. The big question was what to do. I suggested psychotherapy, and since Barbara had no strenuous objections, I went to Zurich to confer with Dr. Carl Jung about her. He agreed to see Barbara, but by the time I got back to Paris she was back in the hospital and Dr. Jung was out of the picture."

Barbara had suffered a relapse of her intestinal ailment and had to be taken to the American Hospital in Neuilly. Three physicians, Drs. d'Alliennes, Loriche and De Gennes (Barbara's personal physician), decided that the only sensible course was the surgical removal of the damaged section of the intestines. Barbara spent months recuperating from the latest operation, and during that period Igor tried to figure out what he could do with himself other than serve as Barbara's nursemaid. After some thought he began toying with the idea of becoming a race-car driver.

Although opposed to the idea, Barbara gave her husband the money for an Alfa Romeo racer, which Alexis bought and immediately entered in a novice-class race at Pau, a resort town in the Pyrenees, where to everyone's surprise he finished a strong second. He was less fortunate the second time around, a road race held in Monte Carlo, during which he collided with another car. He decided to find a safer career for himself.

"I wanted to work," he says, "but Barbara was against my taking a job. She didn't mind me working a few months a year, but that wasn't work I could find."

After mulling it over, Igor came up with the idea of entering the real estate field, where he could dictate his own hours. He planned to acquire old houses, renovate them, then sell them at a profit. The first house would be his own. He would purchase a house for himself and Barbara, a place where they could spend weekends and holidays. It would also serve as a showplace, a model house where he could experiment with some of his architectural ideas.

The house he finally bought, using Barbara's money to pay for it, was in the Paris suburb of Gif-sur-Yvette, a village of brooks, woods and farm land. The house had no plumbing or electricity. After installing both, Igor went to work on the rest of the house. He rebuilt and repainted it, inside and out, and constructed a new garage. He put in a library, music room, country kitchen, game room and guest suites. He furnished it, and made certain that the fireplaces were in working condition. When it was done he invited Barbara to drive out and have a look. One day she was too ill, the next day too tired. Days passed into weeks, weeks into months. Her excuses became more and more lame. Each time Igor asked, she came up with a new one, until it finally dawned on him that his wife had no intention of ever looking the house over, much less living in it. It was a sad but revealing moment for Igor, one that he put best in his own words when he said to a friend, "I had a house but not a home."*

*See Dean Jennings, *Barbara Hutton*, pp. 220-21.

Thirteen

A T THE BEGINNING of June 1949, shortly after Lance joined her for the summer, Barbara attended a party at Elsie Mendl's house in Versailles. There she met Gerald Van Der Kemp, the newly appointed curator of the palace at Versailles who was in charge of a massive restoration effort then being carried out on both its buildings and grounds. Barbara happened to mention that she owned the Savonnerie carpet that had belonged to Marie Antoinette. It was in her suite at the Ritz, and she wondered whether Van Der Kemp wanted it for the palace. "She gave it to me on that night," he recalls, "and I was smiling like a little boy. Even in Versailles it is too fine to be on the floor when the public is admitted." Barbara also donated an ornate commode that had been made for Louis XVI, as well as a substantial check to pay for other furnishings and work that needed to be done to complete the chamber of Marie Antoinette. For her altruism she was made a Chevalier of the Legion of Honor.

Barbara's health was still fragile and she spent the last two weeks of June and all of July in and out of Swiss rejuvenation clinics. She visited the Blue Cross Clinic in Basel to consult with Dr. Walter Pöldinger, an Austrian whose peat-bath treatments had done wonders for Winston Churchill. She later went to the Montreux clinic of Paul Niehans, M.D., whose specialty was the injection of animal cells—mainly those of sheep—into the human bloodstream. Barbara submitted to a series of injections but showed little overall improvement.

By August she was in Venice, accompanied by Lance and Igor, and it was from there that Troubetzkoy telephoned Court Reventlow in Newport to ask if Lance could stay abroad a few weeks beyond the allotted time limit. Reventlow turned the request down and demanded that Lance be returned, as stipulated by agreement, on the first of September.

Barbara had other ideas and when she failed to send her son home, Reventlow went to Surrogate Court in Dedham, Massachusetts, presided over by Judge George Arthur Davis. Barbara was represented in court by John J. Burns of Boston and by Graham Mattison, then with the international investment banking firm of Dominick & Dominick. Her lawyers presented the court with an affidavit from Barbara stating that she was "a semi-invalid, weighing 84 pounds and confined to bed a good deal of the time." Annexed to this document were letters from several physicians attesting to Barbara's ill health, including a notarized brief from Dr. Giuseppe Comirate of Venice, who wrote that Barbara was "in a very fragile and delicate state of health after four major operations in three years ... and it can only be detrimental to her recovery for her to be separated at this time from her son." In addition there was an affidavit from Lance stating that he had been physically abused by his father, and that since the birth in 1946 of his half brother, Richard, his father's attitude toward him had undergone a dramatic change. This statement was accompanied by a medical diagnosis of Lance's asthmatic condition indicating that Newport's cold, damp climate was detrimental to his health and that "he should be transferred as soon as possible to a school located in a warmer and drier climate."

Court Reventlow denied that he had ever abused Lance, or that the birth of Richard had in any way diminished his feelings toward Lance. He added too that his son was currently attending St. George's School in Newport, one of New England's fine boys' preparatory schools, and that his education would suffer if his studies were interrupted. Finally he submitted a number of newspaper articles describing Barbara's "active" schedule on the Lido. One of the articles contained a photograph of Barbara emerging from a swim in the Adriatic. Another photograph showed Barbara and her entourage stepping off a yacht after it had docked. On the basis of this evidence, Reventlow insisted that Barbara was feigning serious illness only to retain custody of Lance.

Following a brief recess Judge Davis ruled that Lance would have to return to the United States as quickly as possible. All other decisions were to be deferred until such time as an impartial panel of physicians could be convened to examine the boy.

According to Peggy Reventlow, Lance returned to the United States, and she and Court drove to New York to pick him up at the pier. But when they arrived he was no longer there. Graham Mattison had already spirited the boy off to the Waldorf.

"We found Lance in a room at the hotel," says Peggy, "encircled by a ring of Barbara Hutton's henchmen—doctors, lawyers, private detectives, bodyguards. Lance looked very unhappy. He was openly hostile toward his father and talked almost as if somebody had hypnotized him. He kept watching the others in the room, especially Graham Mattison, to see if they approved of what he was saying. Mattison had clearly deceived us. He went behind our backs and somehow finagled a court order demanding Lance's surrender pending an official investigation. To this day I don't know how he did it, but we left the Waldorf knowing that Barbara had finally won. She had brainwashed Lance into believing that his father hated him. It was a lie. Lance was only fourteen, and my husband never heard from him again."

Lance's arrival in New York in mid-September was followed shortly by the arrival of his mother aboard the *Queen Mary*. She was still complaining about her health and spent a week in Lenox Hill Hospital undergoing tests. But as far as the medical profession could tell, there was nothing physically wrong with her.

Aunt Jessie finally convinced her niece to see a psychiatrist. Somebody in the family suggested the name of Dr. Gerhart Freilinger, who maintained an office on the Upper East Side. In one session the doctor confirmed that she was suffering from anorexia nervosa. Dr. Freilinger theorized that because she had been ignored as a child, her refusal to eat was a way of drawing attention to herself. But knowing the cause did not of necessity cure the symptoms. Barbara continued to fast.

Igor Troubetzkoy arrived in New York toward the end of October and found his wife sequestered in Suite 3910 on the thirty-ninth floor of the Hotel Pierre. He was kept waiting three days before she agreed to see him. "She was so-o-o-o-o tired," he says, mimicking the reception she accorded him. "She couldn't figure out why she had returned to New York, and I couldn't understand why I had followed." In mid-March 1950, with Lance enrolled in the Judson School near Tucson, Arizona, Barbara returned by boat to Paris. Igor flew back by himself at the beginning of April.

It was through Count Jean de Baglion that Barbara made the acquaintance in Paris of thirty-year-old Prince Henri de la Tour d'Auvergne, a French aristocrat whose grandfather had been Foreign

Minister of France. Henri, a broker in a French securities firm, was refined, witty, fanciful, a writer of poetry and a voracious reader. He and Barbara began seeing each other and were soon spending weekends together, either at his house in Paris or in resorts like Deauville and Nice.

What was strange about the affair was the candid manner in which they carried on, a sharp contrast to Barbara's surreptitious meetings with Freddie McEvoy during the last days of her marriage to Cary Grant. "Troubetzkoy saw what was going on," says Jean de Baglion, "but he was too afraid to say anything to Barbara. He didn't want to lose her."

The end, when it came, was almost anti-climactic. It happened the end of June after a party that Barbara threw in a floodlit garden adjoining the British Embassy in Paris. The Duke and Duchess of Windsor and Jimmy Donahue were among the guests. Jimmy, who could be pretty crude, made a distasteful remark to Igor about Barbara and Henri. The next day the couple had it out. Igor told Barbara everything he had been storing up for months, all the little slights and painful moments that he had let pass by. When he was done he went to his room, emptied his closet, packed his car, and drove off.

His destination was Cannes and when he reached it he locked himself in a hotel room and for the next three weeks he slaved away at a manuscript that he called *Life With Barbara Hutton*. He had no publication plans for the manuscript but when it was done he locked it away on the premise that it might one day come in handy.

It was in Cannes that Igor bumped into actor Errol Flynn, to whom he had once before been introduced by Freddie McEvoy. With Flynn in Cannes was a famous attorney from San Francisco, a specialist in torts and divorce settlements, whose name was Melvin Belli. An hour after meeting Igor, Belli agreed to represent him in his divorce case with Barbara Hutton. He consented to work on a contingency basis—20 percent of any settlement, plus expenses.

By early September Troubetzkoy, Flynn and Belli were all in Paris. Belli contacted Graham Mattison through Dominick & Dominick's Paris offices and requested a meeting. They met twice, the first time in the dining room at the George V.

"After the conference with Mattison," recalls Belli, "I met Igor and Flynn at Maxim's. The three of us went there every night. The food was wonderful and it made more palatable my announcement that the meeting hadn't gone very well. Igor was discouraged but he wasn't morbid. We were taking turns paying the bill, and since Igor was broke he had brought along a half-dozen rabbits from the garden in back of his country house. The chef was glad to take them instead of cash, because rabbit was a specialty of the house. Igor said to me, 'If Mattison doesn't come across, I'm going to have to start breeding rabbits.'

"Anyway, Mattison agreed to another meeting, this time with everyone present. He brought along a lawyer named Samuel Hartman, and I was there with Troubetzkoy and Flynn. We sat there talking for a while, and I could see we weren't getting anywhere. I wanted three million dollars, and they were offering a tenth of that. Then they doubled their bid. After three hours Mattison says, 'Nine hundred thousand. But that's the bottom line. Take it or leave it.' Igor draws himself up at this point. 'I don't want to be nine-tenths of a millionaire. I want to be a millionaire. So start talking a million, or let's forget it.' So they forgot it."

Belli returned to San Francisco. The newspapers were full of stories about the pending divorce. As soon as he could Belli called a news conference and pleaded his client's case. "Igor Troubetzkoy is heart-broken," he said. "He wants Barbara to return to his side and rectify the damage she has done by casting him aside like the proverbial worn-out slipper. Barbara has to learn that she can't just buy husbands the way she goes out to purchase a new dress. She seems to be involved in some new grotesque adventure but unless she resumes conjugal relations with Igor, we intend to sue."

It was strong-sounding stuff, and Barbara, now in Madrid, responded with a threat of her own: "So now he has threatened to sue me. He thinks I'd rather die than go through the publicity. They want to crucify me, but they won't. If they want to play dirty, I can play dirty too. Igor is the cheapest, most mendacious man I have ever known. He's only interested in grandfather's money."

The war of words was still raging in November 1950 when Barbara returned to New York and was confronted by reporters wanting to know if she was divorcing Troubetzkoy in order to marry Prince D'Auvergne.

"Henri is only thirty years old and I still regard him as a kid," responded Barbara. "He is a scion of one of the best families in France and is a true Prince—not a phony Prince like some I could name who have the title. It is really too bad that a woman cannot have an innocent friendship with a man without provoking a scandal."

Barbara's lament about scandals found few sympathetic ears, par-ticularly after it became evident that she was responsible for her own scandal-making. One evening she and Henri (who suddenly turned up in New York) went to El Morocco for dinner. Dinner for Barbara consisted of a dozen gin and tonics. At some point between her eleventh and twelfth drinks she disappeared underneath the table and huddled there beating time to the orchestra with a fork and knife.*

Her comportment was beginning to rival that of her notorious cousin, Jimmy Donahue, whose latest shenanigans involved the Duke and Duchess of Windsor. Early in 1950 Jessie Donahue entertained the Windsors in Palm Beach, and Jimmy met them there. His humor, manner and generosity appealed to the Windsors—so much so that when they returned to their Paris home at 85 rue de la Faisanderie that spring, they took him along. The year he met the Windsors he came into a $15 million trust fund, a fortune that enabled him to be even more flamboyant than usual in his spending; his continual lavishing of expensive gifts on the Windsors could not have failed but add to their regard for him. As a tireless host and gadabout, his duties as the accommodating third member of the household gradually increased, until even the European press took notice. "Jimmy," wrote one columnist, "escorts the D. and D. everywhere and stays up playing cards with the Duchess long after the Duke has retired." In subsequent weeks he was seen escorting the Duchess in public without the Duke. Jimmy and Wallis were hardly inconspicuous at such fashionable Paris nightspots as Monseigneur, L'Eléphant Blanc, Shéhérazade—dancing together, singing, holding hands, passing notes, whispering, giggling, exchanging long looks and private jokes. One of Diana Cooper's stories about this unnatural alliance insisted that at Monseigneur late one night, Jimmy ordered an enormous bunch of red roses for Wallis. At the time she was waving a large white ostrich fan, a gift from the Duke, which she put down. She asked the flower girl to place the roses in a vase on top of the fan. "Look, everybody," Wallis squealed. "The Prince of Wales's plumes and Jimmy Donahue's roses!" Lady Diana, who happened to be with them at the time, noticed that the Duke of Windsor's eyes filled with tears.

With the press beginning to offer speculations as to the metaphysics of the living arrangement *"chez the D. and D.,"* the Duke of Windsor became concerned. But when he warned Wallis that people were talking, she ridiculed him. *"Really,* David? What could possibly be more harmless. I'm old enough to be his mother. And everybody knows what Jimmy is. Why, his friends call me the Queen of the Fairies!"

Her husband did not press the point, not even in the fall of 1950 when she announced that she was joining Jimmy in New York while the Duke remained in Paris to work on his memoirs. With her arrival in

*See Dean Jennings, *Barbara Hutton*, pps. 235-37.

the States, the rumors began to circulate in earnest. A line by Walter Winchell in the *Daily Mirror* summed up what most of café society had come to believe: "The Duke and Duchess of Windsor are finished!" The gossip columns resounded with items coupling Jimmy and Wallis. They were seen together at the Stork Club, El Morocco, Gogi's Larue. Jimmy took her to his familiar gay hangouts—George's and Madame Fox's—and introduced her around. One evening they surprised patrons of The Colony by bringing along two violinists and a harmonica player, as well as Elsa Maxwell and Angier Biddle Duke. This was perhaps the first and only time that diners at The Colony were serenaded by musicians.

During the day Wallis and Jimmy stopped traffic on Madison Avenue as they prowled the antiques shops and art galleries. She shared his enthusiasm for collecting eighteenth-century snuffboxes; he gave her one that had belonged to an earlier King of England, George IV. Jessie Donahue, oblivious to the rumors associating her son and the Duchess of Windsor in a romantic entanglement, was pleased that he was keeping such illustrious company. The Duke of Windsor, besieged by a constant stream of newspaper reports, was outraged, and finally decided to join his wife in New York in time for Christmas. Jimmy now delivered the coup de grâce. On Christmas Eve he led Wallis and the Duke, once the temporal head of the Church of England, into St. Patrick's Cathedral for a midnight mass in Donahue's own Catholic faith.

Jimmy delighted in all the attention the press was paying him, and from time to time added a few of his own tidbits to the clamor. He cracked up a gathering of reporters by saying of Wallis, "She's marvelous! The best cocksucker I've ever known!" Such crudities were lent credence by the eyewitness testimony of a reliable member of Jimmy's circle who claimed that after a party at Jessie Donahue's house, he accidentally strayed into the wrong room and found Jimmy and Wallis in bed together.

Incredible as it seems, the Duke of Windsor never once acknowledged that his "perfect" marriage wasn't everything he had hoped it would be, or that his wife, bored to death by her drably unimaginative husband, could possibly think of ever having an affair with another man, much less Jimmy Donahue. What the obtuse Duke of Windsor did object to was the talk and the whispering and the play in the press that the "friendship" generated, unbecoming publicity for a man of his station and background. Otherwise he was bafflingly blind to his wife's actions.

Jimmy and Wallis could not have been more unsubtle in their sexual dalliance had they rented the Globe Theater and performed their act on stage. They were so steady a duet that Elsa Maxwell publicly cautioned the Duchess on the importance of "appearance" and "discretion." Wallis, stubborn and willful as always, paid little heed to such advice. In New York, prior to the Duke's arrival, she and Jimmy stayed together in one of Barbara Hutton's guest rooms at the Pierre. In Paris Barbara later arranged for them to use the apartment of a friend. Whenever Jimmy traveled with the Windsors, they would take three bedrooms, with Jimmy invariably sneaking in to spend the night with Wallis. On these occasions she would post a sign outside her door: KEEP OUT, OR STAY OUT, OR DON'T COME IN. This astounding bedroom farce went on for more than three years, the Duke remaining mysteriously silent while Jimmy mugged and camped his way deeper and deeper into Wallis's heart.

Some months after the affair's termination in 1954, an acquaintance of the Windsors saw Jimmy on Fifth Avenue, strolling arm-in-arm with his latest "friend," an androgynous boy in his late teens. Donahue, who was about to take the lad with him on a world cruise, had lost none of his biting humor. "Let me introduce you," he said, "to the boy who took the boy who took the girl who took the boy off the throne of Merry Old England."*

❦

Early in 1951 Barbara Hutton checked into the Arizona Inn in Tucson, a few miles from Lance's boarding school. Francis Ryan, the bell captain at the Arizona Inn, remembers serving Barbara, Lance and Ticki in their hotel rooms: "I was in room service then. Miss Hutton and the others rarely came to the dining room but would have their meals served daily from our department. Their eating hours were hopelessly erratic and the meals had to be served individually at their convenience. She made up for it with extravagant tips. One evening she entertained some friends in the dining room. In those days we had live music throughout the dinner hour, and she was so impressed that she called the musicians over and gave each a hundred-dollar bill to play at her table."

*The details concerning Jimmy Donahue and his relations with the Windsors are drawn primarily from the following sources: Steven Birmingham, *Duchess: The Story of Wallis Warfield Windsor;* Iles Brody, *Gone With the Windsors;* J. Bryan, III and Charles J. V. Murphy, *The Windsor Story: An Intimate Portrait of Edward VIII and Mrs. Simpson by the Authors Who Knew Them Best;* Ralph G. Martin, *The Woman He Loved: The Story of the Duke and Duchess of Windsor.*

Henri de la Tour d'Auvergne flew out to Arizona to spend a week with Barbara before embarking on a new position with a Canadian banking firm in Montreal. His departure occasioned an entry in Barbara's notebooks to the effect that she had been left "to the lonely spectacle of lifeless cacti and leaping jack rabbits." The remainder of her stay proved uneventful except for a passing encounter with British actor Michael Wilding, the future husband of Elizabeth Taylor. Wilding was staying at the Arizona Inn with Hollywood newlyweds Stewart Granger and Jean Simmons, at whose wedding he had been best man. One evening Wilding noticed Barbara by herself at a table in the hotel bar. When she smiled at him he went over to introduce himself. They shared a bottle of Dom Pérignon at the bar and polished off a second bottle in her suite. Wilding ended up spending the night with Barbara.

The following day he invited Barbara to join his party for supper around the swimming pool. She arrived punctually, beautifully attired and made up. Apart from a dazzling diamond ring, her only jewelry consisted of what looked like a necklace of black beads, which surprised Granger a little as he knew she owned a magnificent collection of jewelery. After dinner, during which Barbara only toyed with her food, she remarked on the pretty engagement ring Jean was wearing and asked to see it more closely. "While she was examining our slightly flawed stone," writes Granger in his autobiographical *Sparks Fly Upward*, "she made sure Jean was suitably blinded by the blue-white gemstone she was wearing herself. Then she noticed the rather unpretentious pearl necklace I had given Jean as a wedding present and, after saying how sweet it was, asked Jean if she liked the one she was wearing. I tried to kick Jean under the table as I had a suspicion of what was coming, but Miss Hutton got there first. She held out her black beads and thrust them across the table into Jean's face. They weren't beads at all, they were black pearls, a unique and absolutely priceless string. ... I wanted to kick her skinny arse all round the pool as I couldn't stand the way she was trying to humiliate Jean."*

At the end of February, Barbara was staying with some old friends, Ignacio (Nacho) and Lee de Landa, at their home in Cuernavaca, Mexico. The purpose of the visit became clear when Barbara appeared at the civil courthouse in Cuernavaca to file divorce papers against Igor Troubetzkoy. The documents were countersigned by Civil Court Judge

---

*Barbara's black pearl necklace, among her most valuable possessions, originally belonged to Anne of Austria, Queen of France and the mother of Louis XIV.

Alfonso Roqueni and posted on a bulletin board outside the court-house, as required by Mexican law.

Melvin Belli heard of the divorce action only because he belonged to the Mexican Law Association and had friends in Cuernavaca. "At that time the divorce mill in Mexico was a farce," says Belli. "But even they had a law on the books stipulating that all parties had to be notified in writing. When I called Igor in Paris I learned that he had never been served. Then it got back to me that this judge in Mexico was up for re-election and was actively soliciting contributions for his campaign fund. So I gathered my pennies and sent my law partner down there with $2,500 in cash for His Honor's war chest. He hands over the contribution, and the next day Barbara's divorce case goes out the window."

Learning of the court's decision, Barbara returned to New York and under an assumed name took refuge in the LeRoy Hospital, a private sanatorium at 40 East Sixty-first Street. The only friend she saw during her stay was Anya Sorine, whom she hadn't seen since the day she and Igor were married in Switzerland four years earlier.

Barbara was released from LeRoy Hospital on June 3 and returned to Paris three days later. The next time she was seen by anyone was a few weeks later at a cocktail party in an apartment not far from the Ritz. Another guest at the same party was the American composer Ned Rorem, who was meeting Barbara for the first time and subsequently recorded the event in his *Paris Diary:* "....There she was dancing moodily with one of the forgotten gigolos, the two of them trembling slowly in the middle of the floor. She can't have weighed sixty pounds and her...eyes oozed like black wounds from beneath an enormous hat. She fell upon the couch in a daze and asked to be alone with me for a moment, and though nobody liked that idea since I was not famous ... they acquiesced and went away.... We talked about America and how nice we both were. Then everyone came back and I was forced to leave."

Later that summer Melvin Belli received a telegram from Igor Troubetzkoy instructing him to drop all pending divorce claims against his estranged wife. The message confused Belli for several days until he came across a newspaper interview with Barbara, in which she said that Igor had come to see her and had apologized for all the sadness and trouble he had caused her. The interview ended with Barbara denouncing all the "greedy and selfish people around Igor" who had been misguiding him in demanding money from her.

Having been made official scapegoat in the case, Belli was dropped altogether as Troubetzkoy's counsel, and Igor worked out an amicable divorce settlement directly with Graham Mattison. The conditions of the divorce stipulated that Troubetzkoy would receive the deed to the house in Gif-sur-Yvette, a new car and a lifetime trust that yielded approximately $1,000 per month. The trust, according to Igor, amounted to a piddling $250,000, far less than Mattison had originally been willing to pay. He settled his account with Belli, by paying him a total of $30,000 in fees; he paid an additional $2,500 to a second California attorney, Milton Golden, for miscellaneous legal services.

In keeping with the bizarre nature of the protracted negotiations, the case ended with two separate divorce rulings, one in Mexico, another in Paris. Barbara's lawyers appealed Judge Roqueni's decision, and on July 20, 1951, it was overturned and a divorce granted. But because there was some doubt as to the validity of a Mexican divorce, Graham Mattison filed a second suit in Paris, and a second decree was granted on October 31, 1951.

Igor continued to appear on Barbara's doorstep from time to time for years to come. Howard D. Jones, U.S. Consul General in Tangier from 1968 to 1971, recalls a strange encounter he once had with Troubetzkoy in 1969. Jones had received a call from Barbara's secretary one Sunday afternoon asking if he might drop by to help soothe Barbara's nerves after a little crisis at Palace Sidi Hosni. "When I entered her bedroom," says Jones, "there was a gentleman kneeling as if in prayer at the foot of her bed. I nodded a casual greeting, assuming he was a prelate. Barbara promptly accused me of not showing proper deference to Prince Igor, her Fourth."

⁊❦

Don Carlos de Bestegui y de Iturbi—"Charlie" to society—was a mining-rich, Eton-educated Parisian of Mexican heritage with a genius for interior decoration. Before the war he was famous in Paris as a bachelor whose taste ran to beautiful women and beautiful houses, but he outdid himself during the war, which he spent, as a neutral with diplomatic status, restoring a large eighteenth-century château outside Paris, called "Groussay." Then the Germans took over the house and left it in ruins. After the war Bestegui started over, this time in Venice, purchasing the spectacular eighteenth-century Palazzo Labia, overlooking the Grand Canal, with its eighteen ground-floor salons, the largest of which contained the Tiepolo frescoes of Antony and Cleopatra.

On September 3, 1951, Bestegui gave an eighteenth-century masked ball at the Labia that was to become known as "the party of the century." If it wasn't that, it was certainly the party of the fifties. Everyone with even the vaguest pretense of social accomplishment claimed to be invited, whether they were or not, and when the Paris

Herald Tribune published a pirated copy of the 1,500-name guest list, the fibbers were exposed. The more fortunate 1,500 ranged in age from the young Vicomtesse Jacqueline de Ribes to the ageless "Morosine of Venice," a dowager once popularly regarded as "the most beautiful woman in the most beautiful house in the most beautiful city in the world." Others in the crowd included Duff and Diana Cooper, Arturo Lopez, the Aga Khan, Elsa Maxwell, Daisy Fellowes, Bernard Berenson, Cecil Beaton, every Rothschild in France, every Volpi in Italy, and Barbara Hutton.

Barbara's escort was Count Lanfranco Rasponi, a figure in Florentine and New York social life, a music critic and publicist commonly credited with having "discovered" the cosmetics queen Elizabeth Arden. Rasponi attended the Bestegui party as a blackamoor in black face and a costume consisting of black tights and a short-waisted top with petaled hem. Barbara went as Mozart in a $15,000 Christian Dior creation that included a black domino mask and white powdered wig, diamond-spangled lace and solid gold shoe buckles. It was not the most original costume at the party, but it was the most expensive.

The Bestegui ball may have been the last great folly of its kind. The Grand Canal had the look of a movie set brightly illuminated by floodlights as the flotilla of gondolas, ferrying the guests, passed beneath bridges lined with cheering spectators. Grandstands for 4,000 Venetians had been erected in the piazza near the palace. All the streets surrounding the Labia were lit with flares. Servants in eighteenth-century liveries, carrying torches, escorted each new arrival up the grand staircase and into the central chamber to be received by the beaming host.

Barbara would describe the event: "Lots of food and drink, congeniality, three jazz orchestras, dancing, the wondrous effect of so many authentic-looking costumes. Every time anybody went to a balcony the crowd outside burst into raucous cheers. The funniest sight: Marie Laure de Noailles, monstrous as the Lion of St. Mark, dancing with Jacques Fath, hideous in an oversweet confection of gold and white lace covered with thousands of feathers that got plucked off as the night wore on. Most subdued guest: Mrs. Winston Churchill in a black lace gown and three-cornered hat. Most original costume: Salvador and Gala Dali in matching twenty-foot-high cylindrical masks, more twenty-first- than eighteenth-century. The next day Dali was found feeding the pigeons in St. Mark's, wearing nothing but a flaming red wig and a pair of knee-high pink socks."

At the beginning of November Barbara was back in her suite at the Paris Ritz. On the fourth, ten days before her thirty-ninth birthday, she received word that a yacht carrying Freddie McEvoy and his new bride, French fashion model Claude Filatre, had gone down in a storm off Cap Cantin, a hundred miles southeast of Casablanca. The bodies of McEvoy, his wife, her maid and three crew members were recovered a day later.

As soon as she heard, Barbara called Baron Gottfried von Cramm in Hanover, who tried to console her as best he could. He suggested that she meet him in Cologne so they could be together on her birthday. "It will make you feel better," he said.

He was waiting for her when the express from Paris pulled into the railroad station. Barbara, having had too much to drink, practically fell into Gottfried's car to be driven to Cologne's Excelsior Hotel, where he had booked separate suites. Her visit was marred by several factors, not least of which was the sorrow she felt over Freddie McEvoy's death. In addition there were the crowds that daily milled outside the Excelsior to catch sight of the famous Woolworth heiress, making it impossible for Barbara to step out of the hotel. Every day the mailman delivered a large bundle of letters to Barbara's suite, hundreds of letters from strangers asking for money or making frightening threats against her life. Instead of celebrating her birthday, Barbara climbed into bed with a bottle of gin and drank herself to sleep.

At the end of the month Gottfried accompanied her to Frankfurt and put her on a flight for New York with a brief stopover for refueling in London. When the plane landed in London Barbara refused to wait with the other passengers in the air terminal, maintaining her seat and insisting that she had bought a ticket for New York and wouldn't leave the plane until it arrived there.

Barbara's wanderings over the next six months took her from New York to Tucson, Tucson to Mexico City, Mexico City to Acapulco, Acapulco to Cuernavaca, Cuernavaca to San Francisco. By June 1952 she was in Hillsborough, adjacent to Burlingame, where she had lived as a child. With her in a ten-bedroom mansion were Lance, Ticki, Sister, Helen Munier (her personal maid), Antonia (Tony) and José Gonzales (a married couple who worked for Barbara in Tangier and often accompanied her on trips), as well as Bill Robertson who had been hired as Barbara's house manager.

For the most part Barbara kept to herself, venturing out of doors predominantly to take walks or to visit old friends, such as Susan Smith or Harrie Hill Page. On occasion she would drive into San Francisco to go shopping for Oriental fashion in Chinatown.

One of Barbara's favorite shops in San Francisco was Byron Trott's Villa Iris, specializing in European dinnerware. She regularly placed huge orders and had the merchandise shipped to friends as far away as Japan. Another store she frequented was the San Francisco branch of Sak's Fifth Avenue. One day she called from Hillsborough and ordered a dozen full-length blue sable coats. In the end she kept three for herself and gave the others away to her staff and friends. She bought a thirteenth coat for the salesgirl who processed her order.

A few weeks after Barbara's arrival in Hillsborough, she received a visit from Jimmy Donahue. Jimmy took his cousin to the Beige Room, a club with performances by gays and female impersonators. Barbara had been told that one of the transvestite acts was a parody of herself and Doris Duke on an apocryphal automobile trip up the California coast. In the skit the two "heiresses" sit in the back seat of a limousine. Barbara asks the nattily attired chauffeur to pull into the next service station so she can avail herself of the facilities. The car soon stops and Barbara makes a mad dash for the ladies' room. She returns and they are about to depart when Doris decides she too had better freshen up. "Is it sanitary?" she asks. "Clean as a whistle," Barbara assures her. "Only there's no toilet paper." "Oh dear, what will I do?" Doris wails. Barbara rummages through her shoulder bag, discarding various womanly accouterments, before coming up empty-handed. "You should have said something earlier, Dee-Dee," remarks Barbara. "If I'd known I would have saved you a traveler's check. I just used my last one."

Barbara and Jimmy also took in a young Egyptian torch singer named Amuziata Buetti, whose performance at a club called The Deep was receiving raves. After sitting through two sets the cousins went backstage to meet her. Barbara was so impressed that she invited Amuziata to visit her at Hillsborough on her next night off.

Amuziata accepted the invitation. What particularly struck her was Barbara's exquisite taste in fashion. "Her clothes were made with such care. They were Oriental but with ruffles at her face, throat and wrists. The effect was so perfect that no one probably ever bothered to look beyond her clothes. She used clothes to create a smoke screen behind which she enjoyed the best kind of privacy. People looked and didn't see—all they saw were these tantalizing garments."

After two months in Hillsborough Barbara decided it was time to move on. She and her group—consisting of Lance, Sister, Harrie Hill Page and Bill Robertson—flew to Honolulu and checked into the Royal Hawaiian Hotel. Also in the group was Barbara's former companion, David Pleydell-Bouverie, then living in Northern California. Bouverie stayed two weeks and left, convinced once and for all that he and Barbara could never co-exist. Barbara stayed on to attend a costume ball at Shangri-La, Doris Duke's $3 million Diamond Head dreamhouse.

By early September Barbara had moved on again, this time into Irene Selznick's house at 1050 Summit Drive in Beverly Hills, not far from the Buster Keaton mansion she had once occupied. Irene Selznick had moved to New York, and Cary Grant had helped Barbara find her new rental. By coincidence, the Keaton mansion was presently occupied by Cobina Wright, Barbara's early mentor, now a society columnist for the Los Angeles *Herald-Examiner*.

Cobina, as full of energy and optimism as ever, planned a party to welcome Barbara back to the old neighborhood. She hired an orchestra, caterer, several bartenders and security guards. She ordered a massive cake and stocked her refrigerator with magnums of champagne. But on the night of the party Barbara felt too ill to attend—or so she claimed.

In a last-minute bid to try and rouse the guest of honor out of her lethargy, Cobina sent actor Gilbert Roland over to the Selznick house. Roland, as Cobina would later tell it, found Barbara in bed nursing her own bottle of champagne. The actor took stock of the situation and decided to stay. In any event, he didn't return to the party that night and the next day told Cobina that he and Barbara had thrown their own little party.

Cobina was on the verge of breaking the story of a new Barbara Hutton romance when she received further details. The next time Roland called Barbara he was told that she was out of town. He telephoned a second and a third time and received the same excuse. Barbara wasn't out of town but out of sorts. She had retreated into her own impenetrable shell, locking her door and pulling the draperies. With the exception of one or two members of her household staff, she maintained contact only with Dr. Jack Hollins, her Hollywood physician, who stopped by on a regular basis to see her.

"She was back on alcohol, back on pills, back on cigarettes, back on her back," says Hollins. "She was convinced she had less than a year to live, that she was dying of some mysterious ailment. And she was on Seconal, codeine, Demerol, and anything else she could get her hands on. I found I could cut her dependence on sedatives by prescribing a placebo—a harmless sugar tablet—and usually they worked just as well as real sleeping pills. It was all in the mind. If she thought she was taking sleeping pills, she slept."

Barbara's complaints, however, didn't abate. Dr. Hollins finally put Barbara in the hospital for a complete workover, if only to show her that there was nothing physically the matter. The results of the tests re-enforced the doctor's theory that Barbara—not illness—was her own worst enemy.

On February 1, 1953, she returned to her house and climbed back into bed. All the reassurance that medical science could provide couldn't convince her that she wasn't on her last leg. And since she believed that she was dying, she also believed that no amount of medication could do her more harm than had already been done by the rigors of nature.

It happened that Lance had a friend from Switzerland named Leland Rosenberg staying with him at his mother's house, a twenty-five-year-old former trainee with the Department of Public Information at the United Nations. One evening Barbara asked the young man to drive to the nearest pharmacy to fill a prescription for her. Rosenberg, who had no inkling of Barbara's drug problems, did as she asked and returned shortly with a vial containing two dozen Seconal tablets. That evening, frustrated by her inability to fall asleep, Barbara took all twenty-four pills.

The inevitable had come to pass. Dr. Hollins was shaken out of slumber by a ringing telephone. By the time he reached Cedars of Lebanon Hospital, Barbara was barely breathing, her blood pressure a life-threatening sixty over ten. He worked swiftly with the help of an intern and several emergency room nurses, and within minutes Barbara had tubes and needles protruding from various parts of her body. It was dawn before she was out of danger, resting comfortably in a hospital bed.

After her return to Summit Drive Barbara denied ever having tried to kill herself, insisting she had merely wanted "to fall asleep." A wary Dr. Hollins kept a close watch over his patient, visiting her at home as often as two and sometimes three times a day, making himself available whenever she wanted to talk. After a while he suggested that she consider going into psychotherapy. She resisted the suggestion but offered to consider the possibility.

It was at about this time that Doris Duke turned up in California. She had recently purchased Rudolph Valentino's Beverly Hills estate, Falcon Lair, and was having it redecorated. When she heard about Barbara's mishap, she dropped in on her old friend and brought along a strange little man from Mysore, India, who called himself Yogi Rao. Yogi was a teacher of transcendental meditation and he had apparently helped Doris overcome one or two hurdles. Doris was certain that he could also help Barbara.

Whatever form Yogi's help took, it didn't by any means come cheap. Barbara signed up for a series of fifty one-hour sessions with Yogi at something like $1,000 per session. Barbara was never very explicit about what went on during these sessions, although she once indicated that they involved Rigaud candles, a prayer rug and a great deal of monosyllabic Mantric chanting.

At the end of these sessions Yogi Rao returned to Mysore, and Barbara went back to Dr. Hollins. Their dealings transcended the purely medical. The doctor, an older man with white hair, represented a father figure to Barbara. Their relationship was made even more complex when Lance, at seventeen, started dating the doctor's sixteen-year-old daughter. Barbara turned to Dr. Hollins for advice on how to raise her son. Hollins felt, as did others, that Lance was spoiled. He drove around in a high-priced sports car and frequented such Hollywood nightspots as the Beachcomber and Mocambo. Like his mother, he tended to drink too much, especially considering his age. An argument erupted between Lance and Dr. Hollins when the latter attempted to induce his daughter to date other boys.

Lance's teachers at the Judson School described him as a bright but shy student who had difficulty making friends. His best friend at school was Bruce Kessler, whose father, Jack, had founded the Rose Marie Reid Swimwear Company, and whose mother, Nina, was a surrogate mother to Lance. The Kessler home in Los Angeles was where Lance spent much of his time away from school. One of Lance's later acquaintances summed up his familial situation in this fashion: "Bruce Kessler was like a brother to him. Nina Kessler was a mother, Cary Grant a father. On the whole he seemed like a lonely guy. When he graduated from high school, the only person to attend the ceremony in his behalf was Bill Robertson."

Lance possessed Court Reventlow's light brown hair and athletic physique but had the facial features and remote mannerisms of Barbara Hutton. "Lance," says Bruce Kessler, "was protective of his mother but never close to her. They were alike in certain respects but also quite different. Lance was earthbound, and his mother was off in the clouds. Lance spent money on cars maybe but wouldn't dream of splurging on clothes or throwing it around the way she did. He didn't fit the image she had mapped out for him. She thought he should be interested in 'the finer things in life.' She taught him everything she knew about precious jewelry, for example, but he was only interested in making his own jewelry, not in buying it at Cartier. Lance could never understand what drove his mother—the incessant globetrotting, spending, the marriages and love affairs. He used to joke about it. I remember one time ... this was later on ... for his twenty-second birthday, I think it was ... his mother was supposed to take a bunch of us out to dinner. Lance was to get a date and thought about inviting my sixteen-year-old sister. My mom and I told him, 'Your mother will accuse you of cradle snatching.' 'Oh, yeah,' he said. 'Wait till you see what she brings.'"

Much of the turmoil between mother and son arose because neither appreciated the other's lifestyle. Cary Grant was fixing Lance up with a number of Hollywood starlets, while his mother wanted him to date college girls and girls from "better families." The only romance Barbara seemed to condone involved Gloria Gordon, daughter of MGM producer Leon Gordon, a friendship that all too quickly dissolved.

Lance, in turn, castigated his mother for her growing dependence on doctors, especially her dependence on Dr. Hollins. There was a particularly bitter argument between Barbara and Lance when Dr. Hollins told Barbara that she was giving her son too high an allowance. Lance finally asked Bruce Kessler for advice, worried that his allowance would be reduced. In a moment of lightness, Bruce said, "I know what—I'll marry your mother and then I'll raise your allowance."

In the middle of March Barbara received a telephone call from Anya Sorine in New York. Savely Sorine, the Russian artist, was dying of cancer. He was in Mount Sinai Hospital, and the doctors there had given him only a short time to live.

Barbara immediately flew to New York. The sight of this once robust man now reduced to wasted flesh was difficult for her to accept. She went to see Dr. Martin Steinberg, director of Mount Sinai Hospital, and asked him to send all of Savely's medical bills to her attention in care of Graham Mattison, Dominick & Dominick, 14 Wall Street. The day after her hospital visit, a courier arrived in Steinberg's office with an envelope containing a check for $100,000, Barbara's donation to Mount Sinai's cancer research fund. When Savely died a few months later, she made a second donation in the same amount to the same fund.

Barbara had made up her mind to return to Paris. Her only other stop in New York was the Central Park South studio of painter-sculptor Herbert Haseltine to view for the first time a pair of gold-cast horse heads she had commissioned as far back as 1943. The idea for the heads came to Haseltine in 1938 while he was making detailed drawings in the stables of the Maharajah of Nawager of an Arabian stallion named Indra and a mare named Lakshmi. When he saw in the treasure chambers of the Indian princes examples of the jeweled trappings worn by animals in ceremonial processions (such as are illustrated in Mogul miniatures), he decided to carve the figures in a highly stylized manner and have them cast in 24-karat gold, and ornamented with precious stones. The cost of the materials necessitated a patron for the project. He found one in Barbara Hutton.

The heads, weighing more than 30 pounds each, were one-quarter life-size, measuring about 15 inches from the peak of their manes to the bottoms of their rock crystal bases. The stallion head contained 135 ounces of fine gold, the mare 178 ounces. The casting, chasing and setting of the precious stones was done by Joseph Ternbach, a Viennese art restorer whose studio was in Forest Hills, N.Y. Ternbach acquired the jewels from New York dealer Raphael Esmerian. The final count, as indicated by invoices, reads as follows:

STALLION (Indra): 164 rubies, 16 full pearls, 94 half pearls, 69 diamonds (tafel diamonds), 12 emeralds, 82 sapphires.

MARE (Lakshmi): 182 diamonds (tafel diamonds), 24 emeralds, 12 sapphires, 46 half pearls, 6 full pearls, 21 rubies, 13 ruby heads.

From the beginning the horse heads were a source of aggravation to Barbara, starting with their transportation from New York to her suite at the Paris Ritz. These arrangements became the responsibility of Graham Mattison and whether by oversight or simple miscalculation, he appears to have blundered by insuring them for shipment to Europe for only $50,000, more than $1 million below their appraised value.

Another problem arose in the fall of 1953 when the Tate Gallery in London offered Haseltine a one-man show to celebrate his best-known equestrian sculpture, including several works commissioned by Winston Churchill. Churchill also wrote an introduction for the exhibition catalogue. Barbara, however, had grave misgivings about placing her two Arabian horse heads on display, claiming that she hadn't yet had time to enjoy them herself. What she actually feared was a barrage of negative publicity once it became known that she had spent such an exorbitant sum on a work of art. The sculptor and his patron argued. The heads remained in Barbara's possession, but her friendship with Haseltine was hopelessly shattered.

Fourteen

B‌ARBARA ARRIVED IN Paris at the end of March 1953, and in April agreed to an interview with Art Buchwald of the New York *Herald Tribune*. One of the revelations that emerged from the meeting, which took place at the Ritz, was Barbara's saga of how strangers would sometimes spit at her when she was young and growing up during the Depression. Buchwald apparently came away from the interview with sympathetic thoughts about Barbara.

A few weeks after the interview Barbara was marooned in bed again. Dr. Robert de Gennes, her chief Paris physician, visited her often in her suite. She was drinking heavily, hiding the liquor bottles under her bed or in the closet. As fast as the doctor confiscated them, they would reappear. One evening Ticki Tocquet phoned Dr. Jack Hollins in Hollywood, to tell him that Barbara had once again tried to kill herself, this time by slashing her wrist and throat with a razor blade. Dr. Hollins flew to Paris.

He found Barbara in the hospital sitting up in bed, impatiently flipping through an Italian fashion magazine, her neck and left wrist swaddled in heavy bandages. The wounds were not deep enough to be considered lethal. Dr. Hollins concluded that Barbara had not meant to kill herself but was only sounding an alarm for help. She wanted attention, love, admiration. She wanted to be noticed, to be taken care of. Before returning to California, Dr. Hollins again advised Barbara to seek out a good psychotherapist, somebody who could help save her from herself. Once more Barbara told the doctor that she would take his suggestion under advisement. He left knowing her answer before she gave it.

Except for two faint scars, her recovery was complete and she was back at her hotel when Lance arrived to spend the summer in Europe. He was accompanied by his Swiss friend, Leland Rosenberg, and one of Leland's acquaintances, Manuel de Moya, an ambassadorial aide at the Dominican embassy in Paris. On the last day of May the trio departed for London to attend the coronation of Queen Elizabeth. After a week they were back in Paris, staying in Barbara's suite. Two weeks later they decided to go to Deauville to take in the international polo championships. Barbara went along for the ride. The French press accused her of chaperoning her son in an effort to frighten off the young female aspirants interested in his inheritance. Lance was evidently susceptible. He had recently been emotionally involved with a certain high-priced California call girl. When the lady discovered the identity of her John she suddenly became possessive, and it took a substantial sum of Barbara's money to pry her loose.

It was during her stay in Deauville that Barbara encountered the notorious Porfirio Rubirosa. Rubi, a competitor in the international polo tournament, was keeping company with the effervescent Hungarian-born actress Zsa Zsa (née Sari) Gabor, veteran of two previous marital mismatchings—first to Turkish diplomatic employee Burhan Belge, then to millionaire hotelier Conrad Hilton. Now she was estranged from husband number three, actor George Sanders.

Porfirio Rubirosa was an ambassador in the service of the Dominican Republic, having represented his country with no discernible results in Germany, Belgium, Great Britain, Argentina and France. Like Prince Aly Khan, he was among the most famous of a dying breed—the quintessential universal playboy-stud. His sexual exploits earned him the nickname *Toujours Prêt* (Always Ready), and throughout his amorous career no woman ever questioned the propriety of that phrase.

Contrary to the fantasy-laden reports of many gossip columnists, Porfirio Rubirosa was no banana-republic hayseed, born with a scythe in one hand and a machete in the other. He was the son of a well-to-do general-turned-diplomat who became Dominican chargé d'affaires in Paris. Porfirio was born in the Dominican Republic, but he was raised and educated in Paris, attending the finest schools and early in life circulating among the highest ranks of society. He returned to his native Caribbean island at seventeen to study law at the university, but after six months withdrew in favor of a military career. By twenty he was a captain in the army.

His passion for sports was evident early. He led the Dominican polo team to victory over a Nicaraguan team at what was to prove a propitious moment—just after Generalissimo Rafael Leonidas Trujillo established himself as dictator, in 1930. Trujillo took a fancy to the brash young officer. One day he sent the youth on a man's mission—to meet Señorita Flor de Oro (Flower of Gold) Trujillo at the the airport and escort her home. The seventeen-year-old daughter of the dictator was returning from school in France.

Flor de Oro was immediately drawn to Rubirosa. Although neither tall nor classically handsome, he exuded a magnetism, a passion and a *joie de vivre* that she found irresistible. He gave the impression of being a violent and reckless man, overbearingly possessive, yet at heart a true romantic. "He was a tough guy with beautiful manners," said one of his cronies. "He didn't chase women, they chased him," said another. Rubi wrote his own set of rules on what it took to win over a rich and powerful woman. "Never paw a woman," he said. "A woman does not like to be pawed. She likes to be—ah, liked." Rubi was shrewd, manipulative, amusing, self-confident, debonair. He was an easy conversationalist with a continental accent and a sensual voice. Two years after he met Flor, they were married. Trujillo declared the day of their marriage a national holiday, and later dispatched the young couple to his embassy in Berlin.

Rubi's life soon read like a script for an Errol Flynn movie. The columnists tracked his movements through Monte Carlo and St. Moritz, to the gambling casino at Cannes, the night clubs of London, the jazz clubs of Paris. He drove at Le Mans, wagered at Longchamp, organized his own polo team, excelled as an amateur boxer, learned to pilot a plane, played the bongo drums and guitar, collected porcelains and antiques, and fancied himself a gourmet. Those were his hobbies. His business was debauching women, loving and leaving them. "Do you ever work?" he was asked by a reporter. "Work?" he responded. "I have no time for work."

Five years into their marriage, having moved with Rubi to Paris, Flor Trujillo announced her intention to sue for divorce. Rubirosa graciously agreed. Instead of condemning him, his father-in-law rewarded him with a promotion within the Dominican legation, announcing that Rubirosa was an accomplished diplomat. "He's good at his job," said Trujillo, "because the women like him and he's a wonderful liar." Perhaps the dictator felt that anyone capable of spending five years with his daughter had to be a diplomat. Before she was finished, Flor would accumulate a stable of nine husbands.

After the divorce Rubi became involved in a number of unsavory schemes, everything from the smuggling of jewelry out of Civil War

Spain to the sale of visas to French Jews at the start of World War II. As Rubi's brother, César, put it: "He got rich selling visas to the Jews, but didn't everyone?" The price of a lifesaving visa ranged from $300 to $3,000, depending on supply and demand. Rubirosa purportedly sold them by the hundreds. Although he never actually denied the charge, he preferred to point out that he too was a victim of the Nazis: "I was twice arrested by the Gestapo, and twice incarcerated in prison camps, once in France, once in Germany." He neglected to explain that what he called "prison camps" were in fact diplomatic detention centers. He was housed in luxury quarters and spent his days playing polo with high-ranking German brass.

It was in 1940, between arrests, that he met the French cinema star Danielle Darrieux, then married to film director Henri Decoin. Decoin was no match for Rubirosa. Rubi and Danielle were married in 1942, following her divorce, vowing that they would stay together only as long as their mutual passion survived, or until their money ran out, whichever came first. The latter course was averted by Danielle's enormous popularity at the European box office, a plateau that had reached international proportions with her starring role opposite Charles Boyer in the vastly successful *Mayerling*. What came between them ultimately was Danielle's mother, who moved in with them after the war. "Once she entered the picture," noted Rubi, "Danielle and I argued incessantly. It was a very big love and we had said the moment it stops being such a big love we would separate. We would not ruin this beautiful thing. So we separated and later we agreed to an amicable divorce."

Then in 1947, Rubi met and married Doris Duke, whose previous marriage, to playboy James H. R. Cromwell, dissolved with the death in 1940 of a prematurely born daughter. The Duke-Rubirosa wedding took place at the Dominican embassy in Paris, following the eleventh-hour appearance of a pair of lawyers bearing a prenuptial agreement, protective of the Duke millions, for the groom to sign. Despite the contract, Rubirosa fared well financially. His wedding presents from Doris included a check for $500,000, a string of polo ponies, several sports cars, and a converted B-25 aircraft. The marriage lasted thirteen months, during which time Doris also gave him a two-hundred-year-old mansion at 46 rue de Bellechasse on the Left Bank, a prominent Paris address where Princess Elizabeth Chavchavadze had once lived.

It was Manuel de Moya, Rubirosa's fellow countryman, who brought Barbara together with Rubi at a small dinner party in Deauville. Barbara and Rubi had known each other on a casual basis since his marriage to Doris, but now the complexion of their relationship began to change, spurred on by Zsa Zsa Gabor's sudden decision to rejoin her husband George Sanders in Paris. The day after Zsa Zsa's departure Barbara was awakened at dawn by the sound of guitars, bongo drums and loud singing. Rubi had gathered a few friends, including Baron Elie Rothschild, to serenade Barbara from beneath her hotel window. This gesture took immediate hold of her imagination, because only a man in love, she reasoned, would go to such lengths to win a woman.

Barbara had always wondered what it was about Rubirosa that made women so vulnerable to his charms. She had never quite understood Doris Duke's motives for marrying Rubi, or how it was that he never moved about without a retinue of women at his disposal. But she soon learned first-hand what it was about him that made him so irresistible to the opposite sex: "He loves to please women, because by pleasing them he pleases himself. He is the ultimate sorcerer, capable of transforming the most ordinary evening into a night of magic." The same notebook entry describes Rubi as "Priapic, indefatigable, grotesquely proportioned. His lovemaking secret is that he practices an Egyptian technique called *Imsak*. No matter how aroused he becomes, he doesn't allow himself to complete the act. What he enjoys about it is the sense of control he achieves over his own body while exciting the woman beyond control, beyond the threshold."

If even 50 percent of the anecdotes and rumors that persisted about Rubirosa were untrue, there was still enough evidence to lend credence to the myth. Alice-Leone Moats, in researching her book, *The Million Dollar Studs*, interviewed one of Rubirosa's former valets, a Russian named Victor, who recalled an incident that proved particularly embarrassing to his employer: "One afternoon when I thought Mr. Rubirosa was out of the house, I went into his bedroom to put away some shirts. He was there and he wasn't alone. I had interrupted him at a very crucial moment. In his fury, he jumped out of bed and rushed toward me cursing like a stevedore. What a sight! I was stunned ... *E le uova, le uova!* They were so enormous that they bothered him and he usually wore a jockstrap."

The same servant was fired when it came out that he was making money by selling swatches of the diplomat's used underpants. When an Italian newspaper carried an article on the enterprising valet and disclosed that Rubi's briefs were made to order in an ultrathin cotton by Hilditch & Key of London at $15 a pair, the haberdasher was swamped with thousands of orders for the same article.

Rubirosa's prodigal dimensions were so widely and casually discussed that it became usual when ordering freshly ground pepper in the finest European restaurants to ask the waiter for the "Rubirosa." The comparison of Rubirosa's natural equipment to a sixteen-inch carved pepper mill helps explain why he had women on several continents clamoring for his attention. His chorus line of conquests included names no less recognizable than Zsa Zsa Gabor, Dolores Del Rio, Joan Crawford, Veronica Lake, Jayne Mansfield, Marilyn Monroe, Susan Hayward, Tina Onassis and Evita Perón.

In 1952 and 1953 Rubirosa was named as corespondent in two highly publicized divorce scandals. Richard J. Reynolds, scion to a vast tobacco fortune, accused his wife, Marianne O'Brien, of dallying with the playboy. And Robert Sweeny, Barbara Hutton's former swain, made the same charge against his wife, Joanne Connelley, heiress to Texas oil millions. The publicity accruing from these two affairs had immediate repercussions. Charging Rubi with "personal misconduct," Trujillo dismissed him from his ambassadorial post and suspended his diplomatic passport. Without position, salary or expense account, the Dominican found himself in the indelicate position of having no choice but to pursue Barbara Hutton.

⁂

In mid-September 1953 Rubirosa flew from Paris to Bel Air, California, to join Zsa Zsa Gabor, whose most recent reconciliation with her estranged husband had fizzled. Two months later Barbara Hutton arrived in New York aboard the S.S. *United States*, accompanied by Jean de Baglion on his first visit to the States. Barbara promptly came down with bronchial pneumonia and was taken to Doctors Hospital, where she remained for three weeks. Baglion visited daily, ministering to her by reading French poetry and plays. Rubirosa, whose days were now spent flying back and forth between Zsa Zsa in Los Angeles and Barbara in New York, saw her twice. On both occasions he brought large bouquets of flowers.

The day Barbara returned to her suite at the Pierre, Rubi was there to escort her. He was helpful, polite, overbearingly solicitous. It was time for the kill and Rubi went for the jugular. A few hours later he kept a luncheon appointment at 21 with Leon Block, the proprietor of Dunhill Tailors, then located near the restaurant on West Fifty-second Street. Over a thick sirloin he announced that he was going to marry Barbara Hutton and needed a new wardrobe. They returned to the store after lunch, where Rubi put in an order for twenty-five tropical-weight hand-tailored suits at $300 apiece. Block's instructions were to deliver the suits to Rubirosa and the bill to Barbara Hutton.

The next setting in what was fast becoming the most preposterous romantic triangle of the decade was the Last Frontier Hotel in Las

Vegas, where Zsa Zsa Gabor was rehearsing with her sisters, Eva and Magda, for their debut as a night-club act. Zsa Zsa had already announced her presence by posing for photographers in a semi-transparent evening gown specially designed for her debut.

On December 20, six days before the opening, Russell Birdwell, a leading Hollywood press agent, flew to Vegas to call on Zsa Zsa, whose public relations he had been handling for several years. He was concerned about the gossip that was emanating from Hollywood linking his client to Rubirosa. Zsa Zsa assured him that there was nothing to it. Not only was there nothing to it but Rubirosa was planning to marry Barbara Hutton. Birdwell was taken aback. "Oh, come off it, Zsa Zsa," he said. "That's absurd. The man's been chasing you halfway around the world, and suddenly you bring Barbara Hutton into this. It doesn't make sense."

"Don't argue with me, Russ," said Zsa Zsa. "Rubi loves me, but he's going to marry Barbara. He has never lied to me in his life. Besides, he needs the money."

If Birdwell was confused by Zsa Zsa's claim that Rubirosa was about to marry Barbara Hutton, he was more bewildered a few days later when he heard that Rubi had gone to see Zsa Zsa again. He arrived in Bel Air for a Christmas Eve dinner with Zsa Zsa, her sisters, her young daughter, Francesca Hilton, and Zsa Zsa's mother, Jolie. According to Zsa Zsa's 1960 autobiography (written for her by Gerold Frank), the party ended with another guest joining them: George Sanders. Having heard that Rubirosa was in town, Sanders chose Christmas Eve to pay the couple a visit. He apparently climbed a ladder, heaved a gift-wrapped brick through his wife's bedroom window, then casually followed it with his person. He was accompanied by his lawyer and a private investigator conveniently armed with a camera. "Merry Christmas, my dears!" he announced as flash bulbs illuminated the room. Once again Rubirosa found himself cast in the role of corespondent.

On Christmas Day the Gabors, including Mama Gabor, returned to Vegas for their final rehearsal. Rubi followed on the next flight, and with a whole day to kill, took in Lena Horne at the Sands and Marlene Dietrich at the Sahara. When the Dietrich show ended he headed straight for the high-stakes baccarat table at the Desert Inn. Within a few hours he had amassed a pile of IOUs totaling $50,000. As his losses continued to mount, the casino management became concerned. In fact, they wanted to know how Rubi planned to finance his losses. Rubi told them about his pending marriage to Barbara Hutton and even offered to telephone her in New York while they listened in on an extension. If the story was true, said the management, then Rubi had nothing to worry about. He placed the call and got through to Barbara. He asked her whether she still wanted to marry him. "I can't wait, darling," she said. He then told her about his delicate monetary dilemma. Barbara, demonstrating the proper Yuletide spirit, said, "Don't worry, darling. I'll wire them the money at once."

Later that evening, as Zsa Zsa tells it, she and Rubi were relaxing in her hotel suite when the phone rang. It was columnist Igor Cassini. He was trying to reach Rubirosa—did Zsa Zsa know how to find him?

Rubirosa put his finger to his lips. Zsa Zsa got the message. No, she told the caller, she had no idea.

"In that case," said Cassini, "can you tell me if it's true that he's about to marry Barbara Hutton?"

"I don't know a thing about it," Zsa Zsa said frigidly and hung up.

Feeling "humiliated" by Cassini's call and "hurt" by her "rediscovery" of Rubi's marital intentions, she pulled rank on her visitor, stood up, marched to the door, opened it, and ordered him to leave.

"You won't marry me," said Rubirosa. "Why should you care if I marry Barbara?"

"I don't care," said Zsa Zsa. "Now go! Go and marry that woman."

Rubi walked to the door and stood in the doorway. "Just tell me one thing," he said. "Why won't you marry me?"

"Because I don't love you," said Zsa Zsa. "I love George. I always have and I always will. Now please leave!" Zsa Zsa rushed at him and gave him a hard push.

He struck her a glancing blow and knocked her off balance so that her forehead hit the bathroom door, which was ajar. "You're crazy!" she screamed and ran to the mirror. Above her right eye was the beginning of an angry-looking welt.

She turned on Rubi, pummeling him with her fists. "You've disfigured me!" she cried. "Get out of here! Get out!" She shoved him through the door and slammed it in his face.

The following day Cassini's column in the New York *Journal-American* broke the story of the forthcoming Hutton-Rubirosa nuptials.

Not to be outdone, Zsa Zsa called her own press conference, for which she had donned a black eye patch over her right eye. As the photographers flashed away, she proudly announced that Rubi had given her a black eye as a going-away present. "He begged me to marry him," she said. "He said it was not too late. He would drop Barbara and marry me. Barbara chased him in Deauville, and he chased me. He didn't jilt me, I jilted him. And when I said I wouldn't marry him, he socked me in the eye. I'm the happiest girl in the world. The fact that he hit me proves that he loves me. A woman who has never been hit by a man has never been loved."

"What about Miss Hutton?" queried a reporter.

"I wish her all the luck in the world—she'll need it. She's a very brave woman if she marries Rubi. On the other hand, for a rich woman he's the very best pastime she could have."

The publicity snowballed. The photographs of Zsa Zsa in her pirate's disguise appeared worldwide. The eye patch suddenly became all the rage. At Marlene Dietrich's next show, all thirty of her high-kicking chorus girls came out wearing eye patches. When Rubirosa arrived in New York, he was met at the airport by fifty reporters sporting eye patches. On Fifth Avenue in New York and on Rodeo Drive in Beverly Hills the smartest boutiques were selling eye patches of all shapes and shades, many covered with sequins, others with jewels. They were sold in pairs as "his" and "hers" and were worn at social functions, cocktail parties and fund-raising affairs.

Having exhausted the eye-patch routine, Zsa Zsa now threatened to sue Rubi for assault. "Once he marries Barbara," she assured the press, "he'll be worth suing. Without her, he's not worth the shirt on his back."

Some columnists felt that Zsa Zsa had finally gone too far. Louella Parsons branded her "the biggest publicity vamp Budapest has ever produced." Walter Winchell commented on what a pity it was that Rubi hadn't punched her in the mouth instead of the eye—"anything to shut that big yap." Even Russell Birdwell had his say. Dropping her as his client, he remarked, "If they don't stay in line, I don't play with them. You can have publicity, and you can have showmanship, and there is a certain point at which bad taste sets in. And that's what happened to Zsa Zsa."

Barbara Hutton was also about to be put through the wringer, and not just by her long-time critics. The feeling among friends and foes alike was that her decision to marry the Dominican playboy was, for her, another indulgence she was permitting herself, even in the face of certain disaster. Her ex-husband Cary Grant and her friend Baron Gottfried von Cramm sent telegrams imploring her to reconsider. Graham Mattison tried to change her mind. Her uncle, E. F. Hutton, called and in an acerbic tone, not unlike her father's, said, "Have you gone out of your mind, Barbara? Do you know what this man is? And do you realize what that makes you?"

The only nod of encouragement came from Generalissimo Trujillo. The dictator reinstated Rubirosa to his former post of minister-counselor in Paris, and announced that by special edict Barbara Hutton had been granted honorary Dominican citizenship, allowing the marriage ceremony to take place at the Dominican consul's residence in New York without the usual formalities, such as blood tests and a marriage license.

Now it was Aunt Marjorie's turn to give advice. "At least telephone Doris Duke and get some information on Rubirosa," she told her niece. Barbara complied and got back to Marjorie: "Doris says he's charming and wonderful." Marjorie groaned. "If that's the case," she said, "then why did she let him go?"

Aunt Marjorie was concerned about the hold Rubirosa would be able to establish over Barbara's finances by marrying her in the Dominican consulate under existing Dominican law. But Barbara's response to all this was a curt "In spite of what everyone says, I know I'm going to be very happy."

Aware that she was wasting her breath on Barbara, Aunt Marjorie called Jimmy Donahue and induced him to speak with Graham Mattison about the prospect of drawing up a prenuptial contract to protect Barbara's financial interests. Jimmy, an unlikely emissary, learned from Mattison that he had already broached the subject with the diplomat. Rubirosa would sign nothing that didn't guarantee him $3 million, payable in advance. Mattison tried again, however, and succeeded in whittling Rubirosa down to $2.5 million.

At three o'clock on December 30, an hour before the wedding, a band of reporters trudged into Barbara's living room at the Pierre. The lights of a Christmas tree blinked in a corner of the room. Barbara sat on a light-green settee, next to Lance. She wore an upswept hairdo and diamonds that sparkled in a brooch on the scoop neckline of a black taffeta dress by Balenciaga, complemented by diamond-and-pearl earrings and a pair of diamond bracelets. She had agreed to the press conference, but looked as though she now regretted it.

Then Rubi entered and Barbara waved. "Rubi, darling, here we are." He kissed her hand and took his place next to her and Lance on the settee. The first question followed. Who would be Barbara's attendant at the wedding? "My son," she said. "My son is wonderful. He's all in favor of the marriage." Lance smiled but looked as uncomfortable as his mother.

Would her holdings become Dominican property?

"I don't know. I don't think so," she said. "Legally I'm still a Danish subject."

Rubirosa interrupted to note that they were being married under Dominican law. "But in my country her money belongs to her and my money belongs to me. Anyway, I don't need her money. I have enough of my own." He did now, but since nobody knew about the recent transaction and since he didn't elaborate on it, they skipped on to the next question: What did Barbara think of Zsa Zsa Gabor?

She hesitated and then said, "I'm terribly sorry. I don't know the lady. I read the remarks she made, but I have no comment."

Rubirosa again interjected, "Miss Gabor is just trying to gain some free publicity out of all this. It's all a publicity stunt. Everything she says is fabricated."

"When did you and Miss Hutton meet?"

"Some time ago," said Rubi. "But we only started to see each other this summer at Deauville."

"When we were in Deauville he told me he loved me," added Barbara. "I didn't believe him. It's awful to have money. I could never give anyone credit for loving me for myself." Then, almost as an aside, she murmured, "I hate to look in the mirror because I'm so ugly. I used to be beautiful. But I'm not anymore."

Rubirosa made the obligatory comment that his forty-one-year-old wife-to-be was still beautiful and would always be beautiful.

"Do you think the marriage will work?"

"I wouldn't be doing it if I didn't *know* it would work," said Barbara. "I've made many mistakes in the past but now—at last—it is right. I'm so happy, I can't begin to tell you."

The next question was directed at Rubirosa: "What is it that Barbara brought into your life?"

Rubi mumbled for a moment and then broke into French, saying that the word he wanted was "grand."

Barbara raised an eyebrow at this response. "It was sincerity," she said. "I brought sincerity into his life."

On this note the press conference closed. Barbara stumbled as she rose to her feet, and two reporters held her upright. She went to her bedroom and returned presently, wearing a long velvet coat over her dress and a large black picture hat. She was unsteady as Lance and Rubirosa guided her out of the hotel and into a waiting limousine. A large crowd stood before the building at 1100 Park Avenue, home of Dr. Joaquin Salazar, Dominican consul general in New York. Dr. Salazar conducted the ceremony in Spanish, and Major General Ramfis Trujillo (the dictator's son and Rubi's former brother-in-law) was best man. Lance, Jimmy Donahue, Jean de Baglion and Barbara's stepmother, Irene, were also there, as was Leland Rosenberg, recently hired by Rubirosa as an unofficial aide.

After the exchange of rings the couple and their guests drank champagne and posed for the press. Barbara looked exhausted, her eyes drained of emotion. "How does it feel?" she was asked by a reporter. "I feel as though I've been hit over the head," she responded. "I'm so tired I could die."

Another assessment of the day's proceedings came from Zsa Zsa Gabor in Las Vegas. When shown a United Press telephoto of the Rubirosa-Hutton wedding, she said, "Look how unhappy they both look. Barbara looks like she's on a death march. Maybe she should have worn white."

As it was, black may have been an appropriate choice of color. By the time they reached the reception arranged for them at the Pierre, Barbara was out on her feet. Half an hour into the party she collapsed and had to be carried off to bed. The festivities went on without her. They also went on without the groom, who disappeared only to reappear several hours later near Leland Rosenberg's bachelor digs on East Thirty-eighth Street with an exotic showgirl in tow.

The second evening went no better for Barbara. The Rubirosas had invited a few friends to ring in the New Year with them over midnight supper at the Pierre. An hour before their arrival, while dressing, Barbara took a nasty spill in the bathroom and broke her left ankle. The ankle was set in a cast. The common aassumption in the press was that Rubirosa, having blackened Zsa Zsa's eye, had found the act of beating up women so invigorating that he had also slugged his wife. The report was untrue, but the accident did postpone their honeymoon plans.

On January 11 an ill wind blew Zsa Zsa Gabor into town. Zsa Zsa announced her arrival at the Plaza by holding yet another press conference, at which she proclaimed that Rubi, his newlywed status notwithstanding, kept courting her by telephone. In subsequent days she was seen with the bride's former boyfriend Prince Henri de la Tour d'Auvergne and with best man Ramfis Trujillo, giving rise to society scribe Nancy Randolph's tart observation that "Zsa Zsa is acting like a jealous wife, despite the fact that she and Rubi aren't even hitched.

Two days after Zsa Zsa's advent Barbara Hutton, confined to a wheelchair, managed a half-smile for photographers as she, Rubi, Leland Rosenberg, two maids and a registered nurse boarded a chartered Eastern Airlines Super Constellation bound for Palm Beach. The charter cost Barbara $4,500. In Palm Beach she paid $30,000 for a three-month lease on the Maharajah of Baroda's elegant cream-colored villa at 1900 South Ocean Boulevard, a house filled with Oriental art treasures and tended by a residential staff of six. The nurse slept in a small bedroom adjoining Barbara's room, while Rubi occupied separate quarters at the opposite end of the house.

Their physical estrangement, inspired in part by Barbara's injury, in part by Rubi's lack of interest, neither diminished her generosity nor lessened his obsession with spending her money. As a wedding present she bought him a twin-engine North American B-25, the same model Doris Duke once gave him, but which he had since sold. Just before January 22, Rubi's forty-fifth birthday, Barbara asked him whether there was anything special he wanted. As a matter of fact, he said, there was a 400-acre citrus plantation for sale in the Dominican Republic. At $450,000 it was a good investment. Barbara gave him the money.

Besides the plantation, Barbara bought Laddie Sanford's polo ponies—fifteen in all—and tossed them in, along with ruby cuff links, diamond stickpins, as well as a Lancia, which Rubi entered several weeks later in the twelve-hour Grand Prix at Sebring. The birthday party she gave him featured an orchestra and a troupe of flamenco dancers, and as an added treat Rubi's favorite troubadour, an itinerant Cuban guitarist named Chago Rodrigo, who strummed and sang Latin American love ballads. But the party was a dud. Barbara retired long before any of the guests were ready to leave and could be heard weeping herself to sleep in her bedroom. Nor was Rubirosa his usual ebullient self, spending most of the evening alone with a bottle on a dark terrace overlooking the swimming pool.

A week later there was another party, this one at the home of Laddie and Mary Sanford, and one of the guests was Cobina Wright, who had flown in from California the night before. She found Barbara there alone, hobbling around with the aid of a crutch. She was surprised at how pale and unhappy Barbara looked. They sat at the piano together and while Cobina played, Barbara attempted to sing along. In the middle of the song her voice faltered and she began to weep.

"What is it, darling?" Cobina asked.

"It's Rubi," sobbed Barbara. "One of these days he's going to do me in."

Cobina managed to quell Barbara's tears. She didn't bump into Barbara again that vacation, but wherever she went in Palm Beach—parties, restaurants, country clubs—Cobina heard nothing but talk of Barbara this and Rubi that—"hype, hype, hype," as she would write in her column. The disintegration of the Hutton-Rubirosa nuptials was not just the most prevalent topic of conversation that season, it was the *only* topic of conversation.

David Fields, former publisher of the *Palm Beacher*, acknowledges that there was nothing discreet about Rubirosa's womanizing. "It was known that he maintained an apartment on Peruvian Avenue where he would take his dates. He would prowl the Palm Beach nightspots, pick up whatever was available, and drive off in a haze of champagne. It didn't really matter to him if they were duchesses or call girls, socialites, actresses, models, waitresses, salesclerks, manicurists, or what have you, as long as they were good-looking and good in bed. If they were members of the villa-pool-and-patio set, so much the better, but if they weren't, that was okay too. On occasion he would drive down to Miami to party on Ramfis Trujillo's yacht, which happened to have once belonged to Marjorie Merriweather Post. On other occasions he played polo at Delray and met women there. The only time he restrained himself was the day Barbara went to Delray to watch him play. That was when Barbara's stepmother was down and they had nothing better to do."

When Rubi wasn't partying, night-clubbing or playing polo, he could usually be found on Worth Avenue spending Barbara's money. During his short stay in Palm Beach he accumulated sixty suits, twenty pairs of shoes, fifty pairs of silk pajamas, dozens of sweaters, shirts, slacks and sport jackets. Nobody was surprised to learn that he was near the top of the Best Dressed Men's list for 1954.

The bills—including food and beverage charges, entertainment and athletic equipment—began to reach Graham Mattison in New York. When Mattison saw what Barbara was spending on Rubi—or rather what Rubi was spending on himself and charging to Barbara—the lawyer wrote a detailed letter explaining that if she didn't curb her husband's extravagance, she would have to start dipping into her already depleted savings. Although Mattison provided no figures, Barbara's closest friends estimate that she was still worth $25 million, maybe more, a figure substantiated by an article in *Fortune* on America's 500 wealthiest individuals. The fact that Barbara was no longer an American citizen didn't seem to deter the magazine from including her in its rankings.

Mattison's letter to his client went unanswered. Nor was he the only one who had difficulty reaching Barbara. Aunt Jessie tried telephoning her niece at least twice a day. Whenever she called, she found herself trapped on the line with Leland Rosenberg. Rosenberg was seemingly ubiquitous. According to Jessie, he had assumed the unassigned role of majordomo and was running the household and its staff like a drill sergeant, threatening to court-martial anyone who stepped out of line.

An example of his militaristic character was provided during a visit to the house by Sylvia Ashley Gable. Sylvia, whose former husbands included Douglas Fairbanks Sr. and Clark Gable, and who had known Barbara for years, tried to enter a powder room that Rosenberg considered off limits to anyone but Barbara. To everyone's astonishment he hurried after Sylvia, pushed ahead and flung himself against the door. "You cannot enter," he warned. "This room is for Mme. Rubirosa."

Sylvia was not the person to be shunted aside. She gave Rosenberg a hefty shove and said, "You get the hell out of my way." He did.

Graham Mattison also had his doubts about Rosenberg. Although he had nothing concrete to base it on, he suspected Rosenberg of being a publicity seeker who would stop at nothing to get his name in print. He blamed Rosenberg every time the media ran an item about Barbara. He was further alarmed that the publicity had spread from newspapers and magazines to radio and television.

Bob Hope was the first television personality to use the Rubirosa marriage as part of his comedy routine, by cracking, "Well, spring must be near. Barbara Hutton is getting ready to do her annual house cleaning." George Jessel, wearing an eye patch à la Zsa Zsa Gabor, also did a bit on Barbara, spewing out a tired medley of one-liners: "Barbara gets married so often she only buys Minute Rice. But she got smart, she only buys it by the case lot." By far the most strident evocation was sounded by Eddie Cantor. The last scene of one of Cantor's television scripts had the comedian in a black wig impersonating Rubirosa on his wedding night, trying to force his way into his bride's bedroom which is guarded by a pair of armed Pinkertons. The groom laments his bad fortune and decides "to curl up with a good book," at which point he produces three or four bank books. After some more charading and jokes, he says to the audience, "My wife may be sleeping in there, but the best part of her is in here." He holds up the bank books as the scene fades.

A day after the broadcast the real Porfirio Rubirosa climbed aboard his B-25 in Miami and headed for Phoenix, Arizona, where Zsa Zsa Gabor was on location, playing a trapeze artist in an aptly titled Dean Martin-Jerry Lewis comedy, *Three Ring Circus*.

Zsa Zsa informs us in her autobiography that the moment she knew of Rubi's pending arrival she asked a friend, Marylou Hosford (today Mrs. Cornelius Vanderbilt Whitney), for help in hiding the flying Dominican's identity. Mrs. Hosford took a room for Rubi under the name of William Perkins at the Jokake Inn, where Zsa Zsa was also staying. From all indications, the reunion was a happy one.

The following evening after dinner, Rubi, Zsa Zsa and Marylou returned to the inn by way of a narrow path, the two ladies walking ahead while Rubi pulled up the rear. Suddenly a reporter jumped out of the shadows, held up his press card, and stammered, "Miss Gabor, is it true that Mr. Ru-Ru-Rubirosa is in town?"

Zsa Zsa stared at the reporter and with a perfect touch of indignation in her voice berated him for intruding on her privacy: "How dare you! Mr. Rubirosa is married to Miss Barbara Hutton. What would he be doing here?" When he heard the commotion, Rubi disappeared into the shrubbery.

The ladies reached their quarters and broke down with hysterical laughter. They were still laughing when a knock was heard at the door. It was the hotel manager, bursting with the latest news. There was a rumor, he said, that Mr. Rubirosa was somewhere in Phoenix.

"It's not a rumor," said Zsa Zsa.

"It's not?" asked the manager. "But where is he?"

"Hiding in the bushes."

When the manager understood that his guest was telling the truth, he came up with a daring plan to get Rubirosa out of the hotel before he was discovered by the press. A few minutes later Zsa Zsa and Mrs. Hosford emerged from their room, climbed into Marylou's car and drove off, followed by six or seven automobiles filled with reporters. When the coast was clear, Rubi was ushered into the rear of a laundry van and transported to an empty house in Scottsdale owned by friends of the manager. It took Zsa Zsa and Marylou many hours of driving around in circles before they were finally able to shake their pursuers. They reached Rubi's hideaway at two in the morning, only to find him seated in the den, bored, tired, hot and drunk.

He returned to Palm Beach a few days later with the alibi that he had flown to the Dominican Republic on "official business." Barbara said little about the trip. For a week or so there was peace in the Rubirosa household, and there were reports that the marriage might actually be salvageable.

One evening the Rubirosas took the Chilean polo player Emilio Tagle and his wife to dinner in the wine cellar of the Moulin Rouge restaurant. On the way they passed Earl Blackwell, president of Celebrity Service Inc. in New York. Blackwell recalls the evening:* "I had been walking with Mrs. Frank Farrell, wife of the former New York *World-Telegram* columnist. Barbara invited us to join her group for dinner. We went along and spent a nice evening together. Russell Nype, the musical comedy star, sang for us and Rubi accompanied him on the guitar. As we left and waited for the car outside the restaurant, Barbara asked me for a pen. She wanted to jot down her telephone number for me. Without thinking I handed her a ballpoint I carried in my inside jacket pocket. Just as she took it, I remembered that I had picked it up a

---

*Earl Blackwell gave an earlier interview to Dean Jennings, covering the same subject matter. It appears in Jennings, *Barbara Hutton*, p. 279.

month earlier at a press conference for Zsa Zsa Gabor. On the barrel of the pen, in bright gold letters, was an inscription: "With the compliments of Zsa Zsa Gabor." I prayed she wouldn't see it. She wrote her telephone number and handed me the pen and slip of paper. I have no idea if she saw Zsa Zsa's name. She didn't say anything, and I doubt she would have said anything even if she had seen it. She was too well mannered to react in that way."

The Moulin Rouge outing was such fun that Barbara planned a return engagement, this time inviting half a dozen couples, including Sylvia Gable and her cousin, Woolworth Donahue, whose bright temperament could enliven almost any party. But it did little for this one. Rubi had invited Chago Rodrigo to play his guitar during dinner. Chago's first selection, "Just a Gigolo," was hardly appropriate for the occasion. But Rubirosa seemed to enjoy it so much that Chago played it again. Barbara sulked through the rest of the meal, and when it came time to leave, she rose from her chair, went over to Rubi, drew back her right arm and let fly with a slap that lifted him halfway out of his seat. It was a show-stopper, and by the time Rubirosa's head cleared, Barbara was gone.

The next day, February 20, Barbara left the Baroda mansion and moved in with Jessie Donahue at the Everglades Club. She refused to speak to the press, leaving that chore to Jessie. Mrs. Donahue issued a one-sentence summation: "Barbara is definitely through with that disgusting man." A more official statement was tendered three weeks later: "We regret that we have mutually decided that it is wisest for us to separate. Our separation is entirely friendly and any public statement giving a different impression is completely incorrect."

It was the fifth time in her life that Barbara had made such a statement, glossing over the differences to stress the "friendliness" of the occasion. By official count the marriage lasted fifty-three days and effectively marked the end of Rubi's career as a professional stud, while establishing some kind of modern-day mark in the way of a fee. In the seven and a half weeks they had been together, he collected approximately $1 million in gifts and $2.5 million in cash—more than $66,000 a day.

Rubirosa had never dissected his other marriages, but because he now feared reprisals in the press he spoke about life with Barbara: "I do not think Barbara is a sick girl, but she certainly does not want to participate in an active life. She prefers to stay in bed all day and read. After weeks of such an existence I knew our marriage could not last. I tried my best to stand it, because I knew if I left her I would be branded the villain and the betrayer of womanhood. At forty-five I am still a healthy man. My day starts early when I leap out of bed, eat a spartan breakfast, and head for polo practice. I am horrified at the thought of a healthy person who stays in bed all day, as Barbara does. I truly wish that my wife would abandon her way of life."

Sylvia Gable offered the only public rejoinder to Rubirosa's unflattering commentary: "Rubi talks about a typical day! That's a laugh. Why, his typical day starts at eleven P.M. when he rolls out of bed and heads for the nearest night club. Surely he knew that Barbara wasn't in perfect health when he married her. Shouldn't a husband show some compassion for the frailty of his wife?"

Arriving in New York on March 17, Barbara was met at Pennsylvania Station by the press. She limited herself to one droll comment ("It was a lovely honeymoon, thank you") and one acerbic barb ("I would like to be referred to as Barbara Troubetzkoy, not Mrs. Rubirosa"). If she was as depressed as everyone thought, it didn't show. Back at the Pierre she hired Billy Baldwin to redecorate her suite. She then went to Leron and stocked up on towels and embroidered tablecloths. Albert Aferiat of Porthault came by with samples of sheets, pillowcases, blanket covers. The day of his visit Barbara's rooms were filled with fresh anemones, which happened to match the pattern of Porthault's red-anemones-on-white-linen sheets. She ordered ten sets of the anemone sheets and fifty sets of other floral designs, an acquisition she repeated annually for the next dozen years.

She also asked Monsieur Aferiat to design a four-tiered, ivory-handled parasol with handmade lace on the outside, beneath that a layer of white fabric, then a layer of black fabric, and on the inside a layer of pink silk. Barbara saw pink, the outside world saw lace, and the black material acted as a sun shield. Labor and material for the parasol came to $1,500.

Barbara had anticipated using the parasol in Mexico, where she expected to go for her divorce from Rubirosa. But the trip was canceled when Mexican officials ruled that the case was outside their jurisdiction. As an "honorary" Dominican citizen married to a Dominican diplomat in a Dominican-sanctioned ceremony, Barbara had no choice but to wait for Rubirosa to sue her for divorce in the Dominican Republic. The final decree was handed down on July 30, 1955.

As soon as he could, Rubi joined Zsa Zsa Gabor in Paris and for the next eighteen months they were mainstays on the international party circuit, with its profusion of spas, yachts, night clubs, casinos, race tracks and polo ponies. By early 1956 they had run out of steam. Zsa Zsa Gabor returned to Hollywood, married a succession of wealthy businessmen, and rebuilt her sagging career around a series of late-night television guest show appearances in which she continued to make a spectacle of herself—and a bundle of money in the process.

If Zsa Zsa's driving ambition was to "make it" in Hollywood, Rubi wanted to find eternal youth. Late in 1956, at age forty-seven, he took his fifth and last wife, a sparkling, scatterbrained eighteen-year-old French starlet named Odile Bérard—stage name: Odile Rodin—whose picture he had first seen on the cover of *Paris-Match*. Insofar as "pleasure-seeking" and "the good life" were among her main preoccupations, Odile and Rubi seemed to be ideally suited. In fact they were still husband and wife in July 1965 when Rubirosa, buoyed by an unexpected victory on the polo field, went off by himself to celebrate. After hitting most of his favorite all-night drinking locales he jumped into his silver Ferrari (bought with Barbara's money) and headed home through the pre-dawn fog of the Bois de Boulogne. In an accident almost identical to the one that five years earlier had claimed the life of his fellow playboy, Prince Aly Khan, Rubi skidded off the road and smashed into a chestnut tree. He died in an ambulance on the way to the hospital. Some 250 friends, including Mrs. Pat Lawford and Mrs. Jean Smith, sisters of the late John F. Kennedy, attended his funeral in Paris. Neither Zsa Zsa Gabor nor Barbara Hutton was among his public mourners. Asked for a comment by the press, Barbara said she had "no harsh or hard feelings against Rubi. In his own way he was a perfect gentleman. He was born a few centuries too early, that's all."

Fifteen

I̲N THE SUMMER of 1954 Barbara went to Tangier and there met Daniel
Rudd, a twenty-eight-year-old American, an interior decorator and
collector of antiques. At the end of the summer they spent several
weeks together in Spain, before Barbara left with Margaret Latimer for a
month-long stay at the Hotel Nacional in Havana. She spent the
remainder of the year in Cuernavaca and by early 1955 was at the
Beverly Hills Hotel, the so-called Pink Palace, for an intended visit with
her son.

Lance, who was in the process of moving from a garden apartment on
Selma Avenue in Hollywood to a small house on North Knoll Drive in
Benedict Canyon, had dropped out after one semester at Pomona
College in Claremont, on the grounds that he was interested in auto
racing and could see no point in a college education. Barbara had hired
Dudley Walker, Cary Grant's former valet, to help take care of Lance.
Dudley's position turned out to be all-encompassing. "I kept him," says
Dudley. "I paid the rent, electric bills, the groceries, and so on, because
until his twenty-first birthday he had no money. He was getting a
thousand dollars a month from his mother but was running up an
average monthly telephone bill of eight hundred dollars. Like his
mother, he couldn't stick to a budget. At the end of the month he was
always broke. I'd have to pay myself out of my own pocket, though I
knew I'd eventually get it back from Barbara."

Socially speaking, this was to be an active period for Barbara, one might even say hyperactive. She started the month of January dating Michael Rennie, the tall, good-looking British leading man, and ended it with Hal B. Hayes, a millionaire architect and contractor whose money had been made in military installations and other government construction projects. Both were engaging, successful, vain men who wore a beautiful woman on their arm as they might wear a carnation in their lapel.

Michael Rennie, then between wives, took Barbara dancing at Mocambo on their first date and subsequently invited her to spend a weekend with him in Palm Springs. Their two days and nights together must have been somewhat on the unconventional side, because Barbara recorded the following thoughts: "I consider myself quite normal sexually. There are times when I like sex and times when I don't. When I'm in the mood for it, I like nothing better. But I don't enjoy cruelty. I hate it when somebody I think I know comes out wearing a rubber diving suit, with a bullwhip in one hand and a jar of vaseline in the other."

Hal Hayes was more in keeping with the type of man Barbara was used to dating. A perennial Hollywood bachelor whose name cropped up regularly in the columns, he was personable, humorous and distinguished-looking. He had been linked with the likes of Kay Spreckels, Rita Hayworth, Ann Miller and dozens of other Hollywood film and social figures. Unfortunately for Barbara, Hayes was somewhat on the flashy side, given to flaunting his wealth in ways that didn't impress her in the least. His home above Sunset Strip was a gaudy showplace that featured a free-form indoor-outdoor swimming pool, spigots in the bar that spouted scotch, bourbon and champagne, and a tree in the living room with a built-in television.

One evening in mid-January when Hayes was out of town on business, Barbara took Lance and his date to dinner at the Brown Derby. After dinner she returned to her bungalow (No. 6) at the Beverly Hills Hotel and found that the hotel management had sent over two complimentary bottles of wine—a Pouilly-Fuissé and Château Lafite-Rothschild—and a selection of cheeses and tropical fruit. Barbara sampled the wines and was soon feeling light-headed and warm. She had heard of an after-hours eatery in Hollywood called Googie's that supposedly had a very friendly and lively atmosphere and attracted an interesting crowd. Calling a cab, she asked the driver if he knew the place. "It's next to Schwab's Drugstore," he said and drove her there.

Googie's, as it turned out, was a modest bistro with a neon-light jukebox near the door, a cigarette machine marking the intersection of the front and back rooms, tables covered with blue-and-white check-ered tablecloths, the inevitable publicity shots of Hollywood's most popular stars lining the walls. The place was packed, and after a few minutes Barbara was about to leave. As she turned she nearly tripped over a young man in blue jeans, black turtleneck and steel-rimmed glasses seated by himself at a corner table. He offered her a seat and ordered her a drink. He introduced himself as a working actor, a former student of the theater arts at UCLA, whose first major film perform-ance was in the can. The name of the film was *East of Eden;* the name of the actor was James Dean.

Although only twenty-three and virtually unknown at the time, Dean had a way about him that quickly appealed to Barbara. Perhaps it was his irreverent sense of humor. "So you're the lady who gets a little richer every time the cash register rings at Woolworth's," he quipped between chomps on a hamburger. Barbara laughed, and Dean proceeded to spill out a convoluted tale about the week he had spent at a five-and-dime in Los Angeles demonstrating can openers, and how during another dry spell he had sold encyclopedias door-to-door in South Bend, Indiana. Most of the housewives had slammed the door in his face. He did an imitation: "Madame, will you kindly open the door so I can get my tie back."

Barbara felt a surprisingly strong rapport with Dean, who was blessed with a deep sense of curiosity. He seemed avidly interested in learning about Barbara's past, her friends, her poetry, her travels. Although his questions were endless, he seemed sincerely interested in knowing her, and he listened for long periods without interrupting, allowing her to develop her thoughts in an unhurried way. After several hours, when Barbara decided it was time to leave, he followed her into the street and offered her a lift on the back of his motorcycle. Without a second thought, Barbara climbed aboard. It was a short but hair-raising ride, Barbara's dress billowing out behind the speeding machine like a black parachute. "If you pass this test, you can pass any test," Dean bellowed into the wind. She must have passed, because when they reached her hotel, he simply announced that he was coming in.

Once inside, they quickly disposed of a chilled bottle of champagne, picking up the threads of their conversation at Googie's. This time it was Dean's turn to talk and he raved to Barbara about the exhilaration of taking chances, the pursuit of the heightened moment, intensity for its own sake, "something men find only when they're with each other." Real life, he remarked, was experience.

They drank a good deal and spoke easily and openly about a wide range of subjects, including themselves. Dean's effect on Barbara was agreeably bewildering. With him she felt oddly free, whimsical, aggressive yet feminine. He stretched out on the couch with his shoes off and his head cradled in her lap.

"It was late and he was drunk and I was drunk, so I asked him to stay," she explained in her notebooks. "He removed his shirt and pants and climbed into bed, and I snuggled in next to him. We made love and then we made love again. It seemed the right and natural thing to do, although I couldn't help but wonder about his sexuality. He talked so fervently about men and adventure and masculinity. We talked and dozed and made love until long after the sun rose. In the morning he ordered black coffee and scrambled eggs and the waiter served it in the dining room. Then I watched as he climbed on his motorcycle and disappeared around the bend. Forever."*

On February 1, 1955, Barbara and Hal Hayes, with leis draped around their necks, arrived by plane in Honolulu. They stayed for a month and reappeared in Los Angeles, where they were seen dancing together nightly at Ciro's. Barbara took a Slenderella reduction course in Beverly Hills but lost interest in it later that spring when she decided once again to take to the road, stopping briefly in New York, Paris, Madrid, before arriving in Tangier in mid-July. It was from there that she sent Hayes a "Dear Hal" letter, while writing Baron Gottfried von Cramm and inviting him to join her in Tangier for the remainder of the summer. He arrived a few days later.

After Rubirosa, Von Cramm was an absolute joy. As always, he was polite, gentle, refined. One evening Barbara did her Chinese dance for him, the same sequence she had once performed for Cary Grant. Other evenings she sent for her favorite belly dancers and rewarded their gyrations by throwing them jewels. When Gottfried warned her that she was being exploited, she responded, "I've never seen a Brink's truck follow a hearse to the cemetery."

On October 11, having returned to Paris, Barbara wrote a letter to the Kennerleys, announcing that her long fight for her German tennis ace was finished. She had emerged victorious:

> Just a few lines to tell you that Gottfried and I are being married here in Paris on October 25th. Imagine! After all these years—18 to be exact. Of course I would have been far happier in life if I had married him long ago. But I am not complaining, as I am the happiest woman in the world today.

*On September 30, 1955, James Dean was killed in an automobile accident while driving his silver Porsche 550 Spyder to a road race in Salinas, California. He was twenty-four. Barbara sent twenty-four white roses to his funeral in Indiana.

He spent all summer with me in Tangier, and in all my life no one has ever been sweeter or more tender with me.

I hope I am not boring you going on like this, but I thought that if anyone should know about the wedding, it was you ...

Jean Kennerley was genuinely happy for Barbara. "For years," she says, "Barbara had this thing about Gottfried, and I kept urging her to have an affair with him, live with him, anything. I felt it was the only way she would ever get him out of her system. So when I learned they had spent the summer together and were getting married, I had high hopes."

The marriage was briefly postponed until the morning of November 8, 1955, a day of heavy wind and rain, when Barbara, Gottfried and his brother, Siegfried, appeared at the Versailles City Hall for a clandestine civil ceremony conducted by Deputy Mayor André Mignot. The only other witness to the ceremony was Gerald Van der Kemp, who walked over from his curatorial post at the Palace of Versailles. After the reading of the civil code, both parties said *"Oui."* The register was signed. The rings were exchanged. Barbara helped Gottfried. Gottfried helped Barbara. Then the deputy mayor, now addressing Barbara as "Baroness," delivered a brief speech. He thanked Gottfried for a gift of 500,000 francs ($1,400) to be given to the Paris poor and gave him the gift of a *livret de famille,* or official family record book, with space for a dozen children. When Barbara saw the leatherbound book she stifled a laugh. The next day she sent Van der Kemp a check for the Château Restoration Fund in the amount of $150,000, which, added to her previous donations, made her the largest individual contributor to the fund.

Following the ceremony there was a press conference and a reception for twenty friends in Barbara's suite at the Ritz. Dressed in designer's black and banker's blue, respectively, Barbara and Gottfried looked a trifle shopworn—she with puffy cheeks, he with a double chin. While guests feasted hungrily from a buffet of caviar, salmon, lobster à la Parisienne, fowl from Bresse, and fresh vegetables, Barbara and Gottfried answered questions hurled at them by the press.

They were vague when pressed about future plans. Would they reside in Paris? Well, Barbara volunteered, that depended on how much time her husband spent in Hamburg, where he owned an import-export firm and a tennis school. Then she waxed slightly melodramatic: "I'm deliriously happy. I've waited so long for this day."

Von Cramm had apparently waited just as long. "We should have married eighteen years ago," he said. "We wanted to marry after our first meeting in 1937. But somehow it never happened."

"We certainly should have married eighteen years ago," Barbara agreed. "It would have saved me many heartaches—and marriages!" She then added, "Gottfried is the only man in my life who has really wanted me to love him. Now finally I have someone to talk to when I go to bed at night. There will be no more lonely nights."

It sounded cozy and convenient, but as usual with Barbara, there were soon a number of unforeseen dilemmas. She had hoped to spend the winter months with Gottfried either in Palm Beach or San Francisco, yet when he applied for a visa at the American embassy in Paris, his application was rejected. No reason was given, but it was common knowledge that the U.S. Immigration Service was implacable against admitting aliens with records of "moral turpitude."

As an alternative to the United States they spent the winter and early spring in a rented villa in Cuernavaca, where they were soon joined by Lance. Lance disapproved vehemently and perhaps validly of Von Cramm, not only because of his homosexuality but also because of his formal, Teutonic mannerisms, a trait that reminded Lance of his own father. Like Court Reventlow, Von Cramm tended to be stiff, precise, rather grim-faced, not given to spontaneous laughter. He rarely relaxed in public, whether at work or at play, but always stood as if encased in a plaster cast from chin to toe. Even at parties he found it difficult to let himself go. As an associate pointed out, the only place Gottfried von Cramm was able to unbend was between the baselines of a tennis court, where his mind and body seemed to enter a whole new dimension of being. Still, there were compensating characteristics. He was an honorable, decent, kind and tolerant individual. He had no false vanity, no dishonest tricks, no guiles or pretensions, and there was nothing mean, cruel or petty about him. She could tell him virtually anything and he never lost his temper. He was a gentleman, a man of impeccable lineage and demonstrable sweetness, but also a man born under the spell of an unlucky star. Von Cramm had the bad luck of constantly being in the wrong place at the wrong time.

This was true even in the world of tennis. A magnificent athlete, he had the misfortune of gaining prominence in the sport at the same time as Fred Perry of England and Donald Budge of the United States, two of the game's most acclaimed players. Von Cramm's career totals were highly impressive—two French titles, four German titles, the mixed doubles title at Wimbledon in 1933—and yet he gave the ineluctable impression of not being able to win the big one, of succumbing under pressure. He lost the finals at Wimbledon to Perry in 1935 and again in '36, and to Budge in '37. Then came the unhappy events of '38, culminating in his public humiliation at the hands of the Nazis. After the war he returned to the tennis courts of Europe—no longer young, out of shape, out of friends, cash, sobriety, out of everything except courage and integrity.

But when the Von Cramms returned to Paris in May 1956, their marriage showed all the signs of early erosion and decay. Jean de Baglion, thrust into the thankless role of go-between, noted that the root of the problem was Gottfried's preference for men. His inability to relate to Barbara on any kind of meaningful sexual level created a deep schism. "It wasn't that he didn't try," suggests Baglion. "It was just that he couldn't perform. Barbara took it personally. It piqued her vanity and became a constant source of irritation. It wasn't the lack of sex she cared about, it was the idea behind the lack of sex, the notion that he would go with any man and not her. The truth of the matter is that they never consummated their marriage."

Their respective methods for dealing with the dilemma (or not dealing with it) drove them further apart. Von Cramm became an absentee husband, making frequent business trips to Germany or simply disappearing for long stretches without telling anyone where he was going or what he was doing. In the meantime, Barbara occupied herself by throwing the same type of dinner and drinking parties she had always given. They were happenings, events, rituals, a means of staving off the inevitable boredom.

She gave one party for Gilbert and Kitty Miller to which she invited the Duchess of Windsor, the Duke of Alba, and an assortment of maharajahs, museum curators, film producers, socialites and politicians. Dinner was served in the suite. The drinking got heavier as the evening progressed, until by midnight the entire group was thoroughly inebriated. Somebody threw a dozen highball glasses out the window. Somebody else called the police. Kitty Miller and the Duchess of Windsor got into an argument. One of the dinner guests downed a fifth of vodka and collapsed in a heap. The police arrived and the party ended.

A few weeks after the party Barbara received a visit from Michael Duff and Ted Peckham. Peckham's fleeting fame was the result of a male escort service he operated in Europe during the 1930s and early '40s, catering to either sex. Jimmy Donahue was a client, and so was Peggy Guggenheim. Peckham had been introduced to Barbara in the 1930s in Venice by Princess Jane di San Faustino.

Peckham recalls the later meeting: "Michael Duff and I found ourselves at the Ritz during cocktail hour and Michael decided to call Barbara from the lobby. She invited us up. Von Cramm was there with a few of his boyfriends, and they were fluttering about getting ready to step out for the evening. We were uncomfortable so after a few minutes

Michael suggested that we were probably intruding and ought to be going.

"'Don't leave,' Barbara pleaded. 'Can't you see what's happening here?' We stayed and the others left and Barbara immediately started talking about how horrible it all was. She mentioned walking in on her husband and finding him in the sack with another man. 'What did you do?' Michael asked her. 'What could I do?' said Barbara. 'I told him to be more discreet. If a servant or somebody from the hotel had walked in, it could have caused a scandal.'

"She had a kind of double standard about gays. She found her husband's homosexuality threatening to her femininity. Otherwise she had this old-lady's attitude toward gays. They would sit around and compliment her. These rich gals love it. They always have gays hanging around."

Barbara spent August, September and the first two weeks of October at the Grand Hotel in Venice, while Von Cramm shuttled back and forth between Venice and a penthouse apartment in Hamburg recently acquired with part of a $2 million dowry provided by Barbara. On October 18 Barbara joined her husband at Alfeld, in Bavaria, where his mother, Baroness Jutta von Cramm, lived in a fifteenth-century mountaintop *Schloss*. The family gathering was anything but cordial. Barbara later complained that her mother-in-law hardly conversed with her and spoke only German when she was around, although she could as easily have spoken French or English.

Husband and wife returned to Paris at the end of the month, but by late December, Gottfried was back in Germany and Barbara was left to celebrate Christmas with Ticki Tocquet and Jean de Baglion. Ticki gave Barbara a sweater she had knit, and Baglion gave her two volumes of French verse. In return they received a typical Hutton windfall— diamond earrings for Ticki and a gold Cartier cigarette case with a large check inside for Baglion.

"She was constantly giving away fabulous presents, or whisking you off on a glamorous vacation," says Baglion. "As a working man, I would never have seen anything of the world without Barbara's help. I didn't have the means. Barbara made it possible for me to travel. The same can be said for many others. Silvia de Castellane received countless benefits from Barbara, and so did her four children, especially her daughter Bou-Bou, whose real name was Barbara. She was named after Barbara Hutton. The kids called Barbara 'Tante,' meaning 'Auntie,' and Tante was very good to them. But she was good to everybody. She set Tony Pawson up in a $100,000 apartment in Paris. She bought homes for Sister, Ticki, Antonio and José Gonzales. She bought me my apartment on rue Washington. She gave hundreds of thousands of dollars to a fund for the victims of a flood in the Po Valley in Italy. Her generosity was unbelievable. To give you some idea, when Ticki died in 1959 she left behind an estate worth in excess of $2 million."*

Early in 1957 the Von Cramms flew to Cuernavaca. Four weeks later, Gottfried returned to Paris and Barbara flew to Los Angeles to attend Lance's twenty-first birthday celebration,† an occasion marked by his acquisition of an $8 million investment fund that yielded nearly $1 million per year in interest. In addition Barbara had already given him a birthday check for $1.5 million with which he built himself a home in the fashionable Holmby Hills section six hundred feet above sea and smog levels on a triangular peak overlooking Beverly Hills. It was a rambling ranchhouse-style abode constructed from rough-hewn stones and timber with a sloping roof of concave Mexican tiles. An enormous swimming pool that started outdoors extended into the living room. Other features included a bed with built-in console that controlled a sliding front gate and every electrical outlet and appliance in the house. There was a gem-and-jewelry studio, an automotive workshop and a staggering view through floor-to-ceiling picture windows.

Lance's birthday party was also his housewarming. Adhering to his mother's wishes, he gave a formal sit-down dinner for forty. Barbara brought Bill Robertson and several other members of her California contingent. Lance's guests included Bruce Kessler and his parents; Ronnie Burns, son of Gracie Allen and George Burns; Julie Payne, daughter of actor John Payne; Jimmy Boyd, the singer; Gary Crosby, son of Bing; and Chuck Daigh, a race-car driver.

Another guest, Gould Morrison, recalls that Lance's house (dubbed "Camp Climax") soon became the hangout for a number of the sons and daughters of Hollywood's luminaries. "Most of them," says Morrison, "were engaged in the decorative and aristocratic occupation of doing nothing whatever, a function they fulfilled with distinction. Like most of the swinging jet set, they were bored out of their minds. Despite his car-racing career, Lance was also terribly bored. He used to liven things up by indulging in sexual highjinks. His parties invariably turned into orgies and daisy chains. Lance was nice enough, but it's ludicrous to say that he wasn't spoiled. He was one of the most self-indulgent people it has been my pleasure to know."

*Over Christmas of 1956 Barbara also sent checks in $200,000 denominations to such established organizations and charities as Lincoln Center (then being built in New York), the New York Foundling Hospital, the Muscular Dystrophy Fund, and the Venice Restoration Fund.

†At twenty-one, Lance elected to become an American citizen rather than a subject of Denmark or England.

Shortly after his twenty-first birthday Lance met Jill St. John, a redhead with hazel-brown eyes and the requisite complement of measurements, including an IQ said to hover in the "near-genius" range. Jill, whose real family name was Oppenheim, had made her acting debut at age six as Sharon Barbour on the long-running radio soap opera *One Man's Family*; by sixteen she had appeared on more than a thousand radio shows and fifty TV programs. She dropped out of UCLA after two semesters to make her first feature film appearance in a drab little number called *Summer Love*. At seventeen she married laundry heir Neil Dubin, a union that lasted less than a year. At eighteen she became engaged to Lance Reventlow. The diamond in her engagement ring stretched, as she put it, "from knuckle to knuckle."

She was pleased with the ring, less pleased that Lance seemed to be consumed by his fascination with cars. He owned nine of them—a Mercedes for running errands, a Jaguar for dates, a Rolls for formal outings, a Ferrari, Porsche, Cooper-Climax and Maserati for road racing, and an old beat-up Chevy "for the hell of it." Not content merely with driving his own racing cars, Lance sold a $2 million block of stock his mother gave him for his twenty-second birthday and established Reventlow Automobiles, Inc., the purpose of which was to build an American car capable of outracing the European machines that so completely dominated the field. The result of Lance's endeavors was a sports model named the Scarab, after the Egyptian beetle and good-luck charm.

During its first year in competition the Scarab compiled a respectable record. In October 1958 Lance's driver, Chuck Daigh, drove it to victory in the Sports Car Club of America Race at Riverside, California. A month later Lance drove it and won the Laguna Seca Road Race at Monterey. In December, Lance took the Scarab to the Bahamas and there he won his most impressive victories, sweeping both the 225-mile Governor's Cup and the even more prestigious Nassau Cup. It was the first time an American-built car had won both events in the same year.

Just as Lance's hopes were beginning to mount for a victory in one of the major European Grand Prix races, he was involved in an accident. In May 1959 he was making a qualifying run for the Santa Barbara Road Race when he was hit by a Ferrari. Lance emerged shaken up but unhurt. He entered and won several other events later in the year, and by 1960 deemed his racing machine ready for international competition on the European circuit.

The European experiment proved a disaster. The two Scarabs he sent over flopped everywhere they went. They failed to qualify for four of five Grand Prix events (Dutch, Monaco, French and British) and made it into the Belgian Grand Prix only because two other qualifiers were scratched at the last minute. Neither of the Scarabs completed the Belgian race. For all intents and purposes, Lance's dismal European showing marked *finis* to his automobile-racing career. He continued to dabble in the sport, entering an occasional race, but never again attaining the kind of success he had met when the Scarab first hit the course.

In March 1957, after Lance's twenty-first birthday party, Barbara had checked into the Royal Hawaiian Hotel in Honolulu. Her guest on the trip was Countess Marina Cicogna, whose mother was Anna Maria Volpi, of the venerable Volpi family of Venice. "Barbara was drinking," contends Marina. "Mostly gin. The drinking accentuated her frequent fluctuations of mood. At times she could be sweet, gracious, joyful. Five minutes later she would become an impossible tyrant. Social one day, she would turn strange and remote the next. She was heavily into drugs—uppers, downers, in-betweens. Her main problem was that she tried to possess people with her money and wound up transforming them into monsters. In a way she was extraordinarily manipulative, somewhat sadistic."

On the few occasions when Barbara left her hotel suite it was either to visit Doris Duke at Shangri-la, her estate on Diamond Head, or to spend time at the Honolulu Academy of Arts, which from November 1956 through January 1957 mounted an exhibition of more than 150 of Barbara's most valuable samples of Chinese porcelain.

John Gomez, the Hawaiian-born manager of the Duke estate, remembers Barbara as subdued and retiring. "She used to sit around and read," he remarks. "Once while sitting under a hala tree, from which the natives weave baskets and mats, she asked me about the tree's bright blossom. I told her it was called 'hinano.' 'What a beautiful-sounding word,' she said. So after that I always called her Hinano."

Before leaving Hawaii at the end of the month, Barbara and Marina Cicogna engaged in a furious argument. As Marina tells it, Barbara had offered her a pearl necklace if she would accompany her to San Francisco. Marina refused the necklace and asked for money instead. "I felt I was being manipulated, and if she wanted to pay me off, then I wanted something I could use. At first she said nothing. Then she came storming into my room, sat down and simply lost control of herself. She went up like a rocket. She was holding the pearl necklace in her hand and her hand began to shake. Then she threw it at me and began screaming at the top of her lungs. Eventually we made up. She gave me a check and I went with her to San Francisco. When I returned to Milan, there was a new Thunderbird waiting for me, a going-away present from Barbara."

Marina Cicogna stayed in San Francisco with Barbara for only a week. After her departure Barbara began to be seen around town with stockbroker Stanley Page, the recently divorced husband of Barbara's friend Harrie Hill Page. Barbara and Harrie had managed to see each other whenever Barbara returned to San Francisco, but when Harrie found out about Barbara's interlude with her former husband, she confronted her old friend. Their friendship was never the same.

Barbara went back to Paris and back to Gottfried von Cramm, who found her a few days later lying on the floor, dazed, drunk, soaked in blood. She had fallen against the edge of a desk, gashing open the side of her head. At the hospital where she was patched up, a doctor told Gottfried about a sanatorium in Sweden that catered to alcoholics. Von Cramm was dubious about the prospect of being able to convince his wife to travel all that distance to enter a sanatorium. He telephoned Jean Kennerley in London for advice, and Jean responded by flying to Paris. After speaking with Barbara, she suggested that instead of the sanatorium, they find her a nearby apartment, a place of her own, where she would be away from the Ritz and would be forced to fend for herself. The experience would presumably take her mind off her problems.

Since Jean de Baglion worked in real estate, he was put in charge of the search. The first place he showed her was a magnificent house on the left bank that was later bought by the Greek shipping magnate Stavros Niarchos. Baglion became exercised when Barbara praised Winfield House at the expense of this great eighteenth-century French mansion. "But Barbara," said Baglion, "Winfield House was built in the 1930s." The next place on Baglion's list, which he showed her the next day, was at 31 rue Octave Feuillet, near the Bois. It was a third-floor eighteen-room apartment that belonged to André Citroën, the French industrialist and automobile manufacturer. Realizing that Baglion was still angry at her because of her Winfield House remarks, Barbara accepted the apartment with alacrity, and even asked Baglion to find a second apartment in the same neighborhood for Silvia de Castellane. Such an apartment was found a few houses away and Barbara bought both, hiring the famous Mr. Travers of the interior decorating firm of Jansen to do whatever remodeling was necessary.

Barbara remained at the Ritz while the work was being completed. Since it would take time, Jean Kennerley came up with a second idea. She suggested that Barbara get busy putting together a second volume of poetry, a follow-up to *The Enchanted*. Morley Kennerley offered to scout around for a printer who would do the volume justice, and to give whatever literary advice Barbara might need or want. Barbara agreed. She spread hundreds of manuscript pages around her suite and began making a preliminary selection.

One evening in mid-July she took a breather and went to Le Grand Véfour restaurant for coffee. While there, she bumped into Noël Coward, who was by himself. "She was not very drunk but weaving," he discloses in his *Diaries*. "She took charge of me, and I finished the evening alone in her suite at the Ritz, reading her own poems to her. Actually some of them are simple and moving, but she is a tragic epitome of 'Poor Little Rich Girl.' She is capable of great kindnesses but her money is always between her and happiness."

Coward, sensing Barbara's insecurity, was shrewd and thoughtful enough to express enthusiasm for her work. His praise gave her the confidence she needed to make her final selections. *The Wayfarer* appeared in a private edition of 200 copies in December 1957 via R. S. Atterbury's Westerham Press, Westerham, Kent, England. Its sixty-six pages contained forty poems, a dedication to Lance Reventlow, and a four-color cover portrait of Barbara by Edmund Dulac (made from a pen-and-ink sketch by José Maria Sert). The poems were similar in tone and temperament to those in the earlier volume. The second volume, whose unifying themes were love and wanderlust, included odes to Thebes and ancient Greece; a unit of poems on Tangier; another group for friends; a poem on blindness, another on the beauty of hands, a third on a cigarette lighter (*"Le Briquet"*), and several on themes suggested by *The Tale of Genji*.

The most strained verses in the collection are the romantic poems she had written to and for Gottfried von Cramm. It was as though, lacking true romance in her life, she had to strain for it in her poetry. An example of the genre is a poem called "The Proposal," written for Gottfried during their summer together in Tangier. The beginning of the poem is a rapturous celebration of idealized love; it is a moving sequence despite its failure as a work of art:

> *Oh! let us be lovers*
> *Now the nights are clear,*
> *And the moon the sole*
> *Accomplice to fear.*
>
> *Let us blend our bodies*
> *As one blends perfume,*

And challenge the heavens
To enter our room.

Let us love only
As the gods have before,
And make them stand humble
Outside of our door....

Although their divorce was still several years off, Barbara and Gottfried went their separate ways. In late August 1957 Barbara left her husband behind and went to Venice with an entourage that included Silvia de Castellane, Jean de Baglion, Dan Rudd, Tony Pawson and a friend of Rudd's named Claude Eggerman. It was the summer that Maria Callas and Aristotle Onassis met for the first time, introduced at Elsa Maxwell's Headdress Ball on the roof of the Danieli hotel.

Following the Maxwell bash, Onassis threw a week of parties aboard his yacht, the *Christina,* anchored in the entrance of the Grand Canal, where international and café society mingled as one, occasioning Cholly Knickerbocker's tart commentary that "it's nearly impossible to know what's what, who's who and why anyone is where these days in the Venetian social swirl." Even such tradition-bound stalwarts as Countess Lilli Volpi and Countess Marina Luling Volpi found themselves inviting jet-set strays to their annual balls and dinner dances. At a fête for four hundred in her Palladian palace, Villa Barbaro, near Asolo (outside Venice), Countess Marina Luling Volpi was overheard saying to Barbara Hutton, "Barbara, dear, who are all these people?"

One of the people that night was twenty-seven-year-old Jimmy Douglas (James Henderson Douglas 3rd), a Chicagoan living in Paris whose father was the Secretary of the Air Force. Douglas, who like Barbara was staying at the Grand Hotel in Venice, was shocked by the strange types that formed a phalanx around her. "I still have this picture of her," he says, "surrounded by faithful servants, hired jesters, and ne'er-do-well hangers-on. Some of them, like Margaret Latimer and Jean de Baglion, were absolutely devoted. Barbara was evidently having drinking problems. She would stay up nights putting it away. Baglion would implore her to stop. She wouldn't, and so he and Sister Latimer would water down her drinks to dilute the effect. Others kept plying her with straight drinks, gin mostly, in the hope of getting her even more drunk, because when she was inebriated or bored she tended to give things away—furs, cars, jewelry. This indulgence fascinated the less than affluent, who found it hard to fathom wealth so great that the bearer thought nothing of squandering huge figures higgledy-piggledy.

"Her capriciousness would sometimes cause tremendous tensions within the cadre. These came about because everyone watched to see who was getting what. If she was sitting with old friends—all of whom she'd given presents to in the past—and somebody new appeared, she might spontaneously make a present to the new person of something more valuable than anything she'd given her friends. I remember one day in Venice she gave Silvia de Castellane a beautiful emerald necklace. The next evening at a party at the Palazzo Papadopoli she gave an even more beautiful and expensive necklace to a woman she barely knew just because this person had been admiring the article all night. When Silvia de Castellane saw this little transaction—and I'm not at all certain she wasn't meant to see it—she absolutely flipped. Events of this sort took place on a daily basis. Also, Barbara had a soft spot for people with quirks. She liked strange accents, for example. One day in Venice she began talking to an American woman from Alabama who spoke with a pronounced Southern accent. She gave the woman a sable coat because she fancied her accent. All of this made life uncomfortable for those around Barbara. The in-fighting and jockeying for position among the members of her entourage approached total insanity. It never occurred to me then that I might one day become part of it."

Jimmy Douglas left Venice about the same time another young American, twenty-nine-year-old Philip Van Rensselaer, descended on the scene. Philip's ancestor was Kilian Van Reensselaer, the seventeenth-century Dutch patroon who owned 700,000 acres along the west bank of the Hudson, more than any other individual landowner in the history of New York State. Despite his familial distinctions, Philip lived modestly on Manhattan's Upper East Side. What he lacked in capital he made up for in prep-school good looks and social connections. A listing in the *Social Register* and an elder brother, Charles Van Rensselaer, who penned a society column, assured him entrée into the homes of the affluent and influential. His host in Venice was his friend, Count Brando Brandolini, whose wife, Christiana, was the granddaughter of Princess Jane di San Faustino, and the daughter of the late Eduardo Agnelli, founder of the Fiat empire. Her brother was Giovanni Agnelli, acting head of Fiat. It was at the Lido that Barbara first met Van Rensselaer, introduced to him by Marina Cicogna.

Philip's estimation of Barbara's entourage was roughly the same as that registered by Jimmy Douglas. He is quoted by Cleveland Amory in *Who Killed Society?* as insisting that "Barbara didn't know the Right People from the Wrong People, and in fact didn't know people at all." As an example of her inability to gauge right from wrong, Van Rensselaer tells Amory that he caught Barbara's "phony foreign entourage trying to get her in a deal whereby she would buy a spurious Picasso and then they would share the profits with the dealer. I tried to tell her but she didn't want to hear about it. All she could say was, 'I don't want to hear anything unpleasant.'"

In a 1978 interview with Brigit Berlin for Andy Warhol's *Interview* Magazine, Van Rensselaer depicts himself in singularly unflattering terms, freely admitting that his checkbook had been confiscated by bank officials "because I gave so many bad checks." He goes on from there to describe what amounts to a personal credo: "Some people claim that Monte Carlo is the Monte Carlo of the garbage set. It's colorful and vivid. People are always involved in scandals, love affairs and stealing money. It's exciting. It's like a big tapestry.... I'm drawn to the squalid glitter and blackmailing creatures of the international set where everything goes and anything is possible. I've seen hustlers become great millionaires. It's just wild.... I love colorful people. In the '60s I was involved with all these financial wizards. They were involved in shady deals. They bought up companies and made tons of money and had done terrible deals with the Nazis and saw the Windsors and all these people. They became great column regulars.... It fascinates me. Since we're only in this world for such a short time, why not do everything. You're going to be awfully sorry when you get old and you're on your deathbed and you think, 'Oh, if only I'd done all those things.'"

Not long after meeting Barbara, Van Rensselaer went off to Greece with the Brandolinis aboard the yacht of Stavros Niarchos. He rejoined Barbara in Paris and spent a good deal of time listening to her recount the details of her kaleidoscopic past. When Barbara arrived in New York aboard the *S.S. United States* on November 14, the day of her forty-fifth birthday, he was still with her.

From the pier they were driven directly to Broadhollow on Cedar Swamp Road in Old Brookville, Long Island, Jimmy Donahue's 100-acre estate, acquired the year before for $400,000 from Alfred Gwynne Vanderbilt. Three days after their arrival Philip accompanied Jimmy Donahue to the Fan Ball at the Plaza Hotel. It was there that he informed columnist Nancy Randolph of his intention to marry Barbara in Mexico.

This announcement was never confirmed or denied by Barbara. When she left for Cuernavaca at the beginning of January, Philip went along. But it was only a matter of time. Barbara soon telephoned Jimmy Douglas in Paris, having gone to considerable lengths to locate him, and invited him to join her in Mexico. Barbara and Philip, according to Philip, had an amicable parting. "She gave me enormous sums of money," he would tell Cleveland Amory. "She said I was a gentleman and was meant to have lots of money. And anyway, she wasn't paying for me, she said, Grandpa Woolworth was."

Over the next three years Barbara and Jimmy Douglas were in constant motion. "We logged thousands of miles," says Douglas. "There were few weeks when we weren't traveling. Barbara thrived on travel. She was the last of the Great Wayfarers. When Barbara was up and in good form she was overpowering. She seemed to burn. Nothing was enough for her. Nobody could keep pace with her. She could go days without sleep. It was almost superhuman.

"I soon found out that most of the things I had read or heard about her were false. She was an invention of the press. The real Barbara Hutton was quite remarkable, infinitely interesting, a great personality with great imagination. Hers wasn't the woebegone, unhappy life the press made it out to be. Barbara Hutton had more fun than anyone I've ever known. But she lived so intensely that her bad moments were as bad as her good moments were good. There were nightmarish moments, particularly in her later years—suicide attempts, drug episodes, alcoholism. But there were also long stretches when she was on top of the world, and that's the Barbara most people don't want to hear about.

"I also don't agree with the theory that her life was one long quest for the ideal mate. That may have been a factor up through her marriage to Cary Grant, but later on her vision changed. When I knew her she was no longer looking for a man with whom to spend the rest of her life. It was more a live-for-the-moment attitude. If you can be happy today, tomorrow will take care of itself."

Their sojourn started in February 1958 when Jimmy and Barbara arrived in Beverly Hills. There she was introduced to Jill St. John. Privately Barbara expressed the opinion that Jill was using Lance to advance her acting career, an opinion shared by some of his friends. But while his friends were outspoken on the subject, Barbara exercised diplomacy, suggesting only that Lance and Jill "experiment" by spending six months apart before investing in a gold wedding band. When Lance rejected the idea, she said nothing more about it.

At the end of February, Barbara and Jimmy Douglas headed for Honolulu, then flew to Manila, spent two nights there and proceeded to Hong Kong and Bangkok, where they visited James Thompson, who had helped decorate Barbara's palace in Tangier, and who happened to be a brother of Jimmy's stepmother. From Bangkok they traveled to New Delhi. There Barbara acquired a set of rock-crystal plates encrusted with rubies and had them shipped to Tangier. After a leisurely tour of India, including visits with Ayisha, the Maharanee of Jaipur, and with Princess Berar, the granddaughter of the Sultan of the

Ottoman Empire, they spent a month living on a houseboat in Kashmir. They then went to Istanbul, and by early June arrived at the Imperial Hotel in Vienna, where they were entertained by Baron Gecman-Waldeck, an opera devotee who each night took them to another performance. They returned to Paris and in August went to stay with Lady Kenmare at La Fiorentina, her estate near Cap Ferrat. Venice was their habitat for September, and there they stayed with Prince and Princess George Chavchavadze at the Palazzo Polignac.

Toward the end of the month Barbara traveled to England to consult with the pioneering plastic surgeon Sir Hector Archibald McIndoe, chief of surgery at the Queen Victoria Plastic and Jaw Injury Center in East Grinstead, Sussex. McIndoe, known not only for his cosmetic surgery on movie stars and members of the royal family but more importantly for his miraculous work on disfigured RAF fighter pilots during World War II, performed two relatively minor surgical procedures on Barbara—a partial face lift and a reduction mammoplastry (breast reduction), an operation she had been contemplating for years.

She healed quickly, and in the fall she and Douglas arrived in Tangier, where Barbara had hired a new housekeeper, a White Russian woman named Ira Belline, a cousin of Stravinsky's and a close friend of David Herbert's. Herbert visited Sidi Hosni one afternoon, and the three of them—Barbara, Ira and David—were sitting on the balcony just idly chatting away when out of nowhere Barbara said, "Oh, did you know I've had my breasts reduced?"

"Yes, darling, I know," said Ira.

Barbara looked at her. "Oh, that's right," she said. "But David didn't know. I wanted him to see how lovely and small they are." At which point she dropped the top of her dress and showed David her cosmetically reshaped breasts.

She had gone through with the plastic surgery, according to Ruth Hopwood, because of her intense attachment to Jimmy Douglas. "It was a frustrating time for Barbara," says Ruth, "because she was passionately in love with Jimmy, and Jimmy's sexual inclinations were evidently extremely complex. Barbara joked about her knack for attracting difficult men—first Gottfried von Cramm, then Jimmy. I don't think her relationship with Jimmy was completely sexless, but it wasn't what it might have been. She was frustrated, and the frustration made her anxious. She couldn't sleep nights. It wore Jimmy down to have to stay up with her night after night."

By the middle of January, Barbara and Jimmy were on their way to Cuernavaca to view the completion of what had become one of the most heralded architectural projects in Mexico, a $3.2 million Japanese-style house on thirty acres of land within sight of the snow-capped peak of Popocatepetl, an inactive volcano reminiscent of Mount Fuji in Japan. Barbara had bought the land in 1957 from José Villanueva, a Mexican contractor, and hired the Hawaiian architect Albert Ely Ives to design the house, using materials, craftsmen and landscape gardeners imported directly from Japan. She called it Sumiya—translated, The House on the Corner—after the original Sumiya in Kyoto, built for one of the early courtesans of Japan. But Barbara's "house on the corner" had more the air of an emperor's palace than that of a discreet bordello. If was filled with authentic fourteenth-century imperial furniture, priceless Oriental screens, brightly colored silks, interior rock gardens, a Jacuzzi for ten, flower-bedecked moats, bridges that served as passageways connecting one wing of the house to the other. Peacocks and cranes strutted about the grounds, pausing occasionally to dip a tentative foot in the heated swimming pool. There was a kabuki-style theater that seated forty where Barbara showed films (sent to her by Cary Grant) and staged productions of dancers and musicians (also imported from Japan).

After three months amid the tranquility of Mexico, Barbara and Jimmy Douglas arrived in San Francisco. Whatever they did, wherever they went, they attracted the press. Herb Caen traced their daily jaunts in the pages of the San Francisco *Chronicle*, reporting that Barbara walked into Schneider's on Post Street and walked out with an $8000 sable, then went to dinner with Jimmy at Ernie's, and on to the Ricksha for a nightcap, before retiring for the evening to their adjoining suites at the Mark Hopkins. The same columnist, after announcing their plans to visit Japan, wrote about a call they paid to Gump's, Barbara's favorite jewelry store. Looking Jimmy Douglas over, one of the salesmen said to Barbara, "Miss Hutton, your son looks simply wonderful!" "That's not my son, that's my husband," she said, as they departed arm-in-arm.

The Japanese leg of their journey was to be the highlight of their three-year global journey. They went everywhere and saw everything, including sites rarely seen by Westerners. Their tour guide was a Japanese named Hirotaka Hatakayama, whose log (a small portion of which is herein transcribed) charmingly conveys the essence and flavor of the expedition:

> May 4. Visited Hakone Gougen Shinto Shrine. Mr. Douglas wished to take photos inside shrine building. The priest said he has never permitted anyone to take a picture of the inside and refused us permission. So I explained to the priest that Mr. Douglas is not an ordinary tourist but a virtuoso on things Japanese and I gave to the priest 500 yen as a "gift" to

the god. So finally he allowed us to enter the oratory and take some pictures.

May 5. Drive to Atami City. Mrs. Hutton purchased pipes, incense, kokeshi dolls, wind bells, and records of Japanese popular songs...Mrs. Hutton and Mr. Douglas are great fans for Almond Glico and other caramels. They keep chewing caramels most of the time. I'm following the fashion, too.

May 14. Kyoto. Marchioness Hachisuka, a friend of Mrs. Hutton, invites us to Miyako Odori Dance and Dinner. Next day we call at Urasenke, a headquarters of tea ceremony. Mr. Douglas was tall enough to bump against the low lintels sometimes. At Kawahima, most authoritative Nishijin textiles store, Mrs. Hutton bought many rolls of obi material. In evening we went to Sumiya, old Courtesan House, for a geisha party.

May 20. We visited Shugakuin Garden...Mrs. Hutton found a four-leaf clover in the garden. It was the first time for her to find a four-leaf clover in her life, she said...

June 8. The inn at Aikawa, on the island of Sado, appeals very much to Mrs. Hutton's fancy. In the evening the Tatsunami Troupe performed folk dances which were marvelous beyond description. One of the dances is even a sort of "male strip teasing." We laughed and laughed almost to split the stomach. Mrs. Hutton and Mr. Douglas danced to a Japanese popular song.

It was from Sado that Barbara wrote to the Kennerleys: "Japan is a clean, clear, astonishing country...with a refinement of custom I have found nowhere else. We sleep on futons on the floor and prefer inns to hotels. I haven't slept like this since I was a babe in arms. If I have one complaint it has to do with the Japanese toilet. It is very odd. You squat over a low porcelain affair on the floor. Everything in Japan is done on the floor. This toilet business entails some very tricky positions."

There was one uncomfortable moment on the trip and it took place toward the end as they were about to leave Tokyo for Paris. "Barbara had an attack," says Douglas. "She decided that instead of returning to Paris she wanted to go on to Nepal. When I told her it was impossible, that I had to be back in Paris, she had a kind of apoplectic fit and then she froze up on me. She curled into this tight little ball on the couch. I remember thinking that it was as if the real Barbara, the Barbara I knew, were looking out at me from within this shell. Eventually a doctor came. She wouldn't let him examine her, so he left me a hypodermic of some fast-acting sedative to give her in case she became violent. I didn't need it. She fell asleep on the couch and by the next morning she had recovered.

"Despite these periodic flare-ups, I thought I did an admirable job of drying her out. She was taking Valium to help ease the pain of withdrawal. But the key was that you had to exercise a firm hand. At one point I gave her an ultimatum—'You stop drinking or I leave!' Her first reaction was always to try and bribe you. You had to show her that you weren't for sale."

After a month in Paris, during which Barbara worked out the final details of a friendly divorce settlement with Gottfried von Cramm (the final decree, issued in January 1960, awarded Von Cramm another $600,000, in addition to monies previously received), she and Douglas resumed their travels: Tangier, Copenhagen, Oslo (where they stayed with former ice-skating champion Sonja Henie), Venice. Between Tangier and Copenhagen, Barbara managed to squeeze in two days in Paris to attend a fall preview at the fashion house of Lanvin-Castillo, where, for nearly $300,000, she acquired a large number of the 200 items displayed by models. Among the items she selected were sixty dresses, a honey-colored mink coat with sable collar, a black diamond mink, a chinchilla cape, a turquoise negligee embroidered with blossoms of gold. The reason for the wardrobe, much of which she gave to friends, was Silvia de Castellane's position as a public relations consultant to Antonio del Castillo. Barbara wanted to launch Silvia in her new career.

In mid-December Barbara and Jimmy Douglas flew to New York to spend the Christmas holidays in Old Brookville with Jimmy Donahue. Douglas had expressed reservations about staying with Donahue, and as events unfolded, he had good reason to be apprehensive.

Right away Barbara got her hands on some of Donahue's pills and went racing around from one Long Island town to another, cleaning out the stores, buying everything in sight. She spent $250,000 on a collection of Fabergé jewelry, which she presented to Douglas as a token of her esteem. The next day he returned the merchandise, redeemed her check and tore it up.

Exhausted from his guilt-ridden role as Barbara's warden, Douglas accepted an invitation to join his parents for a two-week vacation in the Bahamas. He left in a state of near exhaustion, promising to rejoin Barbara in Cuernavaca by the middle of January. During his absence she began drinking again and was still drinking when she arrived in Mexico with Bill Robertson, Silvia de Castellane, Jean de Baglion and two new employees—a young Frenchwoman named Marguerite

Chevalier, hired to replace the recently retired Margaret Latimer, and Colin Frazer, a burly, handsome Australian hired as Barbara's bodyguard.

Jean de Baglion was surprised to find Barbara back on the bottle. He surmised that it was due to the absence of Jimmy Douglas. "Whenever she drank," says Baglion, "she became overbearingly extravagant. On our second night in Cuernavaca she brought in a group of musicians from Mexico City to perform for us in her little theater. There were three of us in the audience and sixty musicians on stage. It was slightly absurd.

"Then a day or two later I went on a tour of Cuernavaca. When I returned to the house, Barbara was sitting with her neighbor Nacho de Landa on the lanai of the guest cottage. They were watching Barbara's twenty-five gardeners toiling in a distant field. The workers were dressed as Japanese peasants. 'How do you like Japan?' Barbara said to me. Then she went into a long explanation of feudal life in fourteenth-century Japan and it dawned on me that not only was she drunk, she also thought she was the Empress of Japan and that these were her minions. After a bit, Nacho got up to leave. 'And where do you think you're going?' said Barbara. 'I thought I might take a little swim,' said Nacho. 'You'll leave when you're told to leave!' she snapped. And with that she simply passed out."

That evening De Landa called in a friend, Dr. Allesondo, a prominent Mexican physician who replenished Barbara's supply of Valium and put her on vitamin supplements and megavitamin injections in an effort to dry her out again. Because of her anorexia, he also insisted that she drink at least two specially fortified milkshakes a day. She showed definite signs of improvement until Bill Robertson made the mistake of telling her that Jimmy Douglas most likely would be delayed in the Bahamas, because he had met somebody. The person he had met was Lady Jane-Vane Tempest Stewart, the daughter of Lord Londonderry. Barbara became incredibly jealous.

"One has to question Bill Robertson's wisdom in telling Barbara," says Nacho de Landa. "There was no question of Robertson's allegiance to Barbara. What was in question was his judgment. He was the sort of person capable of telling a terminally ill patient that his days were numbered. I mean he was honest to an almost supernatural degree."

This tendency on Robertson's part to divulge everything made itself felt a second time in a letter he wrote to Jimmy Douglas, reporting on Barbara's condition. The doctor's cure, said the letter, had worked for a while but then Barbara had started drinking again. Moreover, she hadn't slept for two nights in a row; he and Nacho de Landa had stayed up with her, because the doctor refused to prescribe sleeping pills. The letter also said that Colin Frazer was away for a few days but that Barbara was much taken with him, especially at those times when she was drunk.

The words "much taken" jolted Douglas. He dropped everything and left at once for Cuernavaca, arriving at Sumiya with a satchel of gifts for Barbara, including a gaily colored garter snake that promptly wrapped itself around her wrist. Snakes were a schoolboy passion with Douglas. He owned a ten-foot python that he kept in his bathtub in Paris. Barbara had misgivings both about Jimmy and her new pet. Offering a statement laden with double-entendres, she asked him why he had brought "a serpent into the Garden of Eden." She carefully avoided talking about his vacation, and he said nothing about Colin Frazer.

On March 24, 1960, Lance Reventlow married Jill St. John in the royal suite of the Mark Hopkins Hotel in San Francisco before California Associate Supreme Court Justice Marshall McComb. Barbara hadn't wanted to attend the ceremony, and it took Jimmy Douglas a good week to convince her of the necessity of being present at her son's wedding. She flew to San Francisco with Nacho and Lee de Landa, and there for the first time she met Jill's parents, the Oppenheims. "She didn't care for the family," says Nacho de Landa, "but she was glad to see Jimmy Donahue, Dudley Walker, Margaret Latimer, all of whom were at the wedding."

The next time Barbara saw the young couple was in May at her new apartment in Paris. Derry Moore, Lord Drogheda's son, was Barbara's houseguest. "You could slice the tension with a knife" remarks Derry. Jill didn't help much. She did nothing but complain. Nothing pleased her. The food, the service, the sights—everything in Paris was inferior to its counterpart in the States. You could see that the marriage probably wasn't going to last. You could also see that Barbara and Jill didn't get along. They agreed on only one subject: the idea that Lance should give up automobile racing. Barbara was so anxious to put an end to his involvement in the sport that she offered Jill a million-dollar cache of jewels if she could convince Lance to quit. But Jill never collected. She was too ambitious to succeed as an actress to give domestic life a tumble."

Barbara had other thoughts on her mind besides Jill St. John. Toward the beginning of July 1960 Jimmy Douglas left for London for two weeks to attend a friend's wedding. After two days he received a call from Bill Robertson. Barbara, in a fit of loneliness, had gotten drunk and was threatening to end it all by swallowing a vial of sleeping pills. Her suicide threats had become nearly commonplace. Several months earlier on the plane from Mexico City to New York she had tried to force open the emergency exit and hurl herself out of the airliner. It was Douglas who restrained her then, and it was Douglas who restrained her now, rushing back to Paris to see her through her latest self-induced crisis.

It was impossible not to marvel at Jimmy's patience when it came to dealing with Barbara, his willingness to play white knight to Barbara's helpless maiden. But it was a situation that everyone knew could not endure indefinitely. "I had too much admiration for Barbara to be drawn into the ranks of her detractors," observes Douglas, "but I could see where others before me had come up against a stone wall. She was sunk in her ways, absolutely enmeshed in them. What I mean is that there was no room for compromise. You couldn't be with her and at the same time have a life of your own. And in a way that makes sense, because if you're so rich that you're famous for it, life really does take on a different dimension. She didn't compromise, because she didn't have to compromise.

"I think we realized simultaneously that it couldn't go anywhere, that I had served my tenure and it was time for both of us to move on. Our friendship was always there, but on a different and less intense level. In early August 1960 Barbara went to Tangier without me. A few weeks later I received a letter. She had met a young impecunious Englishman named Lloyd Franklin. He was sweet and good-natured and down-to-earth. What troubled me was that he was broke. When I heard that, I said to myself, 'Oh oh, here we go again!'"

❧

By the fall of 1960 not only all Tangier but everyone else in the civilized world who read newspapers knew all about Lloyd Franklin. This twenty-three-year-old Londoner had been a trumpeter in the British Royal Guards, but had then decided to leave the military and travel through North Africa. He arrived in Tangier in the early summer of 1960 with an alpine backpack, an old guitar and a letter of introduction to David Herbert. Herbert had him over for lunch at his home on the Mountain and found him to be a solid fellow—quiet, polite, with a slow smile, strongly resembling a blond Clark Gable, even to the protruding ears.* He had taken a small but clean room in a conveniently located hotel and was currently looking for employment, preferably singing and playing the guitar. Herbert proceeded to take him around to the various

---

*In 1961 Barbara paid to have Lloyd's ears "fixed." The perichondrioplasty (or "ear tuck") to reduce the degree of protruberance was performed in the same hospital in England where Barbara underwent her plastic surgery.

nightspots and cafés until they wound up at Dean's Bar, a refuge not only for Tangerino society but for an international coterie of the rich and titled, of actors and artists.

Joseph Dean, the owner of the bar, offered Lloyd gratuities, meals and a small salary for two guitar sets a night. Lloyd took the job. "He wasn't that great a musician," recalls Herbert. "As a friendly joke Dean began calling him 'blum blum' because that's how he sounded on the guitar. He had a pleasant voice, nothing special. But there was something so winning about him that he became very popular. People used to go to Dean's not to hear him play, but to see him."

That August, after Barbara Hutton arrived in Tangier, Herbert gave a dinner party and invited Lloyd, Barbara, the American ambassador and a number of other members of the English and European community in Tangier. "Lloyd had no formal clothes to speak of," says Herbert, "so I lent him a white dinner jacket. All through dinner Barbara conversed only with the American ambassador. After dinner I asked Lloyd to play the guitar and sing, and Barbara never took her eyes off him. At the end of the evening I asked her to give him a lift back to his hotel. She took him back to Sidi Hosni instead, and early the next morning the phone rang. It was Lloyd to thank me for inviting him and also for introducing him to Barbara. Then Barbara got on the line. 'Isn't Lloyd wonderful?' she said."

The ensuing affair wasn't all the typical older-woman-younger-man romance. In fact it was Lloyd who fell deeply in love with Barbara, and though he was many years younger than she and was being exposed for the first time in his life to a world of great riches and luxury, he never became spoiled or greedy. He never forgot his old friends, and Barbara, appreciating this gesture, would always entertain and invite them to her parties.

That consideration, however, did little to prevent the eruption of gossip that took place once the lovers began to be seen together in public. The gossip that was heard in Tangier and elsewhere centered on Barbara's presents to Lloyd: guitars, trumpets, flamenco and voice lessons, a Rolls-Royce embossed with the insignia of the Royal Guards, an MG, a dozen polo ponies, a stable to house the ponies on fifteen acres of real estate adjacent to the Royal Golf and Country Club, a complete wardrobe and a pair of Patek Philippe watches.

Another portion of the gossip was passed on by Barbara's bemused staff at Sidi Hosni, where Lloyd was now a full-time tenant. A Moroccan cook named Addi (who also worked for the author Paul Bowles) told of how Barbara received a steady stream of correspondence from all corners of the world, in which anonymous men paid her court.

They enclosed photographs of themselves, Addi said, both with and without clothing, and their descriptions of themselves caused Barbara great merriment. She would call Lloyd in and show him the more revealing photos, and if a letter was particularly absurd or erotic, she would read it to him, and this routine apparently never failed to arouse him.

Another tidbit that made the rounds involved a cab driver who doubled as Barbara's chauffeur. This man would drive down every morning to the post office to pick up Barbara's mail and drop it off in her private chambers. One morning the driver heard strange and passionate sounds coming from Barbara's bedroom: ohhh and ahhh and mmmm. The door was half open and out of curiosity he peeked in and saw Barbara lying on her back with Lloyd Franklin on top ("platin' her with his tongue up her puss" in the driver's lingo). Barbara looked up and saw the driver and jumped up and covered herself and asked, "What do you want?" "I came to deliver the mail," he said. "Leave it there," she said, and he went out. That same day she called him in and said, "Did you see what was going on?" "Oh yes, Princess," he said. "Did you know what it was?" "Oh yes," he said. "Do you like it?" she asked. "Yes, I like it," he said. "Well, try it sometime," said Barbara.*

It was shortly after meeting Lloyd that Barbara agreed to sit for Cecil Beaton's camera for the pages of *Life*. Wearing her Catherine the Great emerald tiara, she posed on an ornate Moroccan couch in a filigreed room while serenely plucking a Moorish lute. She looked younger, finer, more composed than anyone had a logical right to expect, "as though [wrote *Life*] nearly three decades of notoriety as one of the world's richest women, the uproar attendant on her six marriages and her countless well-publicized journeys over the face of the earth had left her unscarred and tranquil."

That was perhaps stretching it a bit, though it was evident that she had experienced a resurgence of at least some of her old powers. In her ebullient state she gave a season-ending series of banquets and balls at Sidi Hosni, the most memorable of which was a costume party attended by several hundred guests in drag. Lloyd Franklin went as Jean Harlow in platinum tresses, glowing make-up and form-fitting gown. David Herbert appeared dressed as a peasant girl. Barbara went as Peter Pan in a pair of green velvet tights.

*Pulitzer Prize-winning author Ted Morgan, a resident of Tangier from 1968 to 1973, includes this anecdote in his 1981 nonfiction book, *Rowing Toward Eden*. Morgan heard the story first from George Greaves, an Australian reporter in Tangier for the London *Express*, well known for his humorous storytelling manner. Greaves's source was Barbara's chauffeur, who continued to deliver her mail without further incident.

Starting in the fall of 1960 Barbara led Lloyd over roughly the same terrain she had traversed previously with Jimmy Douglas: Venice, Paris, New York, Cuernavaca, San Francisco, Honolulu, London, Paris, then back to Tangier. Her major project in Tangier during the summer of 1961 was an international polo tournament she helped organize to raise funds for the city's volunteer fire department. The trophies were presented by Barbara and King Hussein of Jordan. In addition, she had her staff work overtime stuffing cash into envelopes, which were then taken down to the public hospital wards and distributed among the poor.

Later in the summer she gave one of her typically opulent rooftop parties, a formal affair attended by a glut of guests of all ages and from all walks of life. The roof terraces were covered with colorful tents and flower arrangements, and a wooden dance floor had been laid. Local dancers had been hired to entertain. Finally Barbara appeared, a cluster of emeralds embedded in her hair. She wore several ropes of pink pearls at her neck, and her dress was embroidered in diamonds. She looked, suggested Cecil Beaton in *Self Portrait With Friends,* like "a little Byzantine empress-doll. Her gestures of greeting and affection, her smiles, the look of surprise or delight, were all played in the grand manner. An arm was extended for the hand to be kissed, a graceful turn of the head to greet a Moroccan 'big-wig,' a wide, open-armed welcome to an old friend, head thrown back with lowered lids and a move of the mouth—every sort of smile and coquetry.... She was in need of a director to tell her that she was forcing her efforts too much. None the less, I was fascinated."

Barbara longed for relaxation, for peace, for stability—words that crop up repeatedly in her correspondence. Yet at the same time her letters reflect a restlessness that thrived on uprootedness and instability. Nothing illustrates this point better than her wildly erratic, on-and-off relationship with her son, although it is also true that some of the upheaval originated with Lance.

During the winter of 1962 Lance visited his mother in Cuernavaca and was accompanied on the trip by his valet, Dudley Walker. As Dudley recalls, "Barbara was down there with Lloyd Franklin and Jimmy Donahue, and Lance was saying lots of things he shouldn't have said inasmuch as his mother was supporting him. It had to do with all the publicity that she was getting because of her affair with Lloyd. Lloyd was a nice enough chap but he was younger than Lance, and Lance found it demoralizing. Anyway, one day Lance says to Donahue, 'Where's that drunken cunt of a mother of mine?' Donahue goes straight to Barbara and tells her what Lance said, and that's the end of Lance. She cut him off without a cent, including his trust funds. He had to sell his house in Holmby Hills and buy a smaller one in Benedict Canyon. It wasn't a pleasant period for Lance. He and Jill St. John had separated and she was seeing Frank Sinatra. They divorced in 1963. The only advantage to his new-found poverty was that he got off lightly on his divorce settlement with Jill—it was something like a hundred thousand dollars spread over a span of seven years. Barbara eventually repented and reinstated Lance and helped him fix up his new place."

Despite its effect on Lance, the romance between Barbara and Lloyd continued to flourish. When they returned to Tangier in August they were joined by Ira Belline and David Herbert on an automobile tour across Morocco. "Barbara was very happy during this period," says Herbert. "She and Lloyd drove in a Peugeot, while we followed in a Renault. Barbara was wonderful to travel with, extremely sprightly and easygoing. In the morning she would be the first person up and out. I would find her in the hotel lobby sitting on her valise. She wore her hair up because she didn't want to bother with hairdressers. She was grabbing for happiness while she still could, and she was right to do so."

The first phase of the journey took them through Meknés, Fez, Midelt, Tinerhir and Ouarzazate. There they attended a two-day festival given by the Pasha of Ouarzazate with dancing, musicians, carnivals, feasts. They then drove south to the ancient walled city of Taroudant in the Anti-Atlas Mountains on the edge of the Sahara, a center of fragrant gardens and olive groves set against a stark, sun-bathed landscape of granite cliffs and red earth. They stayed at French Baron Pellenc's swank resort hotel, La Gazelle d'Or, which Barbara had first visited in the early 1950s and which soon became her favorite vacation retreat. When they arrived David Herbert, who had never been there but had heard a good deal about it, was more than a little surprised to find that they were the only guests, and it was only then that he learned that Barbara was in the habit of reserving the entire resort for herself, an extravagance that cost her in excess of $40,000 a week.

After three weeks in Taroudant they drove to Marrakech and checked into the Hotel Mamounia. While there, Ira Belline happened to meet a former acquaintance, Raymond Doan, a Vietnamese chemist for a French oil company located in Gueliz, just outside Marrakech. Doan, who had been educated in France, considered himself primarily an artist, an expressionist whose pastel oils of Moroccan street life showed a considerable if not yet fully developed talent. Married and with two young sons, Doan also had an elder brother, and this fellow, Maurice, an admitted opium addict and homosexual, lived in Marrakech as well; his house was exquisitely decorated, though constructed in a way that might be construed as diabolical. Maurice could lie in bed, and thanks to the arrangement of the rooms plus a complicated system of mirrors, see what was happening in every room of the house—"like a spider in its web," according to one visitor.

When Raymond Doan heard that Ira Belline was in town with Barbara Hutton and several other friends, he invited them all to his house for tea. "It was a dreadful visit," recalls David Herbert. "Doan's French wife, Jacqueline, was in curlers when we arrived. His children were bedridden with the measles. The tea was tepid and bitter. Doan himself was a wiry, nervous, birdlike Oriental, youngish-looking despite some gray, whose sole objective seemed to be to sell us a painting. The paintings were everywhere, covering every square inch of wall. Doan led us from room to room, like one of those hyper tour guides at the Louvre, determined to cover every artifact. 'Oh, let's just buy one and get out of here,' Barbara whispered. Finally she saw something and paid for it and we left.

"One afternoon about ten days after returning to Tangier, I went to visit Barbara at Sida Hosni. She had this strange glint in her eye and said she had something to show me. She then produced an envelope and inside on a plain sheet of stationery was a handwritten poem. It was in French and full of romantic imagery, the sort of garble a love-sick schoolboy might send his girlfriend. Reading it, I had to stifle a laugh. There was no name or return address. 'Any idea who sent it?' I inquired. 'It's from Raymond Doan, of course,' said Barbara. 'How can you tell?' I asked. She pointed to the postmark on the envelope and said, 'Who else do I know in Marrakech?'"

꠸

In early January 1963 Raymond Doan, Maurice Doan, and an American art dealer friend of theirs sat in a restaurant in Marrakech hatching a complicated and unlikely plan revolving around Barbara Hutton. Another diner at a nearby table, Mrs. Bruce Nairn, the wife of the British consul general in Morocco, overhead the conversation and repeated it in detail afterward. The originator, as far as Mrs. Nairn could tell, was Maurice Doan. Raymond Doan was essentially an innocent pawn at this stage, whose only act had been to send Barbara a few love lyrics through the mail. It was Maurice's idea that the art dealer organize a one-man show of his brother's paintings to take place during the summer of 1963 at the Tangier Casino. The dealer would presumably earn a nice commission for his efforts. Maurice Doan, on the other hand, had bigger ideas, most of them involving his younger brother.

One of the first people Mrs. Nairn saw after overhearing the conversation was her husband's friend David Herbert. Herbert said nothing until Barbara returned to Tangier that summer. Then, when he saw an announcement for the Raymond Doan exposition in the Tangier newspaper, he went to Barbara and told her everything he knew. "She was furious," says Herbert. "But she was furious with me. She couldn't deal with the notion that somebody might endear himself to her simply for her money. She called me a gossip and refused to have anything further to do with me. Our friendship came to a temporary halt."

The exhibition arrived in Tangier and Barbara attended the opening. Raymond Doan was there and so was a painting he had done of Sidi Hosni as seen from outside the high palace walls. Barbara purchased not just that painting but the entire show, paying the asking prices without uttering a word of protest. But this was just the beginning. For his role in the enterprise she bought Maurice Doan a luxury apartment in Paris. She gave Ira Belline a charming villa outside Marrakech. Lloyd Franklin, meanwhile, was moved out of the Hutton menage, and Raymond Doan was moved in.

According to David Herbert, Lloyd Franklin was deeply injured by his forced exit. He wanted to marry Barbara, but she wouldn't because she felt he should have his own family and children. This was not simply an empty excuse on her part; it was how she felt. It was a selfless act, perhaps the only such act she ever showed a man she claimed to love. Lloyd Franklin was too young; more to the point, Barbara was too old. Yet to David Herbert the dissolution of their romance seemed a great pity. He couldn't remember Barbara being more carefree or more happy than she had been with Lloyd. In a real sense, he was the one person who truly cared for her.

In time Lloyd married Penny Ansley, a young and pretty English heiress. They moved into a house on the Mountain, a wedding present from Barbara Hutton, and through his in-laws Lloyd was able to embark on a financially secure career as a stockbroker, spending half the year in London, the other half in Tangier. Penny and Lloyd had a child, a boy named Julian, and David Herbert was the boy's godfather.

But the story was to have an unhappy ending. On January 1, 1968, having celebrated the New Year with friends in Marrakech, Lloyd and his wife (pregnant with their second child) were driving back to Tangier. A child suddenly darted across the road. Lloyd turned the wheel sharply to the right, missed the child, but lost control of the car. They were stopped by a roadside tree. Lloyd was dead at age thirty-one, and his wife died of injuries the following day.

Sixteen

O N OCTOBER 30, 1963, two months after Raymond Doan's one-man art show, three Rolls-Royces departed Sidi Hosni carrying Barbara and an entourage of companions and retainers, including her hairdresser (Jean Mendiboure), her dressmaker (Vera Medina), her personal maid (Tony Gonzales), her housekeeper (Ira Belline), her bodyguard (Colin Frazer), and her majordomo (Bill Robertson). Their first stop was the de luxe Tour Hassan Hotel in Rabat, where Barbara marked her arrival by dispersing Moroccan robes, caftans and packets of Berber jewelry to all members of the hotel staff.

A few days later she went to the Loatian embassy in Rabat and made them an intriguing offer: she wanted to purchase a title for Raymond Doan. She was willing to pay $50,000. The Laotian official assured Barbara that the embassy wasn't in the title-selling business. "But how much did you say you would pay?" he asked. "Fifty thousand dollars," repeated Barbara. The official thought for a moment and suddenly remembered that an old clerk at the embassy was a "Prince" and owned a dilapidated palace back in Indochina that carried a title with it, or had in the old days. So they sent for this fellow with the palace and the so-called title and the deal was struck. Raymond Doan was now Prince Raymond Doan Vinh Na Champassak, and Barbara, with her mania for make-believe, could say that her first, fourth, and last husbands were all princes.*

From Rabat the contingent moved on to the Mamounia in Marrakech, where Barbara re-enacted her gift-giving ritual, winning favor with everyone but Raymond and Maurice Doan, who felt she was being heedlessly altruistic. It was perfectly clear at this point that Raymond Doan was no longer an innocent bystander in his brother's grand scheme. Once Barbara had swallowed the bait in Tangier, Raymond of necessity was forced to change, even to the extent of going along with his newly acquired title. So complete was his conversion to royalty that when Graham Mattison later presented him with a prenuptial separation-of-property agreement, he initially refused to sign, claiming that as a modern-day monarch he was not permitted to append his signature to legal documents of any kind, save marriage certificates. His explanation convinced Mattison that he was dealing with either the most humorous or the most corrupt of Barbara's seven spouses. Shortly before the marriage, Doan relented and signed the agreement.

Jean Mendiboure, Barbara's coiffeur in Tangier and one of her closest confidants in later years, was suspicious of Raymond Doan from the first. "By the time we arrived in Marrakech he had already left his job," states Mendiboure. "His wife and kids had already gone off to the Canary Islands and a divorce suit was in the works. He defined himself as a spiritualist—one day he was a Zen Buddhist, a day later he was the son of Allah. Behind his back people called him 'chimpanzee,' because he always wore a dour expression on his face and insisted on being addressed as Prince Champassak.

"In Marrakech we were soon joined by Silvia de Castellane and her recent spouse, Kilian Hennessy, of the French cognac family; also Graham Mattison and his new wife,* a Brizilian named Perla de Lucena. The group then drove down to the Gazelle d'Or, a herd of Rolls-Royces crawling between the mud huts of Taroudant. On our first night in Taroudant, Raymond Doan gave Barbara a huge amethyst ring and matching bracelet as an engagement present. She put the ring on and commented on how attractive it looked, then slipped it off suddenly and hurled it against the wall. 'Give this junk to your wife!'

---

*Champassak (also written Champacak) was located some two hundred miles west of the ancient ruins of Angkor, near Bangkok (in what is today Thailand). Champassak ceased to exist as an independent "kingdom" in 1947. In an autobiographical essay in the French magazine *L'Oeil* (1972), Raymond Doan traces his Champassak ancestry as though he were an actual member of the family.

*Graham Mattison's first wife is today Mrs. Gretchen Nicholas. She is a New York socialite and an heiress of the Knight-Ridder newspaper fortune.

she screamed. The ancient Greeks believed that the amethyst prevented intoxication and that was how she took it—as a commentary on
her drinking. But even more amazing than her action was Doan's
reaction. He stooped to pick up the ring, fumbled it and stooped again.
Thereafter Barbara humiliated him whenever she felt like it. One of her
favorite pastimes was to tempt people with money. And Doan was
perfect for that mode of entertainment."

In December, Jean Mendiboure accompanied the newly engaged
couple from Casablanca to New York on what he described as an
"unusually bad crossing"—foul weather, seasickness, constant bickering between Barbara and Doan. They arrived on Christmas Eve and
went straight to Barbara's suite at the Pierre. The following day they
drove out to Jimmy Donahue's place on Long Island. Woolworth
Donahue was also there, recently divorced from wife number two, Judy
"Baby Doll" Church. Jimmy's French chef had prepared a sumptuous
Christmas Day repast that was marred, Mendiboure recalls, by still
another altercation between Barbara and her intended.

"In the middle of the meal Barbara started raving, 'I'm going to kill
him! I'm going to kill him!' She bolted out of her seat and ran into the
kitchen, where she grabbed a butcher knife and came out swinging at
Doan. The chef managed to wrestle the knife away from her. She then
went to her room to sulk for a few hours and when she returned she
said, 'It's these pills and drinks that are making me crazy.' She decided
she would go into New York for treatment. She wanted to leave
immediately, although there was a good foot of snow on the ground. I
was staying next door in the guest cottage so I went out to retrieve my
suitcase. On the way back I slipped on a patch of ice in the driveway and
came down on my right wrist, breaking it. I was in great pain and
Barbara was leaping for joy. She couldn't have been happier. 'Oh,
goody!' she said. 'Now we can share the same hospital room.' To her it
was all a big game. She had every painkiller known to mankind, and
after she gave me some pills I was ready for the drive into Manhattan.
Her physician in New York was a Dr. Poindexter and he had us
admitted to Lenox Hill Hospital. It was against hospital policy, but
Barbara managed to have us placed in the same room. I slept most of
the time, and Barbara soon became morose and bored. After one night
and two days she was ready to leave. It was eleven-thirty P.M. when she
started trying to reach Poindexter by phone. When she couldn't get
him, she informed the night nurse that she was signing us both out.
'You can't do that,' said the nurse. 'We need your doctor's signature.'
'You don't think we're going to stay in this dump against our will, do
you?' said Barbara. So we left and Barbara's driver picked us up and
drove us over to the Pierre. I rolled her into the lobby in a wheelchair. I

was wearing a hospital gown with my right arm in a plaster cast, and Barbara had on a bathrobe with just a sable stole thrown over her shoulders. There were a couple of tourists at the front desk and one said to the other, 'Well, that's New York for you.' He might better have said, 'Well, that's Barbara Hutton for you.'"

Twenty-seven guests (including Lance Reventlow) arrived in Cuernavaca, Mexico, to attend Barbara Hutton's seventh wedding ceremony, a number fraught with no more magic than any of the previous occasions. On the marriage certificate she gave her age as fifty-one, her religion as Protestant, her residence as Cuernavaca. The groom gave his name as Prince Pierre Raymond Doan Vinh Na Champassak, his age as forty-eight, his religion as Buddhist. At a press conference he revealed that his father had been a Vietnamese viceroy and attorney, and that his mother was French. Although educated in France, Doan maintained that he had made periodic trips to his homeland and was related to Prince Boun Oum Na Champassak. Barbara then told the press that Prince Doan "is a composite of all my previous husbands' best qualities, without any of the bad qualities."

A civil ceremony was conducted at 7 P.M. on April 7, 1964, by Felipe Castrejon, mayor of nearby Jiutepec, in the Jiutepec City Hall, and was repeated at Sumiya the following afternoon for the benefit of Barbara's guests. For the second ceremony bride and groom were bedecked in Laotian wedding finery—Barbara in a green caftanlike garment with gold trimmings; Doan in a white suit with a colorful shawl slung over his shoulder. In true Buddhist tradition, Barbara wore gold rings on each of her big toes, bells around her ankles, red paint on the soles of her feet.

The couple honeymooned in Hawaii and Tahiti. Doan insisted on traveling "like normal people"—without staff of any kind and with only a few suitcases. The trip proved catastrophic because Doan had to cater to his wife's every wish and had to make up for all the missing staff. For one person to deal with her took more sang-froid than Doan could muster. After several weeks Barbara left her husband in Tahiti and returned to Cuernavaca. Doan, fast becoming inured to his wife's unpredictable behavior, followed a day later. The entourage, as he learned, was both a practical necessity and a buffering device that she used when the intimacy of a one-on-one relationship entailed sacrifices she couldn't face. It was the old repetitive cycle: Barbara wanted idealized love, romantic love, without any of the complications or drawbacks that real love entailed; she wanted a forest but not the trees.

Doan, who was as inscrutable as a totem pole, was well rewarded for his perseverance. On marrying Barbara, he reportedly received a check for $1.5 million (Maurice Doan received a similar amount), a new wardrobe, a large monthly allowance and a new house, Villa Barbarina, a four-bedroom, two-story affair built by architect Robert Gerofi on the same property that had once housed Lloyd Franklin's polo stables.

Exactly seven months after Barbara's marriage to Raymond Doan, another wedding took place, this one involving once-divorced Lance Reventlow and his new bride, Cheryl Holdridge, a starlet and one-time Mouseketeer on the Walt Disney television series. Cheryl, the adopted daughter of a retired brigadier general and a New Orleans housewife, grew up in Sherman Oaks, California. Tall, pretty, and blond, Cheryl, known in Hollywood as "an ingenue type," counted Elvis Presley among her former boyfriends. But it was twenty-eight-year-old Lance, with his massive inheritance, that the nineteen-year-old would marry. The ceremony, with more than six hundred guests in attendance, was held inside the Westwood Community Methodist Church in Hollywood. According to stories in the press, the ushers and bridesmaids arrived in a silver hearse. Also present was Cary Grant with bride-to-be Dyan Cannon (she later gave him the child he had always wanted); actress Donna Douglas (of *The Beverly Hillbillies*); television personalities Morey Amsterdam and Russell Arms. Bruce Kessler (who had been absent from Lance's wedding to Jill St. John) was best man, and Doreen Tracey, another former Mouseketeer, was maid of honor.

Notably absent from the ceremony was Barbara Hutton, who was again in bad health and on her way from Cuernavaca to the Presbyterian Medical Center in San Francisco, where one of her doctors was Lawrence Nash,* a specialist in digestive disorders. Nash's unorthodox solution to his patient's chronic stomach problems was a nutritious protein mixture called Spirulina (microalgae found in certain alkaline lakes) that could be mixed with fruit juices or sprinkled over cereal. To break the hold that alcohol had over her, Nash suggested that she stick to soft drinks. This solution worked almost too well. She became a Coca-Cola fiend. She never ate; she just drank Coke, by the case, first at room temperature and in later years on the rocks.

There was still the matter of Barbara's addiction to barbiturates. Cary Grant thought he had the answer: hypnotism. It had done wonders for him. "You will give up smoking, you will sleep well, and you will never have to take another pill," he assured her over the phone. A day later Grant got a hypnotist he knew in San Francisco to visit Barbara in the hospital. The man propped her up in bed and began, "You are getting tired...your eyes are getting heavy...you are drifting off...you are falling asleep..."

*A pseudonym

After fifteen minutes of this Barbara opened her eyes and demonstrated that she was still wide awake. The hypnotist began again, and again Barbara opened her eyes. A third attempt proved equally futile. When Barbara got back to Grant and related her experience, he said to her, "Barbara, you're an impossible woman." And she said, "But you always knew that."

Barbara showed gradual improvement without benefit of hypnosis and by mid-March 1965, she was out of the hospital and on her way to Maui, in Hawaii, where she and Doan celebrated their first wedding anniversary. Raymond presented Barbara with four illustrated volumes of fairy tales; she gave him three heavily ornamented belts, one of which—a diamond, ruby and emerald Naga, the serpent-head symbol of Vishnu—had formerly belonged to Sarah Bernhardt. In addition she bought him a new Jaguar. The car was waiting when they reached Paris at the beginning of June.

A visitor that summer was astounded to find Barbara's Paris apartment filled with bowls of floating carnations. In each bowl were cards listing Barbara's virtues: sensitivity, refinement, beauty, gentility, intelligence. The card that stood out in the visitor's mind had "Largesse" written on it. Doan had ordered the flowers and written out the cards. "It was flattery of the most blatant kind, and Barbara was taken in by it," charges the visitor.

That August the couple went to Evian-les-Bains, a French resort noted for its healing mineral baths, and there were joined by Doan's sons, Jean, twelve, and Gilles, eleven, who hadn't seen their father since the summer of 1963. "We were around only because of Barbara," says Doan's elder son. "My father didn't want to know from us anymore. When Barbara heard that we were attending a tiny one-room schoolhouse in Tenerife, she insisted that we go to school in Switzerland. My father was against it, but she took it upon herself to send us to Beau Soleil, a boarding school in Villars-sur-Ollan. She paid for everything.

"He was what you would call a good artist and a lousy father. Once he had his hands on some money he was a different person. I can give a hundred examples of how he changed. He took up golf, for instance. Barbara would accompany him to the driving range and watch him take lessons. He was a duffer. I doubt he ever broke ninety. But he insisted on having the best of everything—the best equipment, the best teaching pros, the best caddies. At the end of a round Barbara, who generally waited for him in the clubhouse, would tip the caddie the unheard-of sum of several hundred dollars. Neither of them had the faintest idea how much you tipped a caddie, but my father liked to pretend that he had been around money all his life."

Barbara's spending and her bizarre behavior seemed to escalate in direct proportion. That fall in Tangier she began to quibble with the administration of the American School over the way they were handling her scholarship fund. One day she drove to the campus to inspect the new dormitory she had financed. She decided the colors of the dorm were far too gaudy and insisted on having the entire building repainted. She then gave an afternoon tea at Sidi Hosni for the students in the program and was scandalized to learn that they spoke French and English but very little Arabic. The next day she took them out of school and brought them to Asilah, a small town on the coast fifty miles from Tangier, and there she rented a villa to house them and hired a tutor to teach them their native language.

George Staples, a veteran English teacher at the school, was highly amused by Barbara's method of sponsoring children for her fellowship program. "I suppose her method of selecting students was refreshing in this age of machine-graded IQ and aptitude tests; she chose her children on the quality of their smiles as she passed them in the street. It was unorthodox, but it was no less effective than any other criterion."

She used a similar method in selecting nurses and other members of her household staff. If she needed a nurse, for example, ten applicants would be lined up at the foot of her bed. She would look them over and either by osmosis or intuition point out the one she wanted.

The nurses—and there were three in attendance that fall—couldn't get over the way she paid some of the locals to fill their buckets and pails with sea water from the nearest beach in Tangier so she could bathe in salt water. She would linger in the tub for hours, kept company by one or another confederate, usually Ruth Hopwood or Ira Belline or Mrs. Huguette Douglas, a wealthy American widow with a house in the Kasbah. Barbara would talk about her friends in Rome or London or Paris; she would complain of being used by her friends, though of course it was she who made the exploitation possible.

Another acquaintance in Tangier was a large woman in her middle forties, with a shrill laugh and a thousand sob stories, who often stayed up all night listening to Barbara's lamentations. Her nightly visits were evidently well rewarded. Barbara gave her numerous presents, including a gold pearl necklace she said had once belonged to an empress of Japan. The woman, who still lives in Tangier, no longer talks about Barbara.*

---

*The gold pearl necklace was of cultured pearls—but the finest anywhere—and cost Barbara $200,000. Barbara used to pass them off—as a joke—as having once belonged to the Empress of Japan. This was not the case.

But there were people like her wherever Barbara went. Jean Mendiboure reminisces about a woman in Cuernavaca hired when Barbara wanted to improve her Spanish. "This woman," he says, "was already getting well paid, having asked for more than she would have dared ask of anybody else. But she soon realized she could get even more out of Barbara if she played her cards right. She started going on about her five kids and how she and they had nothing to eat. 'I don't know if I'll be able to keep coming because I need another job to support my children,' she told Barbara. Barbara was taken in. 'Oh, my poor dear,' she said. 'I'd love to give you something, but I have no money either. Even though, as you can see, I live in this fabulous house, I'm as poor as you are.' She went on to explain that her lawyer, Graham Mattison, had cracked down on her spending habits. She rarely had cash on hand, and Mattison had control over her checks. The woman was unimpressed. She repeated her story, adding a few new flourishes to make it more convincing. She went on and on until she insinuated herself into Barbara's heart. 'Well, let's see what I can give you instead of money,' said Barbara. She rummaged around and finally plucked this giant ruby out of a drawer and gave it to her. And after she gave it to her, the woman never came back."

During this period Barbara was dispersing her fortune with such gladhanded determination that her associates could only conclude that she meant to discard everything, all her worldly goods and possessions. Whatever it was that drove her to such extremes—whether guilt, generosity, boredom or lunacy, or a combination thereof—seemed to be deeply ingrained in her personality. Her unpredictable sprees made it virtually impossible for anybody, including her attorneys, to know precisely how much money still remained to Barbara. All anybody knew was that the desire to divest herself of riches had seized her with increasing strength and rapidity. Jane Bowles, with whom she was on only moderately friendly terms, visited Barbara one evening and came away with a magnificent diamond ring. But Jane, aware that Barbara was no longer responsible for all her actions, returned the ring the following day. Just as quickly Barbara gave it away again, this time to Cheryl Holdridge, together with other expensive odds and ends, presumably because it was Cheryl who finally convinced Lance Reventlow to give up his auto-racing career.*

Even someone as open-minded as Paul Bowles was struck by Barbara's outré behavior. Bowles, an occasional visitor at Sidi Hosni, remembers seeing Barbara in 1965. She was drinking Coke laced with

*Further testimony to Barbara's openhandedness is provided by Robert Harvey, an American-born artist now living in Spain, who befriended Barbara in 1963. "Barbara offered me many things," Harvey writes in a letter (February 29, 1984), "but I accepted a cigarette lighter only." Harvey, a visitor to Sidi Hosni in 1966, was evidently in the minority.

crème de cacao and was receiving callers in her throne room, where she lay upon mountains of golden cushions, a tiara on her head. Her complexion was powdery, and her arms were as thin as broomsticks. She had difficulty remembering the names of all her husbands. When someone asked her why she refused to walk, she said, "Because I can afford to pay others to do my walking for me." Her eyes were weak and she had a stream of readers come in to read to her. "I was told by one of her servants," says Bowles, "that on certain days she insisted everyone on her staff sing to her. Anything they would normally say they had to sing."

People in Tangier tended to think of Barbara as an institution, and not as a real person. Her life bore the same relationship to the average person's life that a hotel lobby bears to a comfortable living room; it was impersonal, arranged from the outside for her, so as to seem vaguely official. The "throne" that she occupied took different forms. At times it consisted of the golden Oriental cushions; at other times visitors found her reclining on a divan studded with jewels; occasionally she occupied an actual throne, a high-backed gold chair mounted on a three-foot dais lined with Persian rugs. The purpose of all this was to discourage any kind of familiarity that her guests might be inclined to assume toward her. One wasn't allowed to forget that one was in the presence of the Queen.

Ben Dixon, the American consul general in Morocco in 1965, had known Barbara since 1943 when she was married to Cary Grant. "My wife, Frances, and I knew her in California during the war and we consolidated our friendship in Tangier. She could be very funny, moody, angry at people sometimes. She went through periods of being disappointed in her friends. She was going through a difficult period with Raymond Doan, as if the realization had suddenly hit home that he was no better than most of her other husbands. She used to call me at all hours—three in the morning and again at nine—to complain about him. What struck me about Barbara was her staying power. She was extremely self-destructive, but she also had tremendous inner strength and stamina. She perpetually seemed to be on the edge of extinction, but at the last possible moment she would save herself. She overcame one tragedy after another. When it would seem physically impossible for her to face up to her sad life she called on some inner reserve and somehow managed to handle whatever life threw at her."

Ben Dixon wasn't the only American diplomat in Morocco to receive phone calls from Barbara. His successor, Hal Eastman, recalled a series of phone calls he received from her in the wee hours of the morning when the subject of conversation was Coca-Cola. "She didn't care for the taste of Moroccan Coca-Cola," observes Eastman, "and she wondered if I, as American consul general, couldn't import the stuff from the United States. I told her that we drank Moroccan Coke in the embassy, but that answer didn't suffice. Could I at least get some Coca-Cola for her from Gibraltar? Well, I said, I wasn't aware that the Coke on Gibraltar was any tastier than Moroccan Coke. The sweetness of the beverage must have been a drug-related necessity, because she knew the exact proportions of syrup to liquid in every country's supply. Each bottling plant used its own formula and she wanted the company to produce a uniform product. None of this, however, made a great deal of sense at three or four in the morning."

Like her grandfather before her, Barbara became increasingly estranged from reality as she grew older. For her fifty-third birthday she chartered two planes—one for herself, her husband, and several friends; the other for a group of Moroccan dancers and musicians—and flew from Tangier to Marrakech, where she took over the Mamounia Hotel for a gala outdoor celebration. She threw a second party a few days later at the Caves of Hercules on the outskirts of Tangier, erecting a series of large tents and inviting what seemed like half the local population, but refusing to attend the fête herself because an astrologer she sometimes consulted warned her at the last minute against leaving the house. The festivities went on without her.

At the end of November 1965, Barbara and Raymond Doan arrived in London. From Asprey's, the carriage-trade jeweler on New Bond Street, she bought herself what was to be her last major acquisition of jewelry, a 48-carat pear-shaped diamond, one of the largest of its kind in the world. She paid $400,000 for it.

While in London Barbara had a chance to see Morley Kennerley. He was by himself when she saw him and he found Barbara acting very unlike her usual self. She let it be known, in the small ways that women sometimes use, that she was interested in having an affair with Morley. The Kennerleys were not a couple to keep secrets from each other; when Jean heard of Barbara's proposition, she was rightfully crushed. Their long friendship was not a matter that she took lightly. She waited in vain for a telephone call, a letter, some form of communication or explanation from Barbara. None came: the Kennerleys never saw or heard from her again.

Barbara's personal problems continued to mount. On January 6, 1966, while she and Doan were resting at her home in Cuernavaca, thieves broke in and quietly made off with $25,000 in cash, $20,000 in travelers checks, a dozen bottles of champagne, and $125,000 in jewelry. The burglary was bad enough; worse was the discovery that her insurance had lapsed.

The robbery put Barbara in a terrible frame of mind. The fact that it had taken place while she was in the house made her feel vulnerable to all assaults. She took out her rancor on everybody around her, including her lawyer, Graham Mattison.

Starting in 1946, and each year thereafter, she had signed a power of attorney granting Mattison total control over all her financial affairs. Sheaves of paper were brought periodically by Mattison, which Barbara trustingly signed, including his year-to-year contract as her business adviser and chief consul. But when he turned up in Cuernavaca that winter, she not only refused to receive him but refused to rehire him. He returned empty-handed to New York.

Another of her longest and oldest associations also ran into trouble that year when Nacho de Landa apprised her that he and his wife, Lee, had encountered Court Reventlow at a recent social function in New York and had found him "quite charming." The passage of time had done nothing to temper Barbara's antagonism toward Reventlow, and De Landa's disclosure sufficed to land him in the same doghouse already occupied by David Herbert and Graham Mattison.

In April the Doans were back in San Francisco and once more Barbara locked herself in her hotel room, attended by a battery of nurses. The tedium was disrupted by Doris Duke, who offered Barbara use of her Diamond Head estate in Hawaii. Barbara accepted and made arrangements to have a pair of futons sent from her house in Cuernavaca. The Japanese bedding, which she hoped might help her sleep, arrived simultaneously with the Doans. John Gomez, still manager of the estate, found Barbara extremely unhappy and frail-looking. "I tried to encourage her to go to the beach," says Gomez, "but she would put me off and say, 'I'll go tomorrow.' When I returned the next day, she would say, 'I feel a cold coming on.' There was always an excuse."

After a week indoors Barbara experienced an unexpected burst of energy, but instead of leaving the house she decided to redecorate it. She ordered new wallpaper, carpeting, furniture, got rid of Doris' priceless *objets d'art* and replaced them with those of her own choice. Before she was finished with Shangri-la, it bore an uncanny resemblance to Barbara's Japanese showplace in Mexico. When Doris arrived in Hawaii, soon after Barbara's departure, she was at first baffled and then infuriated by her guest's audacity. She began spreading the word that Barbara had finally gone "over the edge."

Doris Duke was soon to become involved in a more serious doings. On October 10, 1966, at Bellevue Avenue in Newport, Rhode Island,

Eduardo Tirella, an interior decorator and close friend of Doris' for more than ten years, was helping refurbish Rough Point, the famous Duke cottage. When they left the house together late that afternoon in Doris' wood-paneled station wagon and reached the ornate wrought-iron front gate, Tirella hopped out of the car to unlock it. While he was fumbling with the mechanism Doris Duke floored the accelerator—"accidentally," she testified—and the car lurched forward, impaling Tirella and crushing the life out of him. Asked to comment, Barbara Hutton served up a rather morbid thought: "Maybe Doris just didn't care for Mr. Tirella's taste. She certainly didn't care for mine."

While Doris was successfully fending off an indictment for involuntary manslaughter, Barbara was in Tangier nursing a badly sprained ankle and preparing for her annual visit to the Gazelle d'Or in Taroudant. When the entourage, which included Raymond Doan, Jean Mendiboure, Colin Frazer and a retinue of servants, arrived, they attended a party given by the Pasha of Taroudant for resident members of the British foreign office in Morocco. Barbara's personal staff wore brilliantly embroidered caftans, emeralds, diamonds, gay kidskin slippers, scarfs in just the right silk and shade. The pasha, an aging relic with failing eyesight, mistook Barbara's elegantly clad retainers for his guests of honor and seated them on the dais at the most prestigious table for all to see.

It was the only light moment on an otherwise grim expedition that ended abruptly the night a waiter at the Gazelle d'Or introduced Barbara to majoun, a confection made of hashish and dates and honey. The majoun was a novel treat for Barbara, although she had smoked hashish on several occasions with little result.

The waiter warned her not to take too much majoun at first, but to eat it sparingly and wait for the results. Barbara responded with a wave of her hand as she wolfed down a large helping and retired to her bungalow.

"She had a bad night," recalls Jean Mendiboure. "She began hallucinating, claiming that she saw colors and forms and objects floating through the air. Then she began hearing things—bells, sirens, whispering voices. She imagined that people were trying to get into the room to do her harm. She became convinced that Raymond Doan would tiptoe into her room and slit her throat in her sleep. I spent the night trying to calm her down but nothing helped.

"At six in the morning she was still hallucinating, but now she insisted on returning to Tangier before any of the others awoke. We got to Agadir Airport, not far from Taroudant, and by midafternoon were sitting at Guitta's Restaurant in Tangier. A few hours later in walked Raymond Doan. He had followed us in the next plane. When Barbara saw him she was perfectly composed. 'Oh, darling,' she said, 'there you are.'"

Relations seemed to have evened out between Barbara and her husband, but within days it got around that she had locked Doan out of Sidi Hosni. It was said that they were separating and that Barbara wanted a divorce. The press in Tangier reported that Barbara had given her husband a $3 million check in exchange for her freedom. Doan confirmed his wife's departure but denied the rest of the story.

On December 5, 1966, flying from Paris to New York, Barbara emerged from the plane and found herself confronted by reporters. Was it true that she had given her husband a three-million-dollar divorce settlement? Were they actually getting divorced? Barbara ignored the questions as Colin Frazer carried her in his arms to a long black limousine.

Early the next day a story would break that would send Barbara into seclusion. On December 6, Jimmy Donahue's body was found in his mother's New York apartment.

At the time of his death he was fifty-one going on ninety-five. His name had virtually disappeared from the gossip and society columns. He stopped visiting his familiar Manhattan nightspots and spent increasing stretches at home on the North Shore. He turned philanthropic, making considerable donations to a variety of charities and public foundations. He still on occasion flew off to some distant part of the world, still gave dinner parties, but his friends noticed a growing lassitude, a dulling of the once sparkling wit. He talked incessantly of his father's suicide in middle age and of the futility and lost connections of his own existence. He drank more, sensed less and complained bitterly about his increasing lack of male companionship.

The question uppermost in people's minds was whether or not Jimmy Donahue had taken his own life. Dr. James Lindsay Luke, associate medical examiner for the city of New York, performed an autopsy and summarized his findings in the following brief report to the press:

> The final cause of death of Mr. Donahue is "acute alcohol and barbiturate poisoning, circumstances undetermined." In other words, we are not able to evaluate the motivation behind the ingestion of the barbiturates, in this case Seconal, although the amount recovered from Mr. Donahue's tissues far exceeded that of a medicinal or therapeutic dose.

Once again the circumstances surrounding the death of a member of the Woolworth family had been obscured. Did Jimmy Donahue commit suicide or was his death the culmination of a lifetime of barbiturate and alcohol abuse? Were there other possibilities? Rumors circulated within the gay underground that he had been the victim of a homosexual ritual murder, his body mutilated and delivered to his mother's apartment in a black steamer trunk. But this, like similar tales, was the kind of fiction Jimmy Donahue himself might have propagated had he still been alive.

When Barbara Hutton arrived in Beverly Hills early in 1967 to have a cataract removed from her right eye, she was accompanied by Raymond Doan, momentarily quelling rumors of divorce. As though the eye surgery were not enough, she then had to have all her teeth removed. As dependent as she had always been on doctors, Barbara shared her grandfather's aversion to dentists and was now paying the price. She convalesced in a six-room suite on the ground floor of the Crescent Wing of the Beverly Hills Hotel. The hotel staff had been alerted to her growing list of peculiar habits and needs.

A desk clerk recalls that nobody on the hotel's large staff was allowed beyond Barbara's front door. The maids were handed the garbage while standing in the corridor outside the suite. Deliveries and pick-ups of food and beverages were transacted in the same manner. Barbara was evidently afraid of something and from time to time her personal employees had to search under beds, behind doors, in closets, although it was never clear to them what they were supposed to be looking for.

One of the problems with the present setup was that Bill Robertson had replaced Graham Mattison as Barbara's business manager, a position he undertook only as a favor to Barbara. Trying to balance Barbara's books and pay her bills were enterprises that didn't very much interest Robertson. The consequences of his lack of interest were occasionally humorous, though rarely from Barbara's perspective. Sandra Lee Stuart, author of *The Pink Palace*, an anecdotal history of the Beverly Hills Hotel, comments that after several weeks of carrying case after case of Coca-Cola to her suite, the bellmen started a strike action against Barbara. It seems they weren't being tipped. "No tips, no Coke," writes Miss Stuart. "Barbara's supply was cut off."

The situation soon had Barbara on the telephone with Graham Mattison. She was ready not only to rehire him but to give him a substantial raise over the $150,000 per annum she had previously paid him. Mattison accepted and flew out to Beverly Hills, where he confronted the hotel bellmen. He wanted to know why Barbara wasn't getting her usual service. When they told him why, he took out his wallet and peeled off five $100 bills. The deliveries resumed at once.

At the beginning of April the Doans and their entourage headed for the Burlingame Country Club near San Francisco, stayed a week, then embarked on another grand tour, this time from California to New York, New York to Paris, Paris to Kyoto, Kyoto to Tangier, Tangier back to New York.

Jean Mendiboure was part of the entourage that checked into the Pierre on December 20, 1967. After Jimmy Donahue's death, Mendiboure became a stand-in for her cousin. Barbara confided in him. She was constantly giving him presents.

"The day after we arrived at the Pierre," says Mendiboure, "she telephoned Cartier and asked them to bring over the finest watches they had in stock. A little while later a man arrived and spread the watches out, many of them covered with diamonds and thick gold. Barbara called me in and said, 'Listen, Jean, I have to make a present to a gentleman friend, and since you have such good taste, why don't you choose for me. Pick out two that you like.'

"I looked them over and selected a pair of ultrathin, very plain Piaget watches. She asked me if I was sure those were the ones I liked best. I said they were my first choice. Then she asked me to leave. Later she called me in again and said, 'Poor Jean. The watches were for you and you chose the two least expensive ones.' And she handed me a package containing two of the fancy watches that I didn't choose. 'But, Barbara,' I said. 'I don't like these. They're too much. I chose the ones I liked.' She became very cold as she took the watches back. 'Well, okay,' she shouted. 'Then you get nothing.'

"I was used to this so I didn't say anything. Barbara and I had spats all the time, but there was never any question of our remaining friends. the next day she called up Gucci and ordered a dozen cashmere sweaters in assorted colors. When they arrived she asked me what I thought. They were adorable but they were all too small. 'Who are they for?' I asked. 'For you,' she said. The sleeves came up to my elbows, but I acted very pleased because I didn't want to upset her again. Then she handed me another small bundle and inside were the two Piaget watches I had chosen the day before.

"By January 1968 we were in Cuernavaca and four weeks later we reached the Beverly Wilshire in Beverly Hills. It was Valentine's Day and Barbara was still on a spending spree. She bought presents for every hotel employee and for everyone else she knew—sable stoles, diamond rings and watches, ruby necklaces, earrings, lizard carrying cases and handbags. Everything was done by telephone. I don't remember how much was spent, but it was a lot. After we finished tallying and divvying it all up, she realized she hadn't given me anything. So she reached into her bag and pulled out of a pair of enormous diamond earrings she had bought for herself at Van Cleef and she handed them to me and said, 'Happy Valentine's Day!' And I looked at them and said, 'What am I going to do with these? I don't wear earrings.' I didn't want to appear ungrateful, so I took them and had them made into a man's bracelet and that seemed to satisfy everyone.

"It was pretty clear that the Raymond Doan bubble had burst for Barbara and that she wanted him out of the picture. The marriage was bankrupt on both sides. Barbara had been a challenge for Doan. Aside from the financial rewards, there was her celebrity. Doan had the opportunity to meet people he wouldn't ordinarily have encountered. Still, it was an unlikely pairing. I found Doan very grim, almost inscrutable. You never knew what he was thinking. He was highly secretive. He would either go off to play golf, or he would go shopping. He had a penchant for gadgets and gizmos, things like electric back scratchers and lint removers. He also had a eye for the ladies, although nobody can blame him for that. He was considerate of Barbara but he lived a second existence quite apart from the one he led with her. Graham Mattison had it in for Doan. They didn't like each other. Mattison wanted to get rid of him but not to the extent of a divorce. He didn't want Barbara to fall prey to another marital mugging. When she fell in love she was capable of unimaginable feats of generosity. On more than one occasion she nearly gave away her entire fortune."

In late May 1968, Barbara, Raymond Doan, and an entourage of seven were whisked off by jet from New York to Milan, where they checked into three large suites at the Palace Hotel. While doffing her shoes, Barbara lost her footing and fell. At first she shrugged off the accident, but when the pain in her right thigh intensified she called for the hotel doctor. He advised her to go to a hospital for a thorough examination.

Accompanied by Raymond Doan, she was taken in a Red Cross ambulance to the Cittá de Milano clinic to undergo X-ray examinations. The tests indicated a fracture of the right hip. Two weeks later she arrived in Paris with her right leg encased in a full-length cast. Raymond Doan was nowhere in sight. Asked to comment on his absence, Barbara told a reporter, "We've had a temporary breach. I believe you call it a trial separation."

When the press managed to track him down in Amsterdam, Doan offered his own interpretation: "We'll be together again as soon as Barbara mends. She's very brittle and accident-prone. She has bones like chalk."

Barbara had, in jollier times, proclaimed Paris the center of the world. But visitors to her apartment came away convinced that she had returned to her old stomping grounds for one last stomp. She was an apparition—an emaciated, caved-in, hobbling creature subsisting on twenty bottles of Coca-Cola a day; alcohol (at intervals); vitamin pills; intravenous megavitamin shots (often mixed with amphetamines); a soybean compound; Metrecal; cigarettes; and a pharmacopoeia of drugs and medications, including Empirin Compound , codeine, Valium and morphine. It was not her first exposure to morphine, but it was the first time she had taken it in such heavy doses.

Barbara's only abiding comfort in Paris was a household staff that included a number of new faces: Kathleen Murphy (head nurse), Jean Flysens (chauffeur), Baroness Evelyn de Schompre (secretary),* Countess Jaquine de Rochambeau (receptionist).† Of these, she was closest to Jaquine, a beguiling and ebullient young lady, whose husband was a descendant of one of the first families of France. Jaquine, like Evelyn de Schompre, worked primarily for pocket money—"and to keep busy." Barbara kept her busy; she kept them all busy.

"I was hired by Barbara about the time she 'fired' Prince Doan," says Jaquine. "My hours were approximately ten to four. Barbara treated me like a daughter, and she even told me she would have preferred having a daughter. But she called me 'Countess,' and I called her 'Princess.' Everything she owned was embossed with crowns. There were times when she couldn't discern between reality and fantasy. She insisted that all the women on her staff wear luxurious clothing. I would sit in my tiny office in her apartment at ten in the morning dressed for a formal ball. It looked absurd. Visitors couldn't stop laughing when they saw me that early all dressed up.

"She used Lanvin mostly. They would send sketches or photographs and from these she would select the fashions she wanted. I had to go to Lanvin to fetch the sketches. Jean Flysens would drive me over in Barbara's Rolls-Royce, with her insignia on the door. It was 1968, a year of political upheaval in Paris with strikes and demonstrations and street violence. One morning we passed a demonstration and they

---

*Evelyn was the widow of Baron Guy Quoniam de Schomprë, French consul general in the Belgian Congo. After her husband's death Evelyn got a job at the American embassy in Paris and was later hired by Barbara.

†Jaquine's position with Barbara was arranged by Eleanor Close Hutton, the daughter of Marjorie Merriweather Post, whose husband since 1954 was composer Leon Barzin. Eleanor, whose marriage to Preston Sturges had created nearly as much of a furor as some of Barbara's marriages, had been Jaquine's employer prior to Barbara.

After working for Barbara, Jaquine was divorced from Count Patrice de Rochambeau and married Charles R. Lachman, a co-founder of the Revlon cosmetics empire. Lachman was forty-five years older than Jaquine and at his death in 1979 left her a fortune of $30 million.

apparently recognized the car because they surrounded us. A window was broken, but when they saw it wasn't Barbara they let us go.

"Every room in her apartment was decorated differently. She let her friends decorate some of the rooms. I decorated one room. She had exquisite furniture and furnishings, including a very old Japanese make-up table, an Oeben lady's writing table, an ornate parlor table that belonged to Madame de Pompadour, an important painting by Titian. To get the Titian she sold a Botticelli of equal importance. Gerald Van Der Kemp of Versailles visited frequently and gave Barbara advice on what to buy and what to sell. She had a crush on Van Der Kemp and spent hours making herself up for him. She always wore earrings, even in bed, because she thought her ear lobes were too long. Other visitors included Jimmy Douglas, Jean de Baglion, Renée de Becker, Henri de la Tour d'Auvergne, Gottfried von Cramm, Igor Troubetzkoy, the Agnellis and the Patinos. Silvia de Castellane and Barbara were at odds during this period, but Silvia's children visited.

"The story I heard about Barbara and Silvia was that they were at Maxim's one afternoon—this was the year before—and in walked a rather well-known Frenchwoman. This person was being kept by a wealthy Spanish grandee, and Silvia said something like 'Oh, there's that unctuous, disgusting Madame X. She's being kept by the Duke of Such-and-such.' And Barbara lashed out at her in the restaurant. 'You're being kept, too—be me!'

"Barbara's mood changed easily and for no reason. She would sometimes invite people over and then refuse to see them. If she had dinner guests, I would have to stay late. And if she refused to join her guests for dinner, I would have to sit in for her. Sometimes Barbara saw them afterward in her bedroom if she was very close to them.

"She could be extremely cantankerous. She would take out her jewelry and play with it for hours, trying on each article, then studying herself in the mirror. Occasionally she would pretend that an item was missing and would have us turn the house upside down searching for something that wasn't really lost. She could be quite sadistic. She owned some intricate Oriental foot jewelry, for instance, that she insisted I try to wear. It didn't fit right and it was very painful, but she wouldn't let me take it off. She also used to call me at home at four in the morning, which annoyed my husband. But the calls didn't bother me too much because basically I was fond of Barbara.

"The one aspect of the job I didn't care for was having to deal with Graham Mattison. Mattison controlled everything. He signed all the checks, except when the amounts were minuscule and then I would sign them. He was the ultimate gatekeeper. Nobody came or went without his permission. He maintained complete files on everyone who had any dealings with Barbara, social or otherwise. Whenever somebody came to the house he consulted his files and gave me instructions. If she had male company, I was to make sure he left by two A.M. Mattison purposely kept homosexuals around Barbara so she couldn't get too romantically involved. She had a gay Parisian hairdresser from 1968 to 1969 who came daily, worked only for her, and was sacked because she grew tired of him. Four nurses worked in six-hour, round-the-clock shifts. Some of them seemed to be there only to spy on Barbara for Mattison. He wouldn't let her do her own hiring anymore, except in rare instances. Colin Frazer went on leave for a while, so she hired a bodyguard—half French, half Moroccan—whose primary function was to gratify her sexually. His employment ended when he tried to steal the two Haseltine horse heads she kept as mantel pieces.

"One of her pet projects was a customized Ferrari she was having built for King Hassan II of Morocco. She knew the king personally and wanted to surprise him with a red-and-green Ferrari to match the colors of the Moroccan flag. This entailed months of bickering with the Ferrari people in Paris, because the factory in Italy could never quite match the colors to Barbara's satisfaction. After two years the car was still in the shop, and it was at this point that Barbara found out that according to Islamic custom the monarch wasn't permitted to accept such a gift from a woman. The project was aborted.

"I can't say it was ever boring working for Barbara. There was the time when she called Sargent Shriver, the U.S. ambassador to France, and told him her employees were trying to poison her food. In reality we were only trying to get her to eat. The ambassador dispatched his assistant, Gerald Culley, who volunteered to be Barbara's official food taster. After he left, Barbara apologized for suspecting us, but the following day the accusations started all over again."

At the end of 1968 Barbara was staying at Claridge's in London. Her sole outing was to the Café de Paris with Lord Drogheda's wife and son, Joan and Derry Moore. Derry and his mother were struck by the transformations Barbara had undergone, not just psychologically but physically. Her earlier face-lift had collapsed completely, leaving pockets of dried dead skin that were blotched over with layers of Pan-Cake make-up. "She was very odd by now," says Derry. "In bed she wore all her pearls at once. She retreated into a strange fantasy world, the result of being completely isolated from normal human contact. She talked incessantly of suicide, and yet she was terrified of death. She wore this very tiny silver whistle around her neck and whenever she wanted her nurse or another member of the staff, she would blow the whistle. The nurse would try to feed her, but she wouldn't take the food. She would chew it and then spit it out, sometimes at the nurse."

At Cuernavaca in the winter of 1969 Barbara gave a party for a hundred. The affair went on much longer than she had expected. The sun was up, but thirty or so stragglers were still dancing and drinking. Of the original band only a drummer and a piano player remained, but their music thumped through the house. The houseboy tried without success to get the last guests to leave.

Barbara, lying in her bedroom, signaled for her nurse, who found her bleary-eyed and sullen. "Can't they be sent away?" Barbara asked. "Have coffee and rolls served for breakfast and then send them home."

"They won't leave," insisted the nurse. "They want to dance."

"But I must sleep. Tell them to leave."

"The houseboy has tried. They won't listen."

Barbara resorted to what of late had become her solution to all problems and all suffering. "Then pay them to leave!" she shouted, rolling over and closing her eyes.*

That August Barbara was in Tangier when word arrived that Court Haugwitz-Reventlow, seventy-three, had died in New York following open heart surgery. The death of her former husband made little impression on Barbara. She had more immediate worries, such as where and how to procure more medication than was currently being prescribed by her physicians. In a fit of pique, she would shout at her servants and announce that she was contemplating some drastic action, such as firing them unless they came up with a large supply of painkillers and barbiturates. She knew perfectly well, of course, that she would be helpless without her servants and instead turned to Howard D. Jones, the newly appointed American consul general in Tangier, imploring him to come to the aid of "a poor defenseless woman" who only wanted access to her own pill box.

A week later she again called the consul general to say that she was having heart palpitations and that her Hollywood physician, the only person in the world capable of saving her life, was ignoring her urgent appeal to make a house call from only 7,000 miles away. She asked that Jones telegraph him to come at once. The official soothed her as best he could and later called her secretary, Evelyn de Schompre, who assured him that Barbara was not in any mortal danger and that her doctor was expected within days on one of his regular visits.

*The same anecdote is recounted fictionally in Rupert Croft-Cooke's *The Caves of Hercules,* a novel based on the life of Barbara Hutton.

There was still another crisis and Barbara once more called on the consul general, this time demanding that he appear personally at Sidi Hosni. The crisis, it turned out, had taken place when the physician finally did arrive from Hollywood. Instead of providing her with more medication, he cut back on what she was currently taking. Barbara responded by igniting a feathery fan she kept at bedside and throwing it at him. Fortunately, the flames were extinguished before any real damage could be done. Barbara always rejected the term "Poor Little Rich Girl," but now she assured the consul general she was on her way to the poorhouse because of the extravagant fees charged by her doctors and lawyers. The lament struck Jones as peculiar, especially since he had heard from a reliable source that Barbara had offered her Hollywood doctor $1 million a year to give up his private practice and stay on as her resident physician, a proposition that didn't appeal to him in the least.

Barbara wound up her stay in Morocco by leasing the Gazelle d'Or for a week and inviting a number of people to be her guests there, including British Consul General Robert Ford and his wife and Mr. and Mrs. Howard D. Jones. "Barbara spent most of the first few days in her bedroom," reports Jones. "One of her activities there was ordering roses so that the petals might be fed to the camels outside her window. She didn't seem to want to be disturbed, so one afternoon several of us made an excursion to Goulimine, site of an annual camel fair.

"Upon our return Evelyn de Schompre told me that Barbara was grumbling because we had not consulted her before taking off. In an effort to make amends, I suggested that I might put on the Blue Man robe and turban I had bought at Goulimine and pay a bedside call on Barbara. Just before Evelyn showed me in, she looked a little apprehensive and warned me to expect a surprise and be careful.

"Barbara was sitting up in bed, looking sternly ahead. She had a number of veils over her face. She more or less ignored my greeting and proceeded to lift the veils one by one. When the last veil was gone I was startled to see all sorts of strange red markings on her face. Adopting a fierce, dramatic tone, Barbara asked if I knew what she represented. I confessed my ignorance and didn't have the presence of mind to compliment her on her great get-up. Now, even more dramatically, she announced, 'I am Siva, the Indian God of Death and Destruction.' While I was trying to guess just what she had in mind she pulled a hand out from under the covers and thrust a dagger into my arm. I felt a painful prick through the sleeve of my robe and wondered that she had such strength in her frail body.

"Pressing the dagger a bit harder, Barbara asked if I was afraid. I acknowledged that I didn't feel this way my bravest moment. 'What,' she demanded to know, 'is a little blood between friends?' 'That depends on which friend's blood is involved,' I said.

"Eventually Barbara withdrew the dagger and shifted gear into her most doleful tone: 'You can't imagine how much I miss having a man in my life.' Barely recovered from the dagger prick, I now felt a serious case of mental anguish. Uncertain about just what game she was playing, I was concerned that a false note on my part would give her the pretext to attack me with the dagger just as she had attacked her doctor with a burning fan. A fantasy tabloid headline suddenly flashed through my mind: MILLIONAIRESS ATTACKS CONSUL GENERAL WITH DAGGER IN MOROCCO.

"Sensing my discomfiture, Barbara apparently decided that this game was not promising either and saved the day in a typical way. She now adopted her most indignant mien and declaimed, 'Did you think I said "man"? I said I miss my maid; I've fired her.' I've often wondered whether Barbara was quick-witted on that particular occasion or whether she had played the game before and developed a polished escape line."

Soon there was a reconciliation, a fence-mending, between Barbara and Raymond Doan. Doan had spent much of his time since their separation as a long-haired cultist at an ashram in the south of Spain, writing poetry and presumably searching for nirvana, ultimately stumbling upon the realization that Barbara Hutton was the next best thing. In the winter of 1969 he visited Marjorie Merriweather Post at Mar-a-Lago and convinced her of his earnest intentions toward her niece. It was Marjorie who took the initiative in bringing the couple back together again. By 1970 they were living in Paris as husband and wife, and at first the arrangement seemed to suit Barbara. She and Doan made occasional appearances at small dinner parties or attended the opening-night performance of a new play. But the resurrection of the relationship was short-lived, and within weeks Barbara began to slide again. Graham Mattison became concerned enough with her medical situation to question the European doctors she turned to because they were once again prescribing what seemed to him too many sedatives. Their theory, as one of them expressed it, was that whether or not a patient could make it after a good night's sleep, without one he was completely lost.

In Morocco that year the Doans attended a celebration given by the Pasha of Taroudant for his newlywed granddaughter. The evening of the party, Barbara's Rolls pulled up to a large tent thronged with people.

Colin Frazer hoisted her from her seat and carried her into a section of the tent that was set up for drinks. But when they were invited to go into the dining section, Barbara refused to move. A dignitary from the American embassy tried to speak about diplomatic niceties to Barbara. She rebelled; she did not care to sit before solid food. Convinced that the honor of his country depended on Barbara's presence at her designated place, the diplomat picked up the screaming and kicking woman and carried her to her table. When the meal ended, the diplomat reappeared at Barbara's side, cockily prepared to take up his duty once again. This time, to his immense embarrassment, he couldn't get her airborne. The wedding party had a good laugh at the American diplomat's expense, until Colin Frazer came to the rescue and carried Barbara to another tent where they enjoyed a spectacle put on by animated dancers. Seeing a hangdog expression on the diplomat's face, Frazer went over to assure him that his failure had nothing to do with a sudden loss of manhood or even too much wine, but was due to Barbara's uncanny ability to make herself almost unbearable at times.

Back in Tangier, Barbara locked herself away again. Feeling wistful about the past, she wrote to Aunt Marjorie, recalling one of her early Florida vacations with Jimmy Donahue: "I remember how we spent that entire December by the sea, broiling ourselves in the sun and how we walked up the beach in search of seashells and other gifts from the ocean. At five o'clock we would lie on the still warm sand and listen to the sound of music from the club as the notes drifted out to sea.

On one occasion that summer, during a visit with Doan to the Caves of Hercules, Barbara broke toward the sharp line of cliffs that loomed high over the water. Doan gave chase and caught up with her just before she could have thrown herself over the edge.

"Another summer has come and gone," she jotted in her notebooks. She and David Herbert had made amends and saw each other two or three times a week. He found her "edgy and morose, but otherwise the same sweet person I had always known and loved."

❧

In late April 1971 Count Rudi Crespi of Rome received a phone call from Graham Mattison in Paris. Crespi, a leading member of the international jet set, dabbled in real estate, and Mattison wondered whether he could help Barbara Hutton and Raymond Doan find a palazzo. It was a sort of going-away present from Barbara to her seventh husband. Crespi was confused by the term "going-away present," until Mattison explained that the marriage was dissolving for good and the palazzo was a gift for remembrance.

Rudi Crespi had never laid eyes on Barbara, but his American-born wife, Consuelo O'Conner, a former Powers model (she and her twin Gloria were among the original "Which one has the Toni?" girls), had met her on several occasions. When the Doans checked into Rome's Grand Hotel a few days later, the Crespis were waiting to greet them. Over the next two weeks Rudi Crespi took Doan on a personal tour of the city's choicest real estate. Since no price limitations had been imposed, everything Doan saw was in the million-dollar range. Doan had narrowed his choice to one of three palazzos when Barbara suffered one of her typical hotel mishaps, tripping over a carpet and fracturing her right femur—the bone of the thigh.

She was hospitalized and her leg placed in a heavy traction cast. Despite her obvious discomfort, her interest in people and her generosity remained intact. When she heard that a nurse in the hospital was about to get married, she sent the woman two first-class plane tickets to Venice and a letter offering to pay for a two-week honeymoon in the hotel of their choice.

The Crespis saw to it that when Barbara returned to her rooms at the Grand Hotel she had the services of a full-time nurse, Signora Chervata, a gentle and decent soul last employed by Mrs. Dino De Laurentiis, the wife of the Italian movie producer. Signora Chervata was amazed by the constant parade of Rome's merchants who were so anxious to sell their wares to Barbara that they appeared almost daily at her bedside. Gianni Bulgari was one of them. To appease the jeweler, Barbara finally bought some sapphires, which she offered to Signora Chervata. The nurse refused the jewelry and Barbara asked Consuelo Crespi what she could give the woman instead. Consuelo suggested money, since Signora Chervata's husband needed an expensive operation. Barbara gave her a check for $5,000, and sent the sapphires to one of her maids in Tangier.

Despite Signora Chervata's loving care, Barbara's right leg didn't heal properly and arrangements were made to transport her from Rome to Los Angeles, where she would undergo corrective surgery at the recently opened Cedars-Sinai Medical Center. Raymond Doan escorted her as far as London, and her doctor flew in from California to take her the rest of the way. Even in her medication-induced stupor Barbara realized she would not be seeing her husband again, and their parting was poignant with unspoken words. Although there was to be no further personal contact between them, Graham Mattison set himself the challenging task of keeping the marriage bond legally intact, thereby ruling out the possibility of another marital splurge on Barbara's part. The price of retaining the pseudo-prince's name and title ran higher than expected. Instead of the palazzo in Rome, Barbara was forced to surrender her Leeds-McCormick emeralds to Doan, as well as the tiara once worn by Catherine the Great. According to Doan's elder son, Mattison also continued to pay Raymond's monthly stipend and agreed to keep it up as long as Doan didn't seek a divorce.

Raymond Doan himself has never disclosed the terms of his "permanent" separation from Barbara, but from all indications it appears that he and Mattison did reach some kind of private agreement. Not long after leaving Barbara, Doan set up housekeeping in Montreal and Gibraltar with a young Frenchwoman he had met in Paris. They had two children, and it was only after Barbara's death in 1979 that Doan (by then known as Prince Raymond Doan-Hué d'Annam) legitimized them by marrying his consort. Raymond Doan's only public statement after his final separation from Barbara was almost courtly in content. "She gave me much more than money," he said. "She gave me love."

Another event kept under wraps involved a bundle of Barbara's jewelry, $5 million dollars' worth to be exact. Because of her sudden departure from Rome she decided to leave several boxes of jewelry with an old friend, a titled Italian who in earlier years had been one of her more avid suitors. Included in the treasure trove left with the gentleman in question were Marie Antoinette's pearls, the Empress Eugénie's ruby tiara, two diamond necklaces, a diamond ring, an Egyptian plaque of diamonds, coral, and jade and a red enamel and platinum vanity case. What Barbara failed to realize about her trusted friend was that he happened to be affiliated with the MSI (*Movimento Sociale Italiano*), the Italian neo-Fascist party, a group dedicated to reviving many of the political principles once espoused by Mussolini.

When Barbara returned to Rome the following year to retrieve her jewelry, the titled friend threw up his arms. He claimed to know nothing about it. Barbara had never given him her jewelry; she was confusing him with somebody else. Reverberations of this latest scandal began to be widely felt. Chubb & Son, Barbara's insurance agent, refused to consider the claim on grounds that the jewelry had neither been stolen nor lost; it had been given away. Rumor had it that the so-called friend was fencing the merchandise and turning the proceeds over to the MSI. Graham Mattison had two alternatives: sue the friend and the MSI or sue the insurance company. But neither choice was acceptable because both were dependent upon Barbara's testimony in a court of law, opening her to cross-examination. The publicity accruing from allegations of her addiction to alcohol and drugs would have been disastrous. Mattison was stymied: there was no conceivable way of redeeming the loss.

Part Four

Queen for a Day

Seventeen

Life is a dream, death an awakening.

BARBARA HUTTON,
Notebooks, 1979

O N NOVEMBER 4, 1971, at age eighty-five, Jessie Donahue died in her sleep in her apartment in New York. The last surviving daughter of F. W. Woolworth, she was entombed in the Woolworth mausoleum at Woodlawn Memorial Cemetery. According to the dictates of her will, Barbara Hutton inherited a pair of pearl necklaces and a Vigée-Lebrun portrait of Marie Antoinette that she had always admired.

Early in 1972, with thirty-four Vuitton trunks and a staff of seven in tow, including Colin Frazer, Barbara flew to Palm Beach to see her ailing, cancer-ridden cousin Woolworth Donahue and his third wife, Mary Hartline, a television personality and former showgirl from Chicago. Barbara's return, her first since the catastrophic Rubirosa honeymoon, energized the sun-baked denizens to the point where Palm Beach Mayor E. T. Smith felt compelled to post a police car outside the block-long Donahue residence at 780 South Ocean Boulevard. The hot ticket that season was a luncheon invitation to the Donahue homestead for a poolside visit with Barbara. Mary Sanford and Charlie Munn made it, as did Mary Lee Fairbanks (Douglas, Jr.'s, wife) and Charles Van Rensselaer (the brother of Barbara's former escort, Philip Van Rennsselaer). Charles Van Rensselaer found Barbara "smashing-looking" in a ruffled red afternoon gown by the Spanish fashion designer Pedro Rodriguez. Barbara's two-month vacation did wonders for her disposition. She not only went swimming in the Donahue pool, but began eating again, mostly Cherries Jubilée, a childhood favorite. She went shopping at Martha's Salon on Worth Avenue, visited Aunt Marjorie at Mar-a-Lago, sipped mimosas (champagne and orange juice) at the Everglades Club.

Although weakened by illness, his face shrouded by a recently grown beard to camouflage the scars of surgery, Wooly Donahue remained the stouthearted trooper, catering to his fragile cousin as though she were the one with terminal cancer. In the course of her visit the cousins attained a closeness they hadn't enjoyed before, discovering a wealth of common traits, including a mutual distrust of society types, in Wooly's subjective lexicon "the pimps and whores of the palmy playground set." The individual personalities of Barbara and Woolworth Donahue were of a single mold, a blend of naïveté and obstinance, tenderness and toughness, plus a touch of the whimsical. Both were highly emotional and sentimental with responsive tear ducts, yet given to periods of petulance and imperiousness.

It was at the Donahues' that Barbara met Bernard Gelbort, an interior designer from Beverly Hills whose business partner was Mary Donahue's uncle, Robert Crowder. "Bob Crowder had known Barbara for most of her adult life," says Gelbort. "I had heard so much about her from Bob that when we finally met it was as though I already knew her. I found her aristocratic, glamorous, intense, yet deeply wounded and alone. She had magnificent eyes that reflected all of her emotions at once.

"She was like a child in many ways, constantly in need of praise and reinforcement. One evening she had her hair styled by Mary's housekeeper and the whole night she kept asking, 'Is it all right? Does it look all right?' She wasn't shy except when people tried to get too close to her who weren't close. If someone said, 'Oh, Barbara, I knew you years ago at El Morocco,' she would instantly recoil."

Barbara's visit to Palm Beach was the last time she saw Woolworth Donahue. He died in early April after Barbara had returned to California. In his memory she made a large donation to his favorite charity, the Waldemar Medical Research Foundation in Woodbury, Long Island. Then one afternoon she turned up at Bernard Gelbort's house on North Beverly Drive in Beverly Hills. She was desperate for companionship, so he invited her to stay. She moved in with her staff of nurses.

"She had three or four nurses," says Gelbort. "There was no room in the house so they used to sit out on the porch. Several of the nurses took advantage of Barbara to the extent of lifting her jewelry, or at least things kept disappearing. Her fortune consumed and destroyed her. It's the kiss of death to be that rich."

Barbara's visitors during her stay in Gelbort's house included Bill Robertson, Graham Mattison (who passed by with his customary slew of papers for Barbara to sign), and her usual team of medical men. When one doctor didn't give her the prescription she wanted, she would call in a second physician, and if need be a third.

She complained bitterly about the treatment she received at the hands of her advisers, medical as well as legal. Among the documents that Graham Mattison placed before his client was a bill of sale for her apartment in Paris. Since she rarely bothered to read what it was she was signing, it came as a shock to learn that her apartment had been sold to wealthy Arabs, together with her best paintings and Haseltine horse heads. Mattison also terminated the scholarship program she had established at the American School in Tangier, stranding dozens of impoverished students without the means to continue their education. Next to be cut was a fund Barbara had set up in Denmark in 1951 to help foster the arts in that country.

Nobody quite understood how Mattison was able to liquidate most of Barbara's assets without drawing more attention to himself. Equally mysterious was Barbara's failure to oppose her lawyer's actions. "She complained," remarks Mary Donahue, "but she did nothing to protect herself. I have no idea how Mattison managed to exert such influence over her. She was no ding-a-ling but it's dumb to let your lawyer walk all over you. He had power of attorney from Barbara, and it was that document that sealed her fate."

Barbara's urge, wherever she happened to be, to get up and go somewhere else, took possession again in early May. She was soon back in Paris, staying in the plush surroundings of the Hotel Plaza-Athenée on Avenue Montaigne. Within a week she went to Charente in the brandy-producing region of Cognac to visit Silvia and Kilian Hennessy, before moving on to Plasencia, Spain, where she sampled the local nightclubs in search of classical flamenco. For a price she learned she could select from among the most talented performers and bring them back to her hotel suite to perform in private.

It was in Plasencia that she encountered Angel Teruel, a twenty-four-year-old matador with a reputation as one of the most exciting bullfighters since the days of the legendary Dominguín. Teruel, with his lithe, agile, tawny good looks, also had a reputation as a ladies' man. Barbara was instantly attracted to him and when he left for the Feria, the annual bullfighting festival in Seville, she went along and was seen at every *corrida* in which he was featured. Colin Frazer carried her through the crowds in his arms to her front-row seat. Nothing, not even her distaste for the brutality of the sport, could keep her away.

One of the signs of her interest, it was said, was that she was wearing many more jewels than usual—an expert counted several million dollars' worth in a day. Had that same observer been able to gain entrance to her hotel suite, he would have seen that it was filled with dozens of framed photographs of the matador, not to mention several pairs of blood-soaked bulls' ears. The observer might also have noticed that Angel Teruel was driving around in a new Rolls-Royce, while on his right finger he wore a recently acquired $75,000 gold-and-diamond ring.

When the Feria ended, Barbara and her young matador vacationed together in Marbella on the Costa del Sol, sharing adjoining suites at the Hotel Los Monteros. Reports filtered out that Barbara's first-night dinner consisted of a dozen bottles of Coca-Cola and one bottle of fresh milk. The Spanish press took a rather harsh view of the friendship, depicting Barbara as a scarlet woman, condemning her for seducing a would-be national hero by waving a wad of dollar bills in the young man's face. After two weeks in Marbella she understood only too well that her sad quest for happiness had once more fallen short. Toward the end of June, Angel Teruel returned to the *corridas* of Madrid, while Barbara, her face haggard with age and her eyes hidden behind large sunglasses, was carried off to Tangier.

⁊❧

It is difficult to say at precisely what point in their marriage things began to go awry between Lance and Cheryl Reventlow. There was no single moment or incident that stood out. Lance simply began to spend more time on a schooner he kept off Hawaii and at a new home he had built in Aspen, Colorado, while Cheryl stayed put in Los Angeles. They talked frequently by telephone, often for hours, running up exorbitant bills. They maintained a close friendship but found living together a strain.

"The only thing legal about our relationship, I guess, was our marriage," Cheryl would later tell an interviewer. "Lance was my very best friend. We had our own kind of relationship, which a lot of people might not understand. He didn't want to be in L.A. and I didn't want to be in Colorado, that's all."

But there was more to it than that. One reason for Lance's restlessness was his inability to fill the void created by his retirement from road racing. He continued to play polo, mastered skiing and sailing, earned a pilot's license. He even tried his hand at charity work, helping finance the construction in Aspen of the Music Bowl, an outdoor stadium for symphony orchestras and touring musicians. But without the full-time challenge of auto racing, he was merely another amateur sportsman, a frustrated playboy and pleasure-seeker whose life lacked real meaning or focus. He turned to drugs as recreational therapy, mostly hashish and cocaine, throwing the same kind of wild bachelor parties in Hawaii and Colorado he had once given in California.

On the afternoon of July 24, 1972, he took off with three of his friends—Philip G. Hooker, Robert Wulf and Barbara Baker—to survey a tract of land he wanted to buy near Aspen. Hooker, twenty-seven years old (nine years younger than Lance), a student pilot and former liquor-store owner, was at the controls of a rented single-engine Cessna 206. There were high winds and severe thunderstorms in the area. According to the National Aviation Safety Board, the craft never should have gone up, certainly not with a student pilot in charge.

A few minutes after takeoff, the Cessna experienced engine trouble, banked sharply and crashed into a wooded mountainside eight miles from the nearest road and seventeen miles northeast of Aspen. The wreckage was spotted by another plane. A rescue crew reached the area shortly after nightfall and confirmed that all aboard were dead. In her first violent explosion of despair, Barbara refused to have Lance buried. She was in Tangier and she wanted his corpse flown to Sidi Hosni. Then she changed her mind and insisted that the body first be embalmed, then flown to Tangier for burial in the tiny mosque next to Sidi Hosni. In the end she relented and agreed to let Cheryl Holdridge take charge and make arrangements for a funeral service in Aspen.

In accordance with Lance's wishes, it was more wake than funeral and was held in a large tent in the Music Bowl. An orchestra, made up of young people, played Mozart and Bach. Cary Grant flew out from Hollywood with a planeload of Lance's friends. Dudley Walker and Margaret Latimer attended. Peggy Reventlow and her son Richard (Lance's half brother) were there. Graham Mattison went in lieu of Barbara, who was too distraught to make the trip. Afterward there was a party at Lance's house with food and drink. Lance was buried in Aspen but was later exhumed and cremated, and his ashes were placed in the family mausoleum at Woodlawn Cemetery.

Although they were not living together at the time, Lance had left the bulk of his fortune to Cheryl. Newspaper accounts and obituaries variously estimated Lance's estate to be in the $50-$100 million range, when in fact Cheryl inherited two homes, four cars, a boat, some real estate, and $4.8 million of a trust fund that turned out to be worth only $5 million; Margaret Latimer and Dudley Walker each received $100,000. Within months of Lance's death, his mother bought back the jewelry she had once given her daughter-in-law, bringing Cheryl's total cash inheritance to roughly $6 million.

Ruth Hopwood remembers Barbara by herself at Sidi Hosni, alone with her bereavement, obsessed by the thought that she was somehow responsible for Lance's death. She kept telling Ruth that she had been a bad mother, that she hadn't paid enough attention to her son. At other times she couldn't bring herself to admit that he was dead. She spoke about him only in the present and future tense ("Lance says ... " "Lance is ... " "Lance will be ... ") as though he had merely stepped out of the room for a few minutes.

Barbara had returned to America and was staying in California in 1973 when the aging Marjorie Merriweather Post passed away. Aunt Marjorie was Barbara's last close family tie, but again she could not bring herself to face the depressing prospect of a funeral and chose not to go. Late in the year she heard from Marjorie Durant, the grand-daughter of Marjorie Merriweather Post.* Marwee, as she was called, visited Barbara at the Beverly Wilshire and was stunned to find Barbara's mattress lying on the floor, college-dormitory style; the floor was covered with Porthault sheets, an arrangement she apparently found helpful in combating her insomnia.

Marwee had heard rumors about the depletion of Barbara's wealth but saw nothing in the way of physical evidence to back up these rumors. If anything, Marwee concluded that the opposite was true. She later informed biographer William Wright that she and Barbara got to talking about pearls: "She had one of her jewel cases brought to her she pulled out this jeweled flower as big as a fist and gave it to me. It was a daisy with pearls for the petals, emerald leaves, and a diamond in the center—at least four carats. I took it, but before I left, I gave it back."

Barbara was still in the habit of giving away valuables on the strength of a whim. The daisy found its way into the clutches of a nurse who worked for Barbara at the Wilshire; after the nurse got her hands on the daisy she was never heard from again. A number of trinkets went to a youngish Hawaiian airlines pilot Barbara had met in California who claimed to be in love with her but seemed to be more enamored of her money. Charles F. Boutelle, manager of A La Vieille Russie, the Russian art and antiques dealer in New York, remembers the pilot returning two pairs of $10,000 cuff links Barbara had previously purchased at the store: "I recall the incident because I thought it peculiar that he would exchange both pairs. But I'm sure he must have wondered what to do with such expensive cuff links when it was the money he needed. So we took the cuff links back on consignment and reimbursed him after they were sold."

The pilot disappeared and Barbara went back into hibernation, emerging on her sixty-first birthday just long enough to be flown by

*Marjorie Durant's mother is Adelaide Close Hutton.

Silvia and Kilian in their private Mystère jet from Los Angeles to San Francisco, where she insisted on a birthday special of cheeseburgers, French fries and Coca-Cola. On the return leg of the journey, the birthday girl locked herself in the lavatory and purged herself of the meal.

In September of 1974 she surrendered the lease on her luxury suite at the Hotel Pierre in New York, another money-saving strategy devised by Graham Mattison. She then headed for Venice to spend several weeks as Marina Luling Volpi's houseguest at the Villa Barbaro. Lanfranco Rasponi, also a guest at the villa, was present during a heated discussion between Barbara and Marina over the former's insistence on playing recordings of high-pitched koto music at all hours of the day and night.

"Barbara could be quite cloying," says Rasponi, "but she was badly mistreated during her later years—and I don't mean just by her lawyers and doctors. By 1974 this once self-sufficient woman, long the object of idolatry among the wealthy, was reduced to dead matter. In a Chanel suit, with a silk scarf around her neck, she was taken from cabana to cabana on the Lido, stopping here and there, attempting to convince former friends to join her for tea. But she seemed as ancient as Venice itself, and people wanted nothing to do with her. On she pushed, supported on Colin Frazer's arm, down the line of tents searching for one friendly face, promising one and all that she planned to throw a last party in Tangier that would surely stand the world on its head. But this crowd no longer cared about Barbara Hutton. She was yesterday's news, yesterday's headline. She was of no more interest to them than a deposed monarch."

Barbara returned to California in time to celebrate her sixty-second birthday. She was sustained and consoled in her suite at the Wilshire by two small acts of kindness: a bouquet of flowers from Gottfried von Cramm, and a letter from Cary Grant telling her how much she had meant to him. With the exception of these tender mercies, the world had forgotten her. Her birthday came and went unnoticed for once by the press. "Nobody cares anymore, and I'm happy about it," she told one of her nurses. But her behavior belied the calm: she had reached an all-time low.

The most minute function became an overbearing task. She would no longer eat or sleep or bathe or change her clothes. In the late afternoon she would go downstairs and sit by herself in the hotel's East Indian-style Zindabad Club and remain there until it closed at three in the morning and then return to her room and drink Coca-Cola waiting for dawn to break. She was seized by the terror of losing her mind and with the desire to kill herself in order to escape her tormenting thoughts. Bright light hurt her eyes and she insisted on having the lampshades covered with towels or pink tissue paper and the windows lined with aluminum foil to reduce the glare."

It was at this point that she added a new physician, a Beverly Hills cardiologist, Dr. Eliot Corday, to her roster of medics. She was also temporarily weaned off Valium and placed on chloral hydrate, one of the safer sedatives on the market, excellent as a daytime tranquilizer at a dose of 500-1000 milligrams every three to six hours. Chloral hydrate has one noteworthy feature—suicide with it is difficult, if not impossible, since a dose large enough to kill an adult usually induces vomiting first. But on the whole, the effect of the switch was negligible because Barbara supplemented the new medication with other, more lethal sedatives. She was as drugged up and dizzy as ever.

Her daily sessions at the Zindabad Club had the unfortunate effect of making the Wilshire a magnet for every gigolo and fortune hunter in Southern California. They would line the bar two and three deep and wait for Barbara to make her entrance. There were times, as one of her nurses later reported, when she visited the bar in a black nightgown with jewelry covering her arms from wrist to elbow. She would always take the same corner table, order a drink, nurse it, and puff her way through a carton of cigarettes, oblivious of the stares of the other patrons. She would examine herself, sometimes for hours, in a gilt-edged compact. Her deeply shadowed eyes, down-turned mouth, paper-thin skin gave her visage the appearance of death mask. The flickering cigarette and the pale-blue smoke rising steadily skyward were often the only discernible signs of life.

Her ongoing decline served to defeat the morale of the two men most responsible for her: Colin Frazer and Bill Robertson. Frazer was known to refer to Barbara as "it" behind her back. "It's in the bar drinking," he would report to Robertson. His allegiance to Barbara was unquestioned, but there were times when her antics became too much and he began talking about switching jobs.

Bill Robertson, envisioning himself as Barbara's keeper, made a concerted effort to keep tabs on her by following her around. His repeated attempts to corral her and drag her back to her suite were met by stiff resistance and an angry scowl. At various times she frightened him off by threating to call the police if he kept badgering her. Then one night she vanished from the lounge. They found her early the next morning in a vacant hotel room, her mouth gagged with a stocking, her hands bound behind her back with a belt, her legs shackled to the bed.

Her clothes had been removed and stolen by a suave playboy type to prevent her from giving chase. Also gone were her purse and jewelry.

༺·ঌ

In the fall of 1975 Barbara departed on what was to be her last visit to Tangier. Instead of the monumental society ball she had envisioned the year before in Venice, she settled for an intimate dinner party for eight. But even this modified gathering proved too much for her and in the end she decided to let her guests entertain themselves. She spent the evening by herself in the privacy of her bedroom listening to Japanese music.

A few weeks later there was another dinner party, this one at the home of David Herbert, and among his guests were Garrett and Joan Moore, the Earl and Countess of Drogheda. "Barbara had been looking forward to seeing them again," Herbert recalls. "But when she arrived at the party she looked like one of those theatrical mad women with layers of rouge and white powder all over her face, mascara smudges around her eyes, lipstick slashed across her mouth and chin. When she went over to kiss Garrett he kind of pushed her away and told her to clean up her face. The poor thing couldn't see anymore and was too proud to let her servants apply her make-up. But she did allow one of them to take it off, and Garrett finally granted her a tiny kiss—a far cry from the days when he considered her his 'dream girl.'

"The one thing Barbara never lost was her sense of humor, and it saved her. Not long after the dinner party I sent a gay friend named Peter to visit her at Sidi Hosni. She received him in her bedroom. 'Do come and sit next to me on the bed,' she said to him. 'But I'm queer,' he responded. 'Didn't David tell you?' 'Oh, that's all right, Peter,' she said. 'I won't bite you, you know.'

"Then one day a large package arrived, gift-wrapped, which contained package within package, maybe a dozen in all. It was like one of those Chinese box puzzles. In time I got down to the last one. Inside was a tiny golden egg and a handwritten note: 'To My Darling David. From the Goose Who Has Laid So Many Golden Eggs. Barbara.'"

༺·ঌ

It was at the Plaza-Athénée in Paris late in 1975 that Barbara met the Spanish portrait artist Alejo Vidal-Quadras and his French wife, Marie-Charlotte. Barbara commissioned the artist to do an oil portrait based on a photograph of her taken in the 1930s—her way, reasoned Vidal-Quadras, of recapturing the past.

"I, of course, made the painting of Barbara I was commissioned to make. But if you looked at her face in the nineteen thirties, rosy, fresh, and then looked at her face forty years later, haunted, blanched, the progression from the first expression to the last was shocking. A photograph of Barbara toward the end of her life should be mounted in every home whose inhabitants envy the rich. Barbara's final years were harrowing. Already when we met her she was in a state of mind where the slightest mishap or incident threw her for a loss. We were supposed to meet her at the hotel one afternoon. She put on all her rubies and diamonds to greet us. But we were delayed in traffic and when we arrived she was weeping hysterically because she thought we weren't going to come. She was wearing a black Dior gown fashionable twenty years before but otherwise passé. She had outlived her age. The glamour and elegance and luxury she once knew had long faded. She used to say of herself, 'I'm like a Venetian bridge that somehow never reached the other side.' What I think she meant was that she hadn't been able to bridge the gap between her own era and the one that followed.

"She was on good terms with Hubert de Givenchy, the couturier, who used to attend her parties in Tangier. When he heard that she wasn't doing so well he asked us to help him arrange a dinner party for Barbara. It was held in his town house, with a dozen guests, very chi-chi, but since Barbara didn't know everyone, she didn't say much. She also refused to eat, although Givenchy had ordered only those foods that she liked. The dinner crawled by, but after coffee and cognac one of the guests, an architect named Count Pierre Sheremetievo, whose family had been rich landowners in Russia, took out his guitar and began to play and sing for Barbara. She absolutely came to life and wound up thoroughly enjoying herself.

"But the next time we saw her she was in bad shape again. Her gynecologist had discovered a suspicious-looking lump near her cervix. It wasn't the first such growth, and so they had made plans to fly her to Cedars-Sinai Medical Center in Los Angeles. She didn't want to go. In fact, she was terrified and wanted the biopsy performed in Paris. I searched out the hotel manager and asked on whose authority she was being forced to leave. 'On the authority of Monsieur Mattison, her attorney,' he said. The manager shrugged his shoulders, and with that single gesture the matter was resolved: she was going."

Ruth Hopwood traveled from Tangier to make the trip with Barbara aboard the Hennessey jet. She was admitted into Cedars-Sinai two days later. To her immense relief, a biopsy showed the tumor to be benign. By mid-January 1976 she was in her former Crescent Wing suite at the

Beverly Hills Hotel, eschewing the Beverly Wilshire because her account there was overextended. She owed the Wilshire in excess of one hundred thousand dollars.

It wasn't long before Barbara was sampling the latest by-products of the "me" generation—Quaaludes, cocaine and a steady flow of nineteen-year-old beach boys. They were paid $1,000 a night to sit and converse with Barbara, although it is difficult to imagine what the two parties might have had to converse about. The trouble with the arrangement was that neither Barbara nor anybody on her staff kept very much cash on hand. Her visitors had to be paid by the front desk, and the charge was then added to Barbara's account. Within several weeks she had run up nearly as formidable a bill as the one still outstanding at the Wilshire. The management requested that she make at least a partial payment. She complained at first but then called Graham Mattison. Mattison, having retired from Dominick & Dominick, had retained the New York law firm of Cahill, Gordon & Reindel to handle the brunt of Barbara's legal paperwork. Barbara's account there was turned over to John R. Young, a specialist in deeds, wills and trusts, whose first priority was to straighten out Barbara's financial problems. Mattison was still calling the shots, but a transference of Barbara's power of attorney designated Young as the lawyer of record. In that capacity, he paid all but $6,950 of Barbara's bill at the Beverly Hills Hotel and cleared her balance at the Wilshire.*

On February 23 Barbara received a telephone call from Hernando Courtright, the owner of the Beverly Wilshire. A residential suite, formerly occupied by Metromedia television giant John W. Kluge, had become available on the tenth floor of the Wilshire's new wing. The $10,000-a-month apartment featured four bedrooms, kitchen-breakfast area, formal dining room, living room, den, wall-to-wall carpeting, semicircular terraces, diverting views of the skyscrapers of Los Angeles in one direction and the Santa Monica Mountains in the other. Barbara signed a month-to-month lease and took possession a few days later.

Barbara Woolworth Hutton, the heiress who had once boasted of having more money than she could possibly spend in a lifetime, now had less of it than she would have liked. Or so it seemed from the steady flow of overdue bills, canceled charge account plates, and lawsuits that poured into her new suite. First on line was the manage-

---

*Barbara's final power of attorney was signed on March 27, 1974. Unlike previous documents of this type, the 1974 power of attorney was not a year-to-year agreement but was revocable only on receipt of written notification from Barbara. On November 18, 1976, with Barbara's consent, Graham Mattison transfered the document to John R. Young.

ment of the Beverly Hills Hotel with a claim for the balance of her bill, plus $536.50 to cover the cost of "several flower pots, bowls, and silk flower arrangements" that had mysteriously disappeared, presumably when Barbara's staff packed up. The suit was settled out of court.

Next came Thomas Creech, Barbara's former chauffeur, who sued to collect $32,290 in unpaid wages. Creech contended in his affidavit that during his employment he had been "forced to perform many chores that had nothing to do with driving, such as lining the windows of Miss Hutton's various hotel suites with aluminum foil to keep out sunlight, keeping lamp shades covered with pink tissue paper and insuring that she was served only round ice cubes, as she disliked square ones." It took several years and appearances in court before Creech collected.

In addition there were pending lawsuits and summonses from any number of merchants and emporiums with whom Barbara had done business, including Vera Medina, her caftan maker in Tangier, as well as Tiffany and Harry Winston in Beverly Hills. She owed Tiffany $40,000, half of it for several dozen tiny gold bells she had ordered, to be worn by her nurses (so she would know when they were coming and going); she owed Winston approximately $30,000. The jewelry department at I. Magnin sued for $660,000, to cover charges Barbara had accrued over a period of less than four months. One of Barbara's accountants described her credit record as a "bog of confusion" and placed the onus of blame on her reckless lifelong compulsion "to throw away her money."

But there was more to it than this. Among other considerations there was the question of Graham Mattison and Mattison's indisputable role in the erosion of one of America's greatest fortunes. From the beginning Barbara assumed, perhaps correctly, that Mattison's complex tax planning and fiscal acrobatics depended on a thorough knowledge of international tax treaties, involving areas of the law that were beyond the ken of the uninitiated. What was stunning about Mattison's manner was the ease and openness of his operation. If Barbara was not always aware of what he was up to, the broad lines of his actions were nevertheless there for all to see.

His methodology is perhaps best illustrated by the way in which he handled the sale of Sumiya, Barbara's Japanese-style palace in Cuernavaca. In late 1976 twenty employees at Sumiya filed an official complaint with Mexico's Ministry of Labor, contending that they hadn't received their salary from Mattison in over ten weeks. The ministry imposed a pay order and an $800 fine against Barbara. A second pay order and fine were levied by the Ministry of Taxation for non-payment that year of property taxes. Armed with the two pay orders, Mattison called on Barbara and soon convinced her that Sumiya had to go, that it was nothing but a drain on her already shaky finances. The attorney even offered to find a buyer for Sumiya. A week later he was back in touch with Barbara. Fernando Hanhausen, a lawyer from Mexico City who had handled several minor cases for Barbara, was willing to take the property off her hands. He planned to transform the residence into a restaurant and build a resort of one-family condos on the surrounding land that he would then sell at a starting price of $300,000 per half-acre plot.

"How much is he willing to pay?" asked Barbara.

"Well," said Mattison, "he'll give us five hundred thousand dollars."

Considering that the house and its contents alone were worth anywhere from thirty to forty times that figure, it didn't strike Barbara as such a promising offer. When she questioned the bid, Mattison reminded her that there was a real estate price war raging in Mexico and that it could take years for a better offer to come along, especially considering the prohibitive maintenance costs on the property. Barbara finally gave in and signed a bill of sale. It is unclear what advantage, if any, Mattison derived by selling the house at this ludicrously low price. But the fact that he and Hanhausen had known each other placed the transaction in a rather dubious light. Nacho de Landa, Barbara's neighbor in Cuernavaca, insists that Mattison turned down higher bids on the property in order to sell to Fernando Hanhausen.

When he wasn't involved in real estate deals, Mattison kept busy with other strategies, from the establishment of dummy corporations in Barbara's name to the investment of some of her dwindling assets in the temperate tax haven of Hamilton, Bermuda. He terminated one account with the Royal Bank of Canada and invested her funds in a munitions manufacturing concern located in Belgium; the concern nearly went into receivership and Barbara lost millions. He removed her possessions from Sumiya, sending some of the larger Japanese furnishings to Barbara's suite at the Beverly Wilshire; he placed her invaluable jade collection in storage at Grospiron (formerly Pitt & Scott) in Paris, but later sold it to private collectors. He somehow convinced Silvia de Castellane Hennessy to return a few of the more valuable pieces of jewelry she had received from Barbara over the years. He talked Igor Troubetzkoy into giving back the trust fund Barbara had set up in his name at the time of their divorce. He induced Jimmy Douglas to return four paintings (two by Hubert Robert, two by Jean Baptiste Greuze) that Barbara had given him as a gift. He approached a number of people who had been the beneficiaries of Barbara's generosity and asked them to send back her presents; not everyone complied.

Mattison's handling of Barbara was generally regarded by her friends as cutthroat and cruel. He warned her repeatedly that she would be in danger of being kidnapped if she left her hotel suite and tried to convince her that only the pistol-packing (but gentle) Colin Frazer was capable of protecting her. He told her that she was "broke" and had no principal and no income. He forbade her to sign even the smallest checks. She was informed there was no money for travel to Paris or even to San Francisco. He made certain that any potential suitors were kept out of range and went so far as to have Barbara's nurses censor her mail and telephone calls. He continued to strip her of personal possessions—to pay, he said, for her hotel suite, her doctors and her nurses, expenditures that came to roughly $300,000 per year, whereas the jewelry he carried away was worth far more than that. Barbara's associates and acquaintances concur that Mattison wanted too large a slice of the pie and was willing to go to practically any lengths to get it. Mattison, too, aroused much envy and resentment. He acquired two magnificent homes, one in Estoril, Portugal, the other at 56 Avenue Montaigne in Paris. He acquired an additional suite of rooms at the stately Hotel Lancaster, also in Paris. He owned a pair of customized Rolls-Royces. He traveled constantly. In the summer he threw parties for Arab millionaires and Hollywood film moguls. In the winter he gave gala luncheons at Maxim's for the likes of the Patiños and Baron Alexis de Rédé. He attended charity affairs; his wife, Perla, went to fashion shows; they were invited to Truman Capote's shimmering black-and-white masquerade ball at the Plaza in New York for Katharine Graham, president and chairman of the board of the Washington *Post* and *Newsweek*. He belonged to the Union Club in Manhattan and to the Traveller's Club in Paris. People began to talk, and to wonder. Where did all this money come from?

Questions about Mattison were asked even more persistently by certain key members of Barbara's staff, especially during one stretch when he claimed there were no funds left to pay their wages, in essence re-enacting the scenario previously played out in Cuernavaca. Colin Frazer, for one, talked about putting a private investigator on Mattison's trail. He also talked about having Barbara's books audited by a certified public accountant and the results made available to her employees. Frazer ultimately settled on another course of action, a one-man mutiny whereby he took possession of a Vuitton suitcase packed with Barbara's solid-gold picture frames. Unless Mattison anted up, he was prepared to raise the necessary funds by selling the picture frames. Mattison paid.

A similar wage freeze was deployed by Mattison once more in the summer of 1977 to terminate the services of a nurse nicknamed Sibylla who worked for Barbara for one year beginning June 1976. It was a trying period for Barbara, a period made more difficult by the death on November 8, 1976, of Baron Gottfried von Cramm in an automobile accident during a business trip to Cairo; he was the third former husband to die in this manner. In her growing isolation and despair, Barbara came to rely increasingly on the few individuals still in her employ, especially on the attentions lavished upon her by her newest caretaker.

No longer able to cope with adversity, to distinguish the relevant from the irrelevant, or to confront even the smallest problems of everyday existence, Barbara withdrew into the security of a hospital-like environment, where she became hopelessly dependent on its controlled setting and on a staff whose only function was to cater to her every whim and to pretend with her that her life was like everyone else's. Isolated, feeding on fantasy and drugs, Barbara suffered a breakdown of psychotic proportions, regressing to a child-like state where only her obsessions and compulsions seemed real.

Like an infant in a crib, she clung to the surface of her king-size bed, convinced that she could no longer walk, refusing to eat or sleep. Her body weight never again rose above ninety pounds. Her refusal to ambulate caused atrophy of the leg muscles (dropfoot), inflamed tendons and painful bed sores. The draperies to her room remained drawn. She sustained herself on Coca-Cola and cigarettes, never looking when she used her butane lighter, burning countless holes in her once fine bedlinens and handmade lace coverlets, on more than one occasion setting herself on fire. When one of her Dior dressing gowns went up in flames, she had to be doused with a fire extingusher. Her Vuitton suitcases, thirty-five of them, were scattered about the suite, piled up in hallways, ready to be packed at a moment's notice. One of the spare bedrooms was transformed into a cloakroom for her fur coats. She kept what remained of her jewelry in three modified attaché cases with built-in combination spin locks. The three cases left the side of her bed. She always wore her Pasha of Egypt diamond and a smaller ring, a pearl surrounded by a cluster of diamonds, as well as a pearl necklace and gold bands around her emaciated upper arms.

"As far as I could tell," says Sibylla, a native Californian of Spanish descent, "almost everyone was taking advantage of her. The head nurse, an Irish woman named Kathleen Murphy, kept a running log of Barbara's medications. When I first saw it I couldn't believe my eyes. A horse couldn't have ingested as much medication and survived. Her doctors were swamping her. Most of her friends had deserted her. She used to complain that Nini Martin never called her anymore from San Francisco. Silvia de Castellane Hennessy referred to her as *la folle* —

'the crazy one'! Cary Grant called only once during the time I was there. He wanted to send his daughter over to visit Barbara, but made no effort to see her himself.

"Graham Mattison was a big question mark. Nobody could figure out why Barbara didn't just fire him and turn her banking problems over to another lawyer or to some reputable financial institution. She was obviously afraid of Mattison. He knew too much about her personal life and might go to the press. Also, she was ashamed to admit that somebody might be taking her for a ride. She stuck with Mattison because there was nobody around to give her advice and she was too old and sickly to start interviewing new lawyers.

"As it turned out, Mattison wasn't even the worst of it. That accolade belonged to the merchants and business people, especially those big-name jewelry stores Barbara had frequented for so many years. Toward the end they either snubbed her completely or tried to swindle her with bogus jewelry on those occasions when she would still buy someone a gift. She couldn't see well enough anymore to tell the difference.

"It happened that I showed a bracelet she gave me to Daniel Ryan, the director and vice president of Van Cleef & Arpels. Ryan had known Barbara for years. He took one look at the bracelet and said, 'Barbara gave this to you? It's impossible! All the diamonds are glass.' He then proceeded to tell me how Barbara had owned the most fabulous collection of jewels in the world. 'She had magnificent taste,' he said. 'I know jewelry, but she taught *me* things. She understood cut, design, appearance, shape and function. She could look at a ring and tell you what jeweler had mounted the stone.'

"Everything went to pot at once. Barbara retreated from life. She felt she had nothing left to live for. She had lost it all: her son, her money, her looks, her closest frinds and relatives. Her universe was reduced to the accouterments of ill health. Everything in that universe was a metaphor for something else. Everything had to be called by another name. She christened the bedpan Belinda. You couldn't just say, 'Do you want the bedpan, kid?' You had to say, 'Would you like Belinda, Princess?' Before she would use it you had to baptize it with Rive Gauche perfume and baby powder. The powder gave her bladder infections, but if it wasn't properly powdered, she wouldn't use it. She would go in the bed.

"When she did use it she would lie flat in the bed. She wouldn't lift a solitary finger to help. You had to do everything for her. She got a charge from having people wipe her. I didn't know that at first and I would just hand her the toilet paper. Of course you didn't dare call it toilet paper. It was Clare, as in Clare Boothe Luce. Don't ask me why. When she used the toilet paper herself, instead of using a few sheets, she would take the roll in one hand and pull it as far as she could. She would do this four or five times and then tear it off. Later it would go into the bedpan and down the toilet, where it invariably stopped up the works. The plumber would be called and Barbara would grumble about the hotel's inferior waste-disposal system. After a while I was told to wipe her myself. This was the pivotal moment of Barbara's day, because if she didn't have a poop to end all poops, she had to do an enema, or, as she called it, a Mr. Harrison; we called it a Harrison Shower. She was a nut on not gaining weight, even at this late stage. And so I was placed in charge of bowel movements. I had to keep reminding myself that I was being paid for this. But in truth I felt sorry for Barbara. Her last days were joyless and dark. The only pleasure she derived was from having her behind wiped and being given an occasional enema. I think it gave her a kind of sexual release. I know it did. This went on until the day Graham Mattison without warning, suspended my pay. I left the job a week later."

Another nurse was Linda Fredericks, a thirty-one-year-old part-time high school teacher who joined Barbara in the summer of 1977 and stayed with her to the end. Linda found the position demanding but not in the sense that it was hard work. "It was tedious work," she explains. "It was difficult to talk to Barbara, to keep her abreast. You would read to her for a while and then try to carry on a conversation or figure out what else to do. At night the hotel was very quiet so I would turn on the air conditioner and hope that it would lull her to sleep. When she sensed that you were sitting around waiting for her to doze off, she would start asking for things. 'Bring me this' and 'Bring me that.' A Coke, a glass of water, a magazine. As soon as you got settled again, she would think of something else—'Oh, Miss Linda, darling, would you mind bringing me my lipstick?' She always wore make-up. Once in a while she would decide to strip and wash her face. Then she would apply all this facial cream, leave it on for a few hours and replace her make-up. Once a week she would have her hair done by Marc, the hotel hairdresser. Mattison had stopped paying Marc, but he continued to pass by, out of allegiance to Barbara. Her hair was very brittle and she would have it dyed a champagne blond. But the dye didn't take well and it looked worse than if she had just left it alone. Kathleen always reminded us to tell Barbara how wonderful she looked, especially after she'd had her hair done. I used to write in the log, 'It looks like a Brillo soap pad,' and Kathleen would write back, 'You're such a naughty girl.'

"There were times when Barbara became totally irrational, exhibiting obsessions, compulsions, wild fluctuations of mood. She'd be talking to you one minute and suddenly something would snap. You could see it in her eyes. They would roll back into her head, then forward again as if she were having a seizure. She'd throw you out of the room. The second you closed the door she'd blow that goddamn whistle. 'Where do you think you're going?' Then she'd start mumbling and cursing you out under her breath. She'd moan that her brain was on fire. She needed a painkiller. You would give her one pill and she would insist on having a second. She would tell you how half the world was plotting to kill her—hotel employees, neo-Fascist agents from Italy, U.S. government officials were all out to get her. She would insist that her phone, her bed, her room, the entire suite were all bugged. Her obsessions could usually be dispelled by insistent logic. But some of her obsessions had obtruded themselves so thoroughly on her psyche that is was difficult to talk her out of them. One of her common complaints was that she heard loud sobbing noises coming from the closet. It was Lance in the closet. So you would open the closet door to reassure her. Five minutes later it would begin again.

"She wasn't always *el zombo*. She could be very sharp, humorous, charming. She and Kathleen had this comic running battle over cleaning Barbara's dentures. Kathleen would want to clean them and Barbara would refuse. Kathleen would tell her to spit them out. Barbara would say, 'I'm not going to.' Then Kathleen would raise her voice, 'Spit out your teeth or I'll take them out.' Barbara would respond by acting like a pouty little girl. She could also blow herself up so she looked nine months pregnant. Nobody knew how she did it.

"One doctor would prescribe one medication, another doctor would prescribe something else. There was no rhyme or reason to the patterns or cycles of when the drugs were administered. They would change day in and day out, from week to week. The list included vitamin E and multivitamins three times a day, morphine by injection, potassium chloride and Aldomet to correct an electrolyte imbalance due to too many years of not eating. She used the laxative Peri-Colace and took four tablets in the morning, and four in the afternoon. Twice a day she drank a glass of Meritene with an egg in it. She took gerovital shots, which is supposedly the elixir of perpetual youth. It slows down the aging process. She was given three shots a week for three weeks, then nothing for a month, then she repeated the series.

"She took about ten tranquilizers and sedatives a day, including chloral hydrate, Nembutal and barbital. On and off she would be given Doriden, a sleeping pill, and Empirin with codeine in it. She was addicted to the painkiller Dilaudid. The normal dose of Dilaudid is two milligrams every four hours. She was taking fifteen milligrams every six hours. Eight milligrams will put the average person into cardiac arrest. She went into respiratory arrest and almost OD'd a few times before she gradually built up a tolerance. In addition, she took Valium and Librium. She was lucky to be around, considering the massive doses she was taking. She was also being given Thorazine three times a day, sometimes in tablet form, sometimes by injection. At first she was given just enough to keep her from climbing the walls. But by the end she was taking the drug in such quantities as are prescribed only to subdue dangerous cases of schizophrenia. We told her it was a drug for blood circulation. Whether she believed it or not, I don't know. She developed some nasty side effects, such as jaundice and body tremors. To control the tremors she was put on L-dopa, a drug often prescribed for patients with Parkinson's disease. Jimmy Douglas was visiting Barbara and discovered the L-dopa. He couldn't understand why she was being given L-dopa or Thorazine. He insinuated it was wrong to give her one medication and call it something else. I agreed with him, but then, the doctors didn't want to alarm Barbara needlessly."

Among Barbara's most frequent visitors during her last years were her cousin, Dina Merrill, and Dina's actor husband, Cliff Robertson. "Whenever we visited," recalls Robertson, "she was in bed. There were dozens of half-empty glasses of Coca-Cola around. She must have read a lot because there were books by Victoria Holt and Barbara Cartland next to her bed. She was definitely alert but you could see her frailness. It was a sad thing. She had a sweet, lost quality, a sensitivity. She also had a strong and determined mind. She was surrounded by sycophants, by people on her payroll. Barbara was in a virtual cocoon. She refused to get out of bed. She would say that she had hurt her leg and couldn't move. That was her determination: her refusal to move.

"I thought a change of scenery would do her a world of good. I said to Dina, 'Why doesn't she just get out of bed? Get her mind off herself. She needs to get involved in helping other people. Why don't you encourage her to walk?' Dina would say, 'You don't know her. She won't do it. She was always that way.'

"During another visit I dared Dina to be firm with her. 'Let's just put her in the car and go for a drive,' I said. Dina shook her head. 'It can't be done,' she said. 'Barbara is too determined. That strong will is characteristic of the family. Her grandfather was the same way.'

"After a point I felt it was not my province to interfere. And maybe my wife was right, maybe it was impossible to change Barbara's mind. She had lost interest in the world. What do you do for an encore after living the kind of life she had lived? She was content to just lie there and drift into oblivion."

Robert Crowder was a freqent visitor at the Wilshire, appearing as often as two and three times a week. Ruth Hopwood made the trip once from Tangier. "Barbara wanted to hear all the latest gossip from Morocco," recalls Ruth. "But her attention span lasted maybe twenty minutes and then she would begin to drift off into reveries and delusions. She would talk in a frenetic whisper, insisting that the walls had ears. She was sure that Graham Mattison was planning to put her in a nursing home. It was impossible to rationalize with her. But just as you were about to give up, she would become herself again."

There were those who found they could still coax an occasional laugh out of Barbara, such as Jon Keating, an executive with Neiman-Marcus in Los Angeles and a long-time acquaintance, who would make light of Barbara's worries by telling her that if she continued to talk irrationally he would be forced to write her out of his will. Toward the end Barbara was mostly in a dream world but sometimes, according to Keating, she was "so lucid it was frightening. She told stories of her life, her loves, her son and her husbands. Some of the details about her husbands were frightening—they made my hair stand up on end."

Barbara was amused by a rash of newspaper articles by West Coast gossip columnist Jack Martin, linking her romantically with Anthony DePari, a thirty-five-year-old Beverly Hills florist. They had met when Barbara ordered flowers from his shop. In more opulent days he supplied her with $2,000-$3,000 of flower arrangements each week. When Mattison finally refused to pay the exorbitant floral bills, DePari kept sending the flowers without charge. It was good publicity for DePari and it kept Barbara in flowers, but there was nothing more to it than that.

Hubert de Givenchy visited late in 1978 and brought Barbara a flacon of his own in-house perfume. "You have to come back to Tangier," he told her. "You must give the parties at Sidi Hosni the way you did before." The idle suggestion seemed to pass over her head, but when Givenchy departed and she had time to think about it, she decided that returning to Tangier to spend her last days was an excellent idea. Sidi Hosni was her last refuge, the only residence she still owned. Morocco was close to her heart. Hadn't she once written to the Pasha of Marrakech requesting that in the event of her death, her body be interred in Morocco?* Like an old elephant stumbling off in search of

---

*The letter (originally written in French) was dated November 6, 1963, and was sent while Barbara was staying at the Hotel Mamounia in Marrakech:

Dear Pasha:
Knowing, Monsieur, your generosity and your goodness of heart, and knowing, Monsieur, that you have the charity to admit that I love your country with all my heart, I wish to ask something very difficult of you. Should it happen that my life ends in Morocco, would you see to it, as my own father would, that nobody views or touches my body, and that I am buried in Morocco, because the greatest nobility and dignity are in Morocco, and the greatest heart. Forgive me, Monsieur, and please, I beg of you, accept all my devotion.

its sacred burial ground, Barbara was determined to wend her way back to Sidi Hosni.

She phoned Jimmy Douglas in Paris to invite him along on the expedition. Jimmy, sensing loneliness on Barbara's part rather than an overt desire to return to Tangier, sent a friend of his to visit her. The friend, a young photographer and fashion promoter from Zandra Rhodes, was named Patrice Calmettes. Given to wearing a crucifix around his neck and a diamond stud in his earlobe, Calmettes spent six weeks in and out of Barbara's suite, speaking French with her, charming her, making her laugh. He apparently tried to get her to walk but couldn't. Nor could he shake her out of her essential loneliness or convince her to eat. It was clear to Calmettes, as it must have been to everyone, that Barbara's was a second-rate fate and that she had run out of steam long before the end.

On March 26, 1979, the wire services carried a notice that Barbara Hutton had been admitted to the fifth-floor intensive care unit at Cedars-Sinai, where she was diagnosed as suffering from severe congestive cardiomyopathy, a condition of the lung marked by distension and impairment of the heart function. Through its spokeswoman, Virginia Bohanna, the hospital released a misleading statement saying that Barbara was being treated for pneumonia. Knowing that she was now alone, Jimmy Douglas flew from Paris to Los Angeles to be with her.

Dr. Jay Schapira, Barbara's latest physician, attributed the severity of her attack to inactivity, malnutrition, compulsive cigarette smoking, poor general health, overall decay. She had been suffering from the illness for a year but continued to abuse herself and refused to do her deep-breathing exercises. In the hospital she seemed ready to give up. She refused solid food and wouldn't allow them to feed her intravenously, ripping the needle out of her arm whenever the nurses turned their backs.

One of the nurses led Jimmy Douglas to her room, then left them alone. Barbara was a wasted figure lying immobile in the narrow bed. Her hair was gray-streaked where the dye had washed out. Her eyes opened. She recognized her visitor.

"It takes so damn long," she said.

"What does?" Jimmy asked.

"Dying."

He sat with her for most of a week, watching the flickering green lines on the electrocardiogram screen overhead and listening to the maddening sound of the electrically monitored heart: *beep ... beep ...* He tricked her into eating, amusing her with pantomime and burlesque while the nurse quickly shoveled another spoon of applesauce into her open mouth.

By the middle of April she was out of intensive care. In her new quarters she seemed almost happy at times, and, in a peculiar way, proud that Jimmy had come. She waved in the nurses and other hospital workers on the corridor, and introduced them to him, each introduction followed by a boastful description of his accomplishments. But on other days she was listless and flat, weary of the dull, deadening routine, too tired it seemed to breathe. On these occasions she would inevitably fasten on many of her old obsessions and compulsions, leading Jimmy through her log of complaints, from fears of poverty to her rampant conviction that "they" were planning to lock her away in a nursing home or metal institution. More than anything she wanted to return to Morocco, to spend her last days in Tangier, but she couldn't possibly go back there now, she explained, because it was crawling with murderers and thieves, government agents and spies.

At other odd moments she would tilt her head toward Jimmy and enumerate sundry possessions she wished to leave her friends. "I'm going to give you Sidi Hosni, whether you want it or not," she told him. Her most recent will, a three-page handwritten document that she had dictated to Bill Robertson on December 8, 1976, would have to be revised.* For one thing, she told Jimmy, she planned to excise Silvia de Castellane's name from its pages. "Do you know where the Hennesseys are at this very moment?" she said. "They're in San Francisco. They've been there for two weeks and they never called me. And do you know what they sent me for Christmas? A plastic duck. My word of honor, a duck made of plastic."

On Thursday, May 3, Barbara returned to her suite at the Beverly Wilshire, and Douglas flew home to Paris, convinced that it would take a miracle to keep her alive. She was a living skeleton, weighing no more than eighty pounds.

Linda Fredericks took care of her the first weekend after her return. "I don't think I've ever seen a worse case of malnutrition," she says. "To top it off, she insisted on having Marc come in to dye and brush out her hair. This was on Sunday, his day off, and I had to turn her at the end of the bed so that he could work on her. She couldn't take it. She wasn't well. I called Kathleen Murphy at home and told her I thought Barbara's lungs were filling up again. She wasn't breathing right. Kathleen sent Dr. Schapira over. He wanted to put her back in the hospital, but she categorically refused. 'I'm not going,' she said. 'And that's final.'"

At the beginning of the week Barbara showed signs of improvement. Her color was better. Her breathing was steadier. On Tuesday she was

---

*Barbara's failing health prevented her from revising her will. The 1976 testament was the one eventually admitted to probate.

propped up in bed to receive Graham Mattison, who had flown in from New York. Bill Robertson was in the room when Mattison arrived. Barbara listened as the two men made small talk and exchanged views on the Iranian hostage situation. Mattison addressed a few idle comments to Barbara, and after a few minutes consulted his watch. "I'd better be going," he said. He took Barbara's hand. "Don't look so glum, kid," he told her. "I'm about to spring a couple of million dollars for you."

Barbara smiled. "Graham," she said in her sweetest voice. "Did I ever tell you what I think of you?" Without waiting for a response, she said, "I think you're the biggest con artist I've ever met. Now get out of here, and let me die in peace."

Mattison looked surprised but didn't say anything. After he left, Barbara turned to Bill Robertson and winked at him, Robertson winked back.

Her brief attack on Mattison represented a last gasp. Starting at noon the following day her condition declined and she was kept under sedation. During one moment of consciousness, she whispered the word "water." A nurse supported her head and helped her take a few sips from a glass, but Barbara choked and coughed the liquid back up.

Dr. Schapira examined her on Thursday morning. Her state of health was poor but momentarily stable. It became worse. She had a restless Thursday night and slept most of Friday morning. In the afternoon she wasn't at all well. Bill Robertson and Colin Frazer stayed with her. Kathleen Murphy, who was also in the room, said to her, "Do you know who I am?" and Barbara responded in a distinct voice, "Indeed I do!"

These were her last words. She simply stopped breathing. Robertson called for an ambulance. At about 4:45 P.M., members of Medic 3 and Ambulance No. 608 arrived and tried to revive her. Kathleen rode along in the ambulance. At 5:10 P.M., on May 11, 1979, Barbara Hutton was pronounced dead on arrival at Cedars-Sinai Medical Center. She was sixty-six years old.

The body was later taken from Cedars-Sinai to the Westwood Village Mortuary, where it was registered under the name Barbara Doan. The press was notified and the expected front-page obituaries appeared the next day, detailing the "poor little rich girl's" bittersweet life and seven failed marriages. Her body remained at Westwood until May 21, when it was shipped to the Frank E. Campbell Funeral Home in New York. When friends and members of the family called John Young, the executor of Barbara's estate, for information on the funeral, they were given the runaround. According to Young, Barbara had wanted a small, private and unpublicized funeral service, and he intended to honor her last request. When asked why Barbara's body was still not buried two weeks after her death, the lawyer gave only the vaguest response, something having to do with the difficulty of transporting a corpse from California to New York. Young was forthcoming only when citing heart failure as the ultimate cause of Barbara's death.

The funeral, which finally took place on May 25 at the Woodlawn Memorial Cemetery in the Bronx, was attended by ten mourners: John Young; Mr. and Mrs. Graham Mattison; Mr. and Mrs. Frazer McCann; Cliff Robertson and Dina Merrill; Bill Robertson; Colin Frazer; Kathleen Murphy. There were no representatives from the press, because nobody from the press had been notified. There was also no clergyman. "I don't want some priest I never met babbling over my grave," Barbara had once told her cousin, Jimmy Donahue, whose body was also interred in the Woolworth Mausoleum.

Barbara's plain chestnut coffin was shrouded by a blanket of red and yellow roses. It was a brief service, highlighted by Cliff Robertson's melodic reading of two poems, one by Barbara, the other *for* her. The first ("Will You Remember?") was from Barbara's 1934 volume, *The Enchanted* —

> *Will you remember when day*
> *Has died upon my leaving,*
> *Will you stay in loneliness*
> *And silent grieving? ...*

—and the second ("Gentle Lady") was by Cliff Robertson:

> *Gentle lady*
> *who searched so long*
> *for that elusive dream*
> *that seemed*
> *forever in her grasp*
> *and yet forever fading.*
>
> *Gentle lady*
> *who looked afar*
> *for one*
> *to hold her fragile heart*
> *away from pain*
> *and understand her.*

Gentle lady
alone and lost
in search of love
so simple.

Gentle lady
console your heart
for in its rest
lies peace and sleep
and gentleness.

Her crypt, located in the same row as that of her mother (Edna Woolworth) and son (Lance Reventlow), bore no epitaph or legend, only her elegantly scripted name and dates:

BARBARA WOOLWORTH HUTTON
1912-1979

Epilogue

Last Will and Testament

Epilogue

T HE *"epuisement"* —the gutting and depletion—of Barbara Hutton's fortune did not end with her death. If anything, her demise
brought the process to a head. Within forty-eight hours Bill Robertson
had the contents of her suite packed up and moved out. Clothing, furs,
gold boxes, snuff boxes, Russian icons, Japanese imperial furniture,
assorted *objets d'art:* everything was shipped off for storage to
Grospiron in Paris. On May 14, three days after Barbara's death, when
California agents for the Internal Revenue Service descended on the
Beverly Wilshire to seal off the Hutton rooms and impound her
possessions, as is customary in certain states, all they found was an
empty apartment. Robertson, whose greatest dereliction was his
chronic fear of Graham Mattison, told the IRS that he knew nothing
about Barbara's personal business dealings and referred them to John
Young at Cahill, Gordon & Reindel. Robertson later confided to
Roderick Coupe, a friend of Jimmy Douglas' in Paris, that he "simply
didn't want to get involved."

But Robertson was involved and was about to get much more deeply
involved. For one thing, he was the only person, outside Young and
Mattison, who was familiar with the contents of Barbara's will. For
another thing, he was the only person who knew the combinations to
Barbara's three jewelry cases. He had already taken the liberty, after
Barbara's death but before the removal of her body, of taking the Pasha
of Egypt diamond off her finger and placing it in an ordinary brown

paper bag. He then emptied the three jewelry cases into the same bag. Several days later he convened with Graham Mattison, turned over the paper bag to Mattison, and the two men boarded a flight for Bermuda. Mattison claimed that he intended to place the jewelry and the original of Barbara's will (also provided by Robertson) in a safety-deposit box at the Bank of N. T. Butterfield & Son on Front Street in Hamilton, one of Bermuda's two main banks. Whether he went through with his plan or not, Robertson never found out. No sooner had they landed in Bermuda than Mattison dispatched Robertson to Tangier, to do at Sidi Hosni what he had already done at the Beverly Wilshire: pack up and ship off Barbara's possessions to Grospiron in Paris.

Essentially Robertson was now out of the picture, and Mattison was very much in it. He and Young had made arrangements with the Bermuda law firm of Conyers, Dill and Pearson to have Barbara's will admitted to the probate division of the Bermuda Supreme Court, a remarkable feat considering that the deceased had never in her life so much as set foot in Bermuda. The advantages of having the will probated there were twofold: first, to avoid the kind of unwanted publicity that usually ensues after a celebrity's death, particularly with respect to the disposition of that person's last will and testament (the carnival atmosphere that pervaded the search for a will following the death of Howard Hughes is a case in point); second, there was the question of inheritance taxes, which are considerably lower in Bermuda than in almost any other country, not including the United States.

John Young explains the decision to probate her will in Bermuda as follows: "At her death she was still a subject of Denmark and a resident alien in America. Her legal residence was Tangier, Morocco. But since she had assets in Bermuda and since Bermuda's probate laws are similar to those of the United States (Bermuda being a self-governing British Crown Colony), we chose to do it there, rather than in Morocco."

Unfortunately, Young's explanation raises as many questions as it purports to answer. How is it, for example, that the government of Bermuda, supposedly stringent in its probate requirements, saw fit to probate the will of an individual who had never so much as visited the island? How, having been domiciled in Beverly Hills for the last three years of her life, was it possible to declare Barbara as anything other than a legal resident of California? Why was it necessary to remove Barbara's jewelry from the United States in such a seemingly surreptitious fashion? At best, the entire operation had a cloudy, mysterious air about it.

Barbara Hutton's will was probated in Bermuda on November 26, 1979. Considering the supposed depletion of her holdings, her bequests were plentiful and numerous:

First 1. I leave the Pasadena Museum [renamed the Norton Simon Museum of Art] the four lacquer chests in my hotel bedroom. And all the lacquer ware in the sitting room which consists of three tables and many gold lacquer boxes, most of them bearing the crest of the Tokogawa. I also leave the beautiful wastepaper basket in my room to the Pasadena Museum ....

Second 2. I leave my two gold lacquer screens with the Phoenix bird on the bottom of one and the gold Chrysanthemum denoting the Emperor to the Legion of Honor Art Museum in San Francisco [also known as the M. H. De Young Memorial Museum], and I leave them also my beautiful jade screens of which there are a pair, and furthermore all the rest of my jade collection which is now in crates in Pitt and Scott [Grospiron] in Paris, France.

Third 3. To Mr. and Mrs. [Kilian] Hennessy of Charente, France, I leave all my silverware, Venetian glasses and twelve silver plates bearing the crest of the Romanovs....

Four 4. To Mrs. Silvia Hennessy I leave my exquisite ruby ring surrounded by diamonds and two matching bracelets as well as the matching earrings.

Five 5. To young Madame Gilles [Barbara] Hennessy I leave my Golconda ring [the Pasha Diamond] as well as most of my other jewelry ....

There were additional bequests. The M. H. De Young Memorial Museum, in addition to her screens and jade collection, was to receive the paintings of Barbara by Alejo Vidal-Quadras. She left a pair of pink pearl and diamond earrings and a matching ring to one of her nurses, Mrs. Joan Hajny. Kathleen Murphy was supposed to get two pairs of pearl earrings, one black and one white. To Nini Martin she bequeathed all her "most beautiful silk rugs" (Chinese and Persian) and a pair of silk prayer rugs. Barbara Hennessy (Silvia's daughter), in addition to the jewelry, was to receive the rock-crystal chandelier that had once hung in Barbara Hutton's Paris apartment.

To these bequests were appended two others:

Should there be any money credited in my name I leave half of it to Mr. William Robertson and half to Mr. Colin Frazer. I also leave to Mr. Robertson the portrait of me done by Master Savely Sorine.

To my faithful servitors Antonia and José Gonzales I leave the sum of fifty thousand dollars each.

The wording of her bequest to Robertson and Frazer ("*Should* there be any money credited in my name ... ") demonstrates that not even Barbara could conceive of there being anything left over in the way of capital assets. At the time of her death her California savings and checking accounts showed a total balance of less than $3,500. Bill Robertson and Colin Frazer had to settle for what modest samples of jewelry Graham Mattison was willing to give them as a kind of "reward" for their many years of devoted service. Strangely enough, Antonia and José Gonzales seem to have been the only legatees (as of December 1983) to receive legal notifications of their inclusion in the will. None of the others, including the directors and curators of the two California museums, were so advised.

While John Young tried to make sense of Barbara's financial statements, Graham Mattison busied himself at the auction marts, dispersing and selling as much of Barbara Hutton's personal property as he could. In June 1979 he auctioned off her eighteenth-century lady's writing table, attributed to the master *ébéniste* Jean-Francois Oeben, at the Akram Ojjeh sale in Monte Carlo. The table, which had once belonged to Madame de Pompadour, went for $228,000. A matching desk was sold that fall at the New York Armory Antique Show for $275,000. Early in 1980 two of Barbara's priceless Japanese paravents, which had been bequeathed to the De Young Memorial Museum, were apparently sold by the Paris auction house of Drouot. On March 24, 1980, Sotheby's of London brought the hammer down on five of Barbara's most valuable gold snuff boxes for a total of $350,000.

What remained of Barbara's jewelry, rugs, furs, lacquer furniture, jade collection, gold boxes, rare screens was sold privately by Mattison, often on terms unfavorable to the estate. The parure of rubies and diamonds once worn by a Portuguese queen that Barbara bequeathed to Silvia de Castellane Hennessy went for a reported $800,000, one quarter of its estimated value. When Silvia heard from friends about the sale, she purportedly threatened to take legal action against the estate. Graham Mattison, defending the estate's actions on the grounds that Barbara still had substantial debts, settled with the Hennessys by turning over jewelry that Barbara had bequeathed to other legatees plus the deed to Sidi Hosni, despite the fact that Barbara had promised it (though not in writing) to Jimmy Douglas. The Hennessys were thus the only ones named in the will to realize anything of real value from their anticipated windfall, itself a profound irony insofar as they were the only people for whom Barbara had nothing but contempt at the end, and to whom she would probably have least liked to leave anything at all.

As to her attorneys, Barbara had foreseen the dilemma years before. In conversation with Cecil Beaton, she had once said, "Lawyers are the dregs. Unless you commit mayhem or manslaughter, you're better off without them. They'll only exhaust your money and your patience." The great folly of Barbara Hutton's life was that while she could sense the future, she could do nothing to change it.

Bibliography

ALLEN, FREDERICK LEWIS. *The Big Change: America Transforms Itself, 1900-1950.* New York: Harper & Brothers, 1952.

ALSOP, SUSAN MARY. *To Marietta from Paris.* Garden City, N.Y.: Doubleday, 1975.

ALTROCCHI, JULIA COOLEY. *The Spectacular San Francisco.* New York: Dutton, 1949.

ALVAREZ, A. *Life After Marriage: Love in an Age of Divorce.* New York: Simon & Schuster, 1981

AMORY, CLEVELAND. *The Last Resorts.* New York: Harper & Brothers, 1948.

———. *Who Killed Society?* NEW YORK: HARPER & BROTHERS, 1960.

ANGELI, DANIEL, AND DOUSSET, JEAN-PAUL. *Private Pictures.* New York: Viking, 1980.

ANGER, KENNETH. *Hollywood Babylon.* San Francisco: Straight Arrow, 1975.

ARCE, HECTOR. *Gary Cooper: An Intimate Biography.* New York: Morrow, 1980.

ARGYLL, MARGARET CAMPBELL, DUCHESS OF. *Forget Not: The Autobiography of Margaret, Duchess of Argyll.* London: W. H. Allen, 1975.

ARNOLD, WILLIAM. *Frances Farmer: Shadowland.* New York: McGraw Hill, 1978.

ARONSON, STEVEN M.L. "Gerald Van Der Kemp." *Interview,* February 1979.

ASTOR, BROOKE. *Footprints: An Autobiography.* New York: Doubleday, 1980.

ATIL, ESIN. *Art of the Arab World.* Washington, D.C.: Smithsonian Institution, 1975.

BACON, JAMES. *Made in Hollywood.* Chicago: Contemporary Books, 1977.

BAKER, CARLOS. *Ernest Hemingway: A Life Story.* New York: Scribners, 1969.

BAKER, NINA BROWN. *Nickels and Dimes: The Story of F. W. Woolworth.* New York: Harcourt, 1954.

BALSAN, CONSUELO VANDERBILT. *The Glitter and the Gold.* New York Harper & Brothers, 1952.

BARDOA, MAHARAJA OF. *The Palaces of India.* New York: Vendome Press, 1980.

BARROW, ANDREW. *Gossip 1920-1970.* New York: Coward-McCann, 1979.

BEATON, CECIL. *Cecil Beaton: Memoirs of the 40's.* New York: McGraw-Hill, 1972.

———. *Cecil Beaton's New York.* New York and Philadelphia: Lippincott, 1938.

———. *Self Portrait With Friends: The Selected Diaries of Cecil Beaton, 1926-1974.* Edited by Richard Buckle, New York: Times Books, 1979.

———. *The Years Between: Diaries 1939-44.* New York: Holt, Rinehart & Winston, 1965.

BEAVERBROOK, LORD. *The Abdication of King Edward VIII.* New York: Atheneum, 1966.
BEEBE, LUCIUS M. *The Big Spenders.* Garden City, N.Y.: Doubleday, 1966.
_____. *Mansions on Rails: The Folklore of the Private Railroad Car,* Berkeley, Calif.: Howell-North, 1959.
BENDER, MARYLIN. *The Beautiful People.* New York: Coward-McCann, 1967.
BENNETT, JOAN, AND KIBBEE, LOIS. *The Bennett Playbill.* New York Holt, Rinehart & Winston, 1970.
BERLIN, BRIGID. "Philip Van Rensselaer: Only Peasants Came Over on the Mayflower." *Interview,* January 1978.
BIRMINGHAM, STEPHEN. *Duchess: The Story of Wallis Warfield Windsor.* Boston: Little, Brown, 1981.
_____. *The Right Places (for the Right People).* Boston: Little, Brown, 1967.
BOCCA, GEOFFREY. *Bikini Beach.* New York: McGraw-Hill, 1962.
_____. *The Woman Who Would Be Queen.* NEW YORK: RINEHART, 1954.
BOCHROCH, ALBERT R. *American Automobile Racing: An Illustrated History.* New York: Viking, 1974.
BOWLES, JERRY. *Forever Hold Your Banner High!* Garden City, N.Y.: Doubleday, 1976.
BOWLES, PAUL. *Without Stopping: An Autobiography.* New York: Putnam, 1972.
BRASSAI. *The Secret Paris of the 30's.* New York: Random House, 1976.
BRINNIN, JOHN MALCOLM. *Sextet: T.S. Eliot and Truman Capote and Others.* New York: Delacorte, 1981.
_____. *The Sway of the Grand Saloon: A Social History of the North Atlantic.* New York: Delacorte, 1981.
BRODY, ILES. *Gone with the Windsors.* Philadelphia: Winston Publishers, 1953.
BROUGH, JAMES. *The Woolworths.* New York: McGraw-Hill, 1982.
BROWN, EVE. *Champagne Cholly: The Life and Times of Maury Paul.* New York: Dutton, 1947.
_____. *The Plaza: Its Life and Times.* New York: Scribners, 1975.
BRYAN, J., III, AND MURPHY, CHARLES, J.V. *The Windsor Story: An Intimate Portrait of Edward VIII and Mrs. Simpson by the Authors Who Knew Them Best.* New York: Morrow, 1979.
CABLE, MARY. *The Little Darlings.* New York: Scribners, 1975.
CALVERTON, V.F., AND SCHMALHANSES, SAMUEL D., EDS. *The New Generation.* New York: Macaulay, 1930.
CAMERON, RODERICK WILLIAM. *The Golden Riviera.* London: Weidenfeld & Nicholson, 1975.
CARNEGIE, DALE. *How to Win Friends and Influence People.* New York: Simon & Schuster, 1936.
CARTER, ERNESTINE. *Magic Names of Fashion.* Englewood Cliffs, N.J.: Prentice-Hall, 1980.
CASSINI, IGOR. *I'd Do It All Over Again.* New York: Putnam, 1977.
CHAKRAVARTY, AMIYA, ED. *A Tagore Reader.* Boston: Beacon Press, 1961.
CHAPLIN, CHARLES. *My Autobiography.* New York: Simon & Schuster, 1964.
CHASE, MARY ELLEN. *Abby Aldrich Rockefeller.* New York: Macmillan, 1950.
CHISHOLM, ANNE. *Nancy Cunard, 1896-1965.* New York: Knopf, 1979.
CHRISTIAN, FREDERICK. "Barbara's Son—Lance Reventlow." *Cosmopolitan,* October 1959.
CHURCHILL, ALLEN. *The Splendor Seekers.* New York: Grosset & Dunlap, 1974.
_____. *The Upper Crust: An Informal History of New York's Highest Society.* Englewood Cliffs, N.J.: Prentice-Hall, 1970.
CHURCHILL, SARAH. *Keep on Dancing.* New York: Coward-McCann, 1981.
COLACELLO, BOB. "Countess of Cinema: Marina Cicogna." *Interview,* October 1980.
_____. "Odile Rubirosa: Oh Oh Odile," *Interview,* July 1979.
_____. "Truman Capote: Is Truman Human?" *Interview,* January 1978.

COLES, ROBERT. *Privileged Ones: Vol. V of Children of Crisis.* Boston: Little, Brown, 1977.

COOKE, ALISTAIR. *Six Men.* New York: Knopf, 1977.

COOKE, HOPE. *Time Change: An Autobiography.* New York: Simon & Schuster, 1980.

COONEY, JOHN. *The Annenbergs.* New York: Simon & Schuster, 1982.

COOPER, DIANA. *The Light of Common Day.* Boston: Houghton Mifflin, 1959.

_____. *The Rainbow Comes and Goes.* Boston: Houghton Mifflin, 1958.

_____. *Trumpets from the Steep.* Boston: Houghton Mifflin, 1960.

COWARD, NOËL. *The Noël Coward Diaries.* Edited by Graham Payn and Sheridan Morley. Boston: Little, Brown: 1982.

_____. *The Noël Coward Song Book.* New York: Simon & Schuster, 1953.

_____. *Present Indicative: An Autobiography.* New York: Da Capo Press, 1980.

COWLES, VIRGINIA. *The Astors.* New York, Knopf, 1979.

CROFT-COOKE, RUPERT. *The Caves of Hercules.* London: W. H. Allen, 1974.

_____. *Exiles.* London: W.H. Allen, 1970.

CURTIS, CHARLOTTE. *The Rich and Other Atrocities.* New York: Harper & Row, 1976.

CURTIS, JAMES. *Between Flops: A Biography of Preston Sturges.* New York: Harcourt Brace Jovanovich, 1982.

DANIELS, JONATHAN. *The Time Between the Wars.* Garden City, N.Y.: Doubleday, 1966.

DALTON, DAVID. *James Dean: The Mutant King.* San Francisco: Straight Arrow, 1974.

DARDIS, TOM. *Keaton: The Man Who Wouldn't Lie Down.* New York: Scribners, 1979.

DAVIES, MARION. *The Times We Had.* Edited by Pamela Pfau and Kenneth S. Marx. Indianapolis: Bobbs-Merrill, 1975.

DAVIS, JOHN H. *The Bouviers: Portrait of an American Family.* New York: Farrar, Straus & Giroux, 1969.

DAVIS, JR., SAMMY. *Hollywood in a Suitcase.* New York: Morrow, 1980.

DAY, J. WENTWORTH. *H.R.H. Princess Marina Duchess of Kent: The First Authentic Life Story.* London: Robert Hale, 1962.

DEFORD, FRANK. *Big Bill Tilden.* New York: Simon & Schuster, 1976.

DE HOLGUIN, BEATRICE. *Tales of Palm Beach.* New York: Vantage, 1968.

DESCHNER, DONALD. *The Films of Cary Grant.* Secaucus, N.J.: Citadel, 1973.

DE WOLFE, ELSIE. *After All.* London: Heinemann, 1955.

DILLON, MILLICENT. *A Little Original Sin: The Life and Work of Jane Bowles.* New York: Holt, Rinehart & Winston, 1981.

DOAN VINH NA CHAMPASSAK, PRINCE RAYMOND. "Un Ensemble Kmer Inconnu: Vat Phu," *L'Oeil*, August 1972.

DONALDSON, FRANCES. *Edward VIII.* Philadelphia and New York: Lippincott, 1975.

DROGHEDA, LORD. *Double Harness: Memoirs.* London: Weidenfeld & Nicolson, 1978.

EDWARDS, ANNE. *Vivien Leigh.* New York: Simon & Schuster, 1977.

EISENSTADT, ALFRED. *Eisenstadt Album: Fifty Years of Friends and Acquaintances.* New York: Viking, 1976.

ELSBERRY, TERENCE. *Marie of Romania: The Intimate Life of a Twentieth-Century Queen.* New York: St. Martin's, 1972.

EPSTEIN, EDWARD Z. *Notorious Divorces.* Secaucus, N.J.: Lyle Stuart, 1976.

EPSTEIN, JOSEPH. *Ambition: The Secret Passion.* New York: Dutton, 1980.

FISHER, EDDIE. *Eddie: My Life, My Loves.* New York: Harper & Row, 1981.

FLANNER, JANET. *London Was Yesterday.* Edited by Irving Drutman. New York: Viking, 1975.

FOLSOM, MERRILL. *More Great American Mansions and their Stories.* New York: Hastings House, 1967.

FONTAINE, JOAN. *No Bed of Roses.* New York: Morrow, 1978.

FOWLER, GENE. *Beau James: The Life and Times of Jimmy Walker.* New York: Viking, 1949.

FRANK, JOAN. *The Beauty of Jewelry.* New York: Crown, 1979.

FREEDLAND, MICHAEL. *The Two Lives of Errol Flynn.* New York: Morrow, 1978.

FRIED, ALBERT. *The Rise and Fall of the Jewish Gangster in America.* New York: Holt, Rinehart & Winston, 1980.

FRIEDMAN, B.H. *Gertrude Vanderbilt Whitney: A Biography,* with the Research collaboration of Flora Miller Irving. Garden City, N.Y.: Doubleday, 1978.

FURNAS, J. C. *Stormy Weather: Crosslights on the Nineteen Thirties: An Informal Social History of the United States, 1929-1941.* New York: Putnam, 1977.

GABOR, ZSA ZSA, WITH FRANK, GEROLD. *Zsa Zsa Gabor: My Story.* Cleveland and New York: World, 1960.

GALBRAITH, JOHN KENNETH. *The Great Crash: 1929.* 3d ed. Boston: Houghton Mifflin, 1972.

GATES, JOHN D. *The Astor Family.* New York: Doubleday, 1981.

GERBER, ALBERT B. *The Book of Sex Lists.* Secaucus, N.J.: Lyle Stuart, 1981.

GODFREY, LIONEL. *Cary Grant.* New York: St. Martin's, 1981.

GOETTE, JOHN. *History of Chinese Jade.* Ann Arbor, Mich.: Ars Ceramica, 1940.

GOLD, ARTHUR, AND FIZDALE, ROBERT. *Misia: The Life of Misia Sert.* New York: Knopf, 1980.

GOLDSMITH, BARBARA. *Little Gloria ... Happy at Last.* New York: Knopf, 1980.

GOVONI, ALBERT. *Cary Grant: An Unauthorized Biography.* Chicago: Henry Regnery, 1971.

GRAHAM, SHEILAH. *How to Marry Super Rich: Or Love, Money and the Morning After.* New York: Grosset & Dunlap, 1974.

GRANGER, STEWART. *Sparks Fly Upward.* New York: Putnam, 1981.

GRANT, CARY. "Archie Leach by Cary Grant," *Ladies' Home Journal,* January and April 1963.

GREEN, MARTIN. *Children of the Sun.* New York: Basic Books, 1976.

GRIFFING, JR., ROBERT P. *The Barbara Hutton Collection of Chinese Porcelain.* Honolulu: Honolulu Academy of Arts, 1956.

GRUND, FRANCIS, J. *Aristocracy in America.* New York: Harper & Brothers, 1959.

GUGGENHEIM, PEGGY. *Out of This Century: Confessions of an Art Addict.* Reprint. New York: Universe Books, 1979.

GUILES, FRED LAWRENCE. *Marion Davies.* New York: McGraw-Hill, 1972.

GUTHRIE, LEE. *The Lives and Loves of Cary Grant.* New York: Drake, 1977.

HALL, WILLIAM. *Raising Caine: The Authorized Biography.* Englewood Cliffs, N.J.: Prentice-Hall, 1981.

HARRIS, ELEANOR. "The Sad Story of Barbara Hutton," *Look,* July 1954.

HATCH, ALDEN. *The Mountbattens: The Last Royal Success Story.* New York: Random House, 1965.

HENDRICKSON, ROBERT. *The Grand Emporiums.* New York: Stein & Day, 1979.

HERBERT, DAVID. *Second Son: An Autobiography.* London: Peter Owen, 1972.

HERNDON, VENABLE. *James Dean: A Short Life.* New York: Doubleday, 1974.

HERRERA, REINALDO. "Jacqueline de Ribes," *Interview,* September, 1982.

HIBBERT, CHRISTOPHER. *Edward, the Uncrowned King.* New York: St. Martin's, 1948.

———. *The Royal Victorians.* Philadelphia: Lippincott, 1976.

HIGHAM, CHARLES. *Errol Flynn: The Untold Story.* Garden City, N.Y.: Doubleday, 1980.

———. *Ziegfeld.* Chicago: Henry Regnery, 1972.

HOFFMAN, WILLIAM. *Queen Juliana.* New York: Harcourt Brace Jovanovich, 1979.

HOLBROOK, STEWART H. *The Ages of the Moguls.* Garden City, N.Y.: Doubleday, 1953.

HORAN, JAMES D. *The Desperate Years: A Pictorial History of the Thirties.* New York: Crown, 1962.

HORST, HORST P. *Salute to the Thirties.* New York: Viking, 1971.

HOSFORD, MARY. *The Missouri Traveler Cookbook.* New York: Farras, Straus & Cudahy, 1958.

HOTCHNER, A.E. *Sophia: Living and Loving.* New York: Morrow, 1979.

HOUGH, RICHARD. *Mountbatten: A Biography.* New York: Random House, 1981.

HOWELL, GEORGINA. *In Vogue: Sixty Years of Celebrities and Fashion from British Vogue.* New York: Schocken, 1976.

HOYT, EDWIN PALMER. *The Vanderbilts and Their Fortunes.* Garden City, N.Y.: Doubleday, 1962.

HUTTON, BARBARA. *The Enchanted*—privately printed. Glasgow, Scotland: R. Maclehose and Company, 1934.

———. *The Wayfarer* —privately printed. Westerham, England: Westerham Press, 1957.

INGLIS, BRIAN. *Abdication.* New York: Macmillan, 1966.

JAMES, MARQUIS. *Alfred I. DuPont.* New York: Bobbs-Merrill, 1941.

JAMES, JR., THEODORE. *Fifth Avenue.* New York: Walker, 1971.

JENKINS, ALAN. *The Rich Rich.* New York: G. P. Putnam, 1978.

JENNINGS, DEAN. *Barbara Hutton: A Candid Biography.* New York: Frederick Fell, 1968.

JOSEPHSON, MATTHEW. *The Money Lords.* New York: Weybright & Talley, 1972.

———. *The Robber Barons.* New York: Harcourt, Brace, 1934.

KADISH, FERNE, AND KIRTLAND, KATHLEEN. *Los Angeles on Five Hundred Dollars a Day.* London: Collier Macmillan, 1976.

———. *Paris on Five Hundred Dollars a Day.* London: Collier Macmillan, 1977.

KAEL, PAULINE. *When the Lights Go Down.* New York: Holt, Rinehart and Winston, 1975.

KAVALER, LUCY. *The Astors: A Family Chronicle of Pomp and Power.* New York: Dodd, Mead, 1966.

KEENAN, BRIGID. *The Women We Wanted to Look Like.* New York: St. Martin's, 1977.

KELLY, KITTY. *Elizabeth Taylor: The Last Star.* New York: Simon & Schuster, 1981.

KEMPER, RACHEL H. *A History of Costume.* New York: Newsweek Books, 1977.

KINROSS, LORD. *The Windsor Years: The Life of Edward, as Prince of Wales, King, and Duke of Windsor.* New York: Viking, 1967.

KIRKWOOD, ROBERT R., AND BERRIDGE, JOHN R. "The Woolworth Story," *Christian Science Monitor,* March 30-April 4, 1959.

KLAW, SPENCER. "The World's Tallest Building," *American Heritage,* February 1977.

KOBAL, JOHN. *Rita Hayworth: Portrait of a Love Goddess.* New York: W.W. Norton, 1978.

KORDA, MICHAEL. *Charmed Lives: A Family Romance.* New York: Random House, 1979.

KUHN, IRENE CORBALLY. "Rubi's Back and Zsa Zsa's Got Him." *The American Mercury,* August 1954.

LANE, WHEATON J. *Commodore Vanderbilt: An Epic of the Steam Age.* New York: Knopf, 1942.

LAWRENSON, HELEN. *Stranger at the Party.* New York: Random House, 1975.

———. *Whistling Girl.* Garden City, N.Y.: Doubleday, 1978.

LEIGHTON, ISABEL, ED. *The Aspirin Age: 1919-1941. The great, the comic, and the tragic events of American life in the chaotic years before two world wars by twenty-two outstanding writers.* New York: Simon & Schuster, 1963.

LESLEY, COLE. *Remembered Laughter: The Life of Noel Coward.* New York: Knopf, 1976.

LEWIS, R.W.B. *Edith Wharton: A Biography.* New York: Harper & Row, 1975.

LIMERICK, JEFFREY, FERGUSON, NANCY, AND OLIVER, RICHARD. *America's Grand Resort Hotels.* New York: Pantheon, 1979.

LINDBERGH, ANNE MORROW. *The Flower and the Nettle.* New York: Harcourt Brace, Jovanovich, 1976.

LINET, BEVERLY. *Susan Hayward: Portrait of a Survivor.* New York: Atheneum, 1980.

LOCKWOOD, CHARLES. *Dream Palaces: Hollywood at Home.* New York: Viking, 1981.

LONGSTREET, STEPHEN. *The Young Men of Paris.* New York: Delacorte, 1967.

LUNDBERG, FERDINAND. *The Rich and the Super-Rich: A Study in the Power of Money Today.* New York: Lyle Stuart, 1968.

MCALLISTER, WARD. *Society As I Have Found It.* New York: Cassell, 1890.

MCLEAN, EVALYN WALSH. *Father Struck It Rich.* Boston: Little, Brown, 1936.

MAGNUS, SIR PHILIP MONTEFIORE. *King Edward the Seventh.* New York: E. P. Dutton, 1964.

MAHER, JAMES T. *Twilight of Splendor.* Boston: Little, Brown, 1975.

MAHONEY, TOM, AND SLOANE, LEONARD. *The Great Merchants.* New York: Harper & Row, 1951.

MAILEY, JEAN. *The Manchu Dragon: Costumes of the Ch'ing Dynasty 1644-1912.* New York: The Metropolitan Museum of Art, 1980.

MARGETSON, STELLA. *The Long Party: High Society in the Twenties and Thirties.* Westmead, Farnborough, Hants, England: Saxon House, D.C. Heath Ltd., 1974.

MARTIN, RALPH G. *The Woman He Loved: The Story of the Duke and Duchess of Windsor.* New York: Signet, 1975.

MATTHEW, CHRISTOPHER. *A Different World: Stories of Great Hotels.* Frome, England: Paddington Press, 1976.

MAXWELL, ELSA. *The Celebrity Circus.* New York: Appleton-Century, 1963.

_____ . *R.S.V.P.: Elsa Maxwell's Own Story.* Boston: Little, Brown, 1954.

_____ . The Truth About Barbara Hutton," *International-Cosmopolitan,* October 1938-January 1939.

MILLER, HENRY. *The Colossus of Maroussi.* New York: New Directions, 1958.

MITCHELL, THERESE. "Consider the Woolworth Workers," *New York League of Women Shoppers,* April 1940.

MOATS, ALICE-LEONE. *The Million Dollar Studs.* New York: Delacorte, 1958.

MORGAN, TED. *Rowing Toward Eden.* Boston: Houghton Mifflin, 1981.

MORRIS, JAMES. *Pax Britannica: The Climax of an Empire.* New York: Harcourt Brace Jovanovich, 1968.

_____ . *The World of Venice.* New York: Pantheon, 1960.

MORRIS, LLOYD. *Incredible New York.* New York: Random House, 1951.

MORTON, FREDERIC. *The Rothschilds.* New York: Atheneum, 1962.

MOSLEY, LEONARD. *Blood Relations: The Rise and Fall of the du Ponts of Delaware.* New York: Atheneum, 1980.

MOSLEY, OSWALD, SIR. *My Life.* New Rochelle, N.Y.: Arlington House, 1972.

MOTT, FRANK LUTHER. *American Journalism.* New York: Macmillian, 1959.

MURRAY, KEN. *The Golden Days of San Simeon.* Garden City, N.Y.: Doubleday, 1971.

NEGRI, POLA. *Memoirs of a Star.* Garden City, N.Y.: Doubleday, 1970.

NICHOLS, JOHN P. *Skyline Queen and the Merchant Prince: The Woolworth Story.* New York: Trident, 1973.

NICOLSON, HAROLD. *Diaries and Letters, 1930-1939. Vol. I.* New York: Atheneum, 1966.

NICOLSON, NIGEL. *Great Houses of the Western World.* New York: Putnam, 1968.

NIVEN, DAVID. *Bring on the Empty Horses.* New York: Dell, 1975.

_____ . *The Moon's a Balloon.* New York: Dell, 1972.

O'CONNOR, HARVEY. *Mellon's Millions.* New York: John Day, 1933.

PACKER, CHARLES. *Furniture by the Master Ébénistes.* Newport Mon, England: The Ceramic Book Co., 1966.

PALEY, WILLIAM S. *As it Happened: A Memoir.* Garden City, N.Y.: Doubleday, 1979.

PALMER, LILI. "Garbo and the Duke," *Esquire,* September 1975.

PALMER, R.L. *Anorexia Nervosa: A guide for sufferers and their families.* Middlesex, England: Penguin, 1980.

PARISH, JAMES ROBERT, AND LEONARD, WILLIAM T. *Hollywood Players: The Thirties.* New Rochelle, N.Y.: Arlington, 1976.

PECKHAM, TED. *Gentlemen for Rent.* New York: Frederick Fell, 1955.

PHILLIPS, CABELL. *From the Crash to the Blitz, 1929-1939: The New York Times Chronicle of American Life.* New York: Macmillan, 1969.

PLAS, S. DE. *Les Meubles à Transformation et à Secret.* Paris: Guy Le Prat, 1975.

POOLE, ERNEST. *Giants Gone.* New York: McGraw-Hill, 1943.

POPE-HENNESSY, JAMES. *Queen Mary, 1867-1953.* London: George Allen and Urwin, 1959.

PULITZER, RALPH. *New York Society on Parade.* New York: Harper & Brothers, 1910.

RAMSEY, LYNN. *Gigolos: The World's Best Kept Men.* Englewood Cliffs, N.J.: Prentice-Hall, 1978.

RANDALL, MONICA. *The Mansions of Long Island's Gold Coast.* New York: Hastings House, 1979.

REED, HENRY HOPE. *Palladio's Architecture & Its Influence: A Photographic Guide.* New York: Dover, 1980.

RENSE, PAIGE. *Celebrity Homes.* Middlesex, England: Penguin, 1979.

REYNOLDS, JAMES. *Pageant of Italy.* New York: Putnam, 1954.

REYNOLDS, RUTH. "The Life of 'Babs' Hutton: The Story of a $50,000,000 Heartache." Chicago Tribune—New York News Syndicate, Inc., 1939.

RHEIMS, MAURICE. *The Glorious Obsession.* New York: St. Martin's, 1975.

ROEBURT, JOHN. *Get Me Giesler.* New York: Belmont Books, 1962.

ROREM, NED. *The Paris Diary of Ned Rorem.* New York: George Braziller, 1966.

ROSS, WALTER S. *The Last Hero: Charles A. Lindbergh.* New York: Harper & Row, 1968.

RUBINSTEIN, ARTHUR. *My Many Years.* New York: Knopf, 1980.

———. *My Young Years.* New York: Knopf, 1973.

RUSSELL, ROSALIND, AND CHASE, CHRIS. *Life Is a Banquet.* New York: Random House, 1977.

RUVIGNY, MARQUIS OF. *Titled Nobility of Europe.* London: Harrison, 1914.

SATTERLEE, HERBERT L. *J. Pierpont Morgan.* New York: Macmillan, 1959.

SCAVULLO, FRANCESCO. *Scavullo on Beauty.* New York: Random House, 1979.

———. *Scavullo on Men.* New York: Random House, 1977.

SCHATT, ROY. *James Dean: A Portrait.* New York: Delilah Books, 1982.

SEALY, SHIRLEY. *The Celebrity Sex Register.* New York: Simon & Schuster, 1982.

SEDGWICK, HENRY DWIGHT. *In Praise of Gentlemen.* Boston: Little, Brown, 1935.

SELZNICK, IRENE MAYER. *A Private View.* New York: Knopf, 1983.

SHIKIBU, MURASAKI. *The Tale of Genji.* New York: Knopf, 1978.

SHIRER, WILLIAM L. *The Rise and Fall of the Third Reich: A History of Nazi Germany.* New York: Simon & Schuster, 1960.

SIMON, KATE. *Fifth Avenue: A Very Social History.* New York: Harcourt Brace Jovanovich, 1978.

SINCLAIR, ANDREW. *The Last of the Best.* New York: Macmillan, 1969.

SLATER, LEONARD. *Aly.* New York: Random House, 1964.

SMITH, JANE S. *Elsie de Wolfe: A Life in the High Style.* New York: Atheneum, 1982.

SMITH, T.V. "A Successful Experiment in Cultural Transplanting: Barbara Hutton's House in Cuernavaca, Mexico." *House Beautiful* (January 1962).

SPRINGER, JOHN, AND HAMILTON, JACK. *They Had Faces Then: Super Stars, Stars and Starlets of the 1930's.* Secaucus, N.J.: Citadel, 1974.

STASSINOPOULOS, ARIANNA. *Maria Callas: The Woman Behind the Legend.* New York: Simon & Schuster, 1981.

STEWART, ANGUS. *Tangier: A Writer's Notebook.* London: Hutchinson, 1977.

STOCK, DENNIS. *James Dean Revisited.* New York: Viking, 1978.

ST. JOHN, ADELA ROGERS. *The Honeycomb.* Garden City, N.Y.: Doubleday, 1969.

STUART, SANDRA LEE. *The Pink Palace: Behind Closed Doors at the Beverly Hills Hotel.* Secaucus, N.J.: Lyle Stuart, 1978.

SWANBERG, W.A. *Citizen Hearst.* New York: Scribner, 1961.

SWANSON, GLORIA. *Swanson on Swanson.* New York: Random House, 1980.

SWINDELL, LARRY. *The Last Hero: A Biography of Gary Cooper.* Garden City, N.Y.: Doubleday, 1980.

SYKES, CHRISTOPHER. *The Golden Age of the Country House.* New York: Mayflower Books, 1980.

———. *Nancy: The Life of Lady Astor.* London: Granada, 1979.

TAGORE, RABINDRANATH. *The Gardener.* New York: Macmillan, 1914.

TANNER, LOUISE. *Here Today.* New York: Crowell, 1959.

TEAGUE, MICHAEL. *Mrs. L: Conversations with Alice Roosevelt Longworth.* New York: Doubleday, 1981.

TEBBEL, JOHN. *The Life and Good Times of William Randolph Hearst.* New York: Dutton, 1952.

———. *The Marshall Fields.* New York: Dutton, 1947.

THOMPSON, JACQUELINE. *The Very Rich Book.* New York: Morrow, 1981.

THORNDIKE, JOSPEH J. JR. *The Magnificent Builders and Their Dream Houses.* New York: American Heritage, 1978.

_____. *The Very Rich: A History of Wealth.* New York: American Heritage, 1976.

TIERNEY, GENE, WITH HERSKOWITZ, MICKEY. *Self Portrait.* New York: Simon & Schuster, 1979.

TIETZE, HANS. *Treasures of the Great National Galleries.* London: Phaidon Press, 1954.

TIME-LIFE BOOKS, EDS. *The Fabulous Century, Vol. IV.* New York: Time-Life Books, 1969.

TOBIAS, ANDREW. *Fire and Ice: The Story of Charles Revson—the Man Who Built the Revlon Empire.* New York: Warner Books, 1976.

TOMKINS, CALVIN. *Living Well is the Best Revenge.* New York: Viking, 1971.

TOWNSEND, PETER, ED. *Burke's Peerage Baronetage and Knightage.* 105th ed. London: Burke's Peerage, 1970.

VAIDON, LAWDOM. *Tangier: A Different Way.* Metuchen, N.J.: Scarecrow Press, 1977.

VAN RENSSELAER, PHILIP. *The House with the Golden Door.* New York: Trident, 1965.

_____. *Million Dollar Baby: an Intimate Portrait of Barbara Hutton.* New York: Putnam, 1979.

VICKERS, HUGO. *Gladys: Duchess of Marlborough.* New York: Holt, Rinehart & Winston, 1979.

VREELAND, DIANA. *Allure.* Garden City, N.Y.: Doubleday, 1980.

WALLACE, IRVING, WALLACE, AMY, WALLECHINSKY, DAVID, AND WALLACE, SYLVIA. *The Intimate Sex Lives of Famous People.* New York: Delacorte, 1981.

WALSH, GEORGE. *Gentlemen Jimmy Walker.* New York: Praeger, 1974.

WARREN, WILLIAM. *The House On the Klong: The Bangkok Home and Asian Art Collection of James Thompson.* New York and Tokyo: John Weatherhill, Inc., 1968.

WATTS, STEPHAN. *Le Ritz: La Vie Intime du Plus Prestigieux Hôtel du Monde.* Paris: Éditions de Trévise, 1968.

WECTER, DIXON. *The Saga of American Society: A Record of Social Aspiration.* New York: Charles Scribner's, 1937.

WILLIAMS, HENRY LIONEL, AND WILLIAMS, OTTALIE K. *A Treasury of Great American Houses.* New York: Putnam, 1970.

_____. *Great Houses of America.* New York: Putnam, 1966.

WINDSOR, DUCHESS OF. *The Heart Has Its Reasons: The Memoirs of the Duchess of Windsor.* New York: David McKay, 1956.

WINDSOR, DUKE OF. *A Family Album.* London: Cassell, 1960.

_____. *A King's Story: Memoirs of The Duke of Windsor.* New York: Putnam, 1947.

WINKLER, JOHN K. *Five and Ten: The Fabulous Life of F. W. Woolworth.* New York: Robert M. McBride & Co., 1940.

WORDEN, HELEN. *Society Circus.* New York: Covici Friede, 1936.

WRIGHT, COBINA. *I Never Grew Up.* New York: Prentice-Hall, 1952.

WRIGHT, WILLIAM. *Heiress: The Rich Life of Marjorie Merriweather Post.* Washington, D.C.: New Republic Books, 1978.

ZIEGLER, PHILIP. *Diana Cooper.* New York: Knopf, 1982.

ZIFF, LARZER. *The American 1890s: Life and Times of a Lost Generation.* New York: Viking, 1966.

Acknowledgments

FIRST ACKNOWLEDGMENT must obviously go to the late Barbara Woolworth Hutton, without whom, for numerous reasons, this book would never have been written.

Next I should like to thank my literary agent, Peter H. Matson, as well as his associate, Victoria Pryor, and assistant, Elizabeth Grossman.

I am greatly indebted to society PR specialist Marianne Strong, of Marianne Strong Associates in New York, for her generous and continual counsel and encouragement, and to my editor in England, Paul Sidey.

A primary source of the material in this book comes from hundreds of hours of interviews, many of them tape-recorded, which were conducted in nine languages with more than four hundred people spread across four continents and some thirty-five countries. Many of these interviews were conducted by a multilingual staff of researchers that included: Vincent Alfieri, Robin Lynn, Madeleine Nicklin, Kathleen O'Brien, Theresa Stanton and Ellen Uter. I am grateful to each of them. Another researcher, Monica Fritz, was responsible for locating a number of the photographs that appear in this volume. I am especially indebted to my friend and colleague Robert Singer, who not only helped conduct and organize the research and interviews but gave unstinting moral and psychological support when it was most needed.

Although it is not possible to list every person who was helpful (since some requested anonymity), I would like to express my thanks to the following:

Irving Abelow, M.D.; Albert Aferiat; Ann Allison (British Information Service, New York); Elizabeth Alpert (the San Francisco *Chronicle*);Cleveland

Amory; The Hon. Walter H. Annenberg; the late Adele Astaire; Brooke Astor; Martha Atcher; Harry Atkins; R. S. Atterbury.

Angelina M. Bacon (The National Gallery, London); A. T. Baldwin, Jr.; the late Billy Baldwin; A. J. Bart-Hood, M.D.; Charles Baskerville; the late Sir Cecil Beaton; Maximilian Becker; Carla Huston Bell; James B. Bell (New York Historical Society); Melvin Belli, Esq.; Marie Bernard; Frances Bitterman; Earl Blackwell (Celebrity Register, New York); Leon Block; T. Dennie Boardman; Virginia Bohanna (Cedars-Sinai Medical Center, Los Angeles); Daniel Boorstin; Antoinette Borroughs; Charles F. Boutelle; Paul Bowles; Count "Brando" Brandolini; Margaret Astor Brent; Frederick Brisson; Lord David Brooke; Walter Brooks; James Brough; Art Buchwald; Amuziata Buetti; Fred A. Burgess; Lytton Byrnes (The British Museum, London).

Herb Caen; Jeanne Capodilupo (Woodlawn Memorial Cemetery, New York); Truman Capote; Pierre Cardin; Frank Caro, Jr.; J.F. Carroll (F.W. Woolworth Co., New York); Oleg Cassini; Suzanne Caster (the San Francisco *Chronicle*); Countess Donina Cicogna; Countess Marina Cicogna; Mrs. C. Coffin; Barry Lee Cohen, Esq.; Gertie Conrad; Lady Diana Cooper; Roderick Coupe; Hernando and Florence Courtright; Countess Consuelo Crespi; Count Rudi Crespi; the late Rupert Croft-Cooke; Mrs. Thayer Cummings; Tom Cunningham; Dr. Kent Cunow; Charlotte Curtis.

Countess Christiana Brandolini D'Adda; Salvador Dali; Emory Davis; Count Jean de Baglion; Count and Countess Guy de Brantes; Hubert de Givenchy; Daniel Delancy; Ignacio and Lee de Landa; Countess de Menront; Rajkumari Sumair de Patiala (Princess Sumair); Barbara de Portago; Donald Deschner; Armand Deutsch; Adolfo de Velasco; Hazel Dews; The Hon. Ben Dixon; Jean Doan; the late Maurice Doan; Mary Donahue; James Douglas; Jean-Paul Dousset; Kenneth Downs (United Press International); the late Sir Michael Duff; Doris Duke; Sir Alfred Dunn; The Hon. Paul Dworkin.

The Hon. Harland ("Hal") Eastman; Diana Edkins (*Vogue*); William Edwards (The Bow Street Court, London); Louis Ehret; Gerald Ehrlich; Jane Engelhard; Lawrence R. Eno, Esq.; R. D. Eno; Matthew Evans; Carol Ezzard.

Douglas and Mary Lee Fairbanks, Jr.; Susan Fein (Surrogate Court of Suffolk County, New York); Miguel Ferreras; David Fields (the *Palm Beacher)*; Jean Flint; Malcolm Forbes; Robert Forbes; Mildred Fox; Joe Franklin; the late Brenda Frazier; Linda Fredericks; Cleo French; Sir Richard Freylinger.

Fatesinghrao Gaekwad (Maharajah of Baroda); Jean Garay; Lilian K. Gardiner; Wilson R. Gathings; Bernard Gelbort; Robert Gerofi; Dorothy J. Gibb; Lois Gilman; Eugene L. Girden, Esq.; Lillian Gish; John Gomez; William Goulet; Albert Govon; Cary Grant; Gloria Gravert (Miss Porter's School); Dolly Green; Robert P. Giffing, Jr. (Honolulu Academy of Arts); the late Winston F. C. Guest; Mercedes Guitti.

His Excellency Hassan Hajoui; Mohammed Omar Hajoui (Moroccan Ministry of Tourism, Tangier); Fernando Hanhausen, Esq.; Marshall Haseltine; Sheldon Haseltine; Robert Hawkes; Silvia de Castellane Hennessy; The Hon. David Herbert; Carlos Herrera; Jane Alcott Holmes; Ruth Hopwood; Frank Horn; Horst P. Horst; the late Curtis Hutton.

Grand Duke Paul Ilyinsky; The Hon. Howard D. Jones; Mrs. Edna Lee Joon; Frank Just.

James M. Kalett; Jon Keating; Diana P. Kempe, Esq.; Morley and Jean Kennerley; Bruce Kessler; Nina Kessler; the late Emilie Keyes; Joseph Kingsbury-Smith (the Hearst Newspapers); Allen T. Klots; Herbert Werner Klotz; John Kluge; Judge James Knott; Jay Kramer, Esq.; Mr. William Kraft, Jr.

Jaquine Lachman; Rita Lachman; Lester Lanin; Mary Lasker; Sir Richard Latham; Margaret ("Sister") Latimer; Wayne Lawson; Leo Lerman; Francis Levy; Doris Lilly; Jack Linett, Esq.; Anita Loos; Merrill Lowell; Milton and Nettie Lunin.

Donald P. Madden, Esq.; Mohamed Maîmouni; the late Gene Markey; Sheri Martinelli; Linda Matula; the late Charles McCabe; David and Judy McClintick; Bruce McDonnell; Joseph A. McPhillips, III (the American School of Tangier); the late Elinor Guthrie McVickar; Vera Medina; Aileen Mehle ("Suzy"); Jean Mendiboure; Mustafa Menehbi; Edward Merhige; Dina Merrill; Daniel Meyer (Musée National du Château de Versailles); the late Kitty Miller; Jim Mitchell; Alice-Leone Moats; Lord Charles Garrett and Lady Joan Moore (Earl and Countess of Drogheda); Constance Moore; The Hon. Derry Moore; Ted Morgan; Gould Morrison; Raymond Mortimer (the London Sunday *Times*); David Mosen; Ned Moss; George Mühler (Reuters); Charles Munn; Harold Munro.

Momi Nahon; Gretchen Nicholas; the late David Niven; the late Merle Oberon; Lea Orth; Saîd Ouriaghli.

Harrie Hill Page; the late Antenor Patiño; Ted Peckham; Lester Persky; Martha Phillips; The Hon. David Pleydell-Bouverie; Dorchy Plume; Ellen Stuart Poole; the late James Pope-Hennessy; Ernest Portenstein; Paul Posner; Special Agent Eric Potts (Federal Bureau of Investigation, Washington, D.C.).

William Rademaekers (Time-Life, Inc.); Howard G. Rapaport, M.D.; the late Count Lanfranco Rasponi; Anna Ratto; Elysse Reissman; Cliff Robertson; J. Robinson (Bermuda Supreme Court); the Hon. Kenneth N. Rogers; Mary Lady Rothermere; Kathryn Ruby; Daniel Ryan; Frances Ryan.

Robert Sack, Esq.; Mary Sanford; Jerovi Vail Sanson; Kraft Sautoy; Myron Schwartzman; Michael K. Scott; F. G. Seligmann; Robert Shea, M.D.; Elaine Shepard; Eugenia Sheppard; Paul Sidey; Ben Silverstein; Martin Singer; Cheryl Holdridge Skarder; the late Ada Beatrice Smith (Bricktop); Arthur Smith; Earl E. T. Smith; Liz Smith; Nicoll Smith; Anya Sorine; George Staples; Martin

Stoppard; Richard Storm; Donald Stover; Edward Streeter; Merle Streit; Capt. V. S. Strong; Carole Stuart; Lyle Stuart; Missy Sutton.

Barbara Tardiff; Rachid Tensamani; Anna Ternbach; Byron Trott; Prince Igor Troubetskoy; Fred Tupper.

Gerald Van Der Kemp; Claudia Van Ness; Alejo and Marie-Charlotte Vidal-Quadras; the late George Vigouroux; Josephine Villanueva; Diana Vreeland; Sacher Vuchs.

Dudley Walker; Anne Ward; Andy Warhol; J.D. Webb; Charles Weeland (Wally Findlay Galleries); Allan J. Wilson; Earl Wilson; the late Harry Winston; Mrs. Norman Woolworth; Richard Woolworth; Stephanie Woolworth; Cobina Wright; Marion Sims Wyeth; The Hon. Franklin Wymarth.

George Yatrakis, M.D.; Walter Young (Bank of N. T. Butterfield & Son, Ltd.); Jerome Zerbe; Angelo Zucotti.

I would also like to acknowledge the following groups, societies and business organizations for providing information and research materials. The American Red Cross, Washington, D.C.; the Burlingame Country Club; Cartier, Inc., New York and Paris; Claridge's of London; *Daily News*, New York; the Damon Runyon-Walter Winchell Cancer Fund, New York; the Danish Consulate General, New York and Washington, D.C.; the Everglades Club, Palm Beach; the Federal Bureau of Investigation, Washington, D.C.; the Flagler Museum, Palm Beach; the Four Arts Society, Palm Beach; Grospiron, Inc., Paris; the Internal Revenue Service, Washington, D.C.; the Japanese Consulate General, New York and Washington, D.C.; Lincoln Center for the Performing Arts, New York; the Mark Hopkins, San Francisco; the Metropolitan Museum of Art, New York; M. H. De Young Memorial Museum, San Francisco; the National Gallery, Washington, D.C.; New York Foundling Hospital; the *New York Times*; the Norton Simon Museum of Art, Pasadena; the Palm Beach Historical Society; the Pierre, New York; the Plaza, New York; D. Porthault, Inc., New York; the Ritz, Paris; San Francisco Historical Society; the San Francisco Opera Company; Scotland Yard, London; Sotheby Parke Bernet, London, New York and Paris; *Town and Country*; the Traveller's Club, London and Paris; the Union Club, New York; the Harry S. Truman Library, Independence, Mo.

Finally, Jeanne, Chloe and Renee Heymann—my wife, my daughter, and my mother—to whom this book is dedicated.

Index